AF334134

Also by Richard Warren Field

The Swords of Faith

The Election

Dying to Heal with Dr. Alan Fluger

Praise for *The Swords of Faith*

[T]he book's skillful rendering of relentless movement towards confrontation accomplished through Field's shift back and forth between the onward progress of the two leaders. I found my heart beating in time with this sense of inevitable clash.

> \- Nan Hawthorne, author, *Beloved Pilgrim*

Meticulously researched…. Author Richard Warren Field penned this incredibly story with such a vibrant simplicity that not only engrosses the reader in the plot, but that endears them to its colourful and intriguing characters.

Field's passion for this period in history is clearly evident on every page. He relays historical facts and details through action and dialogue instead of narrative. In this way, he makes the story literally spring off each page. But the most striking quality of this novel is Field's ability to build three-dimensional, larger-than-life characters. He is able to show the reader all aspects of their personalities, good, bad, and ambivalent, by taking us into their thought innermost thoughts so that we understand what drives each character.

> \- Mirella Patzer, *Historical Novel Review*

Richard Warren Field's novel of the Third Crusade is a balanced, well-researched attempt to show both sides of the story.

One of the best features of this novel is its sense of inevitability, carefully plotted and paced to make the reader feel propelled into the consequences of the meeting of the armies of both faiths.

> \- *Historical Novel Society*

THE SULTAN AND THE KHAN

Richard Warren Field

The Sultan and The Khan. Copyright © 2014 by Richard W. Field.

All Rights Reserved. No part of this book may be used or reproduced, in any manner whatsoever, without the written permission of the Author and Publisher.

Printed in the United States of America.

Library of Congress Catalog Card Number: 2014941749
ISBN13: 978-1-932045-72-7
ISBN10: 1-932045-72-4
First Edition Paperback 2014
Cover Art by Robert Patrick O'Brien
Author Photo by Matt Garcia - dahlphotographers.com

Strider Nolan Media, Inc.
702 Cricket Avenue
Ardsley, PA 19038
www.stridernolanmedia.com

THE SULTAN AND THE KHAN

DEDICATION

Dedicated to my father, Joseph H. Field. During my childhood, my parents instilled in me a love of history and learning, and a sense of tolerance for religions and cultures different from my own, qualities evident in this book and in my previous historical novel, *The Swords of Faith*. Since *The Swords of Faith* was dedicated to my mother, it is only fitting that I recognize my father in *The Sultan and The Khan*.

ACKNOWLEDGEMENTS

My thanks to Strider Nolan Media for giving a home to my historical novels and for their editorial savvy in discerning my author's voice and then polishing my words to make my voice more effective.

My thanks to Mirella Patzer, an excellent historical novelist and blogger on historical novels, for her support and for her critique group at yahoo.com comprised of historical novelists from around the world who helped review and polish early drafts of this book.

My thanks to superb writer Christopher Moss for his support and friendship during the early marketing of *The Swords of Faith*, the precursor to *The Sultan and The Khan*.

My thanks to "Ron's Amazing Stories" for Ron's perceptive interviewing skills and abilities at dramatization.

My thanks to the Historical Novel Society for the wonderful opportunities to connect and network with lovers of historical novels from all over the world.

And thanks to my wife of twenty-five years, Carrie Robin Field, for her loving support, and for her faith in my talents as I kept entering the public arena with a number of creative enterprises. It would be hard to imagine what my journey would be like without her – so much of what I offer is the result of our shared experiences.

TO THE READER

There is one certainty about any civilization's paradigms: eventually every view of the world fades into obsolescence. During the Eleventh and Twelfth Centuries, the Muslim people of the Middle East certainly perceived that the threat to Islam primarily emanated from Western and Central Europe. They considered these anti-Muslim creatures, labeled by history as "the Crusaders," to be a backwards group intellectually and culturally; but they also saw them as formidable fighters—especially in close confrontations where heavy European armor held a devastating advantage over lightly armored Muslim cavalries.

The Muslims also faced onslaughts from the East during the Eleventh and Twelfth Centuries, but these primarily Turkic incursions were no threat to Islam. If anything, the Central Asian peoples who had converted to Islam were often more fanatic than the Arab Muslims. So the most serious peril to Islam itself came from those militant Western Christian warriors, stoked with the single-minded objective of bringing Jerusalem under Christian control within a Christian-ruled territory.

Within a few decades of the Thirteenth Century, the perception of the threat to Islam made an abrupt, one hundred eighty degree turn. In just a generation, the threat of the Western warriors for Christ seemed to become a minor annoyance compared to the calamity coming from the East. There is little doubt that this threat to Islam influenced Sultan al-Kamil's decision to bargain away Jerusalem to Western Christians in 1229, so he could focus on the threat brewing in the other direction. Ironically, al-Kamil was the nephew of the revered Muslim sultan, Saladin, who had crowned his successes against Western Christians with the capture of Jerusalem in 1187.

This Eastern threat might have been inevitable, but it was hastened to a breaking point and accelerated to a fever pitch of ferocity by the arrogance and overconfidence of Mohammed-Shah, ruler of the Khwarazmian Empire of Central Asia. By 1218, Genghis Khan had secured his conquest of much of China, and now looked west. He sent a caravan of ambassadors and merchants to discuss the relationship between the two empires. Were the Mongol ambassadors and merchants also spies, seeking information for Genghis Khan's next conquest? Possibly. Didn't Genghis Khan believe that he and his descendants were destined to conquer and rule the world, and that he expected all sovereigns to submit to him? Would Genghis Khan have eventually launched a Mongol conquest of the Khwarazmian Empire if Mohammed-Shah hadn't submitted? Probably. But when Mohammed-Shah gave permission to the governor of Utrar to execute the Mongol envoys and confiscate all the goods from their caravan—Mohammed-Shah's share being half—he set in motion one of the most devastating reprisals in world history.

Genghis Khan's campaign against the Khwarazmian Empire was one of destruction and depopulation. Though eight centuries have passed since then, this part of the world never completely recovered, including much of the fabled "Silk Route" that once boasted magnificent, glorious cities like Bukhara, Samarkand and Merv. Populations in cities that did not surrender immediately could expect nearly complete extermination—only a very few craftsmen and selected scholars were kept alive for service to the Mongol empire. Even cities that did surrender could expect to be cleared of their populations so Mongol troops could plunder more efficiently.

Specific resisters of the Mongols met particularly terrible fates. The governor of Utrar was captured and punished creatively: Mongol executioners poured molten silver down his throat and into his ears and nostrils. The Mongols were especially brutal to the populations of cities where a relative of Genghis Khan had been killed. An arrow from a defender of the city of Nishapur killed Genghis Khan's son-in-law. His widow presided over the reprisal. Mongol squads created three piles of severed heads: one of men, one of women, and one of children. They killed dogs and cats, and even rats; they allowed no living creature to remain alive. The population of Bamiyan, where Genghis Khan's grandson was killed, suffered a similar fate. Mongols completely destroyed Herat, killing all 80,000 inhabitants. Mongols killed all but eighty craftsmen in Merv, a city along the Silk Route that for a brief time in the Twelfth Century was the most populous city in the world, exceeding even Constantinople. The number of dead in Merv approached one million. It is estimated that the Mongols killed, mostly in cold blood, fifteen million people overall, a significant percentage of the human beings living in the area. This Eastern threat to Islam made the Western Christians seem like genteel dance partners in comparison.

If there was any hope the empire of Genghis Khan would fragment immediately after his death, that hope did not materialize. Genghis Khan set up a process of succession that, albeit with flaws and interruptions, held up for two generations after he died. (As a practical matter, the empire fragmented after the struggle between grandsons Kublai and Arigh-boke. The conflict was technically resolved in favor of Kublai in 1264, but really resulted in a de facto parsing of the empire into four states.)

In 1251, Mongke Khan, the fourth ruling khan of the Genghis Khan dynasty, delegated the actions needed for the empire's next moves. His brother Kublai would head east to complete the conquest of China. His brother Hulegu would head west to complete the conquest of the Muslim Middle East, moving through Palestine to take Egypt, with ambitions of extending the Mongol empire into Western Europe. (Mongols already held most of present-day Russia and large areas of Eastern Europe).

In 1254, after meticulous preparations, Hulegu and his army of 200,000 began the journey west. His plans involved moving through Persia to capture one of the greatest cities of the world, the spiritual seat of Islam, the home of the caliph: Baghdad. On the way, he would finish some family business with the Isma'ilis, also known as the "Assassins"—once allies but now enemies who had tried to kill Mongke Khan. For the Isma'ilis, this threat from the East was a lethal promise—there would be no mercy for them. For the rest of the Muslims in the Middle East, there were serious choices to make. Millions of lives, and the course of history, would depend on those choices.

1

Third Week of January, 1258
Baghdad
Late Afternoon

"They won't leave a soul alive, not a one of us," the young student said from the doorway. Piles of scrolls and bound volumes cluttered the dimly lit room.

Dawud the Teacher—who had also been known as Dawud of Jaffa or Dawud ibn Butrus—did not respond to his student's words. He quietly finished rolling up his prayer rug, then rose from his modest home's stone floor. As he straightened up he grimaced, feeling every one of his sixty-eight years as his aging joints fought his desire to move. He began to smooth his flowing gray beard then stopped, realizing he was indulging in the nervous habit again.

"You know what this means," the student added, clearly wanting some response.

Dawud narrowed the eyebrows of his craggy face, pausing a moment. "Yes," he answered quietly. "It means God has chosen not to answer our prayers. Yet."

"Baghdad will be totally destroyed," the student said. "Just the caliph putting an army in the field has condemned us all. Islam's greatest city, the seat of the caliphate … the libraries, the observatories, the research centers … they will all be—"

"God will not allow it," Dawud told him, refusing to match his student's desperate mood.

The student bowed. "Teacher, I see no way short of a miracle that God can prevent it."

Dawud thought it over. Without any other recourse, he rolled his prayer rug back onto the ground and knelt back down.

Not wanting to accept this as a valid response, the student

continued to speak. "There are still options. They are not perfect options, but better than waiting for these slaughtering hordes to arrive."

Dawud bowed forward until his forehead touched the prayer rug. "Pray with me," he requested as he lifted his head back up.

The student drew in a deep breath, then relented. He took a prayer rug from a nearby table and laid it on the ground next to Dawud. "Of course, Teacher, prayer is always important. But that may not be our most useful option at this time."

"Flight?" Dawud asked. "At my age, am I to sneak through lines of Mongol horsemen, and then outride them? Men who live in the saddle for most of their lives?"

The student's face tensed. "You were a warrior at one time. You can—"

"That was decades ago." Dawud squinted and shook his head slightly, as if he was trying to dislodge memories he had tried many times to leave permanently in the past.

"You can still ride. I've seen you."

"I was a different man then. Certainly, *that* Dawud would have tried to fight his way through them, preferring to die shedding as much infidel blood as possible." Dawud's eyes moistened. "That is not God's desire for me. I don't think it ever was." Dawud turned away from his student, ostensibly to pray. But what prayer did he have to offer, facing the certainty of slaughter?

Maybe a return of the old Dawud was called for. The Mongols—these illiterate horsemen attacking from distant pastures—were coming to destroy Baghdad, a city responsible for humanity's greatest achievements yet. Nearly soulless creatures were coming to slaughter the best and brightest of the Faithful.

Dawud had been born to a Christian father but later embraced his mother's religion. As a young man he had been a warrior, filled with fiery passion for his adopted faith and with a zealous desire to destroy those who would harm it. Wasn't that Dawud needed now? He knew this student respected him as a wise and principled man. He did not want to reveal just how much he was fighting the urge to return to that Dawud from the past. But at sixty-eight he couldn't be that younger man even if he wanted to.

He gathered himself. God tested the Faithful. Dawud's immersion in blood and rage had caused his failures of the past. Even in this situation, such a course would be a coward's way. He forced a gentle smile. "Flight. Not a reasonable option for me."

The student touched his forehead to the prayer rug and came back up to a kneeling position. "Well, then, there is sanctuary at the—"

"Absolutely not." Dawud stiffened at the suggestion. "I will never be that desperate."

"You have friends there who will welcome you and who share your desire to preserve—"

"No. Do not raise this issue with me again."

"But there is so much you still need to teach, so much wisdom to preserve. God will want you to—"

Yet again Dawud interrupted. "I still pray God will not allow this to happen, but at this perilous time, we need to act for Islam—and for God. Now is not the time to compromise."

"We have very little time," the student told him. "There is no longer an army in the field to resist the Mongols. The word is they are surrounding Baghdad as we speak. But they haven't completed their siege preparations yet, and there is still a garrison here to put up some kind of resistance. Our lives are days, maybe a few weeks, from being cut short by Mongol swords."

"Then we'd better complete our prayers quickly," Dawud said. "We will pray to understand how we can best preserve the wisdom of the Caliphate of Baghdad for posterity, for the Faithful, for all people. We must then act on the answer to those prayers."

Dawud lowered his head. He wished he believed what he was telling his student. He wished he really could see some hope for his fate, and for Baghdad's. A tear snuck from his right eye. He looked away from his student, preventing the younger man from getting a close look. Mustering a firm tone he prayed, "There is no God but God, and Mohammed is the Messenger of God."

January 22, 1258
East of Baghdad
Afternoon

"The city is huge, but the first steps for the siege are completed," Ketbugha said to Hulegu. The two men sat on their horses and stared over an arid, chilly landscape toward the distant walls of Baghdad. An armed entourage flanked them. A chilly breeze blew through the men, barely affecting any of them.

Hulegu, the grandson of Genghis Khan, was just over forty. His skin was brownish and leathery from long days of riding in the sun. His round, chubby face held flat, callous eyes. He was barely over five and a half feet tall, with a stocky build. Ketbugha, his top general, was slightly older, with the same leathery complexion, but leaner and taller.

"The siege engineers completed a surrounding barrier?" Hulegu asked.

"Yes. Back in the land of the Rus, there was enough wood to construct a barrier around the perimeters of their cities. No wood here, but the engineers have completed an uncrossable trench."

Hulegu nodded. "That should contain the city's inhabitants."

"Yes."

"How long before we're through the walls?" Hulegu asked.

"Days, maybe a week," Ketbugha told him.

Hulegu raised his eyebrows.

With some trepidation Ketbugha asked, "The usual policy toward the people?"

Hulegu shrugged. "Yes. The usual."

"We may wish to consider that this isn't the Isma'ilis. This is the seat of the caliphate."

"What's the difference? The caliph thinks he has a special relationship with God." Hulegu snorted. "The Eternal Blue Heaven has ordained that my grandfather and his descendants will rule the world. Any obstruction to this destiny must be swept away."

"Of course. But issues are more complex in Baghdad than they were with the Isma'ili castles. There are—"

"The issue is simple. The caliph should have sent tribute and troops when we asked. His soldiers should have been alongside ours when we destroyed the Isma'ilis. And he should never have sent forces against us. He and his people must not escape the consequences of resisting the destiny ordained by the Eternal Blue Heaven."

"Certainly. No doubt. The caliph and his Muslim followers deserve their fates." Ketbugha swallowed. Hulegu did not seem to understand, but Ketbugha knew his superior would not be patient enough to consider an issue that did not capture his interest. How could he frame his concern efficiently? "But not all the people in the city are Muslims."

Hulegu frowned. "Christians?"

"The spies say Muslims, Christians, and Jews all thrive in Baghdad."

"What are 'Jews'?"

Ketbugha had explained this before. Would Hulegu absorb the explanation this time? "They are a small group that sprang from the land of Palestine hundreds of years ago, before there were Christians or Muslims. They have scattered—"

"Palestine," Hulegu interrupted. "That is along the coast, on the way to the Egypt-land...."

"Yes." Ketbugha forced a smile. He sensed his latest attempt to explain the Jewish people to Hulegu would also fail to stick.

"Not a very rich land at all, where those Jews come from. Egypt-land will yield much more wealth."

"That is true. But the Jews' religious traditions ... well, the Christ was—"

"All religions bow to us," Hulegu said, clearly bored with the details and uninterested in any distinctions. "We rule them all. There are only two religious groups that concern me: those who have submitted to us, and those who will."

"But—"

"And those who resist will be exterminated as a lesson to those who will think to resist."

Ketbugha still needed to resolve the issue, and Hulegu's reference to "two religious groups" gave him a new angle of approach. "Suppose you have a religious group that did not want to resist, but were trapped under the leadership of a group that did resist?"

At the sound of an approaching horse, Ketbugha and Hulegu turned almost simultaneously. The mounted entourage also angled their horses in that direction, instinctively protecting their superior officers. A lone rider with a purposeful swiftness was coming from the direction of the walls of Baghdad.

Ketbugha recognized the man as one of his messengers. He quickly finished his question to Hulegu. "Should those people of the trapped religious group meet the same fate as the resisters?"

"You're concerned about the Christians." Hulegu smirked, as if he had just unmasked a guilty secret.

The messenger arrived. "General," the newcomer said to Ketbugha, careful not to address Hulegu directly, or even look at him. "The engineers report the siege engines are ready. The attack troops are in position."

Ketbugha looked to Hulegu. He knew this announcement would brighten Hulegu's mood and smiled. "On your orders, sir."

"Start the attack," Hulegu told him.

Ketbugha in turn nodded to the messenger.

"Um, General?" The messenger seemed uncomfortable, but continued. "I must report to you…. One of the engineers, brought here from the lands of the Chin, says that our strategy of opening the dikes to flood the enemy army, and of digging the containment trench, has caused substantial damage to the farm ditches that surround the city."

Ketbugha glanced at Hulegu.

Hulegu bristled.

Ketbugha looked back at the messenger, hoping the man would sense that he should finish this message in a hurry.

Hulegu stared out toward the walls of Baghdad. He never once looked at the messenger.

The messenger continued, "The Chin engineer said he has only seen farming ditches like this … of this greatness, in the lands around the city of Beijing. He thought we should consider … that we might want to … we might restore the ditches to preserve the wealth of this city for the great khan."

Ketbugha wanted to throttle the foolish messenger for raising this subject in front of Hulegu. He had no idea how Hulegu would view the issue and did not want to offer an opinion until he was sure it would not conflict with Hulegu's.

"Those ditches bring water to farmlands," Hulegu said to Ketbugha. "They help to supply a large city population. But they ruin good pasture land for our horses."

Ketbugha nodded. He could see where this line of thinking was going.

"My grandfather hated cities," Hulegu reflected. "No matter how many territories he conquered, he never saw much use for places concentrating large populations of the soft and flabby. But, grandfather was from another time. We know now that cities have their uses." Hulegu paused, then shrugged. "When we finish our business here, there will not be such a large population. The need for food will be lessened. So the farming ditches do not need to be restored."

Ketbugha frowned at the messenger.

The messenger swallowed apprehensively.

Hulegu looked out over the horizon. He sneered. "For the Chin engineer who honors the ditches so much … make him a permanent part of them. His family, too. This will be a just reward for his misguided focus. We have a thousand engineers and their families on this expedition. This example will help others to avoid troubling their commanders with trifles instead of concentrating on gaining possession of my city."

Ketbugha looked at the messenger.

The other man bowed, jerked his horse into action, and made a quick exit.

"The Christians," Hulegu said, returning to the previous discussion.

Ketbugha waited for Hulegu to express his thoughts.

"Of course we spare them. I know you are a believer in their faith. So is your mother." Hulegu laughed. "So is my wife. We have Christians from the lands of Armenia and Georgia fighting in the ranks of our men." Hulegu paused a moment. "Make sure the order goes out. No harm to the Christians or their places of worship. They are the ones with crosses on them?"

"Yes."

"Is this what concerned you?"

"I wanted to confirm our policy—"

"And so you have your confirmation. Now, with that settled, I want my city."

"I will supervise the attack personally."

2

Late January, 1258
Acre, Kingdom of Jerusalem
Evening

"Aram!" the voice called, accompanied by pounding on the door. "They're calling for us! Now!"

"Damn!" Aram muttered.

The girl underneath him giggled.

The small room was dark except for two candles. Aram and the girl were on the bed, under a light blanket.

"Don't you dare stop," the girl insisted, still giggling.

Aram kept moving.

"Aram!"

"Just a couple of minutes!" Aram called out.

"A couple of minutes?" the girl asked.

"A lot of minutes," Aram grunted to the girl. "A multitude of minutes."

She giggled again as she grabbed his rear end and shifted his position on her.

"Aram! Do you have a girl in there?"

Aram didn't answer.

The girl was no longer giggling, but softly moaning.

"This building is a church! We're visitors here!" More pounding on the door demanded Aram's attention.

Aram was glad he had latched the door.

"Aram! You're going to lose this work! All the way from Baghdad, for nothing!"

"Work?" The girl seemed to be scrutinizing the words. "Prince? Needing to work?"

"Princely. Type. Work." Aram struggled to offer explanations without breaking the mood.

"There are no Christian princes in Baghdad," the girl insisted, seeming to slip out of the mood.

"All right." Aram caught his breath. "I'm not a prince. Do you really want me to stop?"

The girl curled her arms around him. "No."

As Aram emerged into the lit hall, Nestor, the one who had been pounding on the door, said,"If they get on to you defiling their novices, you won't get the job—hell, you might not even leave here alive!" Nestor's thinning hair, dark brown and gray, bounced as he scolded Aram. Nestor wore a blue shirt and black cotton pants in an apparent attempt to look prosperous and modest at the same time.

Aram shrugged. "I was getting bored." Aram was tall, at least six inches taller than Nestor. He had an olive complexion, black hair, and striking greenish-brown eyes. From the reactions of women in most of the places the twenty-six year old had traveled, he knew he was handsome and expected to be admired. Aram dressed in a white silk shirt and baggy blue pants.

The men started walking down a hall.

Aram said, "They've kept us waiting three days. But I do appreciate their hospitality. So I did them a service. That girl is not going to make a very good nun. It's good they find that out now."

"No it's not."

"Fine. You're right. It's not."

"Try to remember, these people take matters more seriously than you do. There is a civil war between the Italian merchant factions that has divided—"

"Italian merchants fighting amongst themselves. That's a new one."

"This is not something to take casually," Nestor said through gritted teeth. "We are in the Venetian quarter. You do not want to—"

"I know, I know. Three streets this way, two streets that way. Don't go here, don't go there. The battle of the monastery of Saint Sabas, a little part of a little hill...."

"It's much more than that now."

"The girl is not some spy from the Genoese quarter."

Nestor bristled. "Let's not go out of our way to offend these people."

"Or you'll lose your commission."

"They will pay expenses for me bringing you to their attention, yes."

"Expenses...." Aram smirked at Nestor.

"Just ... don't spoil this opportunity with the wrong attitude."

"Don't worry."

They arrived at a wooden door to a meeting room. Nestor knocked.

"Enter," called out a voice inside the room.

Nestor pushed the door open. At the back of the room, a long table took up most of the width of the area. Five men sat at the table. Wearing robes of brown hemp, they all darkened the mood with uniformly grim expressions. Though they were not exactly the same height, weight or age, at first glance they all seemed indistinguishable from each other.

The one in the middle spoke. "Sit." He pointed to two stools that faced the table.

Aram glanced around the room as he and Nestor sat. The room was austere: a few plain tapestries, with religious themes, hung on the brown brick walls. But the plainness of the room seemed to match the dark moods and drab appearances of the men staring at Aram.

"We are not accustomed to waiting," said the man in the middle. Aram could now see this one was older than the others, and the other four seemed to defer to him. "Your tardiness caused us all to miss evening services." The man spoke French with a unique accent. Aram could not place it, but he was certain it was not the native French accent. He had to be originally from somewhere else.

"My apologies," Aram told them. "I was attending to a religious matter myself, and lost track of—"

"We do offer apologies," Nestor interrupted.

Aram stopped short of finishing his explanation. He needed to remember: Nestor told him these men had no sense of humor.

"We appreciate and respect your time," Nestor began. "This young man has all the experience you need for your project. He speaks the Mongol language fluently. He is also familiar with Muslims—he grew up in Baghdad."

"But he *is* Christian," the older man confirmed.

"Yes. Absolutely."

Aram raised his eyebrows.

"His name." The older man looked down at a parchment. "Aram." The man paused a moment, in apparent stern contemplation. "It sounds Jewish. A Jew would be wrong for this position."

"My name is Assyrian," Aram explained.

The older man looked puzzled. "Well, it sounds too Jewish," he finally said.

Aram grimaced at the harsh way he pronounced the syllables when he said "Jewish."

"For this mission," the man said, "we will call you Arnaux."

Aram bit the inside of his cheek.

The older man continued. "I am Robert, from Montpelier. You've probably heard of the school of medicine there. It is world famous."

Aram did not know what to say. This sounded like a French location, but he would have no reason to know about a Western European school of medicine.

The man seemed disappointed with the lack of recognition, but he continued. "I have temporarily suspended my duties at Montpelier because the pope has honored me with an important task for Christendom. I have a few questions for you, to see if you are suitable to assist me."

Aram offered a deferential nod. He stole glances at the five men before him. No, they were not a homogeneous group at all. The two men immediately next to Robert seemed engaged with his words, looking at him, even occasionally nodding. The men on the outsides kept blank expressions most of the time. But Aram caught occasional twitches, even hints of grimaces, from both as the meeting continued. And after a few glances, he noticed the man on the far right seemed to be missing his left arm. Aram stored his observations, maintaining a neutral demeanor and attitude.

"You know the Mongol language?" Robert asked.

"Yes."

"You know the other languages of the area?"

"Yes. Arabic. French, obviously." He paused. "Even a little Hebrew." He raised his eyebrows. He saw grins from the two men at the outsides of the table. The man with the missing arm seemed to swallow as a way to make his grin disappear.

"You understand you will be interpreting for me."

"Yes."

"You will be asked to help me communicate the Christian position to the Mongols."

"Christian position." Aram shrugged. "I understand. I have traveled with caravans from Baghdad across the mountains into the Sultanate of Delhi and the region of Tibet. I am familiar with the languages and the customs, and with recent events."

"Good," Robert said, nodding approval. "Recent events call us."

The man at the far left took in a deep breath. Aram waited for an explanation.

"The Mongols have destroyed the Isma'ilis of Persia, a cursed sect of Islam we call 'Assassins.' I understand many Muslims share our satisfaction with this." The man with the missing left arm twitched his nose.

Robert continued. "The Mongols now approach Baghdad, maybe even the Kingdom of Jerusalem and Egypt. They are God's wrath against this blasphemy known as Islam that has been permitted to fester like a pestilence and corrupt this world for over six hundred years."

"God's wrath," Aram repeated, successfully hiding his skepticism. "Oh yes. Of course."

"But we need to set an alliance with them, to make sure they understand their purpose in God's plan."

"An alliance," Aram repeated. The two men to Robert's immediate left and right watched Aram intently. The man on the far right wore an uneasy look on his face, and the one on the far left took in a deep breath.

"Yes," Robert said, seeming to grow irritated. "Against a common enemy. I have heard it said there are Christians among the Mongols?"

"Christians?" Aram paused a moment, then shrugged. "Yes. Not Catholic Christians, but Christians. The Kerait tribe, which has provided wives for many of Genghis Khan's sons and grandsons, call themselves Christian. Some of them believe an ancestor of theirs was one of the three wise men who visited the baby Jesus."

"Ah," Robert said with a nod and a smile. "Well, your knowledge is already enlightening our purpose. We will return that visit to the baby Jesus with our own wisdom. To avoid Hell, they'll simply need to update their Christian beliefs by accepting the religious supremacy of the pope."

Aram forced a smile.

"Good information. Very good, Arnaux," Robert said. "Any questions?"

"Um...." Aram did have questions. If he posed them, though, he had a chance of losing the job. But Aram considered that if this man Robert was really committed to this stated mission, maybe Aram did not want the job. "I may have a question or two...."

Nestor's shoulders squirmed. "Shush," he whispered to Aram.

"Let him ask," Robert said.

Aram raised his eyebrows. He looked at Nestor.

Nestor responded with a look of disapproval.

Aram decided now was the time to be frank, before he committed himself to a job that might be suicidal. Nestor would just have to suffer through it. "In your Christianity, is there a special place in Heaven for martyrs?"

Nestor grunted as he elbowed Aram.

Robert tilted his head. He appeared to ponder the question. "No. I don't think so. Living a good Christian life is the passport to Heaven."

"Then I don't understand the point."

Robert's eyes narrowed.

Nestor quickly interjected, "I'm sure Aram, uh, Arnaux, can learn enough to carry out this mission."

Robert ignored him. "You don't understand 'the point'?" he asked Aram.

"If you aren't trying to become a martyr, no, I don't understand it," Aram said casually. "Because if we go to Mongol rulers and tell them they must submit to the pope or they'll burn in Hell, we have a good chance of becoming martyrs."

Nestor spoke quickly. "Your grace, forgive—"

"You seem to lack faith in the mission, in me, and, I daresay, in God."

Nestor chimed in again. "I'm sure he can be further educated and shown his errors. He's young, and a little—"

"I've learned about Mongols," Aram said, locking eyes with Robert. "Firsthand. Surely you've been briefed by your own people about the recent Christian missions there."

Robert's eyes darted away from Aram. The other four men at the table seemed frozen.

Aram continued. "Very recently, a monk, William, went and—"

"I know about that," Robert said dismissively as his gaze drifted, avoiding eye contact. "It is of no relevance or consequence to our mission."

"But it would seem to—"

"You presume to doubt my ability to successfully complete a Christian mission to the Mongols?" Robert seemed to be begging for a confrontation.

Nestor scowled and clenched his teeth. "Aram," he said quietly out of the side of his mouth. "Not now."

Aram again locked eyes with Robert. "As you've described it, yes, I do question that such a mission can have any potential for success."

Robert's expression hardened.

Nestor whispered, "Aram. Apologize."

Aram was not going to say another word. It was Robert's move. Their eyes remained fixed on each other.

Robert's expression softened as he nodded slowly. He tightened his lips into a grin. "Very good. Very good, Arnaux."

"It's *Aram*, sir."

Robert nodded his head once. "Aram."

"I told you," Nestor said with a tone of relief and forced enthusiasm. "He's exactly—"

"Nestor, wait outside," Robert ordered.

Nestor offered a quick bow and left the room.

"I don't need someone along on this mission who thinks I'm a dangerous fool, but won't speak up," Robert told Aram. "Of course I have studied the reports of the recent Christian travelers to the Mongol lands. I am aware of the story of the Dominican, Ascelin, whose party was almost executed when he refused to walk between two fires and bend his knees to the great khan. And I'm not looking for this to be a mission to Prester John."

Aram smiled his understanding.

"You know of Prester John."

"I was an orphan, and grew up with my adoptive parents in a Nestorian church in Baghdad. I heard about the fabled Eastern kingdom of Prester John," Aram said. "His armies from exotic lands were supposed to sweep away the Muslim domination of the Holy Land. That talk encouraged me to travel east, with caravans, as a helper and interpreter. I never saw any Prester John kingdom, or even a slight hint of Prester John. And I learned—the Mongols are *not* Prester John."

"This is our conclusion as well. But the Mongols are coming. We need contact with this group moving through Persia. We need to determine if they are allies or enemies. We need a clear understanding of their capabilities. And there are still those in authority who believe that a more sophisticated and clever diplomatic approach can yield better results than the past missions. There is a sense that we have just not explained ourselves correctly. We're to try again. So for this mission, I need someone who knows the territory, and won't be afraid to share his knowledge, even when under pressure not to."

Aram started to speak.

Robert added quickly, "Always respectfully, of course."

"Yes, your grace." Aram hesitated. "You must understand, though, that in the Mongol language, the words for alliance and submission are the same."

"A linguistic problem I have no doubt you will find a way to solve."

"It may be more than a 'linguistic problem'...."

"I know our task will not be easy."

"No, your grace."

Robert nodded. "We leave in two days. Please summon Nestor back in here."

Nestor entered timidly, as if trying to assess the mood of the room before deciding how he should behave.

"Thank you for bringing this young man to our attention. We will reimburse your expenses before we leave on the mission, and will firm up the terms of compensation."

Nestor's face broke into a broad smile. "I had no doubts about his suitability. No doubts at all."

Aram rolled his eyes.

Robert smiled.

Nestor bowed and followed Aram out.

"What kind of job have you gotten me?" Aram asked as they walked back down the hall toward his room. "You've dragged me into the middle of a Western Christian civil war. Even those five men did not seem unified. And this mission is led by a recent arrival to the area who seems unaware of what he is walking into."

"It's a good job for an ambitious young man."

"I really try not to cross paths with Mongols."

"You will be envoys. Mongols respect envoys."

"And they have very creative ways of dealing with spies. This is a spy's errand."

"You'll figure it out."

"Are you coming along on this one?"

"I trust you."

Aram stopped and eyed Nestor. "You trust me, so you'll be coming along because you know I can keep us alive? Or you trust me, so you don't need to come along because you figure I'll be able to handle the job without you?"

"The second one."

"Thanks."

The men resumed walking.

Aram arrived at his room. Nestor continued past.

Aram opened his door.

"Did you get the job, 'Prince'?" asked the beautiful dark-haired girl.

Aram broke into a broad smile at seeing that she was still in his room. And she had not gotten dressed.

"Yes. Yes I did."

"Then let's pray for your success." She rose to a kneeling position on the bed. The blanket slipped off of her.

Aram quickly entered and closed the door.

Late January, 1258
One Day Southwest of Kerak, Dead Sea
Night

"How many times do we challenge them?" The question was posed by al-Malik al-Zahir Rukn al-Din Baybars al-Bunduq-dari al-Salahi, known simply as Baybars to many in the region. Baybars crouched with a small group of warriors gathered around a smoldering campfire. The desert terrain amplified the effects of the dry, cold night. "How many times?" Baybars squinted and clenched his teeth. "Until we have our revenge!"

Baybars was a gigantic man with huge hands. He stood over six feet tall and spoke with a low, booming voice. He was about thirty years old—he had no idea of his exact age. His skin was lighter than most Arabs, but darker than most Europeans, the result of his Qipchaq Caucasus-Turkic origins. His unusual blue eyes were even further distinguished by a needle-sized dot prominently visible in his right eye.

The men were wrapped in blankets, huddled around a fire that barely generated enough heat to warm them. All were filthy. They wore torn and faded robes and turbans. Their faces were smudged with the dirt of many days outdoors without shelter.

Swords and knives dangled from their belts. They were Mamluks—former soldier-slaves, now independent warriors. They were originally from an island settlement in the Nile, and were therefore referred to as the Bahriyya: "of the river."

"Qutuz's men keep defeating us—over and over again. They have more men, more weapons," said Sunqur al-Asqar, a short, burly, slightly darker man than Baybars.

Qalawun, one of Baybars' key lieutenants, a well-built man with sparkling dark green eyes and a chisled, strikingly handsome face, widened his eyes and adjusted his position to add a little space between himself and Baybars.

"And so you are losing your desire to regroup and attack them again...."

None of the men offered a comment. They did not move.

"Well, we certainly could make a living providing our services to these flaccid, left-over princes from the Ayyubid sultans. No shortage of work helping them fight each other." Baybars tried to sound casual, testing for agreement, but ready to explode at the first signs of it.

"Life could be much worse," Sunqur al-Asqar finally said tentatively. He was one of the farthest from Baybars.

Baybars burst toward Sunqur al-Asqar, but stopped short of striking him. "We are the Bahriyya! God did not create us to be petty mercenaries!"

The men cowered.

Qalawun shook his head with an almost imperceptible motion as he seemed to be warning Baybars he was going too far.

Baybars backed off and resumed his position crouching at the campfire. "We all share a similar journey," he reminded them. "Many years ago, I was a happy boy, playing in the gentle pastures of my homeland far north of here. Mongols drove my family into exile. Treacherous benefactors who agreed to protect us sold us into slavery. One master rejected me because his wife feared the mark in my right eye. Another master was himself captured and enslaved for a time, making me the slave of a slave. But God reached out and pulled me from the depths, bringing me to the attention of the sultan's inner circle. Like all of you, I attained the honor of becoming an elite slave-soldier. We trained together and lived together, isolated on an island in the Nile Delta, chosen and trained to fight the sultan's most important battles. We all share this in common—raised from meager circumstances to be members of the Bahriyya Mamluks!"

The men nodded and grunted in agreement, including Qalawun and Sunqur al-Asqar.

"Will any of us ever forget the day Faris al-Din Aqtay's head came down to us from the citadel?" Baybars paused and made direct eye contact with the men. "I warned him that dog Qutuz was not to be trusted. God has made me the victim of so much treachery—this has been God's gift to me, that I can smell treachery with the skill of a hunting dog. But Aqtay...." Baybars shook his head. "How many of you were there to see his head flung out like a child's play-ball?" Baybars wanted them to live back in that day, that day when the Bahriyya—bold in battle, strong enough to topple a sultan and install a Mamluk regime— were forced to flee for their lives. Baybars gave his men a chance to immerse themselves in the memories. He inhaled and exhaled tensely as he recalled the treachery of Qutuz, a Mamluk slave-soldier with similar origins to his own, but who had turned on the Bahriyya and engineered the death of their leader, forcing them to become refugees from the center of power in Egypt. Baybars and his men had fought with Qutuz to deal a devastating blow to the French king along the Nile River a decade or so before. They had quelled significant rebellions against Sultan Aybaq. The treacherous Qutuz rewarded their service by making his move with Aybaq, reducing the power and prestige of the Bahriyya by murdering their leader.

"How long do we fight them?" Baybars finally asked. "Until the Bahriyya take power in Egypt! Until that treacherous dog Qutuz is at our mercy, so we can fling *his* head down from the citadel!"

No cheer sounded. The men were too cold and tired to break into an overt demonstration. But many nodded. Some faces clenched in determination.

"Victory to the Bahriyya! Death to Qutuz!" said Sunqur al-Asqar.

Qalawun and a number of other voices repeated the statements, not quite in unison.

"I got all the way through to their standards in the last battle," Baybars reminded them. "Next time, you will provide me lots of company. God wills it."

Qalawun nodded. "We need to settle some business here first, with this al-Mughith Umar who is supposed to be allied with us."

Baybars' eyes narrowed. "Yes. Yes, he will need to supply more resources for our next move against Qutuz."

"He fancies himself sultan of Egypt, but seems unwilling to commit completely to the fight," Qalawun added.

Baybars took in a deep breath. He looked down at a small parchment in his hand. "Sultan of Egypt." His lips tensed. "We will educate him further as to our value to that ambition. And he will treat all if us, including our wives, with the respect we deserve."

Qalawun frowned at the parchment, his face tensing, as if requesting an explanation.

Baybars looked at the parchment again. "A communication from my wife. Some continuing misunderstandings."

"Commander. What of the rumors from the north?" Sunqur al-Asqar asked. "That the Mongols are on their way?"

"Mongols." Baybars nodded, staring grimly out at nothing. "I've heard the rumors." Mongols had indirectly shaped Baybars' life for almost twenty years. It had to be God's will that he would some day confront them directly. "We won't be able to face Mongols with al-Mughith Umar's meager resources. If God wills that we are to confront those creatures, and earn the honor of destroying them, then we will need the resources of Egypt. Qutuz and his puppet sultan must go, and Egypt must be under the command of the Bahriyya!"

Qalawun started a rhythmic chant that began to build. "Victory to the Bahriyya! Death to Qutuz!"

Baybars broke into a confident grin. These men would defeat Qutuz. Maybe not with al-Mughith Umar. But some way, God would deliver victory over Qutuz. Treachery would be met with justice. The failures of the past would only serve to make the successes of the future more gratifying.

3

January 30, 1258
Mustinsiriyah College in Baghdad
Morning

"The positionings are still not predicted by any logical formula," Dawud said to his student. They sat on a wooden bench in a large library situated within the grounds of the Mustinsiriyah College. Before them was a long wooden table piled with stacks of reading material. The morning sun shining through two windows offered the only light into the dingy room. Dawud held a piece of glass over a bound ledger to aid his aging eyes. He and his student were the only two present in a room usually teeming with scholars and students. Dawud shook his head. "God may choose not to answer this dilemma before my time comes."

"The Koran says the sun revolves around the earth and—"

"The Koran says nothing like that." Dawud looked up from his reading glass. "You show me the passage."

"I don't—" The student stopped himself in mid sentence. "This is what I was taught."

"Teachers sometimes overstate and misinform. If there is one task I could accomplish before I am called to paradise, it would be to offer a treatise that separates the truth offered by the Prophet, and by the truly knowledgeable, from the babblings of the ignorant." Dawud held the reading glass up to his eyes and refocused on the ledger.

"Isn't it obvious that the sun revolves around—"

"Of course. But we should be able to reconcile astronomy with mathematics. And we can't. This is God's puzzle."

"God's puzzle?" The student seemed impatient. "God's puzzle is outside these walls!"

Dawud looked up. The student added, "God's puzzle is that we, the Faithful, in God's greatest city, face—extermination!"

Dawud was taken off guard by his student's emotional outburst. He wasn't sure what to say.

"The answer to God's puzzle is not in those ledger books!"

Dawud set his piece of glass down. He smoothed his beard, caught himself, but then smiled and smoothed it again without internally chastising himself for the habit. "The resolution of that puzzle is separated from us by only a few days. It is in the hands of human beings. And the answer will likely be definitive." He shrugged. "The answer will probably be death."

The student tensed. Tears flowed.

"It is a sadder answer for a younger man, with so much talent…"

The student swallowed. "Sorry."

"But this"—Dawud pointed to the ledgers—"I don't think we will have this answer before … before the end."

A booming, crashing sound thudded in the distance.

"It's beginning," Dawud said with the quiet calm of a man who had accepted whatever fate awaited him.

"On the other side of the city," the student commented.

"From the land side. Mongols are not water creatures—I don't see them mounting an assault from across the Tigris."

The student burst into laughter. "The Mongol navy—that ought to be the concluding line of some kind of joke." The smiles turned back to tears.

Dawud put down the piece of glass and stood. "You and I do not control what will happen to us."

Another booming, thudding sound punctuated Dawud's words.

"We can only control how we will react. I prefer not to immerse in misery."

The student nodded his head vigorously. "I know. I know."

"Let's take a walk through the palace, maybe even into town."

The student stood.

"Are they really so foolish?" the student asked. They walked along the Tuesday Market District at the northwestern edge of Baghdad proper, the opposite end from where Dawud suspected the main Mongol offensive was taking place. It was empty of stands offering goods for sale. Some stalls left in the area appeared to have been looted. Wide palm leaves, used to shade the stalls when the markets were active, lay strewn through the area. The market usually bustled with activity at this time of day. But commerce had understandably disappeared.

Dawud shook his head. He looked at the families gathering to leave through the Sultan's Gate, at the northwest tip of the city. "It's hard to say who's foolish," he said. "But this city is surrounded. They're walking into certain death."

"There must be something we can do," the student insisted. "Escaping across the Tigris might offer us at least some hope."

"I will bear no ill will toward you if you wish to take that route," Dawud said, and engaged in a rare tap of affection on the student's shoulder.

"But you won't go."

Dawud smiled and shook his head. "No."

"You are my family here in Baghdad. When I came from Nablus to study with you, with my parents' blessing, at my parents' urging, I linked my fate with yours."

"Your choice." Dawud nodded. "Completely your choice."

"Should we at least consider leaving Mustinsiriyah College to remove ourselves from the palace grounds? To be associated with the caliph could be—"

"Don't start with that Christian church idea again."

"We have friends there. *You* have friends there. There is a rumor they have some sort of protection."

"I do have friends there. No doubt, I have learned to accomplish much good through collaboration with well-meaning, intelligent people of other faiths. But I will not jeopardize my place in paradise by accepting protection from a faith I have so completely, at times even violently, rejected. Death is preferable. I will die as a true Muslim, not as a Muslim who flees to the protection of the infidels when it is convenient."

"Arrows!"

Dawud looked up. A scattered group of arrows came over the Sultan's Gate.

Screams came from the people gathered there.

"Very low concentration." Dawud studied the arrows. "Just enough to let us know they're out there."

The arrows crested.

Panic gripped a number of people in the crowd. "Flames!" one of them shouted. People crouched and ducked, some jostling each other for position away from the arrows.

"They're not flamers," Dawud said quietly to his student. A few of the highest arrows seemed to pose a threat, but the others would fall short. "Flamers do not look like that."

Dawud gently moved his student back from the gate area.

"Something's attached to them," the student said.

"To the middle of the shafts." Dawud watched, barely moving, as one of the arrows impacted a few feet from them. His student flinched and cowered.

The arrow bounced up slightly, then skidded. The tip had not been sharpened enough to pierce and stick into anything. Dawud picked up the arrow. Attached to it was a sturdy piece of paper with writing on it.

"A message?" the student asked from a crouch.

"In clumsy Arabic, but definitely a message. We should get this to someone in authority." Dawud began walking toward the southeastern edge of Baghdad. He did not turn to see if his student was following. Maybe he would. Or maybe he would choose not to walk closer to the main Mongol attacks.

"Yes, yes, we have reports from all over Baghdad," said the commander of the unit resisting at the Halba Gate. He was addressing Dawud impatiently. "We know about the message." Crushed structures and smoldering ruins dominated Dawud's view. Unburied bodies and unattended wounded were evidence of the ongoing hostilities at the southeast end of Baghdad. "They've got to stay up on those walls!" the commander shouted.

The area suddenly shook with the impact of something massive colliding with a nearby section of the wall. Dawud saw a man cascading off the wall, apparently trying to avoid the Mongol barrage. A few others tumbled to the ground, pierced with arrows. Other arrows shot past the walls and stuck into the ground. A ball of fire flew over the wall toward the interior of the city. It crashed into a small building and spread spurts of flames throughout the area. A huge disk followed the flaming orb and tumbled into a cache of supplies about ten feet behind the walls. The impact threw arrows and shields into the air.

"Mongols must not care about dates," Dawud said, more to himself than to his student.

"What?"

"They must not have enough stones for all the catapults. So they've cut up the date trees." Dawud's face offered a dark, wry grin. "Won't be a very good date harvest this year."

The student did not seem in a mood to respond to the dark humor. "We delivered the message. Let's go."

The area shook again with another heavy impact against the walls.

Dawud looked at the commander, but the man did not even seem aware Dawud was still there. Dawud nodded. His student moved hurriedly from the area and Dawud quickened his pace to keep up.

"Teacher," the student said as they walked, "the message says judges, scholars, administrators and Christians will be spared."

Dawud didn't respond. He kept looking up, back behind them, for dangers from the sky.

"We should at least move out of the palace area," the student said. "That might increase our odds for—"

"Over!" Dawud yelled. He spotted a ball of fire heading toward them. Dawud shoved the student roughly across the narrow street. The student flew forward and landed chest and face first. The flaming ball smashed into the ground right where they had been walking. Liquid flames splashed up, hitting nearby structures, starting fires against anything flammable.

Dawud raised his arm as some of the liquid splashed toward him. He grunted with pain, his right forearm burned. A pinch of the Greek fire had found him. He stooped quickly and rolled his forearm on the ground.

The student groaned as he got up. "Are you all right?" he said.

Dawud grimaced. "I smothered it out. The only way to put out Greek fire." He looked at his arm. "It will hurt for a few days. I'll wash it, to prevent festering." Dawud looked at his student. "Are you well?"

"Yes. Thanks to you."

Dawud shrugged. Holding his injured forearm with his left hand, he resumed his survey of the sky above them.

"So, do you think we should move out of the palace grounds?"

Dawud again did not answer. Why couldn't his student understand? Questions of panic, of obsessing over survival, would only lead to distress. Dawud did not want to feel that way. He had accepted that God would handle his fate. If a horrible moment awaited him, he would reduce its duration by not thinking about it until it actually happened. He would face the rest of his time on his terms, by living in the present. How could he get this young man to understand this, so he would stop trying to push Dawud into a horrible moment before its time?

"I know you don't want to go to the Christian churches, but that would assure us—"

"I don't know," Dawud stated gruffly. He did not refuse; he

simply implied, with this response, that he did not want to address the question. Would the student get the idea? Explaining it, elaborating it, would also dilute Dawud's immersion in the present. He had emphatically refused this suggestion before. Now he was saying he did not know.

The student did not speak for a moment.

Dawud surveyed the sky. Another large disk came over the walls, but landed well short of them. It was followed by another flaming ball, but the two men were now far enough removed from the danger area so that it landed a harmless distance from them.

The student smiled. When he spoke, the frenzy had gone out of his voice. He exuded the confident tone of a lesson learned. "If the Koran does not say that the sun revolves around the earth, and our calculations suggest other answers, then should we consider other possibilities, even if learned teachers, blessed by God with wisdom and authority, tell us not to?"

Dawud flashed a quick, slight grin. His student had gotten the message. "Do you consider me to be such a blessed teacher?" Dawud asked.

"Of course. You are one of the most blessed with wisdom by God whom I have ever known."

"Then know this: I have been wrong. Many times."

A smile crept onto the student's face.

February 10, 1258
Just outside the walls of Baghdad
Afternoon

"It is the caliph himself this time," Ketbugha said to Hulegu. They stood just outside Hulegu's tent. Hulegu's area of the Mongol camp consisted of Hulegu's huge blue silk tent, with smaller tents surrounding it to form a makeshift enclosure. About a half mile away, Hulegu could see the walls of Baghdad.

Hulegu nodded. "Finally."

"With a few thousand of his closest friends." Ketbugha smirked.

Hulegu's eyes narrowed in thought. "Armed?"

"No, no." Ketbugha waved off the idea with a dismissive hand gesture. "Retainers. Hangers-on."

"The fool thinks he has safety in numbers?"

"I don't know. If he does believe that, he is *truly* a fool."

Hulegu chuckled. "Well, we *will* greet *this* delegation. Have the guards flank them whether they look threatening or not. And have them work their way among this delegation of thousands. Break it up into segments. If this man believes he has safety in numbers, let us keep him uneasy."

"Yes sir."

Hulegu's servants brought him his mount. Interpreters, top commanders and his elite guards joined Hulegu's entourage without any direct orders from the Mongol prince.

Hulegu's entourage advanced at a regal pace. Hulegu rode in the middle of the group, Ketbugha on one side and his interpreter on the other. Hulegu held a neutral expression on his face. He resolved to maintain a stone-faced courtesy.

The caliph rode in the middle of his own entourage. He wore a bright white turban adorned with a few jewels, and a silk robe intricately decorated with interlocking blue and light green curves. The caliph's bold attire seemed completely contradicted by his manner. He kept looking back at his entourage of thousands as it seemed to melt away behind him, infused with lines of Hulegu's guards. As the caliph arrived, Hulegu noticed the leader of this great religion was perspiring, gulping nervously, almost shaking. When the caliph got within about fifteen feet of Hulegu, the group accompanying him was down to a handful, about half the size of Hulegu's entourage. Hulegu was satisfied the right conditions had been created for this meeting.

Hulegu turned to his interpreter. "Ask him if his health is good."

As the question was translated, it seemed to jolt the caliph. Hulegu was pleased the caliph seemed more and more uneasy and confused. The interpreters continued to facilitate the exchange. "My health is fine."

"I'm glad to hear that." Hulegu nodded with feigned surprise. "I thought perhaps you were ill, and this is why you sent your sons out of the walls to bring tribute, and discuss the terms of your surrender and submission, terms that you yourself should have offered us months ago."

The caliph swallowed. Was he fighting tears? "My sons … are honored representatives of Islam. They offered the tribute in my name. I am sorry this wasn't clear." The caliph tipped his head with a quick bow. "This is why you did not accept their embassy, or their gifts?"

Hulegu eyed the caliph. "Gifts," he repeated. He deliberately forced a laugh for effect. "We have your city, this fabled city of yours blessed by the god you worship." He shook his head. "Under the circumstances, the generosity of your middle son, five days ago, was either the result of laughable incompetence, or deliberate insult. Your oldest son, the next day, brought us nothing to change our minds. Your presence has been required all along, with more substantial gifts, and should have been offered long before this."

"But you will accept"—the caliph stammered, apparently stuck for a choice of words— "our gifts offered today?"

Hulegu shrugged. "Of course. Because they come with your surrender and submission."

The caliph's eyes widened with apprehension at this translation. He swallowed again; his face contorted to fight back tears, but two rolled down his cheeks. "What should we do?" he finally asked with a whimper.

Hulegu scowled. He found the man's tears disgusting. He looked at Ketbugha, who said, "We need the city clear, to complete the next steps of the operation."

Hulegu nodded. He forced a smile as he looked back at the caliph. "Put the word out to all people remaining in the city. They need to lay down their arms and move out of the city so we can count them."

The caliph nodded. He turned to a man with him and gave him orders. The man rode away, joined by a squad of Mongol guards.

"I'm going to put them near you," Hulegu told Ketbugha quietly.

Ketbugha nodded.

"While this process is completed," Hulegu said to the caliph, "you and your sons will pitch tents at the gate near my General Ketbugha's camp. That is all."

The caliph nodded. A squad of guards surrounded the caliph and his entourage and began guiding them toward Ketbugha's camp at the Kalwadha Gate, at the southern end of Baghdad next to the Tigris River.

Ketbugha commented to Hulegu, "He did not even ask about the people."

"He may assume that if we're going to count them, we're going to spare them. But he is too afraid for his own survival to ask the question. Some man of religion he is."

"Are we counting them?"

"Of course not. Kill them all. Set squads to keep the groups herded and isolated to minimize the usual fuss and panic."

"Do you think he believes his action today might spare the city?"

Hulegu laughed. "I can't imagine how he could believe that. He must know we had his army disarm and come out three days ago, then killed every one of them." Hulegu shook his head. "He either harbors some ridiculous hope that we will not exact the justice against this city and its people that his behavior has brought upon them. Or, he knows they will be slaughtered, and only hopes to buy a few more days of his own life by facilitating their deaths. Either way, he is not worthy to be a leader, or even to breathe the air under our rulership. We will deal with him accordingly, when his usefulness to our activities here has expired."

Ketbugha nodded. He started to move away, then looked back. "Should we continue the policy of sparing scholars, clerks, and Christians?"

Hulegu raised his eyebrows. "Of course. But they should have received word they will be spared." He thought a moment. "They should be waiting in enclaves within the city. The Christians should be in their places of worship. But, in case some useful people come out with this group, have some of your knowledgeable agents roaming the activities, looking for those we should keep alive."

Ketbugha bowed and rode away.

Hulegu smiled. Mongol councils had called Baghdad the greatest city in the world. The Genghis Khan dynastic empire, three generations old, was within days of completing the total conquest and absorption of the greatest city in the world. The Eternal Blue Heaven continued to smile prosperity on Hulegu and his family.

February 10, 1258
Mustinsiriyah College in Baghdad
Afternoon

"Throw down your weapons! Come out of the gates to be counted! Your lives will be spared!" The herald spoke in Arabic, with a local accent. Dawud rose from his prayer rug, reacting to this announcement that resonated from outside the library. The act of pushing himself up caused pain to emanate from his burned forearm and he grimaced.

Drums and bells punctuated the repetitions of the proclamation. "Throw down your weapons! Come out of the gates to be counted! Your lives will be spared!"

"We're to be spared?" Dawud's student asked. He also rose from his prayer rug.

The bells and drums, and the announcement, began to fade as the heraldic procession moved on.

"That is the message." Dawud spoke with a detached tone, shielding his conflicted feelings. This announcement, and the herald's accent, told Dawud that the Mongols were now in control of Baghdad, but not yet within the city walls. Would the Mongols really spare anyone, or was this just how they accumulated the people to be slaughtered? And did Dawud want to survive?

"Should we do what they are asking?"

Dawud raised his eyebrows. "We have few options. The area inside the gates will be a very dangerous place when the Mongols start plundering. So we—"

"We could still go to the Christian church over at—"

"If I am to die, I will die true to my faith, not cowering with infidels."

The student nodded. "Could it be that the caliph has agreed to terms that spare Islam's greatest city?"

Dawud smiled. "That would be a miracle."

"An answer to a prayer."

Dawud nodded. He did not believe the student's theory could be correct, but he enjoyed the optimism. If these were to be his final moments, let them be spent with this person, exuding this hopeful emotional state. "Well, if the caliph has come to terms, and a count of citizens is part of it, then we should obey the summons."

"What else could it be?"

If Dawud answered honestly and openly, he would sabotage his student's hopeful mood. His gift to his student would be to help him stay out of the terrible moment, avoid it until it arrived. Dawud shrugged. "Let's go."

Dawud and his student left Dawud's quarters and headed for the Sultan's Gate at the northwest wall of the city. They joined a procession of people moving in the same direction. Some carried belongings, perhaps expecting to be relocated. Most wore expressions of dejection, apprehension, resignation, or mixtures of these moods.

"They need to count us," a middle-aged woman chattered nervously. "They're taking over the city, so they need a count, to know how many of us they now rule. That's a good measure. That's a wise measure."

"They need us out of the walls to loot the city," an elderly man said.

"They can have the loot, I'll take my safety," the woman replied.

She continued to talk but Dawud stopped taking note of the words. The procession grew in numbers as they reached the gate.

Dawud looked at his student. The student drew a deep nervous breath.

"When we get to the gate, and emerge outside, we will know what fate awaits us."

The student nodded.

A crush of people formed at the gate. The smell of sweat and the heat of close bodies increased. Dawud and his student squeezed with the massed humanity through to the other side.

"Move! Move!" The commands were in heavily accented Arabic. "Move to count! Move to be counted!" One yelled directly at Dawud. A horseman urged Dawud forward with a swing of his sword, forcing him to jog to the right, joining a group in front of him. His student was similarly urged forward. People laden with belongings were beaten or whipped until they dropped them. A squad of about twenty Mongols seemed to be working together. When about a hundred people had accumulated, the squad closed ranks behind them.

The squad swirled around the group, forcing them into a jog.

"We're being herded," the student said.

"Yes." Dawud huffed and puffed for air.

The squad's yelling and circling maneuvers created a mood of urgency. Squad members barked out harsh syllables, mostly indiscernible to Dawud. He did hear "move" a few more times, among the other sounds.

An elderly woman was having trouble keeping up with the group.

A horseman rode up to her as she lagged. "Move!" he shouted at her.

"Please." She struggled to catch her breath. "I'm trying."

Dawud looked back.

The elderly woman stumbled, out of breath and out of energy. She fell to the ground. "Please," she sobbed.

Dawud started toward her.

But before he could get close enough to help her, the horseman dismounted. With no more emotion than a farmer cutting a stalk of grain, he pulled the woman up, pulled her head back by the hair, and—oblivious to her yelp—sliced across her throat with his sword. Blood sprayed up. He threw her body down as if he was tossing aside a sack of trash.

Dawud knew he was probably headed for the same fate. But the rage of a past life bubbled to the surface. If he had possessed a sword and shield, he would have rushed the man. But at this time in his life, all he could offer was a defiant outburst. "Hey! Pigmeat! What about the count?" he yelled at the horseman, with his hands out in a grand shrug.

The horseman looked puzzled, as if trying to understand Dawud's comment. He scowled with annoyance, but then smiled. "No need count! She dead!" His eyes reflected his sadistic smile. The horseman remounted and kept looking at Dawud.

"We are all dead," Dawud told his student. "They're herding us, like cattle, or sheep. Herding us for slaughter."

"God forbid it," the student said, biting his lower lip.

A pungent stench caught Dawud's attention. Between gaps in the enveloping Mongol squad, Dawud could see clusters of corpses. They wore the uniforms of the caliph's forces. Others were of Shiite Muslims he recognized. He knew that some of the

Shiites in Baghdad had sought to spite the dominant Sunnis by secretly offering information to the besieging enemy. It did not appear to Dawud that the Mongols made any distinction between Muslim sects. And didn't these fools realize that the Isma'ilis of Alamut, who were Shiites, had been utterly and mercilessly slaughtered two years before? Swarms of flies hovered over the corpses, Sunni and Shiite, together in death.

"The battle was here?" the student asked.

The Mongol squad continued herding the group along the light brown terrain.

"Not a battle."

"Those are dead soldiers."

"All ours."

"They probably picked up their dead."

"No arrows. If this was a battle, there would be arrows."

The student's mouth opened and he turned white, as if slammed in the midsection by a powerful blow. "This … it's what they … it's what happened to the army when they left the city a few days ago? They slaughtered them. Just … slaughtered them! Defenseless!"

"We're all dead in a matter of moments," Dawud said.

The student looked at him, energized and defiant, with a look that said "no, we're not."

Dawud saw that the lead elements of the squad appeared to be looking for an open area to stop. They passed other clusters of corpses, fresher and fresher the further out they went. They were traveling through a Mongol killing ground—Dawud suspected it was one of many. He figured his final resting place would be nearby.

"We're immune!" the student yelled desperately. "We have immunity!"

Dawud let out a long breath. "I'm not sure I want it."

"Well, I do!" the student yelled. "And I believe it is God's will that you—and I—should not die here like this!"

Dawud shrugged. He did not see any other options.

The leaders of the squad halted at the far edge of the perimeter. The final step in the disposition of this group of Baghdad residents was about to begin.

"We are clerks! We are scholars!" the student yelled.

Commands sounded from around the Mongol perimeter. Soldiers turned toward the group and began hacking the defenseless people with battle-axes. Screams of panic, agony, and despondent disbelief filled the area. Dawud noticed the horseman who had killed the elderly woman. He seemed to have his eyes on Dawud, hacking his way through the slaughter to get to him.

"Clerks! Scholars! We are to survive!" the student kept yelling. He could barely be heard over the din of screaming, and commands of soldiers to contain the human herd as they closed in and hacked the Muslims to pieces.

The student yanked Dawud toward the center of the perimeter.

Dawud considered this a smart move. Panicked people were trying to flee through perceived gaps in the perimeter. They made the Mongols' task easier by running right into their axes. The slaughter squad would close toward the middle, so those in the middle would be killed last. This would give the student the longest possible time to get the attention of someone who might spare them.

First to be killed or last to be killed, Dawud was ready. He almost wished he had died a few days earlier, before watching the humiliation of the great city of Baghdad, subjected to conquest by such an evil and inferior group of people. Dawud knelt. "There is no God but God, and Mohammed is the Messenger of God."

The student scrunched his lips together in grim determination. "Scholars! We are scholars! Clerks! Learned men! I am the student! This is my teacher! The great Dawud! You lose the services of a great man if you kill Dawud the Teacher!"

The perimeter continued to shrink. Less than ten remained alive. None of them were shrieking in panic. They quietly awaited their fates, most of them kneeling and praying.

The student kept yelling, now the loudest in the area, clearly audible. "Learned men! He's a teacher! Dawud the Teacher! I'm his student! Mathematics! Law! Government! Scholars!"

Three more people were hacked down.

"We're to be spared!"

Dawud prayed silently.

Two more people died from vicious ax strokes.

"Scholars! Mathmeticians! Astronomers! We have immunity!"

The squad leader yelled a command.

The killing stopped for a moment.

The squad leader trotted his horse over to Dawud and his student. "Astrologer?" he asked with a crude accent.

The student's eyes brightened. "Yes. Astrologer."

Dawud said nothing. He was an amateur astronomer; in no

way was he an astrologer. But he was not going to correct this misunderstanding at the expense of his student's efforts.

"I am his student. This is Dawud the—" The student paused. "Dawud the Astrologer."

The Mongol squad leader frowned and motioned for quiet. He shouted an order to a man who rode away quickly. He gestured disdainfully with the palm of his hand, and a few horsemen killed the rest of the group. Only Dawud and his student remained.

The student knelt down next to Dawud. "We're going to survive. God wills it."

Dawud nodded.

"Help me," the student said.

Dawud nodded again. He could tell the student that maybe real help was not surviving to live in a Baghdad under Mongol rule. But this was not the place or time to ponder such esoteric subtleties. The crude reality of death or life reduced the moment to simplicity.

Another Mongol rode into the area. He wore a more sophisticated uniform, identifying him as someone who probably had more authority.

"Astrologer?" he asked.

Dawud stood. "Yes. Among other things."

"Scholar."

"Yes."

The Mongol looked at the student.

"I am his student," Dawud's student stated proudly. "This is Dawud, the great astronomer, um, astrologer, mathematician."

Dawud nearly laughed. His education included some knowledge in those disciplines, but he was a religious scholar. He hated astrology. He found it to be a nearly heretical pursuit.

The Mongol nodded. He seemed to understand. He spoke a few casual-sounding words to the squad leader, then rode away.

The squad leader motioned both Dawud and his student to kneel. "Pray," he said.

Dawud shrugged. They knelt.

Dawud looked straight ahead. "There is no God but God, and Mohammed is the Messenger of God."

Dawud heard steps behind him. He heard a *swoosh*, followed by the splat and crackle of an ax against a skull. He felt the sticky mist of his student's blood, and bits of brain and skull hit his side.

Dawud continued his simple prayer of submission to God and adherence to his faith. He waited for what he thought would be a sharp pain to the top of his head, then arrival with God in paradise.

Instead, Dawud felt a tug under his armpit. He was being pulled to a standing position by the same man who had just hacked his student to death.

"We have no need of student," the squad leader explained. "But welcome the help of teacher about heavens. We let you student pray before die—respect for you."

Dawud nodded. He looked around at the carnage. That he was the only non-Mongol walking away was either a divine miracle, or a condemnation to Hell. Dawud was not sure. But he would treasure his life, reaping the benefits of his student's desperate attempts to cling to survival. Refusal to embrace his survival would mock his student's death, a death Dawud considered to be a martyr's death. Yes, Dawud's student was with God in paradise. Dawud would try to make his death count for something.

Second Week of February, 1258
Kerak
Evening

"You seem to enjoy this more and more," Baybars said quietly as he hovered over his wife, Adiba. They lay naked under a blanket. Their small tent was well away from the crowded quarters of the Bahriyya Mamluks, within al-Mughith Umar's castle at Kerak.

Adiba blushed, then pulled Baybars back down onto her, covering her exposed breasts. The brown eyes on her round, cherubic face closed then opened.

Baybars grinned, and pulled himself back up. "It's just us. You do not need to hide your beauty from me."

Adiba smiled, but seemed uneasy. "Beauty," she repeated.

Baybars rose up with the blanket on his back, revealing Adiba's entire body. She was a foot shorter than Baybars, solid, with an hour-glass figure, full breasts, and some extra weight including a slight bulge at her tummy. She looked up at Baybars, looked away, then looked back. Baybars enjoyed her apparent admiration of his huge, thick, well-conditioned body. "Yes, beauty. And it's as it should be. We will acquire position and status. You will be the mother of sons to carry on that position." Baybars pulled the blanket over them and lay face up. He pulled Adiba tightly to him.

"Yes. As you always say."

"Patience."

"Life has taught me patience, my dear husband."

Baybars nodded. "I know. And you have been an excellent student." He took in a long breath, then exhaled. "We will be riding out again."

Adiba answered with a nod. But her glistening eyes gave her feelings away.

Baybars said, "I have been unable to speak to al-Mughith Umar about the, the issues you have raised."

Adiba's lips tightened. Tears formed. "Mmm hmmm."

"It is an awkward situation, with his attitude."

"I know." Tears streamed down her cheeks. "Just take us with you."

"I can't. This is not much more than a raid. We need to be able to move quickly. It would be too dangerous for you and the other wives—and for us, if we need to focus on protecting you instead of completing a successful raid."

Adiba looked away.

"It will be all right," Baybars said. "Try to stay clear of al-Mughith Umar and his household as much as possible."

"It's not so easy. We have to interact with them for our basic needs."

"Do what you can."

"We are treated horribly when you are gone!" Adiba's lips trembled. "I cannot assure you that we will all be here when you return! Who knows what depredations al-Mughith Umar will inflict on us!"

Baybars frowned. "He wouldn't dare."

"He thinks of us all as slaves."

"I have seen that attitude. I was freed a decade ago, and placed in a prominent position in the sultan of Egypt's army. He has no call to treat me or you in that manner."

Adiba shrugged. "I was a slave. Not long ago. Headed for a brothel. Part Arab, maybe part Greek or Armenian, or even Turk. Not quite pretty enough for a harem."

Baybars grinned. "I have no complaints about your beauty at all."

"I know you find me modest, even a bit shy."

Baybars tilted his head as he smiled. "You are growing out of it."

"My gift to you, and only you."

Baybars nodded and grinned.

"Lucky for me and my virtue—and for you—I hid my female

development when it started to emerge on my body. I learned to wear loose clothes, keep my eyes down. Dress girlish. Act girlish."

"I know. When I first saw you, you tried that looking-down tactic of yours. But I saw you for the incredible woman you are."

Adiba smiled as she scrunched her shoulders and lowered her eyes.

"I know it is difficult here with al-Mughith Umar. Keep your dealings with that household as meager as possible, like we talked about. Keep the other wives doing the same. I will try to settle all issues with al-Mughith Umar when we return."

Adiba dropped her chin and appeared to fight tears. "Return soon and be safe," she said, almost as if it was a prayer.

Baybars smiled. "God wills it."

Second Week of February, 1258
Acre
Morning

"You asked to see me?" Aram entered Robert of Montpelier's spotlessly clean, tidy and austere office, past two lightly armed guards. Aram wondered why Robert needed guards, but perhaps this was standard for a man in Robert's position.

"Yes." Robert seemed to be stifling a smirk. "Please come and sit with me."

Aram's eyes darted back and forth. He was puzzled by the summons, and Robert's apparently flippant attitude. He nodded politely and sat in a chair next to Robert's table.

Robert had a parchment in front of him. "You must be wondering about the mission."

Aram's eyes darted again. "Um, certainly." Actually he could care less, but he hoped Robert did not sense his attitude.

Robert did. "Ah. Something tells me you are not." He smiled.

Aram realized he needed to do a better job of guarding his feelings. "I figured … I thought we'd leave when you're ready, and that you'd let me know. I have been standing by." Aram tried forcing a charming smile.

"Yes. Well, in case you have been curious, the mission has been postponed."

Aram nodded. "Not cancelled."

"No."

Aram's eyes wandered the room. The man wanted him to ask for more information. Aram truly did not care, but also suspected that whatever purpose this meeting had, he would need to play Robert's game to get to it and end the meeting. "Um, why is the mission postponed?"

"I'm glad you asked. There are military operations underway, and I could not arrange a sufficient armed escort for our journey to the Mongols. It is deemed unwise for us to travel through these battle zones right now without a fairly sizeable contingent of armed men. You are aware of these silly hostilities festering between the Venetians and Genoese? Well, with every group in the city apparently compelled to align with one side or the other, I am finding it difficult to gather much of an escort for our mission."

"The Mongols have reached Baghdad?" Aram said. He knew the Mongols had been on their way. He did not believe they would arrive so quickly.

"They may have taken the city by now."

Aram nodded slowly.

"Your home," Robert said.

"I have few possessions there, nothing worth looting, nothing I even care to check on. And Christians—friends and family—have protection."

Robert scratched his chin. "Christians."

"Yes. As I have said, many Mongol wives are Christian, and—"

"In your Christianity, what is the nature of Christ?"

Aram's eyes widened. He looked away, then back at Robert. "My Christianity?"

"Yes."

"I'm sure it's the same for all Christians, isn't it?"

Robert squinted. "Don't play me for a fool, Aram. You know that the Nestorian Christians have serious differences with the true Christianity practiced under the authority of the pope."

It was at these times, when Robert seemed most emotional— at this point, annoyed—that his peculiar accent emerged most noticeably. Aram swallowed. This meeting was going to be more than just a status report.

"Hmmm." Robert seemed to be sizing him up. "I suspect the differences are a lot more important to others than they are to you."

Aram nodded. "Yes. True."

"I was impressed with you at our first meeting."

"Thank you."

"Others were not."

"I'm … sorry."

Robert flashed a skeptical expression. No, Aram was not sorry and Robert appeared to know it. "They felt I glossed over important potential religious differences."

Aram was not sure how to respond. He wondered if any of the men he had met with Robert had objected to Aram in an effort to sabotage Robert's mission, a mission about which they appeared to harbor some doubts.

"Some were in favor of rejecting your service to us because they do not believe you are a true Christian. We debated and negotiated the problem, and have agreed to a resolution, one I am sure you will not object to."

"Yes?"

"You will take baptism for the true Christian faith, and agree to undergo a course of instruction."

"Well, now." Aram fought for the right words. He smiled and shrugged. "Well, really, your excellency, your holiness—that wasn't part of the terms of my employment here." He shrugged again.

"Hmmm." Robert nodded. His eyes narrowed, and there was that smirk again. "Have you ever visited St. Anne's Convent?"

Aram straightened up. "I believe so."

Robert chuckled, deliberately lingering on the sounds he was making, as if totally in charge of the moment, and enjoying his domination of it. Robert glanced down at his parchment.

Aram wished he would get to the point.

"I have reports about you and two novices. One has visited you here. Poor child, she was orphaned when her parents died of the coughing sickness. The other, a feeble-minded girl, could not manage to sneak away to meet you."

Aram drew a deep breath and grunted. There had actually been three girls. One of them had evidently been clever enough to avoid detection. The other girl—feeble-minded? Possibly. Feeble-minded but gorgeous. Now he knew why she hadn't come to their planned tryst.

"It seems to me," Robert stated, as if appraising some mundane issue, like the cleanliness of a chapel floor, "that you have too much time on your hands, and not enough to do."

Aram scrunched his lips together and raised his chin. "And you have a way for me to fill my time."

"Exactly."

"I might have different ideas about how to spend my time, including...."

"Oh, I would not doubt that."

Aram got out of his chair and started toward the doorway. "So I'll just be...."

Robert barked a strident word in a language Aram did not recognize.

The two guards outside the door entered. Aram stopped.

"Here's the truth," Robert said, with a cool sincerity Aram admired for its transparency. "I am entrusted with a difficult, maybe impossible mission. The farther I get from Europe, the more concerned I am that my task requires me to wander into dangerous and unfamiliar territory. This place is so factionalized between Genoans and Venetians and Pisans, that I have few to rely on here in Acre. You offer me a familiarity with this area, and an attitude of frankness, almost as important as your knowledge, that I have not found with any other interpreter; actually, you will be an interpreter and adviser. But some of my comrades doubt you, and do not care for your lack of deference. Your willingness to be frank and independent comes with some patterns of behavior we simply cannot have."

Aram's head bounced and swayed as he nodded. He looked at the guards. "So, I'm not really offered a choice."

Robert scrunched his face and tilted his head as if pondering the question. "Actually, you do have a choice. You can keep this job, which now involves taking instruction in the true Christianity and living here under the strict supervised behavior of a monk until we leave on our mission, while getting paid handsomely for your services. Or, you can go with these gentlemen to be confined in one of our dungeons as a heretical defiler of Christian girls."

Aram nodded. "Choice. Well, when you put it that way...."

Robert smiled. "Yes?"

"Perhaps these 'gentlemen' could show me to my new quarters, where I can begin my course of instruction and schedule my baptism."

"It is a wise man who makes good choices."

Aram raised his eyebrows and nodded. Robert was not to be underestimated.

Robert stood up and gave the guards another order. They withdrew. The language still sounded unfamiliar. Aram could tell it was not Italian; he'd heard enough Italian merchants speak to be sure of that. He wondered if it was English. He knew some English travelers came to the area, though he had never encountered one. "I'll take you to the director of the monastery," Robert told him. "You met him the night of your interview."

"Thank you."

"It won't be long before we leave to meet the Mongols; your time as a monk should be short."

Aram forced a smile. From service as a monk to engaging with Mongols as part of a delegation that believed the Mongol wives practiced a heretical form of Christianity—what kind of job was this that Nestor had gotten him into?

5

February 15, 1258
Octagon Palace, Baghdad
Mid Day

"You are the host. We are your guests. Bring whatever gifts you feel are suitable for us," Hulegu said to the caliph of Baghdad. Hulegu sat at a banquet table, flanked by his highest ranking commanders, including Ketbugha. A small squad escorted the caliph toward Hulegu.

Ketbugha restrained himself from laughing. He had seen pet cats toy with captured prey before killing it. He had heard that lions and tigers exhibited that same behavior on a larger scale. He considered that maybe a little feline propensity coursed through the blood of the great Genghis Khan and his descendants.

The caliph appeared to be completely befuddled by the circumstances, shivering and quaking with fear, his lips trembling. Ketbugha felt little sympathy for the pathetic man. One placed in such a position of leadership and power should radiate strength and even defiance when facing adversity. Ketbugha had not been born a general. He had earned his position by demonstrating his capabilities during hunts, military exercises, and during the life-and-death duress of battles. This weakling, supposedly the master of an entire great faith, had done no more to gain the leadership of an entire religion than be born. So he deserved his fate. But Ketbugha was bored with Hulegu's game. He wanted to get to the resolution of this matter, and then move on. Of course, Ketbugha had no intention of communicating a hint of this attitude to Hulegu.

Hulegu sneered as the caliph continued to tremble.

Ketbugha watched the caliph's eyes gaze over the scraps of a nearly concluded feast. He smiled as he thought about Hulegu calling the caliph a "host." The palace banquet room had the appearance of a place taken over by people with little interest in it. Plates and cups littered the hall. Hunks of uneaten bread and the bones of various meats were scattered around the room. Chairs and tables had been used by some of the feasting "guests"—cushions and rugs were strewn about for use by others. Two pigs' heads sat on a table, prominently displayed among other platters mostly emptied of their contents. Ketbugha knew how deeply offensive this must have been to the caliph, but he saw no reaction as the caliph silently examined the banquet hall.

"My keys," the caliph said, choking out the words meekly.

"Keys?" Hulegu looked at Ketbugha.

"We have them," Ketbuga said.

Hulegu nodded. "See to this."

"Yes, my khan," Ketbugha said, and rose from the table. Without a command, a small squad joined Ketbugha to escort the caliph. One of Ketbugha's officers handed him the keys as the caliph led the men out of the banquet hall toward the palace treasuries.

They arrived at an area toward the rear of the palace where a series of locked repositories were located. The caliph continued to shiver with fear.

Ketbugha handed him the keys. "Show us our gifts. My men will help you collect them."

The caliph fumbled through the keys. He dropped them. Ketbugha glared at the man.

The caliph picked up the dropped keys and fumbled through them again. "I'm not sure…." The keys started slipping out of his hands again. "I'm not sure which key goes to which treasury."

Ketbugha sneered. If the caliph was stalling, he could almost respect that. But the caliph genuinely appeared to be unable to function because of his fear. Ketbugha took the keys. "Our gifts are in those locked areas?"

"Um." The caliph's face tensed as he swallowed. "Yes. In there."

"Well, we can assist you. We do not need the keys."

Ketbugha's men stepped forward and used axes and lance shafts to break the locks and open the treasury storage rooms.

Ketbugha looked in the rooms, warehouses for various goods. He saw suits of clothing, jewels, jewel-encrusted metal drinking glasses, thousands of coins held in chests and other unopened containers. Ketbugha nodded. "Bring the gifts to the banquet hall and stack them up for the khan." Ketbugha turned to the caliph. "We'll see if the khan is impressed with your generosity, as the host of this momentous occasion." Ketbugha's eyes narrowed. "Or if he thinks you are not such a generous host."

Ketbugha turned abruptly to return to the banquet hall, before witnessing any more cowardly trembling from the caliph.

"You certainly have many possessions," Hulegu said, barely even looking at the stacks of clothing, coins, and other valuables piled up in the banquet hall. "Now we need to know where your buried treasures are."

The caliph's eyes froze. He did not speak.

Hulegu waved disdainfully. "Divide these gifts among you," he told Ketbugha. Hulegu turned back to the caliph. "The buried treasure."

The caliph remained speechless.

"Some of your servants have spoken of it. You don't want to make yourself a poor host by withholding such gifts from us." Hulegu's jaw tensed. "Especially since I have not received my personal gifts from you yet."

The caliph swallowed. "There is a pool of gold. Buried in the middle of the palace."

"A pool of gold."

"Yes."

"You will take us to it."

"Yes."

Hulegu raised his eyebrows. "You have one other treasure."

The caliph could no longer prevent himself from breaking down. Tears flowed.

"Seven hundred women…," Hulegu hinted.

"Some just girls." The caliph sniffled. "Some upon whom neither sun nor moon has ever shined."

Hulegu shrugged casually. "Keep a hundred. You choose."

Ketbugha had to fight to avoid laughing out loud.

"Thank you."

"Well, I will be thanking *you* for that gift of gold."

"Yes."

Hulegu stood up, apparently to join this errand. "It is a pity for your people that you didn't spend some of your wealth on your city's defense, or as tribute."

The caliph did not respond.

"Not very good leadership. Not very good at all. Unworthy leadership."

Ketbugha saw the look of frozen indecision again on the caliph's face. How should a man in the caliph's position respond to such taunts? Ketbugha had no idea. He could not relate to the caliph's behavior at all. Ketbugha knew that he would have spent the fortune on defense or tribute. Wealth locked away and buried in pools was of no use to any of the caliph's subjects. The caliph should simply confess his unworthy leadership. But Ketbugha knew the caliph would be too much of a coward to do so.

Indeed, the caliph offered no response to the taunts. He left the room, leading the squad to the buried pool of gold.

Hulegu took Ketbugha aside. "The operation here is nearly complete."

Ketbugha nodded. "We have emptied the city of all non-useful people. Our men have gathered the valuables and destroyed the structures we do not need."

"Yes. Expertly. My compliments."

"What of this religious leader?"

"I'm not sure he's divulged everything of value, though I think we're very close."

Ketbugha sneered. "He's too much of a frightened coward to hold anything back."

"So, make plans for his execution—him, his sons, his family—any not of value to us."

"I will."

"No royal blood to be spilled."

"Of course." Ketbugha smiled mischievously. "I have picked out some of his most wonderful rugs. We'll sew them up inside and let our horses trample the life out of them."

"Good. Now, for the gold...."

Hulegu and Ketbugha left to follow the squad accompanying the caliph.

Mid February, 1258
Kerak Castle
Afternoon

"Confidence. You need to have more faith and confidence," said al-Mughith Umar, the regional prince, with a smirk that Baybars hated; but he understood that al-Mughith Umar had the power of a regional ruler, and was his superior—for now.

Al-Mughith Umar was a shorter-than-average, paunchier-than-average man, especially for any sort of combat leader. Baybars found him to possess few qualities worthy of his position as an Ayyubid prince, but he was related to the great Sultan Saladin, directly descendent from Saladin's brother, al-Adil.

Baybars scowled. He watched from atop his mount as his men conducted a drill. Poles were stuck in the ground at various positions along the scrubby, arid terrain. About one hundred of the Bahriyya Mamluks completed sharp, coordinated maneuvers in small squads, darting around the poles in simulated attack, retreat and regroup actions. "I know what *my* men can do," Baybars told al-Mughith Umar. "Where are yours?"

Al-Mughith Umar grunted. He squinted and flattened his lips, his expression communicating annoyance at such a challenge from someone he considered an inferior. "They'll be here. They'll be ready."

"They should be here *now*."

"Confidence and faith," al-Mughith Umar said again.

"Without preparedness, your confidence and faith will be but a fool's delusion, leading our forces to slaughter by Qutuz."

"Hundreds more men I have for you my friend, for you and your illustrious Mamluks to hurl at Qutuz. I have no doubt, total faith, all confidence, that our men will find success this time, and that we will restore the Ayyubid dynasty to Egypt."

Baybars tensed. "Whatever you say, Prince." Baybars offered a shallow tip of his head, almost but not quite a bow.

"Here they are," al-Mughith Umar said, smiling and pointing toward the gate at the entrance to the huge castle at Kerak. It was about five hundred yards in the distance.

Baybars considered how, if men under the command of the Bahriyya Mamluks had arrived over an hour late for any function, serious consequences would have followed.

It was hard to count how many of Al-Mughith Umar's men arrived—anywhere between fifty and one hundred—because they approached on sauntering horses, with no sense of formation, and no sense of cohesion or battlefield urgency. "You do have plans for these men to undergo some further conditioning before we go after Qutuz," Baybars said.

Al-Mughith Umar's smile faded. "I told you. They'll be ready. Just make sure yours are. I expect great things from you Bahriyya Mamluks."

"Well then, leave this rabble with us. We'll get them ready to—"

"My men are already trained, battle-seasoned, many with long years of service to me and others of my blood. To place them in some sort of remedial training session commanded by…." Al-Mughith Umar's voice trailed off.

"Slaves. Soldier-slaves." Baybars let out a soft laugh. "It's all right. We know what we were. You also know, very well, we are now some of the most feared warriors in the world."

"My men are already trained."

Baybars nostrils flared as he looked at the approaching soldiers.

Al-Mughith Umar's men finally made their way to the Mamluks' drill. Baybars saw a sloppy group, some slouching in their saddles, some holding their weapons casually, some staring out at nothing, few with any sort of enthusiasm or intensity. He saw men too old, too fat, too young, too fragile-looking to be taken seriously on a battlefield. Maybe one in five looked as if he had any potential to be an effective soldier.

"You don't mind if we at least practice some maneuvers with these men," Baybars said.

"That's what they're here for," al-Mughith Umar replied. "Of course I don't mind."

Baybars nodded.

"Do not underestimate these men." Al-Mughith Umar sounded serious, almost threatening. "I don't care how you think my men appear now. I have seen most of them in action."

"Good." Baybars looked out at his commanders in the field. "Start the drill."

"It's not much more than a raid," Baybars said with disgust as he dismounted from his horse. He handed the reigns to a stable hand. A few of his key commanders did the same. They were inside a small brick stable within the grounds of the huge desert fort, Kerak. "This is not a serious man."

"Not serious about Egypt," Qalawun said.

"Not at all," Sunqur al-Ashqar agreed.

Baybars snorted. "He only wants to use us to slap Qutuz around, steal some treasure, and then make a better deal with Qutuz."

"Exactly," Qalawun said.

"And he knows our patience is thinning," Baybars added.

"So is his," Sunqur al-Ashqar said. "I think he finds us too serious."

"These are serious times," Baybars said.

"Baghdad," Sunqur al-Ashqar interjected.

Baybars lifted his eyebrows and breathed out. "The stories...."

"They killed all the soldiers in cold blood, then most of the people," Qalawun said.

"That is what we've been hearing," Baybars said with a grim nod. "Genghis Khan. Now he was a serious man."

Qalawun wore a look of surprise. "They have destroyed the shining jewel of Islam. They smothered the caliph in a rug."

"Serious people," Baybars repeated.

Qalawun's eyes widened. "You sound like you admire them."

Baybars smiled. "I admire their willingness to do what it takes to achieve their aims, their ruthlessness in not allowing any deviation from their purpose until absolute success has been achieved."

The men with Baybars seemed stunned.

"Relax. I am not confused. Their purpose seems to be the destruction of the True Faith. So while I admire their dedication to success, I also know they are our unequivocal enemy, and that our only possible answer to them is total victory."

The men seemed to relax.

"So it is even more important that we know this enemy, and not cloak ourselves from their many strengths."

Qalawun nodded.

The group left the stable and headed to their quarters at the rear of the large castle complex.

Qalawun shook his head. "It is a shame we meet this threat with such disunity. These Ayyubid princes are such pale hints of the great Saladin."

"The ones in Syria seem to be falling over themselves in a race to submit to this Hulegu creature," Sunqur al-Ashqar said. "There is one, up in Homs—al-Ashraf Musa—who has sought out the

Mongols because al-Nasir Yusuf removed him from his position."

"He is not the only one with those types of priorities," Qalawun said. "Not much of Saladin in any of them—the man who faced down and then made peace with the great Crusader warrior, Lionheart."

"Saladin." Baybars looked up, forming his thoughts on what, for him, was a complicated issue. "The great Saladin. Unifier of Muslims. A compassionate man of Islam. A great diplomat and negotiator."

The men nodded.

Baybars shook his head. "I think this is the wrong time for a Saladin. I think his qualities of negotiation and compassion have distorted into weakness and filtered down to his unworthy descendants to the detriment of Islam."

Sunqur al-Ashqar looked at him with an expression of absolute disbelief.

Baybars grinned. "My friend, this is not a time to immmerse in the petty language of negotiations, in the nonsense of parsing words, all committed to an obsession for peace. Otherwise, how could the son of Saladin's brother have handed over Jerusalem to infidel Christians just a generation or two after Saladin had repossessed the city for the Faithful?" Bayars sneered; his nostrils flared. "Yes. Al-Mughith Umar wants his deal with Qutuz. More women. A softer life. Accomodation with evil. This has been handed down from the great Saladin. First, al-Kamil sells Jerusalem to the infidels for peace. Thank God better Muslims took it back. Now, we labor with this foolish grandson of al-Kamil. We're biding our time. He knows it. We'll go on his raid. But never forget, our purpose is more serious than his."

Qalawun nodded.

Sunqur al-Ashqar spoke. "I wonder—could it be that al-Mughith Umar would rather not take Egypt? The Mongols won't be coming to this place. Al-Mughith Umar can hide away here, dabbling under the veils of his women, while the Mongols go right past Kerak, and even Shawbak, on their way to the Nile Delta."

The men laughed.

Baybars lifted his eyebrows. "I would not be surprised."

The other Mamluk commanders had remained silent throughout this discussion, but now a younger one spoke, with a playful gleam in his eye. "A little of the soft life wouldn't hurt," he said. He grinned at Baybars. "A little exercise with the softer sex. A few babies, to assure the future while we settle the present."

Baybars smiled. He snorted, an apparent laugh. Others seemed to take this as permission to laugh themselves.

Baybars put his arm around the shoulder of the young commander, a smaller man. He kept nodding and smiling. Suddenly, Baybars slipped his forearm around the other man's chest, and brought it up around his throat. The young man gasped for air, and struggled to break the grip.

Baybars barely exerted himself as he continued to hold the man. "The soft life? See? Thinking of the soft life causes you to drop your guard! Little time for the soft life for me. Not with Qutuz ruling Egypt! Not with Mongols on their way! Some day—"

The man was turning from red to blue.

Baybars released him and shoved him forward.

The man staggered and fell. He stayed on his hands and knees as he regained his color.

"We will have our chance to focus on the soft life, to make sons with beautiful women—sons who will carry on our legacy. But we will need to earn the time to focus on the soft life."

Baybars watched with satisfaction as a serious mood once again overtook the group.

Mid February, 1258
Baghdad
Morning

"'Dawud the Astrologer.'" The deep elderly voice seemed full of swagger, as if enjoying a private joke.

Dawud was sitting in a vacated animal pen with about ten other men apparently deemed unsuitable for slaughter by the conqueroring Mongols. He was filthy, sunburned and tired. He sat in the dirt, legs folded, lost in his thoughts, numb to anything but his internal world, making every effort to avoid remembering any of the events of the previous month.

The familiar voice had taken him by surprise. "Nasir? Professor Nasir al-Din al-Tusi?" Dawud swallowed and squinted into the morning sun. He looked up at a gray-bearded, tall man, in his late fifties but still trim, a man who exhibited a mystifying command of the present situation. Nasir al-Din al-Tusi stood at the pen opening with a Mongol officer and a few soldiers. Dawud also found this hard to process.

"I wondered if it was really you, 'Dawud the Astrologer,'" Nasir al-Din al-Tusi said.

"That is what they think."

"It kept you alive."

"God willed it."

Nasir al-Din al-Tusi smiled.

"I thought they killed all the Isma'ilis."

"They did. You know full well that I am not an Isma'ili. I was held captive by them for many years, for my mathematical and astronomical skills, but I am certainly not one of them."

Dawud nodded. So this was the explanation his scholar-friend had used to survive. "How did you, how did you communicate that to these soldiers?"

"Mongols love astrologers. They think astrology can predict the future. They found me in an observatory. I told them the stars foretold their conquest of Baghdad. And when I explained I was a captive, they saw no reason to include me in the slaughter of their enemies."

Dawud stiffened.

"The conquest of Baghdad was not a hard prediction to make," Nasir al-Din al-Tusi continued. "You and I used to speak of the deficiencies of—"

"I never would have believed God could allow it."

Nasir al-Din al-Tusi tilted his head as he pursed his lips in thought. "Come. Walk with me."

Dawud was not sure he wanted to leave the animal pen. He had been hearing noises and taking in odors from the city. Screams. Burning buildings. Rotting flesh. He did not want to see any of it up close.

"It will be all right. The city is not at its best, but the Mongols declared an amnesty days ago. The looting and … the killings … that part is over. I'll show you where the scholars will work."

Dawud stood. "Scholars."

"I am their key science adviser for this region. I'm helping them organize the scholars here. I know how to relate our studies to their requirements. Mark my words, Dawud, these Mongol brutes have the power and resources to construct a truly amazing facility for studying the heavens. I have just the place picked out, up near Mount Sahand."

"Persia."

"Yes."

Dawud nodded. "I used to work and teach at Mustinsiriyah College. We can walk there."

"A lot of damage there, I'm afraid," Nasir al-Din al-Tusi said. "The Christian churches were spared. With your connections—"

"I have no connections at any of the churches."

"I just thought that, with your background—"

"I'm not a Christian. It was the faith of my birth, and my childhood. It is not my faith now."

Nasir al-Din al-Tusi nodded. "All right." He started walking. "We won't go to the churches."

They emerged onto a street in northeast Baghdad. Anything flammable was either smoldering or had become ashes. Brick structures were in various states of destruction, cracked and pulled apart. Torn fabrics, ashen remains of burned books, and broken goods—pottery, tables, chairs, shelves—goods with no value, were strewn about the street. And though Dawud saw no bodies in the immediate vicinity, he could see some dotting the street further ahead.

"Clean up is still under way."

Dawud nodded, studying the degraded Baghdad in front of him.

Nasir al-Din al-Tusi looked at Dawud "They didn't assign you to any corpse clearing detail."

Dawud looked at him. "No. They must think I'm too old. A too-old, valued seer of the stars."

"Right."

"There aren't enough left alive to bury so many dead if they worked for years."

"Birds, dogs and the elements will dispose of them," Nasir al-Din al-Tusi said casually. "We just need to get them out of the streets so—"

"We're talking about tens of thousands, maybe hundreds of thousands of the Faithful, left in the sun to be devoured by birds and bugs."

"And there is not much we can do about it." Nasir al-Din al-Tusi's eyes locked with Dawud's.

"And they're mostly Sunnis," Dawud quipped, "but I did see some of your Shiite brethren out there...."

Nasir al-Din al-Tusi's eyes glared at Dawud. "I told you, there is not much I can do about it."

Dawud did not respond. Nasir al-Din al-Tusi was offering the words and perspectives of a collaborator, a partner with one of the most profoundly evil forces unleashed on the world. Dawud had been a student of this man when he had decided to trade the life as a warrior for a new life as a scholar. They had gone from professor and student to colleagues to friends, as Dawud's own career as a teacher and scholar blossomed. Dawud treasured the intellectual stimuation of their visits to each other over the years. But Dawud could not absorb this development—his brilliant friend, an apparently willing servant of the Mongols.

"So, does an old religious scholar actually know anything about astrology or astronomy?" Nasir al-Din al-Tusi asked.

"Yes. Of course. You know that from our own past discussions. You taught me so much of what I know."

Nasir al-Din al-Tusi grinned. "That is right." He paused. "You know, they value astronomy, though mainly because they think it's useful for astrology."

Dawud became distracted. He saw flies buzzing around four bodies: an elderly woman, probably her daughter, and two small children. Enough of their bodies were preserved from the elements to see they had been felled by battle-axes.

"I'll get a detail out here—these should have been moved a while ago," Nasir al-Din al-Tusi said irritably. But Dawud could not tell if the man was irritated with the lack of clean up, or affected by Dawud's reaction to the slaughtered family.

Dawud nodded, trying to show gratitude for Nasir al-Din al-Tusi's assurance.

"We will be able to make many useful observations and learn much about the world within a Mongol regime. And we do not have to be stationed here. I expect to move out of Baghdad soon after I have the educational centers here reorganized. The Mongols encourage my work, supplying whatever I need to—"

"I doubt they will encourage my work—the teaching of a religion they are trying to destroy."

"You might be surprised. They do not impose their faith in what they call the Eternal Blue Heaven on anyone. Hulegu has a Christian wife. But he doesn't impose his religion on her, or her religion on anyone else." Nasir al-Din al-Tusi raised his eyebrows and spoke quietly, as if offering a profound secret. "We may bring them to Islam someday."

Dawud tensed. "Or these savages will bring us, what's left of Islam, to them."

Nasir al-Din al-Tusi stopped. He glared at Dawud a moment. "I would not make statements like that, even in Persian or Arabic."

Dawud did not respond.

"Men of learning can let these ruler-types play soldier with their armies, especially when we are protected and allowed to pursue the great truths through a method of reasoned investigation. Stay above it, Dawud, as I do."

Dawud thought a moment. He looked at buzzards circling, at a few men with carts trying to clean up—a job that looked hopeless to Dawud. "I don't know if I can."

Nasir al-Din al-Tusi did not comment immediately.

Dawud shook his head. "You know, they have all but wiped this city off the map. Whatever comes back here, if anything comes back here, will be different—it will be a different place. The same space may be occupied, but with different landmarks. They have so destroyed this greatest city of the Faithful, in just a few days ... that...."

"So be part of the rebuilding here if you like. You could be my man here. Help restore this place."

"Under the rule of worshippers of the Blue Sky Eternal Heaven or some other—"

Nasir al-Din al-Tusi stepped nose to nose with Dawud. "You think your faith places you above these people?" His eyes were cold and hard. "You think I must have no faith, or a defective faith, because I work with them?"

Dawud did not answer.

"You have no right to look down on any survivor with some sort of superior attitude. You lied about your occupation to survive! You didn't even start out a Muslim—your father and mother were Christians, part of the Christian state planted among us by beasts from Western Europe! Don't you look down on me!"

Dawud took in a huge breath of air as both men backed away from each other. "I certainly don't look down on any survivor of this satanic calamity."

"See that you don't!"

Dawud nodded.

"You go back to your pen. I will meet you tomorrow and give you some assignments. We will see how you perform. That will determine just what role you will be worthy to play in the new Mongol order here. And foster no doubts, your attitude will be part of my assessment."

Dawud nodded again.

Nasir al-Din al-Tusi walked away, leaving Dawud to return to the pen on his own.

February 20, 1258
Just Outside Baghdad
Morning

"The women keep complaining about the smell." Hulegu's nose twitched as he stood with Ketbugha next to a supply column. Hulegu's personal guards accompanied them. An entourage of servants and attendants bustled around the area, involved in the activities of breaking camp. An endless string of carts carried goods of all varieties: stacks of clothes, piles of jewels and cash, furniture—almost anything moveable, including loose bricks.

"My wife has also been complaining."

"We could stay longer. But we have taken possession of the best of what this place has for us. The rest? Trinkets. We'll let our ancillary forces ferret that out."

"We usually get to the trinkets more quickly," Ketbugha observed.

"Before the bodies start rotting." Hulegu cleared his throat. "There's just so much to take."

Ketbugha nodded.

"Where's that clerk?" Hulegu asked.

"He's coming. I've had him busy with the distribution instructions for the—"

"My requirements take priority! I will not appreciate waiting much longer."

Ketbugha's eyes widened. He motioned to one of his officers by tilting his head.

The man nodded, mounted his horse and rode off.

"The smell is unpleasant." Hulega snorted. "It puts us all in a foul mood."

"We could conscript some labor from—"

"Where is that clerk?" Hulegu grimaced and coughed.

Ketbugha looked out toward the rear of the supply train. "I don't know if your grandfather, or any of his generals, even when we were taking the most magnificent cities of Central Asia, ever sent back this much wealth."

Hulegu smiled. "Il-khan. One step from the great khan. If there were any doubts that I deserve this designation, they are ended with this conquest."

"Yes. Though still answering to the great khan, a khan in your own right, and of this area. Well-earned, Your Highness."

Hulegu looked at his general. "So, as a superior to everyone in the entire world except my brother, who is over a hundred days away from here—why can't I get a clerk for service when I want one?"

Ketbugha swallowed.

Hulegu watched Ketbugha's officer ride toward them on his galloping horse. A smallish man was sharing the saddle, sitting uncomfortably behind the rider.

"Where have you been?" Hulegu yelled as they arrived. "You put counting a bunch of rags and baubles ahead of the needs of your khan?" Hulegu pointed at one of his men, who drew a sword and moved toward the clerk.

The clerk dismounted quickly, falling out of the saddle, stumbling into a kneeling position. He looked desperately at Ketbugha.

Hulegu's eyes widened. "Your insult is against me, not my general! And you will pay for it! Fifteen lashes, and then I decide if you will keep your head!"

"I'm sorry." The man trembled as he choked out the words. "I'm so sorry."

"You will be. Now, you will prepare a message that needs to be dispatched with the expedition to my brother in Qaraqorum. Are you able to handle that?"

"Yes. I'm sorry. Yes."

"Tell him we are delivering these goods as the great khan's share of the spoils from our victory at Baghdad. Our armies will relocate to the pastures of Azerbaijan. We will replenish there, and prepare for our next move, which will be a move through Syria toward the wealthy land of Egypt. Our initial information is that these are lands of territories fragmented under many different princes—untalented, mediocre princes. We will exploit the politics for maximum effect, then make our move. Expect additional spoils in the next two years." Hulegu paused. "Do you have all that?"

"Yes, my exalted lord."

Hulegu squinted.

The clerk withdrew to write out the message.

"Sir," Ketbugha addressed gently. "Il-Khan."

Hulegu raised his chin.

"I ordered this man to complete his accounting of the goods we are dispatching to Qaraqorum, and that we are retaining and distributing. He was on my errand, acting on my orders."

Hulegu eyed the clerk, sitting next to a tent, writing out Hulegu's message. Maybe the man was innocent. But Hulegu had condemned him, at least to a flogging. Everyone had heard his pronouncement. How could he maintain discipline and respect if he reversed his edict?

"Um, I had one other question," Ketbugha added. "There is the matter of Berke."

Hulegu nodded. "I have considered this. I have listened to the advisers. The solution seems plain. Berke is my equal. If he is to have spoils from our victory here, then Mongke, the great khan, who is my superior, will compensate him." Hulegu was annoyed with Ketbugha for raising this issue. Berke was Hulegu's cousin—ruler of his own Golden Horde khanate, also subservient only to the great khan. To send spoils directly to him would be to imply Hulegu was subservient to him. The issue was simple.

"Correct, of course," Ketbugha said. "But you know Berke is fond of this Islam religion here, and so sharing some of our success here could—"

"He's a fool. Religious faiths are irrelevant to Mongols. I'll not behave in some subservient way because he has a weakness for the strange religious beliefs of some conquered people."

"Yes. Understood."

Hulegu looked at the clerk. He looked back at Ketbugha. "Have your men take the clerk to deliver the message to the head of the Qaraqorum expedition."

Ketbugha nodded and turned to a few of his men.

"Prepare for departure!" Hulegu called out. "Right away."

Hulegu's order immediately resulted in a scattering of acknowledgments, followed by energetic action.

No one asked him about the clerk. Hulegu was satisfied that he had maintained his khan-like bearing, and that he could conveniently forget the penalties he had declared for the clerk, penalties the clerk might not have deserved. He wondered if the men knew that by not asking about the matter, they had saved the clerk from punishment, maybe even from losing his life.

Late February, 1258
Baghdad
Mid Day

"It's … hopeless," Dawud said, shaking his head as he held the burnt spine of a book, remnants of what had been part of the library at Mustinsiriyah College. Much of the brick walls of the library still stood, but most flammable elements of the structure were ashes, and some of the walls of the library had crumbled away where plundering operations had caved them in. The black residue of flames was evident everywhere, on piles of decaying debris, and in blotches and streaks on the remaining walls. Tears formed in Dawud's eyes. "Too much. They wrecked, destroyed—too much."

One of the men with Dawud shrugged. "Most of the walls are still there. We'll be able to rebuild."

"A lot of these are burned Korans." Dawud shook his head, now with angry tears and a tense, red face. "How could they? How could God...." He looked up into the sky. "This can't be real!"

"Nasir al-Din al-Tusi told me about you," the man said.

Dawud looked at him, then at the others. They were all Persian. Dawud had never met any of them, and he did know some Persian scholars. "That I'm unhappy about this?"

"Negative," another one of the men said. "Relentlessly, pointlessly, *destructively* negative." Dawud raised his eyebrows. They had been talking about him.

"They're leaving. Today," the first man said.

"With everything they couldn't carry or destroy," Dawud said.

"But they are leaving," the man repeated. "We will control Baghdad, and have the opportunity to reconstitute this Islamic—"

"Reconstitute—with what?" Dawud kicked the ground. Ashes and dust puffed up. Dawud caught a whisp of floating dust in his nose and coughed.

No one commented. But Dawud got the impression his attitude was not appreciated. He walked toward a familiar area, an area of the college that had been largely destroyed. One of the Persian men followed him.

Dawud reached down and cleared some loose, broken bricks off the ground, exposing a mostly burnt stack of books and papers. He took in a deep breath. But as he cleared the charred debris, he smiled. "They missed something." The man who had followed Dawud, a tall Persian of about forty, looked at Dawud, as if soliciting an explanation.

Dawud picked up a flat metal container at the bottom of the stack. He whisked ashes and brick dust off of it, then opened it. He lifted a red silk cover away to reveal a jeweled dagger.

"Yours?" the Persian man asked.

"Yes. From long ago. When I was...." Dawud took in a deep breath and let it out. "When I was a different person. I kept it to remind me...." Dawud did not complete the thought.

The tall Persian man looked annoyed. "Remind you of what?"

"Never mind."

The Persian man squinted.

"I used to do a lot of my work in this room," Dawud told him. He pawed through more piles of loose bricks, and ashes and debris. He found pieces of a broken jar. He knew this jar. He could not help breaking into another smile. "They didn't do a very good job here." He picked up some coins, buried in the rubble.

"You kept coins here?"

Dawud shrugged. "Some cash to buy odds and ends for a modest Islamic instructor."

"The builders will be coming in soon," the man said. "You can advise us on how this was before."

Dawud smirked. "Certainly." Dawud gathered the coins and the metal case holding the jeweled dagger. He walked out toward what had been the outside of the university library, where the other Persian men were. The tall Persian man followed him back. Dawud put the metal case and coins in a small pile with a charred prayer rug and some tattered garments.

A gentle breeze drifted by. The rancid odor of decaying corpses filled Dawud's nostrils. He grunted and swallowed, fighting nausea. He turned to the tall Persian. "Are those builders bringing shovels? It seems to me there should be other priorities."

"Setting priorities is not your concern. Or ours."

"Thousands of the Faithful rot without a burial."

"And this is not what you should be—"

Both men diverted their attention to a small group of horsemen riding up toward the university grounds.

"Georgians," one of the Persians said.

Dawud noticed the men were uniformed differently than the Mongols. They were lighter complected, wore light armor, and had lances as well as swords and shields. The men seemed to be in a jovial mood, passing what looked like a leather wine container back and forth after taking squirts out of it.

"Just don't call attention to us," the first Persian who had spoken to Dawud said. "Stack bricks. They'll leave us alone, as long as they don't think we're hiding anything valuable."

"They hate Believers," Dawud commented.

"Yes," the man agreed. "I've heard them taunting the Faithful and abusing our brethren in despicable ways. They drink, and their drunkenness feeds their bad attitudes. But the khan has declared an amnesty, so—"

"Hey! Cross-worshippers!" Dawud called out.

"What are you doing?"

But Dawud's attention was focused on the Georgians. He held out both arms to summon them. "Hey!"

The squad moved toward Dawud.

"You worship dead bodies on a cross. It's a sham!" Dawud taunted. "You made a man into a God! And he never even died on the cross! You're heretics! And now, you've aligned with the most evil force this world has ever seen!"

The Georgians did not seem to understand, but approached Dawud and the group of Persians with sneers on their faces.

"And you are stupid!" Dawud told them. He picked up the coins, his metal box and his other belongings. "You missed all this stuff!"

The Georgians came over to Dawud. One of the men dismounted. "Give to me," the man said in heavily accented Arabic as he drew his sword.

"No," Dawud said. He dropped the belongings and stepped in front of them. "They're mine. You missed them, you stupid heretic."

The Georgian raised his sword. It wasn't clear to Dawud how much of the taunting the man had understood, or if he was simply going to kill Dawud for the coins and his other meager possessions. Dawud knelt, spread his arms out and pushed his chest forward. "Martyr me."

Dawud heard some insistent voices from a few of the other Georgians. He had some familiarity with the language. It sounded like the men were reminding their comrade of the amnesty. "Amnesty." He kept hearing that word, and an apprehensive tone, along with a lot of other words he didn't understand.

The Georgian swung his sword at Dawud.

Dawud closed his eyes. He felt the force of something pushing him in the chest. As he flew backwards, he opened his eyes to see the bottom of the foot that had just kicked him in the chest. The foot belonged to one of the other Georgians, apparently demonstrating to his friend that there was a more efficient way to take Dawud's possessions.

The Georgians laughed as Dawud landed on his back in the dirt.

The Georgian with the sword reached down and took Dawud's belongings. He put the coins in a satchel. He pulled the dagger out of its case and banged on it until the jewels loosened and popped out, and added them to his satchel. The man then brandished the dagger at Dawud. He grunted as he lunged at Dawud in a stabbing motion, then chuckled as he stabbed the dagger into the ground next to Dawud's head.

The Georgians laughed as they rode away, and resumed passing the leather wine container back and forth.

The Persians seemed to be making comments about their unhappiness with Dawud's actions. He didn't hear their specific words.

He brought himself to a kneeling position. He grasped a handful of dirt in his right fist as his face tensed and moistened with tears. "God has condemned me. To live."

The Persians looked at Dawud. "What did you say?" the tall Persian asked, glaring at Dawud.

Dawud did not repeat his statement, a private thought he had felt only a momentary urge to say out loud.

"We may be able to help with your problem." The tall man moved toward him. Others followed. "I'd prefer not to be with you when you test God's will on this issue again."

He slapped Dawud. Another man kicked him. Blows rained down on him from all directions until he blacked out.

7

Early March, 1258
Acre
Mid Day

"Our monk," the priest said with a grin and a nod as Aram entered the conference room. Aram was wearing a black hooded robe. His hair, what could be seen, had been cut short.

He was facing the same five men who had originally interviewed him for the interpreter position. Robert of Montpelier sat in the middle, his usual place. The priest who had spoken was to Robert's immediate right, and he spoke French with the same accent as Robert.

"Yes," said the priest to Robert's immediate left. "I hear you are doing quite impressively." He also spoke French with the same accent as Robert.

"Thank you," Aram said. He walked forward but there was no extra chair in the room, so Aram stopped about ten feet from the table and faced the panel of priests. Robert of Montpelier raised his eyebrows and smiled.

"So," the priest with the one arm said, "the Mongols have withdrawn to Azure—" The man stammered. "Up past Persia. Azure-ballon."

"Azerbaijan," Aram said. "*A long distance* past Persia."

The priest looked confused. "A long distance?"

"Oh yes."

Robert pursed his lips and narrowed his eyes, but made no comment.

"So." The priest looked at Robert, then back to Aram. "Young monk, what is your recommendation?"

"Well, with the long distance—and I know you're anxious to get this operation going, but—with the long, long travel, it could take years to complete the mission. I understand the pope, um, he wants quicker communication, quicker results."

Robert cleared his throat and twitched his nose, but remained silent.

The two priests on the outside seats squirmed and sneered. The one who was missing an arm turned his head to look at Robert, as if studying him, then looked back at Aram. "I think, um, the pope, um, wants us to go to the Mongols," the priest said. "Immediately."

Robert looked at Aram.

Aram swallowed.

Robert finally spoke. "Well, our new monk here makes a thoughtful point. And the pope has given us room to use our judgment."

The priests on the inside seats, next to Robert, reacted with nods and shrugs. The priests on the outside seats looked uncertain and wary. "We may want to consider an intermediate mission," Robert said.

No one replied.

Aram's eyebrows angled down as he wondered what an "intermediate mission" was.

"I'll discuss it with our, our marvelous monk here."

None of the priests offered a comment.

Robert stood. "I'll walk you to your quarters," he said. He walked around the table and put his arm around Aram's shoulders.

Aram's eyes darted back and forth.

They walked out of the conference room into the hall.

Robert moved his arm back down to his side. "You're making quite an impression."

"Oh, well, that's good, isn't it?"

Robert raised his chin and scowled. "I know where Azerbaijan is."

Aram kept silent.

"I know you hate this mission, and wouldn't mind if we put it off forever."

"Now, I'm not, I'm not *that* against it." It was a weak denial, and Aram was sorry he'd attempted it before the last word had left his lips.

"Quiet. Please. I didn't contradict you in front of the others because I think this is a bad time to go forward with direct contact, and some of the priests and other officials here have expressed questions about why I am not moving ahead more quickly with my mission. But stop playing loose with the facts. Don't play me for a fool. No more."

Aram nodded. "All right." He shook his head. "It seems a difficult thing to do, anyway."

"I think that was a compliment. I'll take it."

Aram smiled.

"I do listen to you, "Robert said. "I heard what you said about the Mongols—submission and alliance being the same word?"

Aram looked at Robert. "Yes. That is true."

"I am listening to you. I want to trust you. I need to trust you."

Aram nodded. Robert continued, "I don't think now is a good time to approach the Mongols about any sort of alliance. They're flushed with victory—swollen with the spoils—confident they don't need anybody."

"True, but they're always like that."

"But if we are to have any success with the approach, our best chance would be to make it when they need us. And they might decide they need us—when they move on Egypt."

"Yes. That would be the best time, if any non-submissive alliance is even possible."

Robert nodded. "Let's work together from now on. I need you to trust me."

Aram forced a smile and hoped it wasn't too obvious that he could not really deliver that trust. But there was one adjustment Aram could make. He needed to stop underestimating the man.

"What I would like to do is go to Baghdad."

Aram snapped his head toward Robert. "Baghdad?"

"Yes. You know Baghdad...."

"Of course. Between various journeys, that's where I lived. But why there, now?"

"I think we need to know what we're getting into," Robert said with a serious look and tone. "I think we need to gather some information about just who we're courting."

Aram took in a deep breath. He knew who they were courting. Why couldn't this Robert understand without a first-hand demonstration?

"We'll go to Baghdad and decide on Azerbaijan from there."

Aram said anything. He had mixed feelings about going to Baghdad, but apprehension was edging out curiosity as his dominant sentiment.

"Oh. By the way, I spoke to the Mother Superior at St. Anne's Convent."

Aram's eyes shifted as he tried to think of where this was going.
"That girl you knew?"

Aram broke into a queasy smile. "The one who—"

"The one who visited you here, yes."

Aram tried to maintain a smile.

"She's missed her time."

"Missed her—" Aram's cheek twitched as he realized what Robert was telling him. "Well, I, um, how do we know...."

"She's confessed you are the only one."

"Oh."

"So, it looks like you'll be ending your days as a monk—and beginning your days as a husband."

They arrived at Aram's quarters.

"Congratulations. We'll set your wedding soon," Robert said. "God knows of your sin, but I'd prefer to leave others guessing." At that he walked away.

Aram grimaced. A trip to Baghdad was starting to sound better to him. If he was going to extricate himself from the growing consequences of this less and less attractive assignment his old friend Nestor had found for him, Baghdad might be the best place for an escape.

Early March, 1258
Baghdad
Morning

"You need to eat something," Nasir al-Din al-Tusi told Dawud with a cold, unsympathetic tone of voice.

Dawud lay rolled up on the dirt in a small, tent-like shelter. He opened his eyes and squinted. "Not much appetite." Dawud forced the words out of his puffy, purple face. His right eye was still nearly swollen shut.

"I would have thought you'd be ready for service by now."

"These old bones don't heal as quickly as they used to."

"Especially when you don't really want them to."

Dawud took a closer look at Nasir al-Din al-Tusi. Hard eyes glared down at him. Dawud took a deep breath.

"When I first heard of your survival, I was quite pleased," Nasir al-Din al-Tusi said. "Yes, I know these Mongols have a talent for destruction. And little talent for building. But it is within this discrepancy that God grants us our opportunity. We can decide what will rise from the ashes."

Dawud pulled himself into a sitting position. He wondered whether he should engage this man in a true exchange of ideas on this subject, or whether he should simply nod his acknowledgement of this lecture he had heard more than once.

"I know you are a worldly man," Nasir al-Din al-Tusi said.

It was clear to Dawud that Nasir al-Din al-Tusi wanted to draw him into a discussion. He decided to offer some conversation, mainly to avoid being blatantly rude. "I've seen a lot, over a long lifetime, maybe a too-long lifetime."

"I know you have." Nasir al-Din al-Tusi paused. "Your many-faceted life is well-known. From your birth to Christians, to a fierce warrior for the True Faith."

"A period of my life that led to excesses—of impulse, of emotion without control, of rank barbarity—not a proud period of my life at all. And not a time of real service to God or the True Faith."

"Yes. So you became a learned man, and shared your knowledge with many. And your teachings carried so much more credibility because of your life experiences."

"Well." Dawud swallowed and let out a long breath. "You seem to have remembered a great deal about me."

"You're a memorable man. A man who should consider that your survival here is God's will."

Dawud shrugged. "What use could God possibly have for me in this wasteland? By what cruel joke would God will me to survive here?"

Nasir al-Din al-Tusi stiffened. "He did, and that is all you need concern yourself with. You should not preoccupy yourself with questions of why. You are here. And you are a potentially valuable man to me. These Mongols will rely on me and my chosen leaders to rebuild and remake this place. You could be one of those leaders. I will leave soon for Persia. Your worldliness, your scholarly attainments—this is a perfect combination of talents for service here. You could rise far in this new order. Even in your advanced years, you could still accomplish and attain a great deal."

"Rebuilding while the bones of the Faithful rot in the thousands outside these gates. Building on their bones, as if they mattered as little as dust swirling in the wind."

Nasir al-Din al-Tusi appeared to clench his teeth. He cleared his throat with a short grunt. "I understand a student was executed, right by your side."

Dawud considered that they had been talking about him, in detail. "A fine young man. His head, hacked in half."

"His efforts kept you alive."

"True. I had resigned myself to the end of my life. The passion to survive was strong in him. It was his idea to live on, not mine."

"Give his death meaning. Join the rebuilding."

Dawud's breathing quickened. His face tensed. "A rebuilding on *his* very bones, that sit outside these gates, his flesh gnawed by all manner of desert creatures." He met Nasir al-Din al-Tusi's eyes. "How would such actions do anything but mock the fact that he ever existed?"

Nasir al-Din al-Tusi sneered. "You are of no use to the Mongols crumpled up on the ground in this pen."

Dawud's eyes narrowed as he grinned. "And of no use to you, either."

"You ungrateful fool." Nasir al-Din al-Tusi's jaw moved forward. "You live when so many others have died. Don't you understand? The True Faith faces destruction. We can live to keep it alive and ensure it will flourish again. God wills this for us of the True Faith who survive."

Dawud slumped back down. "I do not believe God has any hand in this."

Nasir al-Din al-Tusi raised his chin. Dawud sensed a hardening, an abandonment of the discussion. "God has a hand in all things. But God will most certainly desert you, because you have been too weak to maintain your faith. That is your failure."

Dawud did not reply.

"Guards!" Nasir al-Din al-Tusi motioned for some armed men, either Georgian or Armenian from what Dawud could tell, to come into the pen. "This man will be transferred to the East." He looked at Dawud. "They think you're an astrologer. You can go to the court of the great khan and show them your skills."

Dawud snorted. This was a death sentence. Dawud had few astrological skills, and Nasir al-Din al-Tusi knew it. If the long journey east didn't kill Dawud, particularly in his weakened condition, his masters would be likely to finish the job when they discovered his lack of astrological acumen.

"I can't have you taunting occupation troops, angering my best leaders and organizers, talking down and even sabotaging efforts here," Nasir al-Din al-Tusi said, as if explaining the implicit death sentence. "You've given me no choice."

Dawud shook his head. "Staying here to 'rebuild' is no choice for me."

Nasir al-Din al-Tusi snorted irritably. He looked at the guards. "Take him."

The guards picked the bruised and battered Dawud off the ground and yanked him out of the pen.

Mid March, 1258
Baghdad
Mid Day

"They didn't even bury these people," Robert said to Aram. Both men wore pieces of cloth over their faces. "They didn't even draft prisoners to bury them."

"Too many to bury."

Robert looked at Aram. "So these people weren't being punished, executed for some transgression?"

Aram shrugged. "Their transgression was being alive in a city the Mongols have taken by force and having nothing of use to offer them."

Robert looked to his right, at a knight holding the standard of the pope. Just behind the knight was a cart of supplies. A banner with a red cross on a white background rose above the cart. Two knights flanked the cart. Behind them was a procession of another fifteen members of the expedition, all men, all with specific roles for the journey. Robert said something to the standard bearer.

The knight nodded. Little expression showed on his face.

"He told me this was the scene of a slaughter, not a battle."

Aram nodded.

"Will any of their authorities still be in the city?" Robert asked.

"It's unlikely," Aram said. "They aren't occupiers. More likely they left someone in charge, someone answerable to them. The main army is probably off preparing their next move."

The knight bearing the standard gave a slight nod of agreement.

"Whoever is here will know how to make contact with the authorities—where they went, where they are now."

Robert looked around. "I have heard of 'atrocities.'" The cloth over his face moved slightly as his nose twitched. His eyes watered. "I know the heat of battle, the hot blood of fighting for survival can...." He looked at the knight.

The knight held a neutral, unemotional expression. Aram suspected the man understood French, but did not speak it comfortably.

"But this...." Robert shook his head. "Calculated. Unrestrained. Uninhibited deliberate butchery of so many human beings."

"I think, my new Western Christian friend, that you are getting your first lesson in Mongol diplomacy," Aram said.

Robert's face tensed with anger. He turned his head and locked eyes with Aram. "Is that a joke, young man? Do you mock these dead with flip banter?"

"Joke?" Aram looked down. "Hardly. The sooner you realize the seriousness of what I have been trying to tell you about this mission, the better chance—" Aram stopped himself before he could finish the idea.

"What?"

"Not a joke, believe me."

"The 'better chance' what?"

Aram looked at Robert with a stern expression. "That we don't end up in a pile like this." Aram surveyed the rotting bodies strewn out over the dry, light brown landscape. The corpses had begun to wither, with dried flesh shrinking and falling away. Eyes were missing from most of the bodies, obviously pecked out, delicacies for carrion birds. Families clinging to each other in their last moments could still be discerned, with partially disintegrated arms of children clutching adults' near-skeletons. Flies hovered over them all. Processions of bugs moved in dense networks, feasting on their windfall from Mongol military operations.

The group trudged on. Robert looked away, toward the city. Aram looked in the same direction. He had wanted to return to Baghdad to assess his prospects under Mongol rule and maybe even escape an upcoming wedding. But the Mongol destruction of Baghdad had turned it into a foreign place, a place Aram barely recognized, an unpleasant place. He considered that this Baghdad was a worse alternative than his association with Robert and the Western Christians, even a worse alternative than his upcoming forced marriage.

"So who do we look for?" Robert finally asked.

"Someone will find us." Aram addressed the knight next to them. "Keep that standard easily visible."

Robert glanced questioningly at Aram.

"We'll come across a patrol, or sentry," Aram explained. "They'll respect the cross and give us safe passage."

The knight nodded.

"You're from here," Robert said to Aram in a flat tone of voice, as if he had just recalled.

"Yes. I do a lot of traveling, so I don't stay in the city for long periods of time. But yes, Baghdad is my home."

"I'm sorry," Robert said. "I should have realized—you must be facing this visit with a great deal of apprehension."

Aram shrugged. "I'm Christian. My few friends and family? Mostly Christian. They probably made it through." He took a deep breath. "I have little wealth. If it has all been plundered, I can't say it would be of great consequence to me."

Robert smiled. "You are a unique young man. I must say, I am not even close to understanding you."

Aram returned the smile. "I'm really a simple person. I come from a strange background, but I'm simple, just trying to use my wits and experience to make my way in a world of shifting circumstances."

"Strange background...."

"Yes. My parents—" Aram squinted. "I can tell you more later." He lifted his chin out toward the city. "Look. We're about to make contact."

A small, armed group of mounted warriors moved toward them.

Aram nodded. "Georgian. It's the Georgian king's banner."

"Georgian," Robert repeated. "Definitely Christian."

"Vassals of the Mongols...," Aram added.

Robert nodded. "Yes. I remember."

"I'm not clear on your business here," Nasir al-Din al-Tusi said to the tiny Christian delegation. He stood with a small squad of guards at the entrance of a crumbled gate to the city, projecting the mood of a busy man preoccupied with more important matters. He seemed to deliberately avoid offering any sentiment of hospitality or cordiality.

It was Aram who spoke. Persian was not his strongest language, but he could manage. "As I explained to your guards, we are on a diplomatic mission to the great khan. We would like to pay respects to the great khan's brother and gain his approval for safe passage."

Nasir al-Din al-Tusi squinted slightly as he scratched his nose. "You speak for these Christians?"

"Interpreter. Guide. Yes."

"Your Persian has an accent that sounds like you are from this area."

"I am."

"So what are you doing with these fools? These barbarian infidels from the West? They cannot have more than paltry trinkets to offer the great khan. What are you doing with them?"

Robert elbowed Aram. "What is he saying?"

Aram grunted and flinched. "I am fulfilling the duties of a paid position."

"You need to tell me what's going on," Robert insisted.

"I'm explaining what we're here for," Aram said quietly, trying not to move his mouth.

Nasir al-Din al-Tusi raised his eyebrows. "What does this ragtag Christian group want with the great khan, or his brother?"

"This is an advance group, making contact, to recognize the changed circumstances in the area."

"Tell him we are here from the pope," Robert told Aram.

Aram forced a smile and nodded, trying not to let any signs of friction show to Nasir al-Din al-Tusi. "Please let me handle this."

"Did he say the pope?" Nasir al-Din al-Tusi asked, his eyes offering a steely stare.

"The pope," Robert said, broadly gesturing to himself. "From the pope. For the khan."

Nasir al-Din al-Tusi shifted his steely glare back to Aram.

Aram maintained a forced smile, again talking to Robert through a closed mouth. "This is not the group to confront with connections to the pope."

Robert flexed his shoulders back. "You need to let me—"

"These are Muslims."

Robert said nothing more.

Nasir al-Din al-Tusi continued to stare, effectively increasing the awkwardness of the moment.

Aram let the silence remain. He wanted to read Nasir al-Din al-Tusi's attitude before deciding how to salvage the situation.

Nasir al-Din al-Tusi broke into laughter. He nodded toward Aram as his laughter continued. "I don't envy you, young man. You have your work cut out for you!"

Aram nodded.

"You're lucky you aren't a little west of here and running into the Turks."

"Yes. That's for certain."

"The great khan's brother has relocated to the plains west of the Caspian Sea before embarking on his next conquests. I myself will leave to join them shortly. I am only a science adviser, but my superiors here thought I would know better what to say to you." He shrugged. "So I ask again, what could this motley delegation hope to accomplish with this trip?"

"Knowledge of that information is not part of my employment."

"Then ask him." Nasir al-Din al-Tusi sneered and tilted his head at Robert. "Ask the leader, the one who seems so intent on intruding upon this conversation."

Aram turned to Robert. "He wants to know what business you have with the great khan, and his brother."

Robert thought a moment. "Business to discuss with them only," he directed his statement to Nasir al-Din al-Tusi.

Aram took a deep breath. "He says he will state his business to them only."

Nasir al-Din al-Tusi snorted then smiled. "An alliance, no doubt." He paused. "Well, the Georgians and Armenians have their 'alliances'. The alliances of a servant with a master. Come to think of it, that is also my alliance!" Nasir al-Din al-Tusi shook his head, laughing again. "These alliances prevent us from joining the piles of bones bleaching under the sun outside these walls."

Aram nodded.

"Go on to Azerbaijan, then. Seek your alliance."

Aram turned to Robert. "He has cleared us to move on to Azerbaijan."

Robert nodded. "Thank him."

"We thank you," Aram told Nasir al-Din al-Tusi.

"Yes, well these Christians you lead, from the pope,"—he sneered the word "pope"—"are on a fool's errand. You should let them move on ahead and stay out of it."

Aram did not hesitate, knowing that to do so could reveal that he had considered the idea and had decided against it only because of the horrible state of the devastated city. "That would be a breach of my employment," he said quickly.

"You don't seem to be of these people, but also not of the True Faith."

"Assyrian Christian. Nestorian."

Nasir al-Din al-Tusi's eyes opened and his face showed a look of realization. "Ah. Then you may have some friends here. Family."

"Some. A few."

"Christians were well-protected. Stay here with your community and help them rebuild."

"My thanks for your offer. But as I said, that would be a breach of my employment. I will try to see them before we leave."

Nasir al-Din al-Tusi shrugged. "As you wish."

"There is one of the True Faith who I would like to know about, if he survived."

"Yes?"

"Dawud. An old man. Once a Christian who became a Muslim warrior and then a scholar. I learned a lot from him, and came to value his friendship. And I know he had many friends among—"

"Dawud survived." Nasir al-Din al-Tusi's expression tensed. "He has a post as an astrologer. He is on his way east."

"Astrologer?" Aram narrowed his eyebrows. He had recalled Dawud as being hostile to astrology. But Nasir al-Din al-Tusi's terse attitude discouraged him from asking for any more information.

"He is an old man," Nasir al-Din al-Tusi said. "You can ask of him when you and your fellow Christian vacationers reach the great khan. If the old man is still alive."

Aram offered a quick, perfunctory bow. "Thank you."

"I will have a squad of guards accompany you through the city."

Aram looked at Robert. "They're taking me to the Christian quarter."

Robert looked at Aram, his eyes widening. But after a quick moment, he nodded.

Aram turned to Nasir al-Din al-Tusi. "We will go to the Christian quarter. Thank you."

Nasir al-Din al-Tusi flipped his hand with a dismissive wave and abruptly left them.

8

Mid March, 1258
Baghdad
Late Afternoon

"On this side of the walls too," Robert said as his eyes scanned clumps of rotting bodies. The delegation moved away from the walls of Baghdad, northeast. "All around the city."

Aram nodded.

None of the men wore cloths over their faces as they left Baghdad. Aram wondered—were they able to tolerate the odor because they knew they were leaving it, was the breeze flowing away from their noses, reducing the odor's intensity, or had they simply become accustomed to the stench?

Robert looked at Aram. His face was flushed with emotion. Was he on the verge of tears? "I understand now." He let out a deep breath. "And I treasure you, my young friend, for I understand now what you have been trying to communicate to us."

Aram studied Robert. He wasn't sure what the man was trying to say, or whether he really did understand anything. If he did finally comprehend, Aram wished Robert could have accepted what Aram had told him without needing first-hand experience.

"How can our Holy Christian Church, our most Catholic church, steeped in the teachings of Jesus Christ, the savior of humanity, consider any sort of association with these monsters?"

Aram's eyes drifted away a moment, then refocused. "So we will withdraw from this mission?"

Robert shook his head. "I cannot. We are cleared to move on to Azerbaijan. I cannot go back to my superiors and tell them I decided on my own not to complete the mission." He stiffened. "I have made commitments, obligations. There are considerations beyond my, my own sensibilities."

"I see."

"We will go. We will at least meet with the great khan's brother. He is the active Mongol leader in this area."

"Yes. He is certainly the one who gave the order to pile up bodies all around this city." Aram clenched his teeth with anger. "They got some Christians too. You must have noticed that many of the friends I asked for were not present." Aram tried to hold back the emotions welling up inside him, he did not want to give up any self-control around these people. But he could not help himself. "We'll go on ahead, and meet with the one who destroyed one of the great cities of the world as casually as a person might swat a fly or kick a clump of sand." Tears rolled down his cheeks.

Robert paused a moment. "A city controlled by the so-called caliph, a supposed holy man from a heretical faith." Robert sneered as he said the word "caliph." Aram shook his head. He wanted to berate this man for his ignorance. But self-control was coming back to him. "You don't understand the greatness of Baghdad," Aram stated quietly. He wiped his tear-stained face. "I'm the real fool. I took it for granted." He shook his head. His nose twitched as the odor of decay registered again. "I was aware that Baghdad had seen greater days, the golden age, a few hundred years ago." Aram thought about the Baghdad he had been taught about, a place where all varieties of goods were available, where scholars of all different faiths were welcome to explore the boundaries of knowledge and reach the greatest heights of achievement and prosperity to which humans could ascend. Aram realized that, in the Baghdad he knew, parts of the city had deteriorated but hints of past glories remained. And the chance remained, with the right leadership, that the golden age would be restored. His scholar friend, Dawud, had been part of this ambition. He had been involved with some unique thinking about religious matters. Aram closed his eyes and wiped his tears again. "It's all gone now. This place will never be the same. In a flicker of time, it has been swept away."

Robert remained silent.

A breeze delivered another foul burst of odor. Aram frowned and snorted.

The sounds of horse hooves against the turf hung in the air as the two men finally cleared the piles of the slaughtered.

Robert finally spoke. "Why didn't you extricate yourself?"

Aram looked at Robert questioningly.

"I know you are a reluctant future husband, and not entirely committed to this mission. You could have stayed on here. I do not know much Persian, but I got the definite idea that if you had wanted to stay, that al-Tusi character would have made it hard for us to take you."

Aram thought a moment. He shook his head. His lips tightened as he fought a surge of emotion. "I could not endure surviving among the ruins, among the the decaying humanity." He exhaled with a grunt, and the tears attempting to burst from him stayed.

Robert nodded. "So life as a husband and father is not so bad."

Aram looked at him. This sounded like some sort of joke, and Aram usually enjoyed good banter. Not under these circumstances. "No. Nothing could be worse than this." Aram shut his eyes for a moment.

Robert looked ahead. He spoke distantly, as if disconnecting from the moment. "Our mission must go on, but I may not bring the result everyone expects. I must strive to serve my superiors and my God at the same time. I will honor your insight as we complete our mission."

Aram's head jerked back. He looked at Robert with alarm. "Please be careful. A diplomatic mission with no real good faith desire to achieve some form of diplomatic achievement, but that results in the collection of information, is a spy's mission. Mongols respect and protect emissaries, but they are ruthless with spies."

Robert nodded. "I'll keep that in mind." He raised his eyebrows. "And keep these thoughts between us."

"Good."

Late March, 1258
Kerak, Southeast of the Dead Sea
Morning

"Is there permission to pass through?" Baybars called, glaring at an approaching rider. Baybars stood next to his horse with the vanguard of his group of Bahriyya Mamluks. The early morning air remained frosty under the nearly risen sun. Men in the area pulled up tents, doused campfires and gathered supplies. Baybars looked at the huge castle, about a half mile in front of him. The structure stretched out along a small plateau, above a deep, dry moat. It was Kerak, the castle of al-Malik, al-Mughith Umar, and the Mamluks had returned to their families.

The castle Kerak had a clear, dominating view of the surrounding area. The size of the elevated stone-walled fortress, and its prominence over a mostly flat landscape stretching for miles in all directions, gave the holder significant power over the area. No one passing through would escape detection by the occupants of Kerak, and would have a difficult time completing that passage if Kerak's determined forces opposed them.

The rider reached Baybars, dismounted, and bowed slightly. "No. He has declined to open the gates to us again."

Baybars folded his arms. His lips tightened. "Does he expect us to camp outside like vagabonds?"

"The man I spoke to did not specify. He told me an envoy would come out to speak to us."

One of Baybars' officers pointed toward Kerak.

Baybars looked toward the main gate area of the long, rectangular complex. A squad of about ten men, complete with a standard-bearer, rode toward the Mamluks.

"Arms," Baybars said. "Slowly, without panic." He looked at the approaching squad. "But I want armed men around me when they get here."

Two of his men walked briskly away. As the approaching squad arrived, Baybars' men, including Qalawun and Sunqur al-Ashqar, accumulated near him. With sheathed swords attached to their waists, they silently watched the events.

Al-Mughith Umar's squad arrived. About half the men dismounted. They had swords attached to their waists. After these men stood and faced Baybars, another man dismounted; this one unarmed, dressed in silk, with a jewel on his turban.

Baybars focused on this man, who clearly demonstrated by his behavior that he headed the squad, and expected everyone to defer to him. The man approached, flanked by his armed squadmates.

Baybars took a step toward him. "I assume you have come out to escort us through the gates."

"His Lordship, al-Malik, al-Mughith Umar, has asked me to convey his unhappiness that you have again returned in defeat."

Baybars accosted the man with a slient stare, deliberately allowing an uncomfortable silence to develop.

The envoy maintained a stern expression, unyielding to any awkwardness or intimidation.

"Message conveyed. Now you will give the word to open the gates to Kerak for our return."

"Al-Malik, al-Mughith Umar is not willing to readmit defeated, disgraced men. He does not see the honor of it, nor the benefit in it."

Baybars felt his stomach grind up with a surge of rage. He felt a flash of warmth rise from the back of his neck. Energy flowed to every extremity. His eyes widened. His mouth tensed into a taut frown. If this fool had dared to speak these words when not surrounded by armed men, Baybars could imagine picking him up like a tentpole, snapping him in half, and flinging the two parts to the ground. He could imagine taking the man to the ground and crushing his face into pulp with the bottom of his shoe. But such actions were not available, and would have only granted short term gratification anyway.

Baybars looked into the envoy's eyes. Yes, the man maintained a stony facial expression, but the whole manner of his approach told Baybars this man was terrified of his mission. The tough façade appeared to be grafted on.

Baybars allowed his facial muscles to relax. He took in a deep breath and let it out as he brought the grinding in his stomach down to a less extreme level. "Do you think the great al-Malik, al-Mughith Umar would have had the courage to deliver those words to me, the way you have?"

The man's eyes darted. It was clear to Baybars the man did not expect this sort of question. He had been braced for a burst of anger.

Baybars smiled. He had successfully put the envoy on the defensive.

"I am not, um, here to deliver a response to, um, to such a, a bizarre and inappropriate question," the envoy finally said.

Baybars' smile broadened. "Come to me, out from your protectors."

The man looked unsure of what to do.

"I wish to greet a courageous man, sent out to act on a difficult order, and who carried out the order with no hesitation or fear. I wish to kneel with you for a quick prayer for future victories, and that if I am to remain allied with al-Mughith Umar, he has many more men like you in his service." Baybars' smile faded as his eyes looked off toward Kerak. "I have yet to see very many." He glared at the envoy's protectors, making eye contact with a few of them.

The envoy's head swiveled. He appeared to be looking at nothing in particular as he decided what to do. He then nodded and stepped out toward Baybars, away from his armed escort.

Baybars stepped to him, shook his hand, then embraced him in a gripping hug, a hug he deliberately made sure was somewhat painful. Baybars was nearly a foot taller than the man, and may have been close to double his weight.

Two prayer rugs were produced. Baybars and the envoy knelt.

"Praise God for men of courage," Baybars said. "Praise God's will for returning us safely after the trials of the last raid." Baybars paused. "We submit to God's will, and remain the implements of God's will on earth."

Baybars stood, then the envoy. Baybars smiled and slapped him hard on the back, actually propelling the man forward a few steps.

The envoy stumbled, but returned Baybars' smile with a nervous smile of his own.

"I wish all the men in this operation had your courage," Baybars said, signaling he was ready to get down to business. "We will never defeat Qutuz with the quality of forces al-Mughith Umar sends to ride with me."

The envoy drew in a short breath. His eyes flickered. The man apparently just realized that he might still have to deliver difficult news to Baybars, but now out from the protection of his entourage. He looked back at one of them, possibly the leader of the squad.

Baybars looked in the direction of the envoy's glance, then looked quickly back at the envoy. "You do not need them. I would never harm a representative of an ally, particularly a man of such courage and honor. Speak to me. You have nothing to fear."

The envoy nodded. "Al-Mughith Umar said you would likely blame his men. He told me not to accept such excuses."

Baybars grinned and scratched his nose. "So those are your instructions—do not listen to any discussion of the flaws in his men, flaws that have lost me some of my best men, men trained and skilled beyond any level al-Mughith Umar's men can even comprehend."

"Al-Malik, al-Mughith Umar believes you use this explanation to escape taking responsibility for your own failures. He considers this an insult to his men, and his personal honor." The envoy's voice seemed to harden. The man was regaining his confidence.

Baybars nodded slowly. "I see. Well then, ask him one question. One simple question. Does he trust his men to deal with us as opponents? Because if he leaves us out here like wild dogs scavenging the desert in packs, begging for scraps, he will have us as opponents. And trust me, my dear courageous friend, he will experience confirmation of his men's utter inferiority in the most direct and dramatic way."

"He needs assurances that—"

"The only assurance I will give him at this time is that if he refuses us admittance to Kerak, he will have his worst nightmare for an enemy."

"I do not think he will—"

"And if he harms a hair on any of our wives's heads, our justice will be swift and without mercy."

"This is not—"

"That is all. Please return to al-Mughith Umar and make my position clear." Baybars flashed an exaggerated broad smile. He raised his eyebrows and added a slight smirk of malevolence.

The envoy bowed briefly and returned to his men.

The entourage mounted and departed, first at a trot, then at an increasing speed.

Baybars looked at his men. "He'll admit us. This will go back and forth a few more times, but he will open those gates."

He saw looks and nods of acknowledgment and agreement from the men.

"But my brothers, doubts are growing, magnifying, that we will ever defeat Qutuz by throwing in with this fool. We will need a serious change from him, or we will need to consider a new direction."

"Right now, he won't even admit us to Kerak," Qalawun said with a stern expression.

"Even al-Mughith Umar is not that much of a fool," Baybars assured them. "He is doing this to try to keep us in our place." Baybars smiled. "But he has no concept of our place. We do. And we will continue moving toward it, with dedication and determination, until we arrive."

Late March, 1258
Road to Tabriz, Northeast of Baghdad/Southeast of Caspian Sea
Afternoon

"It's the Mongol banner," Robert said to Aram.

Aram focused his eyes on a ragged group of about fifteen horsemen. They approached down a winding trail that led from a rocky outcropping. "It's an old one. It looks worn. Tell the men to have their weapons ready."

"We aren't here to fight them," Robert said. "Maybe these men will know the khan's exact location."

"You need to trust me on this." Aram glanced around at his delegation's armed members. "Be ready to take these men on. Don't make it obvious, but be ready."

Robert's nostrils flared as he frowned.

"Wait here," Aram said to Robert. "Just the standard bearer." He nodded to the man carrying the pope's standard, a dark pole with a golden cross at the top of it.

Robert shrugged, then nodded his assent.

Aram and the standard bearer trotted their horses out to meet the approaching band. It was a motley assembly. Their faded, tattered uniforms seemed to be an assortment of local military attire, not all Mongol. He caught sight of a few Persian shields, what he thought might be an Armenian knife at one man's waist, and some Turkish cavalry swords.

A man wearing a light-colored, leather helmet with one ear-flap torn, called out in bad French, "Christians? You are lost?"

"We are on a mission to see his excellency, the magnificent, triumphant Hulegu, brother of the great khan," Aram called back in deliberately mangled Persian.

The man smiled as his eyes narrowed with a derisive, doubting look. "This group?" he asked. "To see the il-khan?"

"Of course," Aram replied, deliberately looking down his nose at the man. "He has been informed to expect us. An alliance will be the subject of the meeting." Aram continued to stammer through his Persian syntax.

The man turned to a large fellow who wore a metal helmet atop a rubbery-weathered, pockmarked face. "These are fools," the first man muttered in Turkish, in a Caucasus area dialect that Aram could understand with some concentration.

Aram held his expression, making sure not to show any signs of recognition. "If you are with Hulegu's forces, perhaps you will provide us an escort."

"Escort!" The man scoffed at Aram's suggestion. "All the way to Azerbaijan?" He shook his head emphatically. "We are on patrol. We are not here to coddle lost Christians with strange ambitions of alliances."

"Fine, then, we will pass through under your protection."

The man raised his eyebrows. "Do you speak Arabic?"

"A little," Aram said.

"Turkish?"

"Turkish." Aram frowned. "Not much need for Turkish since the Mongols came into this area."

"So," the man said in fluent, unaccented Turkish, "you won't mind if I say your Jesus Christ was a yapping dog and his mother Mary was a whoring bitch."

Aram deliberately shook his head as he shrugged indignantly. "I don't speak Turkish, if that's what you're saying. We can speak in Persian, or maybe Arabic. French, if you know it well enough."

"Look out! Up the hill! Mongol arrows loosed into the sky!" But the man looked down, not up as he tested Aram's reaction to another Turkish phrase.

Aram shrugged. "Persian."

The man smiled. "Fine, Persian." He turned to his larger comrade and spoke in Turkish. "We'll take the gifts and leave these fools here. By the time anyone knows about this missing group, we will be in Syria."

"Starting with these two?"

"No. We don't want to alarm the others."

The larger man nodded.

Aram raised his hands, palms up, with a questioning look.

"My apologies," the man said with a remorse that seemed forced. "I told my bodyguard here what is happening. He speaks only Turkish."

"Ah," Aram said as he nodded, trying to look comfortable.

"We will inspect your gifts for the il-khan," the man said.

"That will not be necessary," Aram said.

"Yes it will."

"Why? Our business is with Hulegu and the great khan, not you."

"We *are* the khan out here," the man said.

Aram looked at the man, his large companion, and the rest of the group. These men were going to "inspect" the gifts whether he liked it or not. To survive this situation, Aram needed to have a scheme that gave his group the upper hand. His advantage was his knowledge of Turkish, and the apparent desire of this group to take the "gifts" with as little effort as possible. After all, they had not attempted to overpower the Christian delegation. Maybe not all these men were up to a fight. Or maybe they did not want to risk injury if they could simply take what they wanted. "I still do not know why you need to inspect our gifts for Hulegu and the great khan. Surely you know that taking the gifts intended for the khan would subject you to grave consequences." Aram looked at the group as if assessing their numbers. "But we do not wish to anger a patrol in the service of the great khan. Give me a few moments to take your request to my superiors. We will signal for you when we are ready."

The man glared at Aram. "How long?"

"Not long at all."

"We will await your signal. Not with unlimited patience."

"If you want to see the gifts, you will grant us the time we need."

The man did not reply. He simply looked at Aram and the standard bearer with a harsh expression. Aram felt they were being measured for destruction.

"We'll give them fifteen minutes," the man muttered in Turkish to his large comrade, not even bothering to wait until Aram was out of earshot. "Maybe they will agree to show us the gifts and we can take them with little effort. But if they don't agree? We'll swoop in."

Aram and the standard bearer moved back toward the Christian delegation.

"We are in terrible, imminent danger," Aram said in understated, quiet French. "They will be watching us. We must gather arms and prepare to resist attack. And we must do it without looking like that is what we are doing."

The standard bearer's eyes widened as panic registered on his face. He jerked his horse forward.

"No," Aram said. He grabbed the reins of the standard bearer's horse. "We have fifteen minutes to prepare, unless we alarm them."

The standard bearer nodded.

9

Late March, 1258
Road to Tabriz, Northeast of Baghdad/Southeast of the Caspian Sea
Afternoon

"Here they come," Aram said. He watched the armed men approach, seven of the original fifteen outlaw riders. "They have decided to approach us peacefully, not wanting to alarm us." Aram nodded. "Good."

"Do we wait for them to get here?" the delegation's key security commander asked. He spoke in labored French with the same choppy, strident accent Aram had become accustomed to hearing from Robert and his close associates.

"No. I will flatten to the ground when they are in bow range. That is when you unleash your bolts." Aram looked at the cart they had turned on its side, and the three crossbowmen behind it. Chests and piles of other supplies lay on the ground in front of the cart, as if arrayed for display. Most of these materials were supplies for the journey, piled up for effect.

Robert watched the activities with his arms folded. "I say again—we should not risk killing Mongol soldiers on what could have been a misunderstanding."

Aram gritted his teeth. "Those are not Hulegu's men, and there was no misunderstanding. They intend to kill us, take everything we have, and probably head on to Syria for mercenary work with a willing Ayyubid prince."

The security knight asked Aram, "See that bush, up next to the white rock?" The man nodded. "Flatten when they get to that point."

Aram nodded. He looked back over to the area behind the cart. A few non-combatants were crouched behind the cart to help reload the crossbows. Two knights stood hidden behind their horses, armored above the waist, helmeted, and ready to mount and move. Robert stood with two other men, his arms still folded, watching dubiously.

The seven men seemed relaxed as they approached, staring at the "gifts" in front of the cart. Aram sauntered a few steps forward to greet them, as if keeping their arrangement.

The enemy riders reached the bush at the white rock.

Aram threw himself to the ground.

Crossbowmen rose up and picked off three of the approaching Turks before they knew what had hit them. The bolts pierced the leather and light metal chest armor. One bolt hit a rider in his unhelmeted face.

The two armed knights had mounted, and now charged. The other four advancing enemies turned to flee. Two had pivoted quickly enough to accumulate some speed. The knights caught the others and hacked them down mercilessly. Seven were now two. Fifteen total would-be thieves had been cut by a third.

The two knights returned.

The crossbowmen behind the cart stood ready with reloaded crossbows.

Aram scrambled back to join the men behind the cart. He wondered if this would be enough of a lesson for this group of outlaw Turks, or if they would try again. Their leader had seemed so smug, so arrogant.

Aram had his answer. Six armed men charged at them.

The knight in command rallied his men in a language Aram did not recognize as French. "Bowmen! Take the men on the edges as soon as they are in range." He looked at the other armored knight. "On my signal, we will take the ones in the middle."

German. Aram finally recognized the language from the word for "bowmen." These men spoke German as their first language. Robert, too, was likely a German. This was an interesting realization, something Aram would need to ponder, but not as important as the unfolding events.

Four arrows lofted into the air from the charging Turks. Robert and the men with him ducked behind the cart.

"Shields!" called out the security commander.

But only one arrow threatened harm, and Robert himself blocked it with a shield.

The crossbowmen picked off two charging Turks on the far left. To the right, a bolt went low and hit the attacker's horse in the neck. The animal squealed and went down, throwing the rider forward onto the ground.

The charging knights propelled toward the attacking Turks in the middle of the spread. The attackers loosed arrows from their bows. Two missed. A third slammed into the torso of the chief security knight, but did not pierce his armor. The security chief seemed oblivious to the impact as he reached an attacker and hacked the man's head in half with a vicious swing from his heavy sword.

Aram smirked. "Mongol arrows would have come at twice the speed from twice the distance," he said. Robert nodded.

The other German knight wreaked similar devastation on another attacker. Before the last of the three could turn to flee, his side was presented to the security chief and the latter hacked at the man's neck, almost completely severing his head.

The unhorsed man fled back toward his comrades, but was not fast enough to escape another knight's sword.

Aram looked out toward the enemy group. They couldn't have more than five or six left. That would make it a fair fight. Aram was sure the Turks would have no desire for that, and so would present no further danger.

Robert put a reloaded crossbow down next to the shield with an arrow sticking out of it. "Recommendations?"

Aram pushed a burst of air from his nose. "The same. We need to rethink this mission."

Robert nodded. "Yes." His lips scrunched. "The Mongols are still consolidating, and their authority over the area seems inconsistent." He looked at the goods on the ground in front of the cart. "And we will need more gifts to make our contact effective."

"More than a box of gold-engraved bibles."

"Agreed. We will go to Acre." Robert's face broke into a mischievous smile. "After all, we have a wedding coming up."

Aram forced a queasy smile.

❧◆❧

Late March, 1258
Kerak
Morning

"You need to tell me how you got bruises on your face," Baybars commanded as he glared at his wife. They stood in a large, barracks-like area on the grounds at Kerak. Baybars and his men had been readmitted so they could reunite with their families.

Adiba hung her head.

"What happened?"

"I was going to tell you. I just didn't want it to be the first thing we talked about on your return."

Baybars took Adiba by both shoulders and nodded. "I understand. But you need to tell me now."

She swallowed. "A guard—hit me."

Baybars' eyes flashed open.

"I—" She seemed to be fighting tears. "I objected to something he was—"

"To some menial chore he had assigned you? This abuse of the Bahriyya wives has to stop!"

She shook her head. "It wasn't chores. We've been doing chores. Some very base chores. It's all right. But—" She seemed to falter with her explanation, as if searching for words, or hoping she wouldn't have to say the words.

"I need you to be the less shy Adiba I have been getting to know," Baybars told her. "I need you to tell me what happened."

Adiba swallowed. "Two guards. Came to me and three of the other wives. We were cleaning the bread ovens. They said you and the others were to be cast away, and so all that is yours in Kerak would be taken by the people here, by al-Mughith Umar's men. They said they wanted to help themselves now."

Baybars maintained a stony expression. "I see."

"One of them grabbed at me. He tore my dress. The second guard said 'no, she belongs to the big brutish one. You wouldn't want him tracking you every day the rest of your life.' So they started toward two others. I stood up, pushing myself between them and my sisters. That is when one of them hit me. There were screams. We screamed, and the men went away. They said they would be back for us after you were sent away, and said they would punish me severely."

Baybars nodded. He clenched his teeth. "I am glad you told me. This is it. We will stand for no more."

Baybars looked around the area and spotted Sunqur al-Ashqar. Baybars raised his chin toward him, beckoning him over.

"Make the approach," Baybars said.

Qalawun joined them. "Time?" he asked.

"Yes." Baybars looked coldly around the area, and at his men and their families. "Maybe past time."

Sunqur al-Ashqar asked, "You're sure this isn't a step backwards?" He met Baybars' eyes.

"It is a step back, but a step toward the familiar at least. That will certainly be an improvement."

"What about al-Mugith Umar's plan for the raid?" Sunqur al-Ashqar asked.

"An interesting diplomatic problem," Baybars said. "One I am sure your talents are up to."

Sunqur al-Ashqar bowed and smiled.

Baybars looked toward Qalawun. "It will be a double game for awhile. We will politely siphon off as many resources as we can from al-Mughith Umar. We will identify and draw in men with potential from his ranks." He raised his eyebrows. "And when the time is right, we will make our move."

Early April, 1258
Shai Island at Lake Urmia, Azerbaijan
Mid Day

"This is the place ordained by the Eternal Blue Spirit," Hulegu said to Ketbugha. The men rode at the head of Hulegu's personal squad. "This is where we will store the wealth of the Ilkhanate. Praise the scouts who found this place. Reward them."

Ketbugha smiled and nodded. "Yes. I certainly will." Their horses carried Hulegu and Ketbugha along the eastern shores of Lake Urmia. Across a small shallow stretch of water stood a craggy, rocky island. Its sharp edges and misty barren shapes contrasted with the low green grass and generally benevolent climate of the area. The jagged ledges and outcroppings radiated a grand ugliness, a power from its lack of symmetry and attractiveness, a fearsome strength emanating from its uninviting nature. "The place is uninhabited except for a few very old tombs."

Hulegu frowned. "Let's not disturb any ancient bones. The Eternal Blue Spirit continues to favor us, but we will retain that favor by respecting departed spirits who may reign as part of the Eternal Blue Heaven."

"Yes. Our shaman's advice on this issue is well worth taking."

"I want orders given to begin moving the treasures here from Tabriz."

"Yes."

"The squads to secure this place have been chosen?"

"Great care has been taken in this process, almost complete now."

Hulegu nodded, then smiled. He gazed at Shai Island again as they continued slowly along the shores of the lake. "Magnificient. Worthy of my family. Worthy of our place in the Eternal Blue Heaven."

"Yes." Ketbugha sensed a gentle, receptive mood from Hulegu. It was a rare opportunity to make a suggestion. "So much wealth. Nearly overwhelming."

Hulegu chuckled with a snort. "But there is never too much. I have learned this from my grandfather. The more spoils a leader has to hand out, the more power that leader accumulates."

"Oh, yes," Ketbugha agreed. "This assures the loyalty of subordinates. Valuable spoils, distributed to subordinates."

Hulegu nodded.

"Some of these spoils have little value to anyone but the followers of the Prophet Mohammed. It seems almost a shame to waste time sorting and transporting all that to this location."

Hulegu's eyebrows raised. "You have an alternative idea."

"Yes, il-Khan. I think we can send those items to your cousin Berke. Word is he remains very agitated with our treatment of Baghdad. Such a gesture—"

"We've been over this."

"I know. And I agree with the general principle. But this gesture would cost us nothing. And Mongke's health…."

Hulegu's eyes narrowed.

Ketbugha decided not to elaborate.

"Concern about succession," Hulegu said grimly.

"Of course. It does not always go smoothly. It is best to keep allies wherever possible."

"Allies with my misguided cousin." Hulegu's mouth tensed into a frown, and his eyes narrowed. "I wonder if my grandfather ever would have made Batu the khan of my 'Uncle' Jochi's lands if he had known the descendants would take on one of the religions of these flabby city dwellers. Just shows, once and for all, that Uncle Jochi never carried my grandfather's blood." Hulegu preferred not to engage himself in his family's past, because a close look would reveal an earthly, fallable aspect to what was supposed to be the dynasty chosen to rule the world by the Eternal Blue Heaven. The strange behavior of his cousin Berke, adopting a local religion, irritated him because it took him back to those stories.

Their grandmother, Borte, had married his grandfather, Temujin—the man who would become Genghis Khan. Shortly after the marriage, Borte had been kidnapped. The young Temujin rescued Borte after a few months of captivity, but due to that period of time there were lingering suspicions through the generations about who had actually fathered Jochi, their first-born son. Hulegu preferred to believe that his cousin, Berke—the son of Batu and grandson of Jochi—did not share Temujin's blood with him.

Ketbugha nodded. "Issues for many years ago. But Jochi and Batu are long gone, and Berke holds much power and capability. His territory is in a strategic position between and around our route to Qaraqorum. Allies with him? Absolutely, especially when it costs nothing of value."

Hulegu drew in a long, deep breath. "Why did that fool adopt this Islam religion? You can see how it limits him. If he had faced that ineffectual twit they called a 'caliph,' he probably would have let him live, and keep the vast treasures of Baghdad!"

Ketbugha nodded and tensed his lips.

"These religions swirl around us," Hulegu said. "I myself was educated by a Christian tutor. My grandfather married our tribe to the Keraits; you are from that line." He was referring to a Mongol tribe that was primarily Christian and supplied many of the wives of the Genghis Khan dynasty. "You know, my own wife is Christian."

Ketbugha nodded. "As am I."

"Yes. But we of the family destined to rule the world stay above choosing among these faiths. The faith of the Buddha … the faith of the Prophet … the faith of the great shaman Jesus, who healed the sick with a touch, and may have defeated death itself. These all are placed within the Eternal Blue Heaven. We do not bow to their limitations—no meat for Buddhists, no wine or pigmeat for Muslims. That was my grandfather's wisdom. It has been every great khan's wisdom since this family came to power."

"And it has served us all well. Which is why I have suggested throwing mere crumbs to Berke."

Hulegu scowled. "In case of issues of succession in the future."

"Exactly."

Hulegu stopped his horse. Ketbugha stopped next to him.

"You are a splendid servant to me." He tapped Ketbugha affectionately on the shoulder. "Kublai, older than me, as you know, is the next brother in line. Arigh-boke is after him. I accept that I will not likely be the great khan." He smiled as his eyes moistened. "I remember the day—I've told this story before, but perhaps not in this context—I remember the hunt. I was nine; my brother Kublai was eleven. He killed a hare, a fast-moving, crafty creature. I killed a goat, a slower and dumber, but larger, more substantial creature. Our grandfather, by then the ruler of the vast lands from one side of the steppes to the other, took us aside and smeared our shooting thumbs with the blood of those kills. I sensed it then—it was confirmed as I grew: Kublai is the smart one, wise but quiet, powerful but not in an obvious way. I am the bellicose one, not as smart, but willing to feature my power and strength to fulfill my family's destiny. I am satisfied with the role mandated for me by the Eternal Blue Heaven. My only claim to succession will be if something happens to both of my brothers."

Ketbugha nodded.

Hulegu gently prodded his horse into resuming its trot. Ketbugha followed.

Hulegu tilted his head up. "Well, your idea will cost us nothing material, I agree."

Ketbugha waited for what he sensed would be Hulegu's final thoughts on the matter.

"Proceed if you wish," Hulegu said flippantly. His face tensed and his expression suddenly grew serious. "But this must be done carefully. I do not want this to look like tribute to my cousin, or some sort of apology. We are not his inferiors. If this is mishandled, and the wrong impression is created, I will level grave consequences against those responsible."

"Understood."

"Tribute is coming from nobles in and around this area."

Ketbugha nodded.

"We are still getting mixed signals from some of the princes between here and Egypt-land. The land is called Syria?"

"Yes," Ketbugha said.

"I want no doubt from anyone about who holds power in this area. It is not Berke; I don't care if he has adopted their faith. Berke does not have any authority over me. It is me, acting only under the great khan, to whom they must submit."

"Yes. I understand."

"Good." Hulegu looked back out over the lake toward Shai Island. He smiled again.

Ketbugha smirked. He realized there could be no gifts for Berke. He would not risk Hulegu's wrath against him, or others, if Hulegu decided at some later time that the actions had been "mishandled."

April, 1258
Azerbaijan
Mid Morning

"We're waiting for your contributions," a slightly balding, chubby Mongol guard said to Dawud in broken, heavily accented Persian. The guard was part of a squad of five.

Dawud was alone in a tent he shared with eight other souls, kept alive for some kind of service to the Mongols. From what Dawud had been able to discern, most of the others were also considered astrologers. His other tent-mates had left to perform various tasks. Dawud had not decided what tasks he should be performing, or if he was really inclined to accomplish anything. And it seemed to him that no one had been concerned about him either, until this guard had questioned him.

"My 'contributions'?" Dawud asked.

"Yes." The guard's sneer revealed yellow teeth, a few short of a full set. He looked at his fellow guards and made a comment in a language Dawud recognized as the Mongol language, but he did not yet know well enough to understand all the words. The tone, however, was taunting. The man turned back to Dawud. "We are all waiting for the great pronouncements of the wise old astrologer of Baghdad! Speak! Show us your connection to the future!"

Snickers came from the other men.

"My contribution." Dawud nodded. He closed his eyes, then stiffened and convulsed as if he was in a trance. "Mongols win. Much tribute for all," he said in their language. He'd picked up a few words, enough to offer some phrases.

Dawud opened his eyes to see puzzled looks on the faces of the squad, except for the chubby guard, who glared at him.

Dawud grinned and winked.

The men laughed. "Wonderful prediction," one of them said.

"You mock me?" the chubby guard asked.

"You doubt my prediction?" Dawud smirked. He knew he risked the man's wrath, but could not help teasing him.

The chubby guard reached for a club attached to his waist. Another guard reached for the first guard's club hand and said something Dawud did not understand.

The chubby guard clenched his teeth as he raised the club. Dawud understood the Mongol word for "defiance" or "resistance," and another word for something like "insolence" or "arrogance."

The second guard shook his head. He looked at Dawud. "Nomolun have no sense of funny," he said to Dawud in barely decipherable Persian. "You are funny. I like funny."

Dawud smiled and nodded, then glanced at the chubby guard named Nomolun.

"But no more joke. You need read stars—tell us signs from heavens."

Another man, taller and thinner than the chubby guard, but with some resemblance to him—possibly a younger brother—stepped forward. His face radiated hostility and malevolence. He pulled his club from his waist and raised it, bringing it down toward Dawud's face with sudden motion.

Dawud raised his hands to protect himself.

The taller, thinner guard stopped short of striking Dawud, then broke into a smile.

Dawud realized he had closed his eyes.

As he opened them, he heard snickers form the other men. The chubby guard was particularly enthusiatic with derisive laughter.

Dawud broke into laughter of his own, trying to match the most boisterous of the group. "Funny," he said, waving his finger at the taller thinner guard. "You fooled me. You truly fooled me. See? This fellow can be funny too!"

The chubby guard, Nomolun, followed with a fake blow of his own.

Dawud flinched and toppled over, laughing again. "And you fooled me too!"

The laughter subsided.

"Funny," the second guard said again. "I like him." He reached over and helped Dawud to a sitting position.

The chubby guard and his brother stood over Dawud, clubs still drawn. Dawud understood the next words in Mongolian. "But he's not here as a jester," the chubby guard said. He squinted, then said in clumsy Persian: "I want your contributions about heavens."

"You want a contribution?" Dawud told him. "I can offer you something more valuable than all the wealth of Baghdad."

All of the men in the tent fixed their eyes on him, except for the chubby guard and his brother, who sneered. Dawud would try, for the first time since he had been splattered with his student's brains, to have some positive impact on the world. They did not understand Persian well, but he hadn't picked up enough of the Mongolian language to say what he wanted to say fluently. So Persian it would be—simple, straightforward Persian. "This is the story of tribes from the desert, tribes that rose from modest circumstances to rule much of the world."

Most of the men had looks of understanding on their faces. Dawud figured he had maybe two or three more sentences before the men would lose patience.

"A man, Messenger from God, received communications from God Himself, building on the faiths of earlier prophets. With the power of that faith, these tribes joined together and spread the True Faith, building great empires of wealth, but also of learning and wisdom. Those tribesmen were not very different from you. God Himself will welcome you to the True Faith, and all the power that submission to God and belief in Him and His will brings. There is no greater treasure."

No one responded. Dawud wondered if his Persian had been simple enough.

The chubby guard said something to his brother in the Mongol tongue. The tone was unmistakenly dismissive and hostile.

"You think you are a shaman, yes?" the friendlier guard said. "You speak of the faith, Islam. We do know of it. It is less powerful than the Eternal Blue Heaven."

"This is not earthly power I speak of," Dawud said.

"Stars," the chubby guard said. He kicked Dawud over, more of a shove than a determined blow.

Dawud grunted as he sprawled onto the ground.

The chubby guard placed his foot on Dawud's back and pressed down. Dawud groaned.

"Stars. You are to read stars. Not joke. Not tell stories of warriors in deserts."

The friendlier guard pulled Nomolun away. He said a few words in a calming tone to the chubby guard. Dawud picked up Mongol words for "older," "wise," and "bad," but maybe with "not" in front of the word. He caught the names of the two brothers. The chubby guard's brother was apparently named Shingkhor.

Nomolun looked at Dawud. "You fool these, but not me. You give us stars reading. Or I make you my … my project." Nomolun stormed out with Shingkhor close behind.

As he sat up, Dawud looked at the friendly guard and nodded, very slightly, a nod of thanks.

"I like you, old man. But you must show us skills reading the stars or your fate will be … will be troubled."

Dawud nodded his understanding. Suddenly, he felt more vulnerable than he had since his student's execution and his own reprieve. Telling that stripped-down story of his faith had moved him. God's will demanded he use his time left on earth for advancing the True Faith, regardless of the circumstances faced by the rest of the world.

Now that he had purpose, he had fear that death at the hands of these unsophisticated creatures would stop him short of that purpose. And fear made him vulnerable. He wanted to survive. He would need to develop some semblance of astrological competence in a hurry.

Dawud sighed. His fellow "astrologers" had reached out to him at first, but had given up when Dawud had shown no desire to interact with them. He would correct that behavior and glean what he could. Survival would grant him the opportunity to further God's will, even in the midst of the calamity the world now faced.

10

"Aram."

Aram cringed as a sharp elbow jammed into his side. It was Robert, standing next to him at the altar of the Church of St. Peter, not far from the beach side of the city, near the Pisan quarter.

"You have to say 'ego mos'," Robert whispered.

Aram looked at Robert, then at the priest and the veiled bride standing across from him. Aram's lips tightened. "Ego mos." He wondered what he had said—probably something like "I agree," or "I will." Here he was, swept up by circumstance, about to become husband to a girl who was no more than a casual partner in lust, married in a ceremony that was little more than a patter of syllables to him. The language was Latin, the language of the Western Christian religion. He had received rudimentary instruction in the tongue during his training as a monk, but had given it little focus. For Aram, this was the language of a long-ago fallen empire, of an ancient civilization hundreds of years past relevance. Aram knew Greek. Greek was the language of an ancient Western intellectual tradition, a tradition of knowledge preserved by Muslims when Western Europeans had failed to preserve it. He might have even understood Greek, though he had rarely heard it spoken. But Latin? Not a relevant language for Aram—until his wedding day.

As the ceremony progressed, Aram's mind drifted again. He thought back to Nestor, his Greek opportunist friend, and Nestor's contact with him at the first of the year. Aram had just returned from a trip to Central Asia with traders from Baghdad. Nestor's suggestion of a job with Western Christians had sounded interesting. Now, a few months later, he was a married man committed to a possible suicide mission to the Mongol court. Maybe life did need to be taken more seriously, especially during serious times.

Aram had always thought of himself as a man of options. He knew many languages, and knew a great deal about the world, even possessing some credentials as a scholar. He felt infused with strength and youthful energy. What were his options now? How would he extricate himself from these circumstances? To the east were more Mongols, more devastation. His home of Baghdad was no longer a possibility. Western Europe could be his best option, back to the land of his ancestors. But fleeing faction-torn Acre and the gentle clutches of the church establishment was not going to be easy.

The syllables kept pattering on and on, seemingly without end. He stood when everyone else stood, sat when everyone else sat, and knelt and bowed in prayer along with everyone else.

There was one set of syllables he did find himself listening for, and he finally picked them out as he focused toward the end. "Jeannette, daughter of Alexandre the Merchant from Tyre." His bride's name. He had heard it before, he was sure—he just hadn't remembered it.

"Aram." Another elbow from Robert caught his attention. "The bride," he whispered. "You may kiss the bride."

Aram lifted his head with recognition. He looked at her, her face covered with a white veil.

"Lift the veil then kiss her," Robert whispered.

Snickers rippled through the small church. Aram overheard someone remark, "I hope for her sake he isn't so shy in the marriage bed." Aram flashed a quick grin. He could imagine that the person making the remark probably had not been involved with as many women as Aram.

Aram lifted the veil. He saw a beautiful girl with dark brown hair and crystal blue eyes, a combination not often seen in the Eastern Mediterranean. His previous contact with her had been months earlier, and in dim light. He looked her over again. He was actually marrying a stunning woman. How had he failed to notice?

She had a filled-out, shapely body, with modestly covered cleavage unable to hide a bountiful appearance. She was about four inches shorter than he was, with thin legs and a narrow waist that flared out to wide hips. There was a slight bulge at her belly.

Aram knew why that was there.

Aram kissed her—a warm, slightly lingering kiss. He smiled at her. She smiled back, although he thought he detected a touch of embarrassment.

He pulled her to him, held her tight, and kissed her again. The immediate future would be just fine, Aram considered.

Music sounded—the recessional from the church—monks chanting one-line modal melodies.

"Aram," Jeannette began as they entered a small bedroom. They were alone for the first time since the night Nestor had introduced Aram to Robert and the Western Christians. She sounded awkward with the name, as if pronouncing a word from a foreign language. "I am so ashamed." Tears streamed down her cheeks.

He reached for her face and touched her tears, affectionately drying them. "Jeannette. What a beautiful name for such a beautiful girl. Jeannette." He smiled. "You just recently learned my name, too, didn't you?"

She smiled and chuckled, but then more tears flowed.

Aram pulled her to him.

"I'm just a girl who lost her parents and didn't want to be a nun," she said. "And now, I have trapped a man into marriage, a man who clearly wants little to do with me."

Aram squeezed her. She was right. But the ease with which she knew and expressed this made Aram realize his attitude and behavior through the wedding ceremony had been too transparent, and so painful for this sweet young girl. "This is not your fault. We are both victims of a rigorous church hierarchy."

"I will not hold you," she assured him as she gently pulled out of the embrace, and took a small step back. "You have salvaged some of my honor with this marriage. If you were to go off, to whatever eastern place you are from, I would just be a deserted wife with a child. There will be help for me."

Aram looked at the girl closely for the first time, seeing the entire girl instead of just a body to quench his lust. She had a sweet, selfless demeanor. She had a conscience, probably more developed than his. There was more to treasure about this young woman than her beautiful body. He would focus on that in order to make this night, and the immediate future, as pleasant as possible.

"So many dreams a girl has, of the man she will wed, of the wedding day. And I cannot even offer you the mystery of this being my first time with you."

Aram smiled. "On that, my wife—yes, Jeannette, my wife—I believe you are wrong. It was dark and rushed when we were together before. I believe we can make this brand new." Jeannette looked puzzled but intrigued. She tilted her head, apparently waiting for an explanation.

"What I mean is that I did not see you very well that night."

Jeannette nodded. "Just … shadows in the dark."

"I would like to see you now. All of you."

He took her hand and walked her over to the bed. He sat down and waited.

She seemed to develop a sweet shyness. "My belly is starting to swell."

"And we know who's responsible for that.…"

She took in a nervous breath, but now showed signs of anticipation. "I think you will still be pleased with my beauty," she assured him.

"I'm sure of it. Let's see."

"Just like that."

Aram nodded. "Just like that. Just like a bride, coming to her husband for the first time."

"You will need to unbutton the fasteners at my back."

Aram nodded again, got up and circled around behind her. He unbuttoned a series of eight hooks. He did not remove the dress. He could see there was an undergarment that went from her chest to just below her waist.

He came back around and sat at the bed.

The dress was starting to fall off of Jeannette. She clutched it to her chest shyly, as if covering herself for one last moment of mystery.

Aram lifted his eyebrows. Beautiful, along with a sweet disposition. He had considered himself unlucky to be trapped at this place and into this marriage. But maybe he could find a way to enjoy himself and celebrate some good luck at just how pleasant this young lady was. The right words and actions could serve to create an enjoyable immediate future.

Jeannette removed her dress. A thin white undergarment covered her breasts and fell below her waist. Aram could see her dark nipples, full-sized breasts protruding erect into the undergarment, and the dark hair below her waist showed through the material.

"The rest," he commanded softly.

Jeannette did as she was told.

Aram saw the slight bulge right at her belly button. He'd seen girls who were not pregnant with a more curved belly than his new wife had. He stood, took her into his arms, and lifted her up. He gently set her lengthwise onto the bed, then quickly removed his own clothes while she waited. He needed no encouragement at all to rekindle his passion for the girl. But this time, the experience was not hurried.

Aram and Jeannette lay naked, tangled in each other's arms under a sheet.

"I meant it, you know," she said to him. "I feel bad that you were forced into this. I don't want you that way."

"It was not your doing."

"It doesn't matter. I'm the one who completed the marriage."

Aram shook his head. "You were forced, too."

She fell silent. Her lips scrunched toward her nose and tears flowed again. "I was given options. You weren't."

"Options?"

"Have the baby, put it up for adoption, then stay with the convent. Have the baby, keep it, and move to a brothel. Marry an old Pisan merchant who didn't mind and was going back to Italy where people would assume the baby was ours. Or marry you."

Aram did not speak. So this beautiful young vixen did have options, and chose the one that entangled him. A point against her.

"I thought, 'He's a Christian man, he's a young man, smart from what I could tell, good-looking.' When I started to regret my decision, they told me I was too late."

"Started to regret it?"

"Yes. When I realized—" She paused. "I realized how they had hooked you in."

"Hmmm."

There was a moment of silence.

"You realize my Chrsitianity is nothing like yours," Aram said.

"Christianity is Christianity."

"Nestorian Christians believe Jesus is divinely inspired, but not God. We also prohibit idol worship—these crucifixes all over your church are blasphemies to Nestorian Christians."

She was silent for a moment. "It sounds like what I've heard Muslims believe."

Aram smiled. "Smart as well as pretty, my new wife. Yes, those tenets are closer to Islam than some forms of Christianity." He paused. "Still think 'Christianity is Christianity?'"

"I don't know."

"Jeannette, I am your husband. I wish that situation to remain. I am on this mission with Robert of Montpelier. It is a dangerous mission. If I do not return, you will be the widow of a heroic man who died in the service of your pope. You and our child will suffer no disgrace."

"I understand."

Aram squeezed her. She squeezed back. He believed she did understand, by what she said as well as what she didn't say. Aram wanted options. He had them. If he decided not to return, the girl would have an out. He could escape from this predicament with relative tidiness.

Late April, 1258
Acre
Early Afternoon

"We've got them on the run!" Baybars yelled. He led a mounted squad over rocky ground dotted with only an occasional clump of greenish brown vegetation. "Watch out for the re-form and counter!"

"They're put to flight!" one of Baybars' officers yelled.

Baybars nodded. He and seventy men had rallied the center and averted disaster. Now he needed to exploit the developing victory of this skirmish.

Baybars spurred his mount to catch up to one of the enemy soldiers. He raised his sword to hack the man down, but had another thought. Coming up on the man's right, he used the shield he held in his left hand to slam his opponent off his horse. The rider fell to the ground. "Take that man!" Baybars ordered. "I want him alive!"

Baybars saw two of his soldiers peel off from the pursuit and surround the dehorsed soldier. Satisfied his orders had been heard and understood, Baybars rode ahead. He wanted more prisoners—the higher ranking, the better.

Baybars' squad grew in size as more men accumulated behind him. He circled back and a few of his men passed him. He watched to make sure the counterattack and pursuit were gaining momentum, and checked one more time to make sure his enemies were not re-forming after a feigned retreat.

"Pursue!" he yelled as a few more of his soldiers rode by. "Take more prisoners!"

Baybars urged his horse into a gallop. He overtook some of his men as they continued pursuit of the disorganized, panicked enemy.

"How many?" Baybars asked as he trotted his horse toward the Bahriyya camp. He watched remnants of the fleeing enemy disappear like specks fading over the horizon. A few of his own men trailed back toward him. Dead bodies and horses dotted his view.

"About twenty," an officer said. "Two emirs. A few are not in good shape."

"Are the emirs all right?"

"Yes."

"Good. Make sure all are treated well. Give the wounded prisoners the best care we have."

"I'll pass along the order." The man rode toward concentrations of Mamluk officers and squad leaders.

Baybars turned his horse to survey the field. The victory was complete. Battles, small or large, could turn on such shifts in fortune. Both wings of his small army had collapsed, and it looked as if Baybars and his men would be surrounded. But Baybars had harnessed a white hot determination and found a way to step up his efforts. His attitude had spread through the men around him like a sudden magic spell of transformation. His center was able to turn the enemy center, and this left the enemy's wings over-extended and isolated from the rest. Baybars had never doubted he would achieve victory. His certainty had been rewarded again. He allowed the energy of the moment to dissipate.

Only a handful of al-Nasir Yusuf's men had escaped the raid. Baybars shook his head and grinned. He had once served under al-Nasir Yusuf, before joining al-Mughith Umar. He had traded one Ayyubid prince for another. Now he had demonstrated his value to the one he had left by opposing and defeating his forces in battle.

Qalawun rode up alongside. "Orders are received," he said. "The prisoners are ready for your inspection."

"You saw the two emirs."

"Yes. Brave men, caught over-extending their lines."

"We will treat them with respect," Baybars said.

"Commander, this opens up Gaza, Nablus, and Hebron to our power."

"Yes. Yes it does," Baybars told him. "It is a great day for the Bahriyya."

"There is no authority to contest us for miles. We can establish this as our territory. You as our ruler."

Baybars smiled. "I like the idea, my friend. Our day for that will come. But this is not the right time."

"Will we leave these territories as they sit within our grasp?"

"No, no, of course not," Baybars assured him. "We will occupy the territories in the name of al-Mughith Umar."

Qalawun raised his eyebrows.

"If we declare ourselves independent, al-Mughith Umar's men serving with us now will likely defect. Some of them are worthless—good riddance. But a few fought well, and with more training, though they will never match the competence of the Bahriyya, they may get close. And eventually develop more loyalty to us than to al-Mughith Umar."

"I see. Bide our time. Serve al-Mughith Umar but wait for opportunities."

"Exactly. And al-Nasir Yusuf is that opportunity. He is technically our enemy now, because we serve his rival, al-Mughith Umar. But al-Nasir Yusuf looks like he will be the better Ayyubid prince for our long-term goals. Sunqur al-Ashqar made contact with him and was turned away, but from what he said, I do not believe that is the end of it."

Qalawun nodded and grinned. "Yes. I see it."

"I'll have a word with those prisoners."

Baybars would send a few prisoners back to al-Nasir Yusuf, explaining the new circumstances in southern Syria, but also assuring him his emirs would be held at Kerak, under al-Mughith Umar's protection, and would be treated with respect.

11

Early Autumn, 1258
Tabriz
Early Afternoon

"Stargazer."

Dawud awoke to the whispered Persian word delivered with a thick Mongol accent. Nomolun, the chubby guard, stood over him. Dawud looked around the small tent. His four astronomer-scholar tentmates remained in their slumber.

"Come with me. We need an early morning forecast."

Dawud spotted one of his tentmates open his eyes, glance at Dawud and Nomolun without moving his head, then close them again.

Dawud took a deep breath. No one wanted to interact with this guard. He gathered himself and grunted as he rose slowly from the ground.

"Come," Nomolun demanded. "The morning forecast is needed *now.*"

Dawud grunted again as he straightened up. He walked out of the tent. Nomolun's brother, Shingkhor was also there.

"This way," Nomolun ordered gruffly, motioning toward an open area where the ponies grazed.

"Who am I offering my predictions to, the ponies?"

"Officials will meet you out there," Nomolun barked. "I will tolerate none of your insult-jokes."

Dawud considered that the man's Persian had improved.

Nomolun looked around. Shingkhor mumbled something in the Mongol tongue. It took a moment to register. The words meant something like "the others are sleeping; let's not wake them."

"I'll complete this task," Nomolun said to his brother. "There will be no problems with this feeble old man. Just make sure no one interrupts."

"Bind his hands at least."

Dawud frowned. This was not a meeting to gather his predictions. "Why do you need to bind my hands to take a reading of the stars?" Dawud asked loudly.

Nomolun smashed Dawud in the face with a backhand stroke of his left forearm.

Dawud toppled to the ground and groaned. Pain from his nose and mouth immobilized him.

"Quiet," Nomolun barked. "You will wake people!"

Dawud felt his arms being grabbed. He looked to see Shingkhor tying his hands. Dawud grunted with pain from his face, and the indignity of being restrained.

Nomolun yanked him up by his wrists, now bound together in front of him. Shingkhor tied the other end of the rope to a horse.

"This will be completed before breakfast," Nomolun said.

Shingkhor nodded.

Nomolun mounted his horse and nudged it forward. The horse walked slowly, pulling Dawud along.

The pace was a little quick, and Dawud was slightly winded trying to keep up, but in no jeopardy of being dragged. They moved along a meandering trail through pastures spread out over gently rolling bright green hills.

There was only one reason Dawud could think of for this treatment: Nomolun was going to execute him. This was being done in a way not to alarm the other astonomers and scholars, and away from any guards who might not agree with the action. A few months before, he had resigned himself to the end. But the day he offered Islam to the Mongol guards, and saw receptive eyes among them; followed by other individual incidents of Dawud sharing his wisdom with fellow astronomers and scholars, and receptive guards—all of these recent developments had energized him, giving him a renewed passion for a purpose in life, a reason to continue living regardless of the horrible turn of events. And now, this ignorant savage, this spiteful tiny-in-stature, barely human being, was going to take it away from him.

Dawud's nose dripped blood.

They approached a clump of bushes, then rounded into an open area of dry dirt. On the ground were bones, a few partially decomposed bodies, as well as detached skulls and headless torsos. Dawud smelled the unmistakable odor of decaying flesh.

An execution ground. Maybe a private execution ground for the two brothers.

Nomolun stopped his horse. He dismounted and untied the rope from the horse's saddle.

"I need stars to look at," Dawud said through a stern stare.

"You are a fraud. Fake. I have confessions from your comrades. They give you what to say. You do not know how to read men's fortunes in the stars."

Dawud did not respond. He felt rage burning—his teeth clenched, his fists tightened, and energy surged through his veins as his mind raced.

"See the birds circling for a feast?" Nomolun pointed up into the sky. "They will be eating your eyes out in just a few moments. I will enjoy watching that!"

Dawud felt his anger building. He welcomed the feeling.

"Kneel."

Dawud did not move.

Nomolun pushed down on Dawud's shoulder with his left hand while brandishing a long, curved sword in his right.

Dawud fell to his knees, his hands still bound in front of him.

Nomolun stood behind the kneeling Dawud. "Beg. Beg for your life."

Dawud said nothing. He let his rage build further. He would likely die, but not while begging. If he could manage it, he would die fighting, with all the strength his rage would grant to him.

"I have killed thousands of you. City people. Useless, soft city people. It is my life's work to kill all city people. Baghdad. That was the best. I went out with as many squads as I could. They all die begging. Either to me, for a few extra moments of their measly lives, or begging to their God. Prayers. Begging to their God for something worthwhile after their useless lives are over! Beg, old man! I want to hear you beg!"

Dawud waited. The time was almost right. His energy was almost at its peak. He could feel rage infusing him with unstoppable strength. And the fool was becoming overconfident. Complacent. Distracted.

"Who knows, I might spare you if you beg."

Now. Now was the moment. With a quickness Dawud had not contemplated for many years, he thrust his elbow back, into the man's kneecap. He heard a crack and a yelp. Dawud turned to see the guard crouched in pain and surprise. Time was moving slower for Dawud than it was for his would-be executioner. Dawud grabbed the guard's jacket with his bound hands and pulled himself off the ground, bringing his knee into the man's testicles. The man screamed, dropped his sword and doubled over. Dawud moved with catlike quickness to the sword and grabbed it with his right hand. He whirled around and made a two handed slash at the backs of Nomolun's feet, slicing his Achilles tendons. The man cried out again as he fell to his arms. Dawud kicked underneath the man, turning him over onto his back.

"Help! Help!" the guard cried out.

Dawud measured Nomolun's throat. He stabbed the sword through Nomolun's neck, right at the spot he wanted.

Nomolun's screams ended, but agony continued to register on his face.

"You fool!" Dawud told him, in the Mongol tongue. "Do you think I've always been an old man?"

The man continued to show agonized expressions and spasms of pain, but could only gurgle.

"I was once a great warrior for the Prophet!"

Nomolun grunted and gurgled.

"You like this? You're just a hacker. I bet you didn't know this one. Yes. I cut your throat right at your voice. You'll die soon. You'll feel all the pain of your wounds as your life slips away. The only thing you won't be able to do, you piece of human filth, is scream."

Nomolun grunted and gurgled again.

"That's the rage. I see it in you." Dawud maneuvered the sword until it was held between his knees, tip embedded in the ground. He used the blade to cut the ropes from his hands. His own rage dissipated as he watched the dying man weakening. "And I am sorry for my taunts. That was your way; it will not be mine going forward. I will let you leave this world with my thanks. My gratitude. I hope I have that word correct. Thanks to you. Sincere. Thanks."

Nomolun seemed to relax, but his eyes still blinked; hanging on to one last thread of life.

"Thank you for the rage. I see now that, channeled properly, rage can be a gift from God. In my past, I allowed rage to lead me to unspeakably terrible acts. I tortured, in slow increments, the Christian man who killed my father. I made him welcome death. I killed Christians in retribution for what should have been that man's sin alone. And I paid for it with a terrible emptiness in my soul."

Nomolun's breathing became shallower.

"Now, I dedicate myself to God's will. God's will was that I would live, and you would die. God's will was that I would gather your lesson on rage before your death, and use it for my future enlightenment. Thank you."

The ropes around his wrists fell to the ground. He reached up and wiped drying blood from his face.

He watched as Nomolun's shallow breathing came to an end.

Dawud looked over at the horse. He was grateful for the mild climate. He would be able to ride some distance away from the Mongol camp in Tabriz before needing water. He figured he was on borrowed time, time that had been obtained for him in Baghdad by the courage and determination of his dear, departed student. He determined to use that gift to the greatest extent possible.

Late Autumn, 1258
Southern Coast of Syria/Palestine
Night

"Bring that man to my tent." Baybars sat on his horse. He moved at a trot past a flickering campfire, leading a small squad of his inner circle.

"He was the highest-ranking one we captured," Qalawun said.

"Yes." Baybars smiled. "The raid went very well. We are making much progress here, tormenting al-Nasir Yusuf's territories, establishing a devastating cadre of dangerous warriors."

Qalawun smiled at the compliment.

"Al-Mughith Umar himself may bring forces north to join us," Baybars said.

"He will have to if al-Nasir Yusuf decides to bring his full forces against us."

Baybars shrugged. "That is why we will hedge our bets. And so will he. This raid will annoy him, maybe even embarrass him. But he has much bigger concerns than us further up north."

The lieutenant chuckled. "No doubt."

Baybars continued to ride toward his tent. The man he had requested was brought before him, hands bound, accompanied by guards.

"Has he been searched?" Baybars asked.

"Of course, commander."

"Remove his bonds."

One of the guards untied the prisoner's hands.

"Not a good day for your squad," Baybars said.

"Better day for me than the ones dead on the field," the prisoner said. "For now."

"You think the day will still go badly for you?"

"I expect you to abuse us, to further embarrass my sovereign. Then you'll execute us, the way Qutuz treated your Bahriyya."

Baybars nodded. "Qutuz treated our captured men without respect or mercy. He killed my great friend and mentor, Aqtay, when he was head of Sultan Aybak's Mamluks. But you ride for al-Nasir Yusuf."

The captured soldier shrugged. "Does it matter who I am with?"

"It might."

The captured soldier shrugged again.

"Would you like to live?" Baybars asked.

"Of course. But I don't expect to."

"You think I will kill you?"

"Not personally. You'll put out a casual suggestion and walk away while some younger fanatic murders me."

Baybars scratched his cheek. "I have not been treating captured prisoners this way. Why would you think this?"

"We have been told this is the way you are."

"You've been told wrong."

"We'll see."

"So you think you will die. But wouldn't you rather live?"

"It's a trap question. If I say yes, you will torture me, and make me regret choosing life over a quick death."

Baybars grimaced with genuine surprise. "I went to some trouble to gain control over some of you. You must think me a bloodthirsty animal if you believe I captured you for torture."

"You're a Bahriyya Mamluk. Your people killed Turan Shah, great grandson of Saladin. You have no respect, only brutality. Brutality is expected. You have allowed me to live for some purpose. Perhaps there is some information you want."

Baybars raised his eyebrows. "No. There is some information I want you to have, to take to al-Nasir Yusuf."

The prisoner scowled.

"You will take a note with my words on it. You will deliver the message that the Bahriyya are alive and well, and ready to cast all infidels from our lands. Al-Mughith Umar is not committed to this goal. We would like to join with someone who is. Tell al-Nasir Yusuf he can stop the Bahriyya raids on his territory by bringing us under his banner."

The prisoner though a moment, then grinned. "Not such a bad day for me after all." He nodded. "I will gladly carry this message. You have caused a lot of grief for al-Nasir Yusuf, and Turan Shah was his uncle…. But as one who has faced you and your men more than once, I can assure you that, for me, it would be most gratifying to be fighting with you instead of against you."

"Good. Mention that to your sovereign. I will have my men provide nourishment for you and one other of your men while I have some written words prepared." Baybars motioned to a few of his soldiers. He looked back at the prisoner. "Have al-Nasir Yusuf send an agent with his reply. We will await his answer here." Baybars looked the man in the eyes with a serious glare. "We have Mongol hordes—packs of savage mounted warriors— with designs on Egypt and God's Holy Lands in and around Jerusalem. We must be ready to face them. The Bahriyya will commit to the best option available."

"I'll communicate that to al-Nasir Yusuf."

"Tell him I will always be available to his contacts."

The man nodded. Baybars' men escorted him away to get the promised supplies before leaving.

"But we will continue to harass al-Nasir Yusuf's territories?" Qalawun asked.

"Oh, yes. To be a threat gives us power. But al-Mughith Umar will never have the resources or courage to match forces with the Mongols. These Ayyubid princes are submitting to Hulegu like a row of flimsy tents falling from a light breeze. I can see al-Mughith Umar considering the same alternative. Al-Ashraf Musa up in Homs submitted long ago. Right now, al-Nasir Yusuf is our best option. We will need to keep our options flexible. Our value is as fighting men. So we will continue to demonstrate our value." Baybars paused. "But I think it is time for Sunqur al-Ashqar to make another trip."

Qalawun nodded.

Late Autumn, 1258
Tabriz, Azerbaijan
Late Morning

"You look good, like the wife of a khan," Hulegu said to his wife, Dokuz Khatun.

She was a woman approaching forty, with a plain, weathered face starting to show wrinkles and a wide-waisted figure. On this day she was adorned with jewels and costumed with brightly colored silks of red, blue, and purple. She looked every bit a Kerait princess married to a Mongol prince. "Thank you," she said. "This will be a great day."

Hulegu smiled. "No doubt. And a long one. We have a line of submissions from princes as far south as the land of Syria."

Dokuz Khatun nodded. "I am honored to be included."

"You are the first wife of the il-khan. It is always appropriate that you join in these events."

Dokuz Khatun grinned and bowed slightly.

Hulegu gave her a quick kiss on the lips.

Dokuz Khatun raised her eyebrows.

"You're surprised I offer my wife a kiss?"

"I'm no fool. You have been well-entertained by your younger wives, especially the new ones from the caliph's harem."

Hulegu shrugged. "But never doubt who the *first* wife is." He beamed with pride. "Our son is on his way to Mayyafariqun to take that city, a city that still defies us." Hulegu clenched his teeth. "This will clear the path to Syria, Palestine, and the rich land of Egypt. Our son will bring glory to both of us, as well as to my grandfather, and your line of Kerait princesses."

Dokut Khatun gave her husband a return kiss. "Come visit me sometimes. I can still be ... entertaining."

Hulegu laughed. "I know you can." Hulegu looked toward the tent opening. "Squad! We are ready!" He took his wife by the arm and led her from the tent.

"This is the one who will give you earrings," Ketbugha whispered in Hulegu's ear. Hulegu sat on an elevated dais at the back of a large tent. Stacks of gifts—jewels, linens, rugs, gold-embroidered wood chests, porcelain, perfumes, silver and brass drinking vessels, and wine to put in them, to name a few—covered much of the tent floor.

Hulegu nodded. "Oh, yes. This should be amusing."

"Al-Malik, al-Rahim Badr al-Din Lu'lu', Prince of Mosul," an announcer called.

An elderly man approached, head bowed. He was dressed in an off-white robe and a white turban, and his face bristled with a white beard poking down to a thin point. "Permit me to approach His Excellency?"

The interpreter made the request.

Hulegu nodded. He knew what was to come, and had pre-approved it.

The elderly man spoke, outwardly firm, but occasionally cracking with fatigue and possibly nerves. Hulegu took in the speech with the aid of an interpreter. "As His Excellency Hulegu knows, I have been a friend of the great khan for four years now. This was not always the case." He took a deep breath. "When I first heard the great khan was sending his younger brother west, to spread their empire into the areas where the Faithful live, I said I would take the young upstart by the ears." The man paused. A hush came over the tent.

Hulegu smiled.

"Well, I am keeping my promise." The old prince raised his hands and displayed gold earrings. "Pure gold. Gifts for the khan, for the il-khan." The old prince placed the earrings on Hulegu's ears.

Hulegu nodded.

The old prince knelt at Hulegu's feet.

"Thank you, my dear old friend, my honest forthright friend," Hulegu said.

The man bowed, rose, and left the tent.

"Al-Aziz Mohammad, son of al-Nasir Yusuf, Prince of Syria," called out the announcer.

In walked a young man wearing brightly colored silks and a white turban with a red jewel. His black beard looked like it was still filling in. A small entourage of nobles and emirs trailed behind him. The young man carried a stack of cotton linens. He walked with a nervous haste and placed the linens on the ground, then bowed. "There are five carts of other gifts outside, Your Excellency, a token of my father's friendship."

"His friendship," Hulegu said. It wasn't clear from the translation if this meant he was submitting, or trying to declare the friendship of an equal.

The young man, seeming more like an overmatched young boy, swallowed. He drew in a deep breath. "Yes. Friendship."

Hulegu held a stern expression. The reply still sounded ambiguous to him. "Where is your father?" Hulegu asked, hoping his grim tone had come across before the interpreter translated.

"He sends, um, his regrets, um...." The boy took in a shallow breath, then another. "His territory is under siege, um, Christians, infidels, from the West."

Hulegu deliberately froze his expression with a skeptical look. He thought of challenging this assertion, an assertion he was certain was either outright false, or at best, exaggerated. But he realized little would be accomplished by bullying the young prince-to-be in front of this gathering. "I see," he finally said. "Thank your father for his gifts, and tell him I look forward to meeting him at some time in the future. Soon."

"Yes, Your Excellency, Sir. I will tell him." He bowed again.

Hulegu nodded.

The young man left the tent, with his entourage close behind.

"Of course it was a good day," Hulegu said to a small gathering of close advisers and high-ranking subordinates. They sat in the middle of the tent, eating lamb chops and drinking some of the recently delivered wine. "Any time we are able to gather so many rich gifts from so many subservient local leaders, it is a good day. But now, we must discuss what we did not receive."

"Mayyafariqin," one of the men said.

"Yes, well, that was not expected." Hulegu grinded his teeth. "And it is particularly galling. We have besieged that location twice before. Years ago, we raised our siege only after a promise from al-Kamil Muhammad that he would submit. We still wait for him to fulfill his promises." Hulegu sneered. "My son Yoshmut will deal with that problem."

Hulegu saw nods among his men.

"We have other small pockets not submitting who will be dealt with over the coming months, with the appropriate sized forces."

The men nodded.

"The other one we need an answer from is al-Nasir Yusuf," Hulegu said. "Another one who has made promises. Almost a decade ago he sent his envoys all the way to Qaraqorum and agreed to submit; agreed to send tribute. Still, to this day, nothing but ambiguous contacts and dithering. And this one holds the key cities in Syria, along the way to Egypt."

"His son came," Ketbugha said.

"Yes. With not much of a submission." Hulegu smiled. "Did you all happen to see this?" Hulegu held up a pair of gold-inlaid slippers. "This man knows how to submit. This gift leaves no doubt." Hulegu turned the slippers to show that the soles were embroidered with images of a dignified, bearded middle-aged man wearing a turban.

"Where is he from?" Ketbugha asked.

"He's Prince Kasi-Kawus. From...," Hulegu looked puzzled. "I don't remember. Somewhere nearby," he said.

His companions laughed.

"The man gives new meaning to the idea of groveling at your feet," one of them said.

The others laughed again.

When Hulegu's smile disappeared he said, "But al-Nasir Yusuf. He does *not* know how to submit."

"He did not submit at all, il-Khan," Ketbugha said.

"No." Hulegu scratched his chin. "He did not. And some of those nobles who came with his son are no friends of his. They seem to understand how to submit."

"But they are weasels," Ketbugha said. "Behind their sovereign's back, they implore you to invade. And what do they have to offer to the effort? Nothing I could discern, other than disrespect and treachery."

Hulegu nodded. "Exactly." He shrugged. "But we are not ready to move on Syria just yet. Keep the al-Nasir Yusuf mission entertained. Keep them happy. In the meantime, al-Nasir Yusuf knows our demands. He has our letter demanding submission. We will entertain this group a little longer—miss no opportunity to demonstrate our power. Then, we send another letter back with them, demanding submission again. And this time, I expect to see al-Nasir Yusuf in person." He smiled. "With earrings. Or *slippers.*" Hulegu again lifted the gift from Prince Kasi-Kawus.

His men laughed and raised their glasses in toast to the soles of the slippers.

12

Early November, 1258
Acre
Mid Day

"I prayed to God for a late term birth. I'm pleased God granted my prayer," Robert said secretively as he greeted Aram just outside the latter's living quarters with Jeannette. They were alone in a hall on the grounds of the Church of St. Peter.

"Yes," Aram said. "A May wedding date, November birth, six months. By the size of my son, many will question that he was premature. But, respectability can be somewhat argued."

Robert chuckled. "You care about respectability?"

"I care for her sake."

Robert's eyes flashed as he smiled. "Very nice. A little consideration." He nodded. "I am impressed with your growth and maturity."

Aram forced a smile.

Robert peeked into the room.

Aram looked over his shoulder. His son was asleep, cuddled on Jeannette's chest. Jeannette looked tired, but her eyes were open. She wore a weary smile.

"Remember Robert of Montpelier?" Aram asked as the two men entered the room. "From the wedding?"

Jeannette frowned.

"I stood with your husband," Robert reminded her. "But your sight was covered by a veil, and you had other matters on your mind," Robert said. "Congratulations on your son."

Jeannette appeared as if she was trying to force a smile, but ended up with a tight-lipped expression. "Thank you."

Aram looked at his wife. Her expression told him she was experiencing more than just a lack of recognition.

Robert smiled and walked up to her. "Let us see him."

"Don't wake him," Jeannette requested. She pulled some covers from him to show as much of the infant as possible.

"Looks like a strong one," Robert said. "And with the good looks of his parents."

Jeannette answered with a barely polite smile.

"Well," Robert said, "I'll leave you two to rest." He looked at Jeannette. "I am sorry to say that I will be taking your husband away soon. But it served my purpose, and I think God's purpose, that we wait until after the birth of your son."

"Thank you," Jeannette said with another smile that barely registered sincerity.

Robert nodded to both of them and left the room.

Jeannette waited a moment. "*That* is Robert?"

Aram's face showed a puzzled frown. "Yes...."

She shook her head. "I heard things about him at the convent."

"About Robert?"

"I think so. He's from back in Europe, from a city with a famous school for healing?"

"I'm not sure where he's from. He says he's from a French city that has a famous school of medicine. But he speaks French with a German accent, and his chief associates appear to be German."

She shook her head. "I've heard he's not a straight talker. Some think he is not everything he says he is."

"Could be. Where did you hear this?"

"The ladies clean at the monastery, and around some of the churches. They hear things. Some of us—we get friendly."

Aram smirked. "I know about that."

"Not just that," Jeannette said, with a frown that scolded Aram. "We care what happens to each other. This Robert came in with some mission from the pope, but some of the people think there's something wrong about it. There are intrigues and schemes related to the Italians and their fight."

"That was settled last June in the battle fought in the harbor not far from here. The Venetian fleet drove the Genoese out of Acre completely. So what purpose—"

"It's never settled between the Italians. They are always fighting over trade issues. Money." Jeannette's face tensed; her eyes narrowed. "My parents." Her lips moved up as her nostrils flared. She fought tears.

"Your parents?" Aram looked at her, puzzled.

"Killed."

Aram tilted his head. "By the coughing sickness."

Jeannette glared back at him. "Coughing sickness. Where did you get that?"

"Robert."

Jeannette raised her chin. "He must have made that up. My father was an agent for a group of Pisan merchants. He and my mother were killed when they got trapped between the soldiers." She snorted. "I had been the little girl of rich traders. Suddenly I was nothing."

Aram looked at her. "Why would Robert lie about the details?"

"You think I'm lying?"

"No! I am sure he is the one with the wrong information." Aram drew a deep breath. "Maybe he didn't want me to realize just how dangerous it is here."

"It will be less dangerous since that battle you mentioned," Jeannette said. "But like I said, nothing is ever really settled between those Italian merchant cities. My father made a fortune feeding off their greed. And then died when he got caught in the middle of it."

"And Robert seems oblivious to it."

"Or is trying to ignore it because it is inconvenient to his purpose."

Aram shrugged as he nodded.

"I hear them talk. People don't think he is here for the reason he says."

Aram's lips tensed and his eyes narrowed. "Well, what exactly is he here for? Honestly, I don't always agree with him, and I find him to be a little heavy-handed with his techniques of persuasion, especially against me. And I think he's less than straight about his background. But until this lie about your parents, he's been otherwise straight with me, sometimes brutally straight. What—" Aram exhaled a short burst of air from his nose. "Is this anything more than just baseless chatter?"

"Something about a William Report," she said. "The William Report he doesn't want anyone to see."

"'William report.'" Aram pondered. His eyebrows arched inward. "And he's hiding it."

"Something about it not being consistent with what he says his mission is."

"William of Rubruck," Aram said. "That must be it. He went east recently, and wrote a report on it." Aram shrugged. "I asked about that when we first met. He said he'd seen the report and that it had no real meaning to what we're doing. The report was for the French king—William's mission was for the French king."

"That's what I heard them talking about. The report does have meaning. People who have seen it say it does."

Aram frowned as he considered what his wife was telling him. "I'd like to see the report. Have you heard anything about if there is a copy anywhere in Acre?"

"Ask Robert."

"If he's hiding something, he is not going to make it easy for me to see the report."

"I don't know."

"You say someone did see it. Someone here in Acre. Can you find out who, and where it is?"

Jeannette took in a deep breath. "It won't be easy, and it won't be right away. I can't just start asking about this."

"I know."

"I'll try." She smiled. "After all, I'm not a widow yet."

Aram smiled and shook his head. She was indirectly thanking him for not running away from her before the baby was born. But Aram wanted to get accurate information on this Robert he'd gotten tangled up with. His suspicions were growing that the objectives of Robert's mission were not what Robert claimed. Aram wanted to learn more about what the real mission was. It might just provide another compelling reason to flee his current circumstances and make a fresh start somewhere new.

Early November, 1258
Small Village South of Lake Urmia
Morning

"We are looking for an old man. He masquerades as an astronomer."

Dawud ducked back into a small stable, part of a modest residence. The Mongol soldier who had spoken was Shingkhor, the brother of Nomolun—the chubby guard who had gone from being Dawud's would-be executioner to dying at Dawud's hands. This was no coincidental village visit, no random search for tribute. These Mongols were specifically looking for him. Nothing had been forgotten. "He would have come here within the last four months. He killed a Mongol guard, my brother. He needs to pay for his crime."

Dawud listened for a reply. He heard none from the villager being questioned by Nomolun's brother. The villager had taken Dawud in, and had eventually set him up with modest quarters. Dawud now paid rent for those quarters, from wages he earned by tutoring village children and even some adults. Dawud exhaled and saw his frosty breath hang in the air of the gloomy, overcast morning.

"Speak! Villagers say he lives with you!"

Dawud's heart pounded. He looked around for a weapon.

"I don't know," the villager/landlord said in a bewildered tone.

"Liar!"

Dawud heard the sound of fist hitting face. He took in a short breath. He could not allow this to go on. He started forward.

"I, I don't know," the man said again. "There was an old man who came through here. He offered lessons for money." Dawud heard a chuckle. "Can you imagine? I let him stay with me for a while, but he ran off when he couldn't keep up with the rent. I'm sure he hasn't gotten far. You will find him."

Dawud stopped. The lie was cast. He would do more harm than good if he surrendered now. He would be executed, along with his landlord for lying.

"I hear from your fellow villagers that he has been here during the last week."

"I'm sure they're telling you what they think you want to hear. He's been gone longer than that."

"I think you lie," Shingkhor said. "We will search the village, your home in particular. If you lie, you will suffer this man's fate alongside him. So will your family. And this village will burn."

"Search away. He's not here."

Dawud couldn't believe his landlord was taking such a risk. They had discussed the best hiding places on the property. One of them was an underground storage bin in one of the horse stalls. Dawud moved quickly to it, opened it up, and crawled in. It was cramped and airless. He wondered if this would be his final resting place—whether the Mongols found him or not. He tried to put the stuffy, snug conditions out of his mind by focusing outside of himself.

Just as he pulled the covering over him, and got it over the hole as well as he could, he heard people enter.

"What's in here?" Shingkhor demanded.

"Horses. Hay." The landlord sounded polite, but also had the tone of someone impatient answering a question about the obvious.

"I can see that! What else? What storage bins?"

"What you see."

Dawud heard footsteps toward the horse's stall. He heard the rustling of some of the large piles of hay. He assumed the man was running a sword through them.

"He's in here, isn't he," Shingkhor demanded.

"Do you see him?"

"You will tell me where he is or I will kill you now!" Dawud heard the sound of Shingkhor drawing a dagger.

"He is not here. I cannot tell you what I do not know."

Dawud heard another man enter the stable. "Nothing in their house. Some signs of the possessions of a scholar in one of the rooms. Books. Papers."

"He left them when he ran off," the landlord said.

"Why would he do that?" Shingkhor asked.

"He's an old man. Maybe he could not carry them. How should I know?"

"And you just left them there?"

"I am hoping to find a buyer for them. If I can't, I will dispose of them."

"No signs of him," the second guard said in Mongolian. Dawud was pleased he had picked up so much fluency in the language. "He's probably off to another village."

"I don't think so," Shingkhor insisted. "Bring his family."

Dawud breathed in hard, then coughed. He couldn't allow it. He wiggled his way toward the storage area opening.

"To do what?" the second guard demanded. "To pile up bodies and still have them say he's not here? Like you have in the other villages?"

There was no audible response from Shingkhor.

Dawud tensed into immobility. Maybe he would get a reprieve after all. And he reminded himself again that if he emerged right now, he probably still wouldn't save his landlord or his family. Dawud waited, a sweating, suffocating delay.

"Burn the stable. That will drive him out."

"Out of where?"

There was silence.

The second guard spoke again. "The old man who you think killed your brother is not here. I would like to get through at least two more villages before nightfall."

Dawud heard no other conversation, just the sound of steps walking to the stable entrance.

❧ ◆ ❦

"That was one of the more foolish things I have ever seen," Dawud scolded in between gulps of water from a leather flask. He sat on a cushion in the middle of the stable. His face was caked with dried sweat. His robe clung to him, sticky and wet. The landlord and his family—a wife, a son and two daughters, all pre-adolescent—hovered around him. Dawud shivered.

"No thanks are necessary," the landlord quipped.

"Of course." Dawud grunted as he drew in a deep breath. "Of course I thank you. But the risk you took to preserve this old life...." He shook his head.

"Dawud the Teacher, Dawud the Wise, the man who has so enriched this village since your arrival—you are not the only person who treasures the tenets of the True Faith."

"How does risking your life, and the lives of your family, advance God's will?"

"Preserving the life of a great sage of the True Faith? Of course it advances God's will."

Dawud took some more water. He frowned in thought. This was God's will. God had granted his landlord an opportunity to test his faith, his goodness, his courage. And the man had passed all the tests with glowing success.

"And now you can stay with us permanently," the landlord said, smiling. "They searched, and moved on."

Dawud shook his head. "My courageous friend, great and honorable servant of God, you are wrong about that. This guard is on an obsessive mission to make me dead and was clearly not satisfied that I was not hiding here. They will come back when they do not find me in one of the other villages. I must leave you. Leave my possessions right where they are until you can find someone who will pay you for them. When they return, you will aid in their search of every bin and orifice of this place. You will be gracious and charming, respectful to the point of being obsequious. You will convince them I am not here. Because, at that time, I will not be here."

The landlord's eyes moistened. His lips tightened. But he nodded. "I'll provision you. Where will you go?"

Dawud shrugged. "Away from Mongols. I have a sense I am in northern Persia, possibly up toward the Caspian Sea and Azerbaijan. To the west are Christian Armenia and Christian

Georgia. They will have no use for an old Muslim teacher of the True Faith and they have submitted to the Mongols. To the north and to the east is where I just came from. So south. Past Baghdad. To Syria. Palestine. Maybe even Egypt."

"Sad that an old man, a great sage—that you need to flee so far from your home."

Dawud grinned. "I am fleeing, but I am fleeing toward my home. Toward my original birthplace, where I was formed, where I suffered my greatest indignities and failings. It may be God's will that I be forced to return to these places, one last stop, before my time concludes."

The landlord and his family looked puzzled.

"Thank you, my friend. I will leave you at dawn tomorrow. I will be grateful for whatever you can provide for the first legs of my journey."

"You will receive whatever you can comfortably carry," the landlord's wife promised.

Dawud smiled.

13

February, 1259
Acre
Morning

"Jeannette!" Aram entered their living chambers and closed the door. "I have orders."

She took in a deep breath. "I knew this day would have to come." Their son stirred and squeaked a few soft, short cries. Jeannette stepped to him and covered him, then stroked his neck.

"We both did. But…," Aram paused. "We're going to Antioch."

Jeannette's eyes narrowed in thought. "Antioch?"

"What's the latest on the William report?" Aram still needed to know more about Robert's mission. Now that he had new orders, discovering all he could about recent events in the area became more compelling.

"Nothing different. We know where it is, where copies are, but can't think of how to get it."

Aram nodded. "I really need to see it. If there is something about this mission that isn't right, I need to know."

Jeannette stepped away from their child and sat on their bed. "They still talk about Robert—they think I don't hear. They say he keeps to himself, and gets a lot of messages from across the sea."

"Well, he is the pope's man here in Acre."

"I don't know, they think it's strange. Something about seals."

"Seals. The pope's seals?"

"I don't know."

Aram shook his head. "This is all too mysterious. I don't like mystery, especially when I'm walking into and around battlefields that include creatures like Mongols."

"I can understand."

"If you'd seen the handiwork of Mongols firsthand, you'd understand it even better."

"I know what you've told me," Jeannette said, with a little bite in her voice. "Even though I haven't traveled as much as you." Aram wondered if she was sensitive to him referring to all of the places he was familiar with because she had experienced little outside of a few streets in Acre.

"Believe me, you don't want to have seen the deeds of Mongols firsthand."

She did not answer. Her stern expression with her lips pursed told Aram she was pouting.

Aram had no patience for what he perceived as Jeannette's little bouts of over-sensitivity. He had more important issues to address. "I'll be out until our evening meal." He left their quarters.

"Aram." Robert looked up from a table at Aram across the room.

Robert was holding a small magnifying piece of glass. He put his hands over the papers he was looking at. Was Robert trying to hide them, hold them in place, or did he just choose that spot for his hands? "You got the orders."

"Yes. Antioch."

After a few awkward moments of silence, Robert finally shrugged.

"Why would we be going to Antioch?" Aram finally asked.

"The pope's orders."

"Oh, well, that explains it all." Aram sneered.

"Just what do you think you're entitled to?" Robert demanded.

"Some reasoning. Some logic. This sounds like a new mission."

"You are in my service. Your pay continues to accumulate. You are only asked to do the most minimal chores while standing by. I will decide what you need to know."

"I see. What happened to my value as an adviser who will speak frankly about what he knows? I have never been to Antioch. There are no Mongol leaders there."

Robert tilted his head, as if making a silent challenge to the assumptions in Aram's quip.

"Mongols in Antioch?" Aram's eyes shifted.

Robert frowned. "In a manner of speaking."

"So Bohemond made it official…." Bohemond was the ruler of Antioch, long a Western Christian state at the northern end of the territories controlled by Western European Christians since the late 1000s. Aram had heard that Bohemond had been wavering with his loyalties. But this was a big step, breaking with "Catholic" Christians to submit to the approaching Mongols. Maybe Bohemond had no choice. Maybe the example of nearby Georgian and Armenian Christian rulers had influenced him. But the decision was not going to be welcomed by the still-independent Western Christian area that maintained loyalty to the pope.

"He submitted. The pope wants me to deliver his objections."

Aram shrugged. "And you're not fond of the mission."

Robert did not reply, but his general bad humor seemed to confirm Aram's assertion.

"No one should be surprised," Aram said with a shrug. "Bohemond's father-in-law is King Hethum of Armenia. The king submitted to the Mongols even before they moved on the Isma'ilis a few years ago. Bohemond's father used to pay tribute to the Mongols."

"But full submission? In effect, becoming part of the Mongol state? No. Antioch is a coastal state. A Western Christian state. The pope objects to such a prerogative taken by a prince under his religious jurisdiction."

"And you?"

Robert sneered "And I what?"

"You seem to be in a foul mood about the whole enterprise."

Robert squinted at Aram. "It is not what I have come here for."

Aram let slip an amused grin. "Ah. The pope changed the mission."

"Just what are you here for?" Robert asked, arms folded across his chest. "Don't you have preparations to complete?"

"Yes. Part of that is determining what this mission is about."

"Mmm-hmm. Well, then I have told you."

"Sort of."

Robert sat back in his chair. "There have been some peculiar occurrences recently. Someone snooping around. Trying to get ahold of a certain report?"

Aram felt a chill as he tensed.

"I told you, William of Rubruck's report is not important to our purpose. You do not need to concern yourself with it."

"Then why are there whispers that—"

"In a place like this, there are *always* whispers. Even when everything is *completely* open and honest, someone will conjure up whispers."

Aram nodded. "Granted. So why not let me see the report? I can then put this—"

"You do not need to see the report," Robert growled back. "I forbid you to look at it. I forbid you to try to look at it. I forbid you from discussing it, or discussing that you want to look at it. Am I clear?"

Aram shrugged. "I would say so."

"Good. Now get your mind out of 'whispers.' And prepare for this mission."

"Why am I going on this mission? There are no Mongols to talk to. I am unfamiliar with—"

Robert let out a long breath. He seemed to be releasing tension to regain control of his temper. "Fair question. You are my adviser on all things Mongol. I am interested in your observations as this contact proceeds."

Aram nodded.

"I will notify you the day before we leave. It will be soon."

Aram took this as a dismissal. He nodded again and left the room.

"He'll be all right now," Jeannette assured. She patted their crying son.

"Something has him upset," Aram said. He followed her through the door to their quarters.

"Thank goodness he let us get through dinner," Jeanette said, laying the child down in a small, enclosed bed.

"And too bad he let us get through the after-dinner chores."

Jeannette smiled. She stroked their son'shis neck with the back of her index finger. His cries diminished.

Aram's attention was diverted to the top of their bed. He saw a small satchel. "What's that?"

Jeannette followed Aram's eyes. "I don't know. I've never seen it."

Aram picked up the satchel and opened it. Out came a bound sheaf of parchments. The first page was blank except for *Itinerarium fratris Willielmi de Rubruquis de ordine fratrum Minorum, Galli, Anno gratia 1253 ad partes Orientales.* Aram felt stunned surprise as he looked at the satchel's contents.

"What is it?" Jeannette asked, urgency in her voice.

"The report. The William Report, as we've been calling it."

"Robert?"

"Not likely. I'm forbidden to look at this."

Aram opened the bound sheafs. The title page alerted him to a potential major problem with the document, a problem he hoped he was wrong about.

"If not Robert...."

"One of your friends, maybe." Aram interrupted.

"I doubt it."

"Well, I doubt it was Robert." Aram thumbed through the pages, more and more desperately as he reached the end. "Damn."

"Aram?"

"It's in Latin. The whole thing is in *Latin*."

"What else would it be?"

Aram clenched his teeth. "Educated people write in *Greek*. Or *Arabic*. I can't read this." He thumbed through it. "I can see from what little I can pick up: it has some dates, locations. I think I even see the great khan's name."

"You don't know Latin?"

"I've never had a call for Latin, not in the *civilized* world."

Jeannette chuckled. "Oh. I see."

"I'll request instruction."

"Don't let it uncivilize you."

Aram glared at Jeannette. He softened. It was a clever remark. Aram liked clever remarks. He was usually not on the receiving end. "More education never hurts, my darling. And, well, as you Western Christians become more and more civilized, the more you learn from us here in the East."

Jeannette laughed. "Yes. Of course."

Aram grinned and shook his head. He looked again at the sheaf of parchments. "I know a man who could help me with this," Aram said, looking off to a corner of the room, but his mind projecting farther than that.

"You do? Who?"

"He's from Baghdad. Educated Christian. Converted to Islam. Went from soldier to brilliant scholar. He was fluent in Greek and Latin. The kind of friend who would help me and not ask a lot of questions."

"A Muslim?"

"Yes." Aram smirked. "There are good Muslims, you know. He

was definitely one of them."

"You say 'was.' Is he dead?"

"I have no idea. He could be anywhere from Baghdad, to some captured Persian observatory, maybe even all the way to the land of the Chin."

"Land of the Chin."

"Farther away even than the Mongols. Much of it also conquered by the Mongols."

"Is there a way to find this man?"

"I don't think so." Aram shrugged. "I'll ask of him among any Mongol contacts in Antioch. He's impressive. If they didn't slaughter him—and one of their people in Baghdad told me they didn't—then he will come to their attention." Aram paused. "But that's a distant possibility. I'll have to take Latin instruction. It's the slow way, but I can control the information."

Jeannette nodded.

Aram's lips tensed. The more obstacles that materialized to his reading the William Report, the more he wanted to read it.

April, 1259
Between Jinin and Ayn Jalut/The Springs of Goliath, Northern Syria
Late Morning

"Prepare for battle, Commander?" Qalawun asked. Baybars rode at the head of about one hundred twenty of his best men.

Baybars narrowed his eyes. Further back were supply trains and the families of the Bahriyya mamluks.

"Those are al-Nasir Yusuf's men,"Qalawun said nervously. "We should be—"

"We should be respectful to our new superior," Baybars told him. "Call a halt."

"Call for a halt!" The command passed back through the ranks.

Baybars turned back and addressed his men. "If this is moving forward according to plan, shortly, we will see one rider emerge in front of al-Nasir Yusuf's group. I will move to greet him. I do not expect treachery, though I request keen observations from all of you, in case the unexpected happens."

Baybars heard some rumblings of conversation among the men, but mostly silence.

Al-Nasir Yusuf's men approached: a smaller group, but all fighting men.

"So somehow we have now achieved what two previous contacts by Sunqur al-Ashqar failed to achieve," Qalawun said. A hint of doubt colored the tone of his voice.

Baybars understood Qalawun's trepidation. The Bahriyya had fought alongside al-Nasir Yusuf before. During recent clashes, Baybars had ordered his men to treat al-Nasir Yusuf's men with respect. Al-Nasir Yusuf's slow and difficult agreement to take them back under his banner could be considered troubling. But Baybars was certain this was not an indication of treachery, and that al-Nasir Yusuf wanted and needed the Bahriyya. Baybars knew the man and believed that al-Nasir Yusuf simply wanted to make enough of a fuss to assert his authority.

Qalawun's fear of treachery was not unreasonable. The Bahriyya had placed themselves in a vulnerable position to make this move. But Baybars trusted his instincts, and sometimes a leader had to take risks based on well-informed instincts in order to progress toward the group's ultimate goals. Al-Mughith Umar was not a viable route to defeating Qutuz and power in Egypt; al-Nasir Yusuf was.

Al-Nasir Yusuf's men continued to approach. Baybars did not see any sign of the lone rider he expected. He wondered if Qalawun's doubts would be justified after all.

"So this is just a choice between two princes." Qalawun drew a nervous breath.

"Yes, it is."

"Our only choice."

Baybars nodded. "It's a good choice, with Al-Mughith Umar on the verge of joining many of his northern relatives in submitting to the Mongols." Baybars shook his head and clenched his teeth.

Qalawun's lips tightened. "But this move is so fraught with, with risk. We are so vulnerable...."

There was still no sign of a lone rider as al-Nasir Yusuf's men were now within arrow range. Baybars considered ordering his men to battle alert, but held off.

"I will not deny it," Baybars said. "This will be a setback. We had to make concessions. But it will yield the potential for steps forward, with much more possibility than we had before. Possession of Egypt. Defeat of the Mongols. That is the goal."

Qalawun smiled. "You have always thought big, commander."

Baybars looked ahead, then smiled. "See." Baybars pointed ahead. "A lone rider. Approaching."

One horseman approached, slowly, holding the reins of his horse. A sword was attached to one side of the animal; a shield was attached to the other side. He wore no helmet, and no armor, not even the leather outer garment often worn by Turkish light cavalry.

"Stand by," Baybars said. He nudged his horse into a slow walk. Baybars also left his sword and shield attached to the sides of his battle horse.

Baybars approached close enough to see the rider more clearly. He beamed a smile of recognition. "So, it *is* you." This was the same man he had released months before to take a message to al-Nasir Yusuf.

"I asked for the honor of greeting and welcoming you," the man told Baybars.

"My men are ready."

"Have them follow us. Al-Nasir Yusuf awaits you in camp, to accept your services under his banner."

Baybars nodded, a deep nod, almost a bow.

"So by now, al-Mughith Umar is aware of your change in masters," al-Nasir Yusuf said with the tone of a ruler issuing unchallengeable, binding edicts. "The terms are set." The man sat on a plush cushion, flanked by armed guards. He was a flabby, middle-aged man with a graying beard. He wore bright silks and jewels, but his clothes hung on him like capes, and his turban seemed slightly askew.

Baybars stood facing him, uniformed in battle attire, his sword at his side. He held a courteous expression. He knew he was supposed to ask his superior what the terms were, but asking would accentuate his subordinate position. He would not ask. He was sure al-Nasir Yusuf would spell out the terms without prompting, like a little boy who couldn't wait to pull the wrapper off a gift.

"The terms," al-Nasir Yusuf repeated, seeming to sneer for effect. "You will retain these one hundred twenty men with you today."

Baybars held a neutral, deferential expression. The men with him were hand-picked and agreed upon before he had left Kerak.

"You will be posted here at Jinin and Nablus. You will be in charge of these territories under my banner."

Baybars nodded.

"The other Bahriyya Mamluks, still with al-Mughith Umar, will be surrendered to my custody. They will be confined at the citadel in Aleppo, well out of potential for mischief."

Baybars felt his stomach grind, but nodded again. This was al-Nasir Yusuf's slap at Baybars for the grief from the raids over the past half year. He would miss these men and regretted their circumstances. But he knew this was one of the steps back he had to take to clear the way forward. And he also knew the men would rejoin him when al-Nasir Yusuf saw the potential of their service to him under Baybars' command. He would work for that result, sooner rather than later.

"This completes the peace between my cousin and me, and clarifies your place in it."

"Yes, Sultan. I thank you for the honor of serving you, once again."

"Good. Dismissed."

Baybars bowed and left the tent.

14

Spring, 1259
The Eastern Mediterranean Coast, West of the County of Tripoli
Morning

"A word with you?" Aram requested. He swallowed as the Venetian ship beneath his feet rocked gently. Aram was grateful for the gentle seas of recent days, his first ever on the ocean.

"Why not," Robert said, smirking. "You seem to have finally conquered seasickness."

"Yes, well, the water is gentler today, and I decided not to take in any food during the voyage."

"No food." Robert chuckled. The two of them stood looking over the starboard side of the ship. The Eastern Mediterranean coast was a dim outline in the distance.

"I ask again: what was the purpose of this visit to Prince Bohemond? Why was I along?"

"You're not only a translator," Robert told him. "You're my key expert on all things Mongol."

"Mm-hm. From what I saw, you barely spoke to him about anything."

"The Prince was a man of few words."

Aram felt a wave of nausea surge through him as the ship listed on a larger than average swell.

"What was there to say?" Robert continued. "There is not much to say when you're being told you've been excommunicated."

"Not much to say."

"Not much to say to me, at least." Robert shrugged. "He knew it was not my decision. He wasn't going to argue me out of it. And he wasn't trying to sell me any justifications for what he did."

"So the pope excommunicates Prince Bohemond for submitting to the Mongols, but he also sends you out here to contact the Mongols about some sort of alliance...."

Robert scrunched his lips and looked away. "Alliance. Not submission. Not to become a vassal."

"I didn't hear you discussing that with him."

"Both the pope and Bohemond have taken immovable positions on these matters. What were we going to accomplish with a lot of cross words?"

Aram raised his eyebrows. The ship rocked. Aram felt his stomach jump, but swallowed hard. "So, if there wasn't much to discuss, what was the private meeting about?"

Robert's head snapped over and he looked directly at Aram. He seemed to be sizing up the question, searching for hidden meanings and contexts. "A private meeting, my dear young friend, is a private meeting for a reason."

"But nothing to accomplish with a lot of 'cross words.'"

"Prince Bohemond got a clear message from the document we delivered from the pope."

Aram breathed in and out. He was not feeling well, and was not interested in hearing any more vague statements from Robert. He could pursue this subject when he had the energy to decipher the conversation. Aram swallowed. "Well, this may be the worst place for me to be," he said.

"Above deck is good," Robert said. "But not at the edge."

"I think I'd rather just lie down and sleep away as much of the voyage as possible." Aram pivoted to leave.

Robert reached out and took his shoulder. "So were you able to learn anything useful from my gift?"

Aram turned back. It took him a moment to realize what Robert meant. "So it was you."

"Of course."

"I wasn't sure."

Robert tilted his head slightly to one side, a noncommittal gesture. "What have you learned?"

Aram snorted. "That I don't read Latin."

Robert's eyes narrowed at first, as if analyzing the remark. He then broke into boisterous laughter. "I see." He nodded. "Yes." He chuckled. "And that is why you have been taking instructions—in Latin!" He shook his head. "Of course."

Aram scowled. "Why don't you just tell me what it says?"

Robert's smile faded. "I told you. It is of no consequence. And you're taking instructions, so you'll know what it says soon enough."

"The language is difficult. The instructor is indecipherable. And the report, from what I can tell, seems to have been written with difficult phrasings and style, and copied down with a barely discernible calligraphy."

Robert smirked.

Aram wondered how much of this Robert knew already. Probably all of it.

"When you think you've figured it out, come talk to me," Robert said.

"Why the puzzle? Why don't you just tell me? How can I be an effective adviser without a complete understanding?"

"There's nothing to tell."

"Sure there is. The 'it.' The 'it' you told me to come and talk to you about when I figure 'it' out. What is 'it'?"

"Nothing. Nothing at all."

Aram took in a long breath. The nausea, temporarily suppressed by his concentration on Robert's "gift", welled up again in his jumpy stomach. "I'm going to lie down."

"We shouldn't be taking any more sea voyages," Robert said. "I'm sure we'll be moving inland soon."

Aram nodded, then walked away.

Mid Spring, 1259
Mayyafariqin, Northern Syria
Late Afternoon

"What is your business, old man?" The Mongol officer spoke nearly perfect Persian. He stroked a thin black beard that covered only his lower chin.

Dawud was flanked by a squad of Mongols who had been out patrolling the area around the besieged city of Mayyafariqin. Dawud could see the tactical advantages of this town, with high sturdy walls to protect it and a clear view of the wide travel lanes through the generally hilly region. He wished he had sensed the importance of the location before arriving, because then he could have avoided it.

Mongol siege operations were evident, though Dawud could see this was only a fraction of the Mongol forces. Dawud figured that they probably expected to take this place quickly and easily.

The fact they hadn't taken it yet would create a sour mood, not good for Dawud's purposes.

Dawud wore a torn, dirty robe. He carried only a water flask and some dried meat which had not yet been taken from him. "Passing by," Dawud replied to the officer. "Just passing by."

"You look like an enemy spy," the officer said.

"Kill him," said a tall man in the Mongol language. His face bore a scar that crossed his right cheek almost up to his eye. "That will settle the matter."

Dawud took care not to show his understanding of the language. His mind raced, trying to find an answer for this brewing crisis.

The Mongol officer looked at him. "What do you think of that?"

Dawud shrugged.

"They wouldn't send an old man who doesn't know our tongue to be a spy," the officer said to his comrade.

"Either way, if we kill him, the matter is solved."

"Lazy," the officer said. "We could be killing a friend."

The second squad member shrugged, as if to say losing such a friend would not be a big loss.

"What is your business?" The Mongol officer's tone was harder; he barked with impatience.

"Passing through, um, not part of this fight."

"He had a dagger, and a few coins," said another of the squad members.

A subordinate raised the dagger for the Mongol officer to see. The officer narrowed his eyes with a suspicious gleam.

"Bandits," Dawud said, explaining the dagger.

The officer laughed. "How many bandits can you fight off with such a weapon?"

"As many as I need to."

The officer laughed again.

"Bandits attacked the caravan I was traveling with."

"What caravan?" The officer looked around. "Did anyone see a caravan?" he asked in Mongolian.

"I slipped away during the attack," Dawud said.

"You deserted your comrades."

"I traveled with them. But I had my own purpose."

"And what is that purpose?" The officer seemed suddenly tense with rage and impatience.

"I have word my son in Aleppo is ill. Very ill. I am on my way to see him."

"Where are you from?"

"Mosul."

"Mosul! Why would you be out here?"

"A more direct route is not available."

The officer nodded. "Yes." He looked at Dawud. "Describe the bandits who attacked you."

"I was not up close to them. From what I could see, they rode in a Turkish style, with Turkish weapons. One wore a helmet I am not familiar with. I know they tried to say they were operating under the great khan's authority."

The officer stroked his beard.

Dawud sensed he might have won the man over. His travels toward Syria, maybe ultimately Egypt, had been slow. He passed a number of villages on the way through southern Azerbaijan, northern Persia, and up the Tigris River to Mayyafariqin, situated at the main route south to Syria. He had taught lessons to many grateful villagers. But more importantly, he had listened. He had absorbed information about the area, exactly in case of this type of confrontation.

The Mongol officer looked at him again. He smiled, but it was not a friendly comforting smile. It seethed with malevolence. "I suspect you are a very clever man. I suspect you have a background as a scholar. I suspect you are using your brain powers to fool me."

Dawud measured his reaction to the officer's comments. "I do not believe you would be an easy man to fool. I think you are a very discerning man, clever enough to learn Persian well."

"Not your tongue either?"

"Arabic, the language of the Prophet, is my first language."

"Go on. I am 'discerning'...."

"Yes. You are right. I am a scholar. I teach in Mosul."

"And are you trying to fool me?"

"No, no. I am trying to see my son."

"So you're known in Mosul...."

"Oh, yes."

"Troops are on their way, from the Prince of Mosul, to aid in this siege." The Mongol officer studied Dawud, looking for a reaction.

"Good. I hope they get here soon. They can verify my story."

"Fine. You will stay until they arrive."

Dawud's eyes darted.

"You don't want to wait?"

"When will they arrive?"

"I believe in a week, maybe slightly longer."

"Sir, please, my son in Aleppo is ill and may be dying. I wish to—" Dawud took in a quick breath. "If I must wait, so be it. I will abide by your decision, of course. But I wish to delay as little as possible."

The officer nodded and thought it over. "All right." He frowned to one of the men in the squad. "Take this man, wide around the city so he sees no troop dispositions, and with his eyes covered, then release him on the road to Aleppo."

"We should just kill him," the man with the scar said. "The city has stubbornly refused to yield and we make little progress."

"So you would have us kill a citizen of Mosul, a subject of one of our best friends in the area, because you find dealing with him inconvenient?"

"I would kill a liar." He glared at Dawud. "Sending a squad away to escort an old man, clearly lying about his purpose … well, it is a waste of resources."

"And is it a waste of resources to kill productive people within territories loyal to us?"

The man did not reply.

"Take him," the officer ordered. He looked directly at the man with the scar. "You stay here." He turned to the rest of his squad. "I want no harm to come to him."

Dawud took care not to exhale a huge sigh of relief. He was not supposed to be able to understand this exchange.

The Mongol officer looked at him. "I am having these men escort you to the road to Aleppo. If I ever discover your purpose was other than what you stated, you will find yourself facing an unpleasant end."

Dawud nodded. "Thank you. And my son will thank you."

With a wave of his hand the Mongol officer dismissed him, and the squad that would lead him around the city.

Dawud felt a warm glow of inner morale as he realized he would be out of Mongol territory, back within Muslim-governed principalities, in a very short time.

Summer, 1259
Damascus
Afternoon

"You wanted to see me." Al-Nasir Yusuf sat on a raised dais in a large room within his main palace. Two guards stood at either end of the dais, staring ahead, as if part of the building unless needed. Al-Nasir Yusuf had two more men to his right and two men to his left.

Banners hung from the ceiling and on the walls. Baybars recognized them as having come from various territories in the area.

"Yes." Baybars was dressed in his sharpest uniform. He wore a bright blue, full-length robe with a pattern of interlocking, light blue circles on it. Under the robe was his light armor, worn not for protection at this meeting, but as part of the effect he wanted to create. On his head was a low, turban-like hat with gold trim. The top white strips were folded down into the front. With this attire, Baybars sought to present himself as a fighting man, ready for duty. "Thank you for your time this afternoon."

"Please state the reason for requesting an audience with me."

The formal tone was certainly a concern to Baybars, but not a concern he was going to mention. "I want to thank you, Sultan." Baybars lowered his head for a quick bow. "My forces are at full strength. We are as ready for combat as ever, awaiting your next orders."

"Good."

"The reason for asking to see you." Baybars gathered his thoughts. He walked toward the dais. He needed to change this atmosphere, and hoped closing the distance would help. He wanted to give the impression of being an intimate adviser, not a distant subordinate.

No one discouraged Baybars from approaching, but al-Nasir Yusuf gave no indication of a warmer, more receptive tone.

"The Mongols. They are my concern," Baybars said.

"Yes." Al-Nasir Yusuf seemed impatient, bored with the obvious.

"We need the resources to defeat them," Baybars said. "You have, now at your service, the Bahriyya, the greatest warriors in the world. But to build the kind of force necessary for success, you need the wealth and resources of Egypt."

Al-Nasir Yusuf raised his eyebrows.

"We need to take Egypt from Qutuz and his puppet, teenage sultan," Baybars continued. "We Bahriyya have serious grievances with that treacherous fiend, and will fight passionately to end his rule there, and put those resources under your command."

"Yes, we all know what Qutuz did to you and your Bahriyya Mamluks." Al-Nasir Yusuf shrugged. "But this has been tried. Recently by you and my cousin. Longer ago by me. It is not an easy task, and may be a bad idea when we are facing such a terrible threat from the north."

"We will succeed this time." Baybars met al-Nasir Yusuf's eyes with a serious, stern expression.

"Your passion is admirable."

Baybars looked to al-Nasir Yusuf's right to see who had spoken those last words. The delivery had sounded patronizing, like a pat on the head for an obedient but ignorant child. It was an immaculately groomed man in a red turban and purple robe; but all the costuming could not hide the man's softness, his flabbiness, his look of weakness in the face of any real challenge, especially a physical one.

"This is al-Zayn al-Hafizi, one of my most important advisers," al-Nasir Yusuf said.

Al-Zayn al-Hafizi nodded to al-Nasir Yusuf. His black beard had a few streaks of gray in it. He looked back to Baybars. "You bring us a formidable military capability, and we are pleased to have you under our banner."

Baybars tipped his head to acknowledge the compliment.

"But there are political matters. Well, there are so many options. I know these people. I have met the great khan in Qaraqorum. Sometimes brute force is not the best option."

"Sultan." Baybars clenched his teeth as he directed his remarks toward al-Nasir Yusuf, not looking at Al-Zayn al-Hafizi. "Against Mongols, brute force is the *only* option, and we need to bring the maximum amount of brute force under our control."

"Spoken like a true soldier," Al-Zayn al-Hafizi said, seeming again to praise and patronize at the same time. "Your bravery, your willingness to stand tall to defend your sultan, and the True Faith—you are truly a magnificent credit to us all. As we decide on our options, your strength and determination will be considered."

Baybars squinted at Al-Zayn al-Hafizi, but quickly relaxed his expression. "What other 'options' are there?"

Al-Zayn al-Hafizi answered, "An accommodation. With Qutuz. With the Mongols. On terms favorable to—"

"The only terms Mongols will accept will place us as their servants," Baybars said. He shifted his attention back to al-Nasir

Yusuf. "Placing the True Faith, the Holy Cities, all under the rule of Non-Believers."

"Baghdad is under the rule of Non-Believers now," al-Nasir Yusuf said. "Destroyed entirely by the Mongols."

"Yes, but the caliph was *not* a fighter. He failed to defend that great city, and God no doubt has a place of shame reserved for his spirit. We, in contrast to him, will be *ready*."

Al-Zayn al-Hafizi spoke again. "The Koran instructs us to explore peace—"

Al-Nasir Yusuf raised his hand up to stop Al-Zayn al-Hafizi from engaging further with Baybars. He looked at the leader of the Mamluks. "My great-grandfather united Egypt and Syria. And with those resources, he took back Jerusalem for the Faithful and resisted Richard the Lionheart, the greatest Christian warrior to come east."

"Exactly."

"And his grandnephew—my cousin, al-Mu'azzamTuran-Shah—was murdered in Egypt. And my family's rule was—brutally and against all codes of honor and decency—violently terminated—by *you*."

Baybars swallowed. He was not sure how to respond to this challenge.

"In fact, I understand it was you personally who ended Turan Shah's life." Al-Nasir Yusuf's face reddened. His lips tightened.

"Rumors," Baybars finally said.

"Rumors!" Al-Nasir Yusuf bristled even further. "Well-circulated rumors, soldier."

"Yes. Well-circulated rumors intended to sew discontent between us," Baybars said. "Enemies trying to undermine our relationship."

"From my understanding, these 'rumors' sounded like bragging, like men expressing pride in the deeds of their commander."

"I'm sure you've misunderstood."

"And I'm sure I haven't."

Baybars did not reply. Al-Nasir Yusuf did not present such a clear path toward effective resistance against the Mongols after all. And Baybars wasn't going to discuss the last moments in the life of Turan Shah. He had been there. He had attempted to kill Turan Shah.

The prince had come to Egypt after his father's death in order to assume rulership. But he showed an utter disregard for the Mamluks who had fought and defeated Christians attacking the port city of Damietta on the Nile Delta. Turan Shah had tried to move his own people into positions of authority at the expense of those who had given their blood for Muslim victory. Drastic measures had been needed. So when Turan Shah had escaped Baybars' initial attempts to kill him, Baybars and a group of fellow Mamluks chased him into the Nile River and killed him there. It had not been clear which of the swarm of Bahriyya Mamluks had actually ended Turan Shah's life, but word spread that Baybars had personally accomplished the deed. He had never discouraged the stories, but now it seemed a good idea to end this meeting before al-Nasir Yusuf decided it was a good time to demand an answer from Baybars for the crime of sultan-cide.

After a few moments, al-Nasir Yusuf said, "If we decide to fight the Mongols, I will call on you. You may be assured of that."

Baybars nodded, then bowed. He did not like the word "if." But now was not the time to make an issue of it.

"Dismissed." Al-Nasir Yusuf waved the back of his hand as if shooing away a fly.

Baybars left.

15

Summer – 1259
Near Tabriz, Azerbaijan
Night

"I like when you ask me to visit you, even though it isn't very often," said Dokuz Khatun, Hulegu's first and primary wife. They lay together under blankets within Hulegu's tent.

"I know you do. And I treasure you for that." Hulegu squeezed her. She was bulkier than she had been as a young bride, and her face gave away her age. But the same eyes sparkled back at him, as if her inner essentials could never be changed. And, truth be told, though her body was a little heavier, the sensuality of her private parts still responded to his touch, and in turn sparked his desire. The younger wives were more outwardly beautiful, but could not match this inner connection.

"I know you also come to me when you are troubled, when you need more than just a pretty body to satisfy your urges."

He looked at her, smiling suspiciously. Could she read his thoughts? Did she really know him so well? He was Hulegu, the il-khan, brother of the great khan, grandson of Genghis Khan. He could not allow her to know how well she had deciphered him, or at least could not admit she had figured it out.

"I always have concerns," he said, as if dismissing her suggestion. "Our youngest son has not been able to finish taking Mayyafariqin. I had intended to march our troops right through there into Syria. Now I fear he will not complete the conquest before we are ready to move." He shook his head. "It is a difficult position. And the stubborn prince who could have submitted, who promised submission before, who knows he will eventually lose, who should know the destiny of this family...." Hulegu tensed with rage. This was nothing short of a petty prince's humiliation of his son, the great-grandson of Genghis Khan, the dynasty destined by the Eternal Blue Heaven to rule the world.

"Yoshmut is capable," Dokuz Khatun said.

"But it's beginning to look like he isn't. And I begin to look weak. The family begins to look weak. Al-Nasir Yusuf responds to me defiantly, without fear, when I demand help at Mayyafariqin."

"I know why you're upset. And I know why you've come to me."

Hulegu stiffened. She was reaching into his private thoughts again, and had the audacity to flaunt it. "These are upsetting things, woman."

"I know. And your attention has to be turned north."

"Every message I get, every report: Mongke is not going to recover his health. When he passes on, I do not know how the grandsons of Genghis Khan will behave. I know how they *should* behave. I do not know how they *will* behave."

"It's Berke. That branch." Dokuz Khatun shook her head bitterly. "Adopting Islam. Adopting heresy. Rejecting the Christ."

Hulegu smiled, then pulled it back. But this was why he had come to her. She knew the issues and could offer informed and supportive commentary, despite her bias toward her own Christian religion. Sure, she was a woman. But his mother, Sorhitani, had nearly run the great khanate at times between great khans. Women could be quite talented. Yes; Dokuz Khatun, she did know him. He needed her to stop enjoying it so much. "Of course, woman, this is obvious. If I move south and commit to this operation, I could be left out of position for whatever happens back home."

"Is there someone you can trust to handle the operation in your absence?"

Hulegu grunted. Now she was trying to pretend she didn't know things because she sensed he was irritated with her overly familiar comments. "Woman, you know well that Ketbugha can handle matters in my absence. He is a gifted commander, and loyal. My grandfather used trusted generals to handle important missions independently. But this should be my operation, if at all possible."

"Let me comfort you," she said to him as she moved closer to cuddle.

He enjoyed the warmth of her touch, and sensed the depth of her loyalty to him, of her connection. He allowed himself a few moments of ease, of comfort in her clutches. But he feared enjoying this too much. "I have given instructions for the fate of al-Kamil Muhammad." This thought made him tense with rage.

Dokuz Khatun faced him with a puzzled look on her face.

"He is the one making a fool of me, and our family, at Mayyafariqin."

His wife nodded.

Hulegu got out of the bed. "I have Armenians and Georgians enthusiastic about the task."

"They are under Yoshmut's command?"

"Everyone there is."

"Are they giving Yoshmut their full effort?"

"I have no reports to the contrary. And they should be motivated. Certainly, this al-Kamil Muhammad has insulted me and this great empire by committing to his submission, then refusing. But his method of demonstrating his disrespect...." Hulegu shook his head. His eyes narrowed and he raised his jaw. "He crucified a Christian priest, traveling under *my* protection, traveling with *written confirmation* of my protection with my seal clearly visible. To subject a man of your faith to that fate...."

"Despicable." Dokuz Khatun's breathing became shallower and her teeth clenched. "Muslims have ruled too much of the world for too long."

Hulegu nodded. "We will put an end to that. They will pay. Al-Kamil Muhammad will pay. I have asked that when they capture Mayyafariqin, they reserve a creative fate for al-Kamil Muhammad"—Hulegu spit out the syllables of the name with a staccato of contempt—"a fate that befits his crimes of defiance and brutality."

"For me, and my fellow Christians as well."

Hulegu dressed. "And for this family's empire, ordained by the Eternal Blue Heaven to rule the world. You can depend on it. I will share the report with you when it comes." He nodded to her and left.

Summer, 1259
Acre
Night

"I'm packed. I'm ready." Aram looked at Jeannette. "I'll be off at dawn." He sat down next to her on the bed. Their son was already sleeping in his own small bed.

"You haven't spoken much about this one," Jeannette said. "Where is Robert taking you this time? Is he finally trying to get a meeting with Hulegu?"

"Not yet."

"What is he doing?"

Aram didn't answer. His lips tightened; he was uncertain how much to tell her.

"I know he's kept you busy. Did you have time to get enough instruction to make any sense of that report?"

"Not really." He took in a deep breath. "I may be on to some of it." He shook his head. "What I figured out doesn't make much sense to me. Robert's approach doesn't make sense to me. It's like he's playing for time in some way. Hulegu took submission after submission up at Tabriz. The whole area is buzzing with the news. We could have gone up there. True, he doesn't have instructions to submit, and maybe that gave him pause. We don't really have enough gifts. I assume he's sent to the pope for more, but I'm not aware of anything coming in. These things didn't seem to bother him before. But now? I just don't know."

"So where are you going this time?"

Aram did not immediately respond, and then it was by trying to change the subject. "Don't forget, they owe me a lot of money. You know who to see."

Jeannette confronted Aram with a serious stare. "You're not coming back, are you? I'm going to be a 'widow' after all."

"I never know if I'm going to make it back," Aram told her. "These travels are dangerous. These times are dangerous."

"Robert isn't with you on this trip. He doesn't even know you're going. That's why you're avoiding my questions." Jeannette's eyes moistened, then filled with tears. "I thought maybe…." She turned away and sobbed.

"It's a trip I need to make," Aram said. "I thought we had an understanding."

"That was a long time ago."

"Not that long ago."

Jeannette shook her head. "You'll leave your boy without a father. You'll leave me...."

"I'm not—" Aram stopped himself. "You're assuming too much. You should think of this like any other trip."

Jeannette's lips twitched and her eyes narrowed. She clearly didn't believe him, and was not going to placate him by saying she did.

"If something does happen to me, you and our son will be fine. Look at my crazy family background. I've been able to make my way in the world."

She searched for a way to delay his departure. "Tell me about your family. You've never really said much about them. Leave me with something to tell him."

Aram frowned. "I told you, you're assuming too much."

"Just tell me."

Aram shrugged. He sat down next to her. "For years, I believed I was an orphan. That's what my parents told me. It turned out they were my actual parents, but they raised me as if I was someone else's abandoned child!"

"That is strange."

"You can see why I haven't offered much about them."

She nodded, but beckoned him with a grin and expectant eyes to continue.

Aram shrugged. "My father was an older fellow. He was supposed to be something special, because his mother—I guess my grandmother—died giving birth, and my grandfather thought that meant something special. So the man who I eventually found out was my true father devoted his life to trying to figure out what that special purpose was. He decided he was destined to determine ultimate truth, and he would search the world's knowledge to find it. He was lucky enough to be born in Baghdad, where such quests received toleration and the resources to indulge them."

"Born in Baghdad? Was he Muslim?"

"No, no. My grandmother was some sort of refugee from the West. From a Western Christian background! She even had an uncle or brother who was a knight with Richard the Lionheart. So, back to my father. He taught at one of the colleges for a living, and spent every hour of his spare time absorbing all the knowledge he could gather. I have no idea if he ever made any progress toward ultimate truth. But he found time to have, um, relations, with a servant girl. A girl he was not married to."

Jeannette smirked.

Aram couldn't help but let his own grin sneak out as he thought of their first evening together. "Those relations led to me."

"And they never married?"

"Unless it was a secret, I don't believe so. That's why I was the 'orphan child' adopted by my mother. My father was known to me as a smart, kindly old man who helped her out. She died of an illness when I was eleven. He died of just being old when I was seventeen. I thought he'd been kind to take me in. I guess that was true, but he spelled the whole thing out in a long letter he left for me: 'To be opened by Aram after my death.'"

"My, my."

Aram shook his head, a rueful smile on his face. "Oh yes. A sordid, strange background for me. So, our son—he has a much easier, simpler background to explain."

Jeannette glared at him. "You don't have to pass along a background. You can stay and raise your son."

"And I will, if I come back. But if I don't...."

Jeannette blasted some air out of her nose. She looked at him. "How much of that is actually true?"

Aram looked at her, confused.

"Your parents lied to you all your life. How much of their story do you think is true?" She grimaced. "I mean, Aram, the Nestorian Christian, with a Christian knight's blood? A Western Christian?"

"Why would my father have lied? He clearly left the letter so I would know the truth about him and my mother."

"Maybe so."

"Family backgrounds, in these times, can get a little crazy."

Jeannette nodded. "Aram. Tell me. Where are you going?"

"Just a quick trip. I'll be back in a week."

Jeannette raised her head and shifted position as she appeared to consider the remark. "And if we never hear from you again, I'm a widow. A respectable widow. With back wages to collect."

Aram nodded slowly. She understood. Good. He would have the option of a clean escape from this weird life into which he had stumbled.

"Aram," she said more firmly. "Where are you going? Don't leave me with a lie. We've shared too much. Where are you going?"

He paused as his eyes drifted away from her face. "Away from Robert. Possibly back to Baghdad."

Jeannette let her tears flow. "And away from me, and our son."

Aram let out a deep breath. "I don't know everything about that document yet. But what I can figure out makes me very dubious about what Robert has in mind, and whether he is a person I want to be aligned with. I'm...," Aram paused. "I'm going to try to get some sort of confirmation on what I'm reading."

"In Baghdad?"

"Maybe."

Jeannette folded her arms. Her hard eyes glared out at him through her tear-stained face.

"I'll reach back for you if I can. But this could be a nasty trip. A woman and a baby would not make optimum traveling companions."

"Or companions for your life."

"A woman and child—"

"Your *wife*, and your *son*."

Aram sent a burst of air through his lips. She wasn't going to make this easy after all.

"I'll tell Robert," she threatened.

Aram looked at her. "If he believes you, I will likely be punished in a way that takes me away from you. If I convince him you are acting silly, that you may be possessed, you will lose the ability to care for our son. He'll probably be raised at the convent, where you will be kept under constant scrutiny."

"You would do that? To me? To our son?"

"You would tell Robert of plans I have confided to you?"

"Confided after I dragged it out of you."

"Because I couldn't lie to you."

"You tried."

"And I couldn't."

Jeannette paused a moment. Her expression hardened. She stood and moved away from him. "Then go. Get on with whatever it is you need to do. I'm still young and pretty. I'll be a respectable, desirable widow. I'll find a *good* man, not one I have to beg just to stay with me." Tears flowed again. She threw herself face down onto the bed.

Aram stood. "I tell you again. I think maybe you're assuming too much. I'm not—"

"Aram, stop it. I understand. I did trap you at the beginning—

I've admitted that to you. I thought our time together had changed things. But it hasn't. Not enough. Don't hurt me any further with false hopes to spare my feelings."

Aram nodded. "Wish me well. As I do you, and our son."

"Of course I wish you well."

"I will sleep in the library."

"You can sleep with me. One last time."

Aram wondered what that meant. He got onto the bed next to her. He quickly discovered, as she moved on top of him and aggressively manipulated the most sensitive and arousable parts of his body, that she would make the most of "one last time." Maybe she thought it would hold him there. But the following morning, just as the sun came up, he left their quarters without waking her or their son.

16

"Magnificent," Hulegu Khan said to Ketbugha. Atop their horses, they overlooked a gentle rolling terrain and a huge group of Mongol warriors arrayed in a large circular formation. Riding with them were some scattered divisions of Turkish, Georgian and Armenian troops, distinguishable by their different uniforms and mostly larger horses. The non-Mongols did not have the legendary Mongol ponies that were small, quick, and able to survive solely on the grass of the steppes.

Hulegu smiled. A training hunt. They would gather food and sharpen battle maneuvers. Short of battle, this activity distinguished the Mongol army from any other army on earth. The non-Mongols could watch and learn, and if they did try to participate, make sure they did not get in the way.

The integrity of the formation's boundaries held, but its members kept moving, surrounding anything within it, and shrinking its size.

"These men are well-prepared for our next move. The foreign units we have retained for the main striking force are blending well," Hulegu said.

"The ones not up to our standards have been assigned to auxiliary duties."

Hulegu nodded.

"The mood is good," Ketbugha said. "The men are ready for the next move."

"My compliments to you and your commanders."

"Thank you."

Ketbugha followed Hulegu Khan's eyes as they diverted to the outer edges of the swirling, shrinking perimeter of Mongol soldiers. At one point, a rabbit scurried through the perimeter, only to be impaled by two arrows from nearby riders. At another point, about a third of the circle away, a similar scenario played out. Hulegu wasn't sure if it was another rabbit; it could have been a smaller creature. He looked at the center of the shrinking perimeter. Mounted archers picked small animals within the circle and angled arrows down to avoid striking soldier-hunters on the other side of the perimeter. Prey had become scarcer because so many animals had already been hit. Cooks and cooks' assistants began the process of collecting carcasses now outside of the collapsing perimeter. Squads seamlessly withdrew from the shrinking circle of armed humanity, forming organized groups of spectators. As the perimeter shrank, most, then all, of the non-Mongol troops had slipped out of the swirling mass.

"Magnificent," Hulegu repeated. "Reward these commanders and this group with the first servings of tonight's feast. This continues to be the best group."

"Yes. But I must say, all the divisions are close to this level of performance."

Hulegu smiled. "That is also my observation. This is the greatest army the world has ever seen. My grandfather would have been proud to command this group."

"No doubt."

The squads continued to peel out of the shrinking perimeter. The men who remained in the formation were mainly armored, close-quarters soldiers, armed with lances and clubs.

Ketbugha grinned. "They have grown restless up here on the plains. We have nearly hunted the area dry."

Hulegu looked at his general and frowned irritably. "You're saying we should have moved into Syria sooner after Baghdad?"

No." Ketbugha's usually accurate reading of the il-khan's mood had apparently been faulty. He had touched a nerve. "Not at all. Please, I'm sorry, you misunderstand me."

Hulegu raised his chin and sneered, as if waiting for an explanation and a more elaborate apology.

But what nerve had Ketbugha touched? "I mean, now is the time to move. The restlessness of the wait works to our favor as the men have had plenty of time to enjoy the fruits of Baghdad, and other tribute."

"The wait has been necessary," Hulegu said in a monotone. His eyes were hard.

"I meant no criticism. I agree."

Hulegu looked at him. "In a month or less, we will go. Make sure they are all ready."

"Yes. You can see; they will be ready when you give the word."

Hulegu looked at the concluding hunt. "The wait was needed."

Ketbugha finally understood. Hulegu had not been comfortable with the delays, and worried that his decision not to follow up more quickly on the victory at Baghdad may have showed weakness, or a shade of incompetence. Ketbugha knew exactly how to deal with this mood. "Il-Khan, I have thought the, the time interval between campaigns, has been masterful."

Hulegu looked at Ketbugha, then turned back to the now-concluded hunt. Cooks and cooks' assistants were the only ones left in the area where moments before had been swirling formations.

Ketbugha suspected Hulegu wanted more reassurance. "The ponies have had time to grow fat and multiply out here on the grasses of Azerbaijan. We know the deserts of Syria and Egypt will not be so amenable to them. We may need to forage for fodder."

Hulegu nodded.

"We also wanted that route through Mayyafariqin."

Hulegu bristled, because this hinted at the failure of Hulegu's son. Ketbugha needed the right emphasis for this issue that he now wished he hadn't raised. "The prince of that city, the treacherous one, al-Kamil Muhammad—he will pay dearly for his duplicity when we take that city. He had submitted, and now reverses. He has killed men traveling under your protection—Christians. His intransigence has—"

Hulegu held up his hand. "Measures will be taken that will spread as a lesson to anyone thinking of defiance and duplicity."

Ketbugha did not say it aloud, but knew that Hulegu's rage was particularly acute because his son, Yoshmut, was involved. "And it was also wise to collect as many submissions as we could," Ketbugha said. "More wealth and men have flowed in, and we have gathered it together and used it to—"

"But couldn't it be said that the long time interval between campaigns has reduced the impact of Baghdad? Al-Nasir Yusuf—sometimes submitting, sometimes not—now seems to be settling on a policy of resistance."

Ketbugha thought a moment. "I believe this vacillation on his part is a sign of his character, the character of a weak man. Our recent contacts tell us he has now taken into his ranks some militant slave-soldiers."

"The Turks. Mamluks, they call them. Turk slave-soldiers." Hulegu snorted. "We have conquered Turks from here to the eastern steppe. *They* give him courage?"

"Or they are imposing their ideas on him."

Hulegu shrugged. "Whatever the reason, we will not gain a submission from him before we move into Syria. We will wait no longer. After we have taken some Syrian territories, and given some convincing lessons on the consequences of resistance, more submissions will follow."

"Another reason the timing is superb."

"Yes. We gathered wealth and used it to acquire even more allies. That is the key. Grandfather understood this. Generous distribution of the spoils taken from flat and flabby cities and given to loyal, effective allies. That, my dear general, is how you build an empire."

Ketbugha nodded and smiled. "He was the master."

Hulegu clenched his teeth.

Ketbugha bowed atop his horse. "My most exalted Il-Khan, you know this better than anyone, but I will take the honor of commemorating this with you. Your grandfather waited long periods between campaigns. He collected information, readied troops, fattened the ponies, then devised masterful strategies to shock and distress his enemies. Il-Khan, he would be proud of your handling of this campaign."

Hulegu raised his chin. His lower jaw pushed slightly forward. "I think you are right."

"You know I am."

"One of three wise men," Hulegu said with a boisterous laugh in his voice. He slapped Ketbugha on the back. "You always say you are a descendant of one of the three wise men who visited the Christ out here so many generations ago."

Ketbugha smiled. Hulegu had gotten the reassurance he needed. Ketbugha held back any further comments. He felt the spirit of the long-ago visitor to the Christ, conferring wisdom on him, to leave Hulegu's mood where it stood right now.

"I am glad you have been so perceptive about our strategies to advance the Genghis Khan dynasty to its destiny under the Eternal Blue Heaven. We will retrace the steps of your ancestor. And this time, we will stay." Hulegu looked at Ketbugha. "And if succession calls me back to Qaraqorum, I may call upon you to command our forces. In the tradition of my grandfather's legendary generals, Subotei and Jebe, on the occasion of this return trip of your bloodline."

Ketbugha felt a welling of emotion within him, to be mentioned in comparison with such icons of the Genghis Khan conquests. "You honor me, il-Khan."

Hulegu grinned almost imperceptably and nodded.

Mid August, 1259
Gaza
Morning

"Was it the lamb last night?" Baybars asked.

Adiba wiped her mouth as she returned from the bathroom of their quarters. "I didn't have any lamb. I ate a great deal of rice and fruit."

"Too much, maybe." Baybars watched from their bed. Adiba stood in front of him wearing only underclothes.

"I don't think so."

Baybars' mouth tightened with a puzzled frown. Why had she become ill? The food here had actually improved from their living situation at Kerak.

"My love, I have missed two monthly periods." She shyly fought back a grin.

Baybars smiled. He motioned her toward him.

Adiba sauntered over, raising her eyebrows. She lay down next to him.

Baybars pulled off her undergarment and patted her belly. "A son."

She grinned. "Maybe."

"I'm sure of it. A son.

"See what happens when you're not away so much."

Baybars gave her a lustful laugh. He kissed his wife, then fondled her. Adiba breathed in deeply and moaned.

"I will expect your duties to be lightened," Baybars said to Adiba, who continued to lie in their bed. Baybars stood over her, wearing his uniform. "I will speak to—"

"I have it under control," Adiba assured him.

Baybars frowned. "Does everyone know about this except me?"

"No. Just one or two of the women."

Baybars glared at her, then grinned. "That child will be my successor."

"I know. Believe me, things are different here. There is respect for us. There is respect for me because I am your wife."

Baybars scratched his beard. He did not feel better respected here. But he was glad his wife did. He shrugged. "Good. Take care of that child."

"Of course."

Baybars nodded, then left their quarters.

Late August, 1259
Damascus
Early Evening

"It really is you," Aram said in Arabic. He shook his head with disbelief. "I couldn't believe it, but I had to find out."

Dawud looked up. He sat at a table in the corner of a small room, part of a library. Stacks of books and parchments sat on the table. He put down the piece of glass he had been holding. As his eyes adjusted he squinted, then offered a smile of recognition. "The intrepid one." He stood. "From my more treasured memories of the old days."

Aram stepped toward him and Dawud moved out from the table. The men embraced, gently at first, but the embrace seemed to grow tighter from Dawud. Aram found himself tightening his grip as well.

They ended the hug. Aram saw a glistening in the old teacher's eyes.

"The old days," Aram said. "It was not much over a year ago."

"It seems like another lifetime," Dawud said. He motioned to a cushion. "Sit. Please."

Aram nodded, put his satchel on the ground next to him, and sat on the cushion.

Dawud sat on a chair. "Forgive me. If these old bones sit on one of those, it will take me the entire afternoon to get back up."

Aram smiled.

"You must wonder why I didn't come to the Christian quarter," Dawud said.

Aram frowned. He did not understand the comment at all.

"The day they killed everyone."

Aram's mouth opened as he raised his chin. "I wasn't there."

"Ah. I didn't see you. In the days after."

"I had been hired for what was supposed to be a quick undertaking. I'm still working for them. Well, maybe...," Aram paused. "It was bad. I saw the bodies, weeks later."

Dawud shook his head. A tear rolled down each cheek. "I still can't get my mind around it. I was there. I went through it. And it seems... unreal, then vividly real, like it happened yesterday." He paused. "They killed Abdul-Mohammed right before my eyes. And he saved me. A young man, full of life, saved an old man ready to die."

Aram was frozen, unsure what to say.

Dawud seemed to sense Aram's awkwardness with the emotions and gathered himself. "It was unreal, an unreal nightmare intruding into the world from the depths of hell."

Aram nodded. "How did you get from there to here?"

"A long, twisted route, I assure you. That tale will take time to tell."

"I heard you were on your way to China."

Dawud raised his eyebrows. "I was. You were there? Talked to someone?"

"Yes, after you'd left, I think. Part of this work I've been doing."

Dawud smirked. "Strange work."

Aram nodded. "That is an understatement. It gets stranger as I go. It ended up involving me with a wife and child."

Dawud's face contorted into a twisted smile of disbelief. "The intrepid one? The world traveler. The young man who never saw a caravan he did not want to join. Married?"

"Well, maybe not much longer."

Dawud sized him up with a puzzled expression. "What do you mean?"

"I mean, I think this job has to end."

"And you are taking flight from it."

"I think so. I think back to Baghdad where Christians, particularly those of my branch, are welcome—where I have the best chance of a gentle prosperity."

"With Mongols."

Aram shrugged.

"Because there may be Christians among them."

Aram did not respond. He sensed disapproval from his old friend and teacher. He should have anticipated this.

"Mongols have a peculiar slant on Christianity," Dawud said.

Aram shrugged again. "I haven't completely decided yet."

"Then I will offer advice. Don't go to the Mongols. For the sake of your soul."

Aram was about to thank Dawud for the advice when he recalled he wanted more input from the old scholar. "You know Latin, don't you?"

Dawud raised his eyebrows, surprised with the sudden change of topic. "It's been awhile, but yes, I can still handle a Latin text."

Aram reached into his satchel and pulled out a sheaf of personal papers. He had taken only a few possessions with him, to allow for light travel. Most of what he carried were mementos and personal papers he could not replace. He handed Dawud a parchment wrapped in cloth.

Dawud took the object. He stepped over to his table and took the piece of glass he had been using to read when Aram had first arrived. He removed the cloth and opened a leather binding. The title read: *Itinerarium fratris Willielmi de Rubruquis de ordine fratrum Minorum, Galli, Anno gratia 1253 ad partes Orientales.*

Dawud's eyes widened. He seemed instantly captivated by the document. Aram remembered why he loved this old man. He was of a different faith, open to all sides of an issue, consistent with the spirit of Baghdad, even years after what Aram had heard described as the "Golden Age." And he was an intensely curious man, ready to indulge in a mystery, ready to search for an answer to a question.

Dawud nodded and seemed to be smirking as he worked his way through the manuscript.

17

Late August, 1259
Damascus
Early Evening

"I took some Latin instruction," Aram told Dawud. "I think I made some headway, but I still couldn't make sense of it."

"Hmmm." Dawud's lips tightened. "It's a report by someone—'brother,' so a Western Christian man from a religious order—someone named William who went, well, east of their lands." Dawud opened past the title page. "A strange script, and written in a style I'm not accustomed to. But I can translate this." He looked up. "The travels of a Western Christian priest? To the East? To the Mongols?" Dawud frowned. He could think of nothing constructive that could be gained from such a journey.

"I think so."

"Why? Why do you have this, and why is it important?"

Aram looked down. "That, my friend, is my twisted tale." He looked up. "I'll fill you in as you review it."

Dawud nodded.

"You're a good pupil," Dawud said. "Your translation of that passage is absolutely correct. The great khan's letter to the French king clearly describes the Mongols as believing they are supreme in the world. This is consistent with your other observations about this document."

"But it makes no sense."

Dawud shrugged. "I agree some of this writing flows in a way I am not accustomed to. But the writing is clear."

"I'm sorry." Aram paused. "I didn't mean it that way. The passage makes sense. It's Robert. It's Robert who doesn't make sense."

Dawud looked off toward the ceiling. He considered Aram's statement. He'd been concerned about an accurate translation for his friend, but Aram was trying to place the document in the context of the assignment he had been working on for Robert of Montpelier. "It would seem this mission of Robert's has already been undertaken, and recently."

"Absolutely," Aram agreed. He gestured at the manuscript. "William met Mongke Khan himself. He learned there that Mongols do not have allies, only servants. The Mongols are pledged to conquer every corner of the world. They believe it is their immutable destiny."

"That is all clear."

Aram shook his head. "The great khan goes on about his understanding of Christianity. I'm sure Mongke Khan was trying to impress his guest by introducing him to Christians. But William notes in this report of his, the Mongols' Christian representatives at the royal court don't even know what their own Syriac religious texts mean! They have money lenders at court, polygamists—they charge money for religious services! And thank goodness they do not engage in that wretched practice of icons with the crucified Jesus on it. But this is another example of how little Mongol Christianity has to do with the pope's."

"It is strange that a bloodthirsty group like the Mongols has such an aversion to depicting blood or death in their art or religion."

Aram looked at him. "You do ferret out the most insightful connections. That is your talent."

Dawud smiled.

"So what is the answer here?" Aram flailed his hand at another passage. "And Mongke Khan lectured William about tolerance! Religious tolerance! He says 'just as God gives us five fingers for a hand, he gives men many ways'—many religions."

Dawud considered that such an idea from Mongols did not sound so bad; maybe the first idea from Mongols he had ever heard that sounded less than terrible.

"Of course, the great khan makes these pronouncements with the idea that all religions are answerable to him."

Dawud nodded.

"So why is Robert here to try to make an alliance with these people if it does not include submission? Why does he pretend not to know that this has already been attempted, and has failed? I know this William was working for the French king, not the pope, but the lessons in this report would apply to a mission from the pope, or from any other authority."

Dawud scratched his beard under his chin. "Good questions. Good questions to ask *him*."

"I don't know that I'm going back to ask him anything. Whatever he is trying to do, there is some deviousness in it. I don't want to get caught up in it."

Dawud frowned. He studied Aram a moment, wondering how much advice he should offer his surprise visitor. "And you are, after all, 'the adventurous one.'"

"What's that supposed to mean?"

"You wouldn't want to stay in one place for too long, now would you?"

Aram scowled. "That's not the issue."

"Well, it's not the issue that consumes you right now."

"Are you going to help me figure this out, or not?"

Dawud grinned. He had touched a nerve, a nerve he would revisit if he needed to, but not now. And it seemed to him Aram had invited his advice. Dawud knew now—he would offer a full dose of it before they were through. "He's secretive. So his mission is not what he says it is."

Aram's eyes drifted as if in thought.

"Are you sure he is really an agent of the pope?"

Aram frowned. "He has to be. He receives dispatches from Rome all the time. He has authority at Acre, though some of the priests there grumble about these same issues."

"So either he is on a mission for the pope that he does not want to disclose to everyone, maybe under instructions to keep it secret; or, he has a stated mission for the pope, but has his own purposes."

"How would we know which it is?"

"Does he get dispatches from only the pope, or from others as well? If he has a purpose outside the pope's purpose, he would certainly have allies in this purpose, allies he would need to continue communications with."

Aram shook his head. "I have no idea how many dispatches he receives, where they come from, if they come from the pope, or Rome, or other places."

"Well, that is what you need to find out. When you go back."

Aram lowered his chin, and narrowed his eyes. "I told you, I may not go back."

"You have asked for my guidance on this document. I have given you my best information on this. Now I will offer some advice you didn't ask for. *Go back* to your wife, and your child, Intrepid One."

Aram picked up the report they had been looking at and put it in his satchel. "I don't think that's wise."

"For you."

Aram gave Dawud a wary look.

"You don't think that's wise for *you.*"

Aram shrugged, as if to ask, *what else?*

Dawud shook his head. "I have always liked you; you know that. You are smart. You are funny. Usually. And I've seen the goodness in you. I've seen you show compassion for the poor and sick, with more alms than some nobles. I've seen you pay courteous attention to an old scholar capable of going on and on and on."

Aram smiled. "I have little need for money. I am not so much the Intrepid One as I am the restless one. I don't stay places very long, so I don't want large caches of wealth to weigh me down. And old scholars—they can be very entertaining."

"It isn't just about you!" Dawud said with a burst of emotion. "If you're grown up, if you care about the world, about those of us daring enough, foolish enough to have affection for you, you will understand it isn't just about you! The Intrepid One—at a crossroads! The choices you make now—the wrong choice, you will live to regret into your old age!"

"I told you the circumstances that—"

"You talk about leaving a wife and child behind as if deciding to give away a pair of shoes! Leaving that boy without a father. Leaving that kind girl you describe without a husband. This is not a casual decision."

"I grew up without parents. At least he'll have—"

"You had parents, Aram," Dawud told him sternly. "They took care of you, both of them, in the only way they could."

"You know about that?"

"Many more knew about it than your parents ever realized. Resemblances, affections impossible to disguise—the truth was evident. We who did know treated those good people with dignity, in an atmosphere of tolerance, with a will not to embarrass when embarrassment would serve no purpose."

Aram took in a deep breath.

"I *did* grow up without a father," Dawud told him. "The void in my life shaped my early adult years, maybe more, in ways that...." Dawud was not sure he wanted to go further into this subject.

Aram looked at him.

Dawud rarely spoke of this. But this young man needed to hear his story. If Dawud was going to offer his dose of personal advice to Aram, he had to be willing to share some personal perspective with him. Dawud needed to relive these events, for Aram's sake. "My father was taken from me by a crazy, demonically fanatic Christian knight named Armande. I watched my brilliant, intelligent, vivacious mother worn down by a bad second marriage to a man possessing less than a fingernail of my own father's character. And I took abuse, from him, from others, that I know my father would have protected me from. My mother suffered. I suffered. I needed that good father."

"This was during one of the holy wars between Christians and Muslims?"

"My father was a Christian knight."

Aram's eyes widened.

Dawud grinned. "Pierre of Jaffa. A great man. Served Richard the Lionheart. Grew to hold small estates in and around Jaffa. But he always spoke of the goodness of men, and told my mother the greatest lesson of his life was the possibility that there could be more than one path to God."

"Like the Mongols...."

"No. I can't help it if they have perverted this idea to mean all faiths are equal under their domination."

"Did you say 'Pierre'?"

"Yes."

Aram tilted his head with a quizzical look. He reached for his satchel and opened it.

"The story is not complete," Dawud scolded, thinking Aram was merely not interested. "Not even close." Aram stopped what he was doing with the satchel.

"My mother died, drained of strength and vitality, never going a day without missing my beloved father." Dawud felt himself shaking. Tears snuck out. He let them flow. "So as soon as I was old enough, I went out to exact justice, to gain retribution. First, I rejected the faith of my father—also the faith of my father's murderer, and of those who had exploited my mother. I joined the True Faith, one positive act amidst an embarrassing torrent of rage. I trained in the military arts." Dawud actually felt a twinge of pride. "My father was a formidable combat knight. I inherited his prowess. I was a great fighter for the True Faith. A most effective one. I killed the enemies of the True Faith under the service of the great al-Adil, Saladin's brother. And all the while, I hunted Armande."

Aram's eyes fixed on Dawud, confirming that Dawud's words had captured the young man's attention.

Dawud swallowed hard. "I found him. He had relocated to a small Christian village outside of Beirut. He was married to a teenaged girl. My revenge would be complete."

"It sounds like he deserved justice."

"I took him one day; he was on his way to the local markets. I told him who I was, and that by my hand, he would never see his family again—he would die in agony."

Aram seemed to flinch at the word "agony."

"I took three days to kill the man. I abused him in every way you can imagine. By the time he died, he had no ability to see, no ability to express desire for women, was missing fingers, toes and had blistered flesh from burns. He begged for mercy so many times...." Dawud burst into tears. "I still hear his cries in my mind, to this day. He had done a terrible thing, but my supposedly personally delivered justice had exceeded his transgressions by exponential magnitudes."

Aram reached out to comfort Dawud, and touched his forearm.

"I'd planned to take seven days to kill him. But after three, I had completely lost my lust for blood. For his blood. For any blood. It was time for me to get on to the next phase of my life, and to try to account to someone for the overreaction my rage had brought about."

Aram nodded.

"I had come face to face with the darkest evil in my soul, and the evil had triumphed. I knew, from my own personal experience, from my own behavior, that this capacity for evil existed within me, and it had triumphed. I resolved never to allow that to happen again. I never married, for fear that evil side of me could infect a family. I sought to hide—from my commander, from my sins of rage—from myself. All because my father was taken from me. All because my mother was left alone to struggle." Dawud looked at Aram. He sniffled. He used the sleeve of his robe to dry his tear-stained face. "I haven't shared that with anyone, not in that way."

Aram nodded again.

"This world is not always easy." Dawud sniffled again, but regained his scholarly bearing. "And truth is not always simple. But I do know for certain, you need to stay with that family of yours. The Intrepid One needs to become the leader of his Intrepid Family."

"Family," Aram said.

"That's right."

"My old friend, I need to ask you something. Was Pierre a common name at that time?"

Dawud frowned. What had Aram taken from his heartfelt personal story? "I suppose."

"Then it could be just a concidence." Aram reached into his satchel. "There is a Pierre-knight in my family background too. Not a well-liked person, according to this long letter my father left me, to be opened after he died, when he decided I could learn the truth."

Dawud watched as Aram held the paper.

"This Pierre left his family, his blacksmith father, to go off and fight for Christianity as a knight. He was supposed to take over the family trade, but he deserted them. Word was he was killed at Hattin. My grandmother, this Pierre-knight's sister, and the rest of the family, were allowed to leave Botron with whatever they could carry. For Europe, a place none of them had ever been. They left behind a lifetime of possessions and reputation. They got caught in a storm and ended up shipwrecked, up along the southern coast of Anatolia. They worked their way back down, struggling as foreigners through the Byzantine state, then through Greeks, Armenians, and Turks. Years later, they made it back down to Acre. They found out there that this Pierre who had deserted the family was now some sort of noble in the Western Christian 'Kingdom of Jerusalem' under King Henry. And he never even tried to make contact with anyone. He just pretended as if he never had a family. It must have been a different Pierre from the one you describe."

Dawud took the letter. He looked grimly at Aram. "Pretended he did not have a family, like you want to do."

"It's different."

"How?"

Aram gritted his teeth, but then relaxed into a casual grin. "It probably runs in the blood."

"Charles the Smith was Pierre's father. And my grandfather." Dawud paused. "Marie, your grandmother, was my aunt."

Aram looked stunned into speechlessness.

"But it isn't in the blood. My father *did* make inquiries. My mother used to tell me that getting final word on his parents, and his brother and sister, were burning issues for him."

"So we—"

"We are family. The old scholar and the Intrepid One."

"Impossible," Aram said.

"Well … highly unlikely, but not impossible. Still, according to this…." Dawud held up the letter he had taken from Aram. He reread it and looked up at Aram. The smile on his face confirmed the familial connection between the two men.

"Well, then," Dawud continued. "Now I am telling you, as your uncle, or cousin, or something, that you will go back to your wife and son. You will find out what this Robert character is up to, or if you flee him, you will take them with you." Dawud paused. "And I will be available to help you in any way I can."

Aram seemed to take a moment to ponder his choices. His beloved teacher was now a newly discovered relation. Why would the man lie?

Dawud watched his face and let him process the information.

"Yes, um, I suppose I prefer Uncle." Aram grinned. "You're too old to be my cousin."

"Oooh. That sense of humor. I thought it was funny before. But, well, it could be disrepectful."

"No disrespect meant. You know that."

"All right. Nephew." Dawud paused. "Does this letter explain how your father ended up in Baghdad?"

"Of course. My father was nothing if not long-winded."

"He was my cousin. Be nice."

"My grandmother—your aunt—got married off to some blacksmith type, someone who had more in common with Charles the Smith than with his daughter. He was cruel to her, but a great smith. Her father was not going to lose another heir to the family business. He did nothing to intervene. Traders out from Baghdad used old Charles' services when they came through the area. My grandmother fell for one of the traders and went with him. The Nestorian Church in Baghdad granted her a divorce, and she married the trader, but promptly died in childbirth. Her husband— my grandfather—so adored her that he thought some great purpose must be ordained for my father since God would not take such a beautiful, blessed soul unless the new soul entering the world was even more special."

"It explains a lot about your father."

"Strange. You were cousins and never knew it."

"Yes. All that time. Closely related people thinking they had little in common. The Eastern Christian student of spirituality. The reformed Muslim warrior secluded in studies of the True Faith, trying to make amends."

"Make amends?"

"You have heard it … nephew. I have much blood on my hands. Some of it spilled beyond proportion. Some of it spilled with deliberately added suffering." He smiled—a weary smile, of a man trying to relieve himself from a burden, close to achieving his intention, but not there yet. Dawud considered he might never fully arrive at total resolution.

"Dawud … Uncle … you are a good man. Look forward. We both will." Aram stood. "And right now, I will go back to Acre. I will get word to you on my progress."

"Good. I will look forward to it. I knew there was a purpose for my survival—somehow outliving unspeakable catastrophe—I'll tell you more about that another time. But this… this is why I have been spared."

Aram nodded. "I will share that belief with you, Uncle. Be ready, because we may come visit you."

"I insist on it. You are my only family."

September, 1259
Azerbaijan, outskirts of Tabriz
Twilight

"You're late!" Ketbugha barked at Shingkhor. "We did not promote you to command a unit of Georgian auxiliaries so you could fail to perform!"

Campfires that had just been lit covered the flat plain. Green grass, cut short by grazing Mongol ponies, covered the terrain. There were a few gently rolling hills in the distance. The area bustled with activity, preparing for well-organized, efficient travel.

"Forgive me, General," Shingkhor said.

"Your commander recommended you as one of the best squad leaders we have, and you very well could be if it weren't for this obsession with avenging a dead brother!"

"I'm sorry, General. But I seek justice for—"

Ketbugha was not interested in explanations or excuses. "This is my first notice of you, as we try to prepare for our departure for Syria tomorrow. This is not how you want to introduce yourself to me!"

The man bowed.

Ketbugha looked to a commanding officer standing to one side, his arms folded. He was a tall thin man, with a weathered face showing more than the man's stated age of thirty-two. There was a scar from a small burn below his right eye.

This second man glared at Shingkhor. "You are embarrassing me," he said. "I pushed for you."

Shingkhor bowed again. "I don't mean to. I will fulfill my duties, I promise, Commander, General. But my duties involve punishing crimes against the il-khan. A prisoner, a man who masqueraded as an astronomer in the service of the il-khan, who killed my brother as he escaped, committed just such a crime. I intend to punish the man responsible."

"That old man is long ago dead!" the commander said.

"We haven't found the body," Shingkhor said. "And we have looked extensively, over the entire—"

"You have terrorized nearby villages. Gone out with your squad late at night. And despite *looking extensively*, you have found nothing."

Ketbugha looked at the squad leader. He appeared to be a serious man.

"You will promise the general—"

Ketbugha held up his hand. "How long has it been since your brother was killed?"

"Just over a year," Shingkhor said.

"A year!" The commander faced his squad leader. "You have been wasting the il-khan's resources for—"

Ketbugha held up his hand again. "Squad leader. It is good you are concerned with justice for your brother. It is good you have a long memory, and that you are persistent in pursuing the il-khan's justice, and your family's justice. You are a warrior of principle and substance."

"Thank you, General."

"But it must not conflict with your duties to your unit. I have a large task tonight, to assure a smooth departure for all of us. If all squad leaders were late—whatever the reason, even if it is a good, justifiable reason—and delayed me this way, I would have no chance of completing my task tonight, and would have to deliver that news to the il-khan. Then, consequences would necessarily follow for all those responsible for the delay."

"I am sorry. It won't happen again."

"Good." Ketbugha looked to the commander of the chastised squad leader. "Do not be too hard on this man. He was not late out of slothfulness."

The commander nodded.

"Chances are your brother's murderer is dead, long gone from this area. But as we move forward, you have my blessing to seek this criminal … as long as it does not hamper your performance of your assigned duties. If you find him, we will make an example of him. No transgression against us will be taken lightly, nor will it be forgotten." To the commander he said, "See to it the other units are on the lookout for this man. He was with the astrologers? Put some guards who recall him into any of the search parties."

The commander nodded again. "Yes, General."

"Thank you, General," Shingkhor added.

"You will thank me by fulfilling your duties, and doing everything in your power to make this expedition a glorious success for the rulers of the world ordained by the Eternal Blue Heaven."

Shingkhor bowed. "Of course."

Ketbugha said to the commander, "I need to inspect the squad that will handle weapons transport."

"Yes." He led Ketbugha toward that squad, and the carts for which they would be responsible.

"Tomorrow morning," Ketbugha said, "we finally move."

"Yes," the commander said. "More wealth. More glory."

Ketbugha looked up at the full moon. "The time is exactly right."

"It is."

Ketbugha said, "You understand the implication of our continued problems at Mayyafariqin." Ketbugha reflected that this night of preparations would have been so much simpler if Hulegu's massive army could move through the crossroads at Mayyafariqin. Without possessing that key location, the army would need to split in order to advance into Syria.

"Yes. Our supply formations will be spread a bit more. I have worked with my squad leaders. They are prepared for the complications."

"Like the one I just spoke to?"

The commander shrugged. "No. He's part of a security squad. For captured enemies. For surrendered towns and villages."

"And dedicated to his work."

"Yes."

Ketbugha took in a deep breath and let it out. "All right. Good." He smiled at the commander. "Mayyafariqin has complicated this move, but there are many good leaders like you to manage it."

"Thank you."

Ketbugha squinted as he grinned. "I would not wish to be al-Kamil Muhammad when our men take that city."

"No. But he will deserve his fate."

"Without a doubt."

Ketbugha moved on to the next inspections.

❧ *18* ❧

"Daniel." Aram spoke quietly as he stood over his son, who slept in his small bed. Aram had never liked the name Daniel. He hadn't protested because he thought it unfair to insist on a name for a son he suspected he would not stay with. But Daniel was the boy's name; Aram now accepted and embraced it. "Daniel, my precious son."

Aram heard the rustling of blankets from the larger bed in the quarters he shared with Jeannette.

"Aram?"

"Anybody tell you, you're too young to be a widow?"

"People are asking about you," she said with a cool tone of voice. "I told them you were probably dead."

"Well, I'm not."

"That's great. You're not dead. How wonderful."

"Jeannette, I do not expect you to become a widow for a long time. I expect us to grow fat and ugly together, watching that one sire us grandchildren." He pointed at Daniel.

"Oh, is that right…?"

"I mean it. You're stuck with me." He looked at her. Anger seemed to radiate from her face. "If that's what you want."

"You have treated me insensitively."

"I know."

"I was very angry at you. There are suitors waiting to come after me."

"I have no doubt."

"Suitors who are not looking to leave me behind."

"Any man would be foolish to leave you behind."

"You did."

"I came back."

"Should I bow down and kiss your feet? And wait until the next time you decide to leave me?"

Aram steadily looked at her. "I won't leave you again."

"Maybe I don't care."

"You have a suitor already?"

"Maybe I do."

Aram grunted as he felt a surge of anger. His face tensed. If she really had a suitor, why didn't she just tell him? The "maybe" irritated him.

Jeannette let slip a smirk, seeming to enjoy his annoyance.

"Well, do you?"

"Oh, how nice. You're finally asking how *I feel*? Where *I stand*? The great Aram is back. What is *my* response?"

"Well?"

"Well, I'll tell you what I think."

Aram nodded. He restrained his impatience. He had discerned that Jeannette was adopting Aram's own cavalier manner. She was not going to let him saunter back into their life together, seamlessly, with a smooth, casual attitude. She was going to get some authentic emotion from him. She needed to be certain that he was truly serious about her.

"Here's what I think. I don't want to grow fat and ugly with you. You can do that yourself."

Aram was not sure what to say. He had thought she would jump to take him back.

"*You* can," she continued. "Well, you can grow ugly. But not fat. And not me. Not either one."

Aram frowned, but started to understand. She was toying with him. It was her chance to be the casual, cavalier one.

"I intend to remain thin and pretty for a long time."

Aram laughed, and that broke the détente.

"Please come to me," she requested seductively.

He smiled, then looked over at Daniel.

"He's sound asleep." Jeannette slipped off the blankets and in one motion removed her sleeping gown.

Aram had his clothes off and his wife in an embrace seemingly with one quick move of his own.

∽◆∾

"Shhh," Aram said. "We're going to wake him."

"And the entire wing of this residence," Jeannette said as she almost simultaneously giggled. She lay on Aram's chest.

Aram was grinning. "It is good to be back."

"Yes. All right. So what happened?"

"Oh, well, I found an uncle in Damascus."

"Uncle. In Damascus." She shook her head. "I never quite know what to expect from you."

"Well, you're signed on for the ride now," he said. "Next time I leave Acre, I will have my family with me."

"Are we going somewhere?"

"Maybe. Who was asking about me?"

"Well, of course the people who had to do the chores you were doing. And Robert. And two of the other priests."

"Hmmm."

"What will we tell them?"

"I went on pilgrimage to Jerusalem."

"That's not funny."

"They won't buy it?"

"No. Of course not."

"Would they buy Rome? Mecca?"

"Aram…."

"I know. I need a story."

"You were in Damascus." Jeannette puzzled it over. "What brought you to Damascus?"

"It's a stop on the way to Baghdad."

"Yes, but what's in Damascus?"

"A lot more than here. Better books. Better medicines. Better food."

"Medicine…."

"Absolutely."

"We could say Daniel had a rash and you went out to get a special potion?"

"Um, then why would you have said I was dead?"

"Oh. Yes."

Aram shrugged. "Let's keep it to the truth, or something close to it. I felt my time on this assignment was up and I decided to go.

I missed my family and decided to come back."

"Robert will probably lock you up."

Aram's eyes narrowed and his nostrils flared. "Robert has a few questions to answer. I'm not sure he'll want to lock me up."

"You learned something?"

"What I learned leads to more questions than answers. Why is he on a mission for the pope that was already completed almost five years ago by William of Rubruck on behalf of the French king?"

Jeannette was silent.

Aram squeezed her.

"Where would we go?" she asked.

Aram took a deep breath. "I don't know." He paused. "I don't know, or we'd already be packing to leave."

"It sounds like I'd better have us ready to leave at any time."

"I think that's a good idea."

Jeannette frowned. "You said something about an uncle?"

"Yes. Remember, I told you about that old Muslim scholar who I thought might be able to help me with the Latin translation? Turns out, he is actually my uncle. My blood-relation uncle." Aram shook his head. "An extraordinary man. Lots to say. Lots to teach."

"In Damascus."

"Right."

"What will you do about Robert?"

Aram's lips tightened. He took in a deep breath. "I'd like to know more about what he's up to, so I can figure out how to extricate myself with as little risk as possible." He paused. "We'll let everyone know I'm back, but offer as little explanation as possible. Leave it to me. Just say I mysteriously popped up again."

"Well, you did."

Aram smiled. "We need to snoop around for information. Look for people who fancy themselves the Robert experts, and are willing to talk about it."

"I can help with that. The girls love to talk."

"But not just chatter. Get me something I can use."

"I'll try."

"Good."

Jeannette smiled. "You really have come back to me. To stay."

"You can depend on it."

❧ ◆ ❧

Mid September 1259
Acre
Almost Midnight

"You will wake!" Pounding on the door roused Aram from his sleep. "You will open! The accent was harsh. The *w* was pronounced almost as if it was a *v* sound. The tone was commanding. The words rattled off like short smacks of a drum.

"Aram?" Jeannette sounded fearful.

"I'm coming," Aram called out. He shook his head, trying to come fully into awareness.

"You will open! You will wake!" The pounding now changed. Someone was trying to break open the door. Aram heard barked words of a foreign tongue. These were Robert's men.

"Be patient—I'm coming!" Aram called out, now showing irritation in his voice. He threw a one-piece nightshirt on over his body. "Don't break it!"

The sounds of banging continued.

Aram moved to the door. "I'm opening the door!"

The sounds stopped.

Aram opened the door. He recognized three of Robert's knights from their previous expedition to Baghdad in early 1258. "Gentlemen, please. It's a bit late for a reunion."

"You come. You will come with us." The tone was commanding and scolding at the same time. The faces were completely humorless.

Aram nodded.

One of the men grabbed Aram by the arm.

"There's no need for that," Aram said.

"Aram?" Jeannette sounded frantic. "Aram!"

Aram heard his son start to cry.

But he was out the door, led briskly away before he could say anything to reassure his wife.

"Could you have possibly found a better way to summon me to Robert?"

But these men were not going to answer.

19

"The dungeon?"

No answer came from Aram's tight-lipped escorts. They continued to guide him along by gripping his upper arms.

Aram felt a surge of trepidation rush through his body, almost like a potion warming his blood. These men were leading him toward the entrance to a dungeon.

A squat, short-haired man with a ring of keys met them.

"Where to room?" one of Robert's guards asked.

The man smiled, showing four teeth. "This hall."

The group moved down the dungeon hall, lit only by a torch the key-man carried. One of the guards continued to tug Aram along by his upper arm.

They reached a door. The key-man put a key in the latch to open it.

"Let me talk to Robert before you—" But Aram stopped his likely-to-be-fruitless plea as the door opened. Inside was Nestor, who squinted at the influx of light and grunted. His face was puffed with bruises under his unshaven stubble. His feet were chained to the mucky dirt floor. A plate of bread and a bowl of water lay across from him. Nestor's hands were tied behind his back, so the only way for him to eat or drink would be to fully extend his body and use only his mouth, as if he were an animal. The room stank of urine and excrement. The conditions of captivity seemed designed for maximum humiliation.

"Aram?" Nestor's face contorted into a relieved smile. "Aram, it's you. My God. I'm so glad it's you!"

"What—" Aram stared at his friend, then jerked his arm away from the guard and stepped toward him. "What's going on?"

"They couldn't find you. So they took me. They thought I would know where you were."

"They found you?"

Nestor grinned sheepishly through his grimy, unshaven face. "They put out the word that you had done a great job, and had a big bonus coming. I found them."

Aram looked at the guards. They seemed to be waiting. If they were going to confine him, they would have started the process by now. The key-man had walked away. Aram's eyes narrowed. They had to be waiting for Robert. Aram moved up to Nestor, ignoring the rank odors coming from his friend. "Quick. I need to know some things," he whispered, though he doubted Robert's men understood their language.

"Well, I—"

"About Robert."

"He's German. They're German."

"I'd figured that."

"They—"

"Why do they find me so important? Enough to confine you here like this? Enough to watch for my return?"

"Where did you—"

"Why?" Aram's voice rose to a volume he didn't want. He looked back at the guards, who eyed him but did not intervene.

Nestor shook his head. "I … I'm not sure."

Aram dropped his voice back to a whisper. "You've got to help me with this. What did they say they needed?"

"To find out where you—"

"No, all the way back. When they contacted you about my assignment. Before this whole thing started. What did they say they needed?"

Nestor's face reflected thought. "Oh." He appeared to search his memory. "No entanglements. That was big. Christian, but no entanglements. Familiar with Mongols. Fluent in languages."

"Entanglements." Aram frowned. This was a vague term. It could mean personal, political, or religious. "What do you mean, 'entanglements'?"

"No loyalties either way, to the Venetians or the Genoans. No contact with the pope, or any of the rival factions in the papacy. Preferably no family. No—"

"So truly *no* entanglements of any kind."

"You were perfect."

"I see you're getting reacquainted."

Aram turned to face Robert, alerted to his presence by his stern voice. Robert was dressed in night clothes, as if hurriedly summoned from his sleep.

"Why is my friend held this way?" Aram asked in his own firm tone.

Robert gave an order in the discordant sound of his apparent native language.

Two men moved to Nestor and began removing his chains.

Robert turned to Aram. "Your friend took money for a job you haven't performed yet. We held him here"—Robert seemed to measure his words—"as encouragement to supply your whereabouts."

"You now have my whereabouts."

"Yes."

Nestor stood and grimaced, stiff from long periods chained in awkward positions.

Aram looked at Nestor. He steeled his expression as he looked back at Robert. "Nestor and I will return all advances immediately. My employment will terminate immediately. My family and I will be leaving as soon as the sun comes up."

"Um, well"—Nestor looked up at Aram with a squeamish smile—"I, I don't have any funds. Perhaps … you do?"

Aram frowned before turning back to Robert. "I will apply my back wages to repay any advances Nestor took on my behalf."

Robert nodded. He stepped toward Aram. He shrugged. "Where will you and your family go?"

"I have an uncle in—"

Robert's face perked up at the word "uncle." Aram quickly realized he was becoming manipulated into yielding a morsel of information he might want to hold closely. "I'm not sure where we will go."

Robert grinned. He grunted. His smile broadened. "You're not sure."

"No."

"Hmmm. Well, apparently you also don't know that all your 'back wages' have been paid to Nestor, as has been my agreement with him."

Aram looked at Nestor. "All of them?"

Nestor again flashed his squeamish smile.

"Yes," Robert said. "Why do you think we never handed you any money?"

"I thought it was being held for me."

"It was. By your friend. So he could take his commission."

Aram looked at Nestor, wanting to ask the question, but afraid he wouldn't like the answer.

"The back wages...." Nestor took a deep breath. "They are not available right now."

"It should be a simple matter of getting them from whatever secure location you have stored them at." Aram glared at his friend.

"Um, well, they're stored, um, as investments." Nestor flashed a smile.

"Investments...."

"Three expeditions. We will triple the money."

Robert laughed.

"What expeditions?" Aram clenched his teeth as he stared daggers at Nestor.

"Two to Persia. For rugs and silk, the silk from the East. One back to Europe. We are backers! Of some traders with great connections to my family."

Robert laughed again. "Yes, well, that is impressive. But until you powerful businessmen receive the fruits of these expeditions, Aram owes me service." Robert leveled his eyes straight at Aram. "Your friend will be held to assure your performance. And you," Robert squinted with menace, "you will be watched. In case you decide to visit any more uncles."

"You will not hold my friend in this dungeon," Aram insisted. "My performance—"

"Of course he will not be held here," Robert told Aram. "You have returned. However, your departure before fulfillment of the obligation could change your friend's circumstances. Severely. As he would be guilty of theft. Otherwise, he will be my guest. In exchange for a few chores, and under watchful eyes to make sure he does not leave, he will have a much more pleasant stay in Acre."

"How long of an advance did my *friend* take for *my* services?" Aram asked.

"Through to Christmas of this year."

Aram's nostrils flared.

"With an option to extend your service for another year." Robert nodded to his guards who took Nestor by both arms.

Aram stepped to him. "I should take off again and leave you here," he snarled through his teeth to Nestor.

"Quiet," Robert ordered. "I deem it in my interests that you two schemers have no contact with each other during this time."

"Fine," Aram said. "That suits me just fine. But all future wages are to be paid directly to me."

Robert chuckled. "We'll address this issue—after Christmas." He paused. "Do you need help returning to your residence?"

"I know my way around Acre."

"Good. You are free to go … back to your quarters. I'll have a few of my men join you, just in case you get lost."

Aram nodded.

As he returned to his quarters, he considered Robert's order to keep them separate. Robert was guarding secrets. Aram needed to know what those secrets were if he was to escape, or even survive, this job for Robert and the Acre Christians. For a young man who had been hired for his lack of entanglements, Aram had managed to become entangled beyond anything he had ever imagined.

20

Late November, 1259
Gaza
Mid Day

"You've done well in my service," al-Nasir Yusuf said. His tone was welcoming as Baybars entered al-Nasir Yusuf's tent.

Baybars looked at the three men who accompanied him, his eyebrows raised, then back at al-Nasir Yusuf. He was surprised that the sultan had actually greeted him at the entrance. "Thank you," Baybars said. "I appreciate your acknowledgment of my efforts."

"Come. Sit with us." Al-Nasir Yusuf motioned Baybars and his men to cushions around a low table that was topped with water, fruit and bread. "Important developments, and issues, have emerged. Nothing is easy in these turbulent times. I need you to know what is happening." Al-Nasir Yusuf paused. He added an apparent afterthought. "And I value your input."

Baybars nodded, even bowed slightly. "Of course." He and his men moved to positions around the table. Baybars recognized most of the men with al-Nasir Yusuf, including his adviser al-Zayn al-Hafizi. Baybars' nose twitched tensely as he recalled his initial impression of al-Zayn al-Hafizi—a soft man with a patronizing attitude. Baybars shifted his sword at his hip; he had been allowed to keep it. But he also noticed the squad of over twenty men in various stations around the tent. Al-Nasir Yusuf was showing partial, but not complete, trust.

Baybars and his men reached for the refreshments.

"Your friend Qutuz is now sultan of Egypt."

Baybars stopped in the act of raising a goblet of water to his mouth. He grinned, then took a sip. "He cast aside the pretense. Al-Mansur Ali is no more than a child; he was a puppet anyway."

"Qutuz cited the Mongol threat as the reason for him to steal the position."

Baybars shrugged. "To my mind, he is only stealing what he already possessed, even if not officially."

"I suppose you are correct."

"One thing this does signal to the world: Qutuz takes the Mongol threat very seriously, even at the gates of Cairo." Baybars looked pointedly at al-Nasir Yusuf. "Do we?"

Al-Nasir Yusuf bristled. "Of course we do."

Baybars looked over to al-Zayn al-Hafizi, but the adviser glanced away the moment their eyes met.

Al-Nasir Yusuf continued, "They did not wait to take Mayyafariqin. They are advancing on the Euphrates as we speak."

Baybars shrugged. "Mayyafariqin would have made it easier for them, but we knew they would be coming one way or another." Baybars raised his eyebrows. "Mayyafariqin will isolate and fall. I suspect al-Kamil Muhammad will pay a terrible price."

"As we all may," al-Zayn al-Hafizi said, "if we handle this incorrectly."

"We must contest these monsters, these destroyers of Islam," Baybars said. "But I heard rumors he actually crucified an envoy from the Mongols?"

Al-Nasir Yusuf nodded. "Yes. It's true."

Baybars shook his head. "I would do such a thing only if I had the means to back it up."

"You think my cousin should not have objected to an ultimatum delivered by a Christian priest?" Al-Nasir Yusuf sneered. "A disrespectful ultimatum?"

Baybars considered the question. "There's a line between courage and suicide, between defiance and pointless vanity. Al-Kamil Muhammad may have found that line, and stumbled over it, into disaster."

"And that is why *we* are considering all options," al-Zayn al-Hafizi said.

Baybars looked at al-Nasir Yusuf, lips tensed. "*All* options?"

"Calm yourself," al-Nasir Yusuf said, but in a tone that was not calm itself, but rather scolding. "I have sent envoys asking for help from Qutuz. They are requesting that help in the strongest possible terms."

Baybars nodded. "Good. We will need his help. And I think we can count on it. He realizes Islam is at stake. We hold the last positions of power for God's great religion. We must not fail this duty God has cast to us. We may be all that stands for the one True Faith."

"I can count on you to serve with Qutuz?" al-Nasir Yusuf asked.

"Yes, of course! For the survival of Islam! Of course!" Baybars felt insulted that al-Nasir Yusuf would have even asked the question. Yes, Baybars had differences with Qutuz. He had fought bitter battles against forces commanded by Qutuz. But among brothers in faith these were squabbles compared to the confrontation to come.

"And you would support other policies of this sultan, if calculated to assure the survival of Islam?" al-Zayn al-Hafizi asked.

It was an oblique question, but Baybars understood the subtext. He looked at al-Nasir Yusuf, to determine how frankly he should answer.

Al-Nasir Yusuf seemed apprehensive, maybe even uncomfortable that al-Zayn al-Hafizi asked such a question. The Mongols were coming his way and he was plunging into fear. He was rallying his subordinates, looking for solidarity.

That was how Baybars would answer. "I would have a hard time supporting any policy of capitulation—to the creatures who destroyed Baghdad and trampled the caliph to death inside blankets; to the creatures who elevate their Christian allies and allow them to dishonor and disrespect our fellow Believers; to the creatures who have massacred hundreds of thousands of Believers and allowed them to rot in the sun, food to worms, dust to the wind." Baybars paused, dropping his impassioned tone down a notch. "But, to my great joy and relief, no such policy is contemplated. You, Sultan, as a great leader of Islam, as a servant of God with power and influence, have chosen to fight. You, in your great wisdom, have recognized that to become servants of the Mongols is no survival at all. It would be the death of Islam, and an affront to God. I honor my service to you, to your policy of victory."

Al-Zayn al-Hafizi raised his chin up and his jaw moved forward. Baybars read disapproval in the man's grim expression—he had clearly expected Baybars to declare support for al-Nasir Yusuf no matter what course he chose, even if it was submission to the Mongols. Al-Zayn al-Hafizi looked over at al-Nasir Yusuf, but said nothing.

"Thank you, my worthy and noble servant of Islam," al-Nasir Yusuf said, tears forming in his eyes. "Your pledge to this struggle is treasured, and I will call on you."

Baybars raised his goblet of water. "My men and I will be ready." He tilted the goblet toward al-Nasir Yusuf. "We *are* ready." Baybars took a long gulp of water.

Late December, 1259
East of the Euphrates River
Mid Day

"Two weeks or less now," Ketbugha said. He and Hulegu rode together among the latter man's entourage, returning from the front of the huge army that moved through the crisp winter air along a hilly, arid terrain. The advancing men kept pace with the easy tempo of a simple chant.

Hulegu nodded. His upper lip twitched. "And so what do we know of this uncle of al-Nasir Yusuf?"

"Nothing new. The advance scouts tell us the defenses at the city will be easily overcome, especially compared to what we've seen in recent campaigns."

"Good. I know Aleppo is not Damascus, and certainly not Baghdad, but it is the first major Syrian city we will encounter. A quick victory is necessary to send a strong message throughout the area."

Ketbugha assured him, "We will have it."

"We will have no more situations like at Mayyafariqin. It makes us look weak, and foolish, and defiable, not to mention the less convenient route into Syria we have had to take as a result." Hulegu ground his teeth. "I sent other messengers; I want that al-Kamil Muhammad to suffer a fate that will be spoken of for centuries."

Ketbugha flashed a malevolent grin. "I think you have been very clear about this, and our troops there will not disappoint you."

Hulegu nodded. He listened to his chanting army. He had heard these simple traveling songs since he could remember, sounds that seemed to transcend mere humanity, as if from the Eternal Blue Heaven itself. These chants, emanating so effortlessly from this massive flow of human beings—could there be any doubt that it was their fate to rule the world, to continue the succession of conquests that would lead to this destiny?

Hulegu's ears registered something else, rising in volume through the singing. It was the sound of horse hooves. Both men turned their heads and reined in their horses.

"From the East," Ketbugha commented.

"From Mongke," Hulegu agreed.

Five riders approached. They wore colorful uniforms, and held an arrow-like formation. The riders at the edges of the formation carried banners reflecting their affiliation with Mongke, the great khan.

The man in the middle of the formation dismounted and completed a deep bow, then handed a circular container up to Hulegu.

Inside was a rolled up message. Hulegu unrolled it, then glanced at it. He had a good idea of what it said, but did not want to express the message himself. He handed it back to the messenger and said, "Read it."

The messenger completed another deep bow before he began: "Mongke Khan, Great Khan, ruler ordained of the Genghis Khan lineage, destined by the Eternal Blue Heaven to rule the world, has succumbed to illness. This occurred during a campaign against the Sung at the eastern part of the lands of the Chin. He contracted an illness of the bowels, and could not be healed despite all manner of potions and shamanic incantations. He now joins the Eternal Blue Heaven." The man rolled up the message.

"How long?" Hulegu asked.

"Four months ago."

Hulegu frowned. Whoever had control of power had not made it a priority to notify him. The next great khan would have to be chosen by a formal council of high-ranking family members, and he wondered if that had also taken place without his knowledge. "Has the *kuriltai* occurred?"

He bowed. "I do not know, il-Khan,"

"Do you have any other information?"

"No, Your Majesty."

"Stand by."

The man bowed again. He signaled to his squad and they dismounted to wait with him.

Hulegu motioned for Ketbugha to follow him and they led their horses a small distance away.

"It should take some time to put the *kuriltai* together," Hulegu said. "My brother died a long way from the homeland."

Ketbugha nodded.

Hulegu felt a lump in his throat. He sneered and clenched his teeth, attempting to stifle even a hint of tears. He had loved his brother Mongke. He knew Mongke's faults: overindulgence, especially overindulgence of drink. But Mongke had been a fair older brother, and as great khan he had allowed Hulegu a free hand in Persia, Mesopotomia, Syria, and Egypt. He would miss his brother, but tears were not an option for the il-khan. If an enemy had killed his brother, Hulegu could have used that anger to stamp down the tears of grief. But his brother had been taken by a humiliating disease. Hulegu swallowed. "Bowels. Sickness of bowels. What fool shaman allowed such a sickness to take my brother, to take a great khan?"

"Unfortunately, we are not in a position to make such inquiries."

"No." Hulegu stared ahead. "Sickness of the bowels." He flared his nostrils. Anger, to stamp down the tears. "A silly way to die."

"Yes."

Hulegu let out a burst of air. "So, succession is an issue."

Ketbugha nodded slowly and raised his eyebrows.

"But our move into Syria, and toward Egypt, is also important," Hulegu added.

"Yes, this is the decisive move for this campaign."

Hulegu looked up into the sky. "My brother Kublai is in line to be the great khan. I have no quibble with that. Kublai is a good brother, and will show the same attitude toward my interests out here. He is the obvious choice. The *kuriltai* will choose him. My presence will not change that result."

Ketbugha nodded.

"My presence is more important here."

Ketbugha nodded again.

"Call over the messengers. And I want some of our own, some of our best."

"I'll see to it."

"I'd like to see them right away."

Ketbugha bowed. He jerked his horse over toward his own subordinates.

Hulegu looked out over the massive column of Mongols moving toward Syria. A slight grin slipped onto his face as he heard the continued simple chant. At least 200,000 human beings—soldiers, support staff, families—this was a moving nation, as great as the massive forces and teeming humanity led across the steppes of Eurasia by his grandfather. In a sense, he was nearly a great khan himself. If this was his position in the dynasty ordained by the Eternal Blue Heaven to rule the world, he could accept it. Then the grin disappeared as soon as he again thought about the death of his brother.

Ketbugha returned. "Our messengers will join us momentarily."

"Good."

"Il-Khan, you have not asked my counsel on this."

Hulegu looked in surprise at his trusted general. "What would that advice be?"

Ketbugha grinned uneasily. "Unrequested advice is…."

"Consider it requested."

"I agree with what you are doing. As always, your reasoning is sound. This route into Syria will complicate our move against our enemies there. Mayyafariqin *still* holds out."

"I'd like to give that al-Kamil Muhammad a sickness in *his* bowels."

"Mayyafariqin will fall. It would have been better for our purpose if it had fallen by now. But this is why your continued presence here is wise."

"Yes. That is what I have said."

"What I also wish you to know is that I can command our forces if your presence back at the homeland is needed. It would be my honor to serve you, the dynasty ordained by the Eternal Blue Heaven to rule the world, in that way, if I am needed."

Hulegu allowed himself a slight smile. "I will continue bringing you in on every aspect of this operation so you are ready to serve if needed."

Ketbugha bowed. "You honor me."

The squad of messengers rode up at a trot. The five original messengers who had arrived were joined by fifteen of Hulegu's men.

Hulegu addressed them. "At this time, my duties here compel my continued presence. I will send a representative to act for me at the *kuriltai,* if it has not yet taken place. That will include my pledge of support for the rightful successor, my older brother Kublai. I will send a message with my condolences, and my memories of the great khan Mongke. I will expect continuous updates from messengers on developments. If needed, send messengers every day." Hulegu slowly looked at their faces. They seemed to understand. "Dismissed."

Hulegu said to Ketbugha, "Make sure the news is passed among our people. I want a meeting with all officers at the setting of the evening camp. I want an assessment of where this expedition stands at this moment."

Ketbugha nodded and left to complete his duties.

Hulegu remained alone on his slow-trotting horse. He let a few tears slide down his cheeks at the thought that he would never see his brother again. But these few brief tears would be all the indulgence in grief he would allow himself.

January, 1260
Damascus
Early Evening

"We need an observatory," Dawud said, shaking his head. "And my ledgers." He scowled.

"Observatory?" the student asked.

Dawud looked up from perusing a bound manuscript. He and the student sat at one of two tables in a small room cluttered with papers and manuscripts. The room was lit by a dwindling sun and a few candles. Some worn rugs were spread out on the stone floor.

Dawud smiled. Did the students get younger everywhere he went, or did they just seem younger because Dawud was getting older? Dawud also felt as if he had aged two decades in the last two years. "An observatory is a place where astronomers can view the heavens and make observations." Dawud pointed at a book in one of the stacks. "Like the ancient Greeks did."

"Greeks? From Europe? Byzantines? *Christians?*"

Dawud chuckled. "Greeks long before Christianity."

The student raised his eyebrows, then raised his head. "Ah."

Dawud wondered if the gesture of understanding was genuine. "Young man, doesn't a person such as you have more interesting pursuits than spending time with an old eccentric collector of trivia?"

The young man looked hurt. "Am I disturbing you? Distracting you from important work?" The student stood. "I am sorry."

"No, no, no," Dawud corrected quickly, concerned he had hurt the young man's feelings. "I really do wonder if you can find any value in spending your free time with—" Dawud cut himself short. "Young man, if you wish to spend time with me, if you find value in it, then remain." Dawud looked down at the papers in front of him. "It is just that I will never reconstruct what we had at

Baghdad. Years of collecting observations, and records of the observations of others. Relating those observations to the theories in the books. Theories of great thinkers of the True Faith, and yes, some theories of the Greeks and other great thinkers from centuries before the True Faith." Dawud shook his head. "I will never reconstitute that."

The young student sat back down. "As long as I am not bothering you. From important work."

Dawud considered that his entire monologue had gone right over the student's head. "You're not keeping me from anything important."

"What observations are you talking about?"

"The ones that confirm our world is the center of the universe. I have tried to duplicate them, to confirm the idea but...," he looked at the student. "I like to see the systematic investigation of our world confirm what God has revealed."

"Any way I can help, I would be pleased."

"I'm not sure what help there is." Dawud smiled. "But I will tell you if I need it."

"Good."

"Are you caught up with your studies for your regular courses of instruction?"

A guilty look on the student's face was answer enough.

"For my courses at least?" Dawud asked.

"Almost. I am still hazy on the period just after the Prophet."

Dawud shrugged. "An important period. We'll go over it again before you leave."

"Thank you. Teacher, can we build an observatory here?"

Dawud chuckled. "I don't think this is high in priority for our sultan, with Mongols approaching from Aleppo."

"After the Mongols, then."

Any hint of lightheartedness drained out of Dawud's face. He stifled the temptation to suggest that "after the Mongols" there would be nothing left in Damascus. "You remind me of someone," he said in a monotone, his eyes focused on nothing but the past.

The student looked puzzled.

"A former student of mine. In Baghdad. Very dear to me." Dawud smiled. "Hung around and asked a lot of questions." Dawud swallowed a lump in his throat. But he knew his eyes glistened with a hint of tears.

"He died, didn't he?"

"Yes. In the slaughter." Dawud's nostrils flared. "A bit older than you. Maybe a little taller. Inquisitive. Loyal."

"I am those things?"

Dawud looked into his student's eyes. "You need to consider leaving Damascus, before the Mongols come."

"I'll leave if you leave."

Dawud's nostrils flared again. He understood the student thought of this as loyalty. But Dawud found himself irritated with the young man's attitude. He almost snapped at him, but realized his irritation was not the student's fault. Dawud didn't want to be responsible. The student reminded him of how he had survived at Baghdad, splattered with the brains and blood of his student-friend who had made Dawud's survival possible but had not survived himself.

Dawud harnessed his churning emotions. "Do you have family in Damascus?" He tried to keep an even tone, but wondered if the student could hear a slight tremble in his voice.

"Yes. Shopkeepers."

"Mongols are reportedly at the Euphrates, at the entrance to Syria. You and your shopkeeper family should make preparations to leave—before the rush to leave overwhelms this place, and the Mongols are in position to make leaving more difficult."

The student looked blankly at Dawud.

"Tell your family," Dawud said gently. "With all the lessons I have learned, maybe the most important one I can impart to you at this moment is my lesson of recent contact with the Mongols. Please. Take that lesson to your family and get out while you can. *Survive*."

"Then why aren't you preparing to leave?"

Dawud rolled his eyes and tensed his lips. "It's a fair question, I suppose. But you must understand that an old man, on the run for two years, has different concerns and priorities than yours. Or at least they *should* be different."

"The rumors are that we may negotiate, and keep peace with—"

"Negotiate with Mongols? We will be negotiating for slavery. No responsible leader of an Islamic government will ever agree to such a thing."

"Teacher, let us not dwell on unpleasantness. Let us talk of observatories."

Dawud drew in a deep breath. He leaned back. "Here? An observatory here? When I have gathered information from the great observatories in Persia and Mesopotamia? Foolishness."

"I'm sorry." The young man appeared on the verge of tears.

"Go home to your family. Leave a tired old man alone with some space."

"Yes. Apologies." The student stood. "May I come back tomorrow after my instruction sessions?"

Dawud contorted his face into a stern, chastising look. "You don't come back to visit me until you can tell me truthfully that you have discussed what I have told you with your family. And don't think I won't check."

The young man looked angry and insulted. "I would never lie to you."

"Tell them."

"If I say I have, then I have."

"Just do it."

"I will." He sniffled.

"Good."

The student gathered a few papers he had brought with him and started for the door.

Dawud called out, "Wait."

The young man turned. His tear-stained but angry face confronted Dawud, suggesting this attempt at tough love may have been overdone.

"Have you completed your evening prayers yet?"

"No."

"Do them here. With me." Dawud rose from his chair and moved to a shelf holding rolled prayer rugs.

The student smiled with tears flowing freely.

Dawud spread two prayer rugs onto the floor in the least cluttered corner of the room.

21

January 1260
Acre
Night

"What do you mean *he* doesn't trust *me?*" Aram asked, his voice raised. He and Jeannette lay in bed next to each other, their room dimly lit by a single candle.

Daniel started crying in his small bed next to theirs.

"Don't yell at *me*." Jeannette got up and moved toward their crying child. "I'm trying to arrange this."

"But what did you tell him? To make him—"

"I didn't tell *him* anything," Jeannette insisted. "I don't even know who he is. Sarah told me he is a very suspicious type."

"The sad thing is, I suspect this mystery man and I are on the same side of this."

"I think that's true."

"So what is so damn difficult?"

Jeannette picked up her child and held him, patting him on the back. She tensed. "Aram, you're not thinking this through. This man does not know you. He only knows you're with Robert, and that you've been in his service for almost two years."

"Because I'm being coerced! I ought to leave Nestor here to rot."

"What makes you think this man knows that you've been coerced? Or knows anything about Nestor? You think Robert is giving that information out to everybody?"

Aram shook his head. "Maybe I should talk to Sarah. I don't think you're explaining—"

"You're going to have to trust me on this. I have explained what I can to her."

"Then why isn't she—"

"She's a gossipy girl. That is why I have been dealing with her. She blabs and blabs with everyone about everything. There's only so much we want to tell her, and even *that* could be risky. We need to consider that anything we tell her will be known by everyone else."

Aram grunted.

Jeannette asked, "How much of our situation do you want everyone to know?"

Aram scrunched up his mouth and nose. "Honestly, I don't care. I just want information on Robert. I don't really care what anyone thinks."

As Jeannette opened her mouth to counter his statement, Aram headed off her rebuttal. "But I understand the advantages of secrecy."

"Of course you do."

Aram paused. "Still. Let me talk to Sarah. Maybe a direct approach to her will—"

"You're not listening to me."

"I am. I understand. But I think—"

"Sarah doesn't know it's you. She doesn't know the anti-Robert contingent involves us, or that we even agree with it. This contact that she talks about, we may have to set up whatever information exchange we can in some convoluted way so he feels protected. And Sarah has to know as little as possible."

Aram's nostrils flared as he exhaled impatiently. "Then how can this ever work?"

"I'm not totally sure yet, but I think I'm getting closer. If the approaches are circuitous, and protect everyone's identities, you will have a better chance of getting the information you want."

"I need to know what this man is up to."

"I know, Aram. I understand. I may be some silly orphan girl you got trapped into marrying, but I am not stupid. Especially when you've explained this a hundred times."

"You haven't seen the world the way I have. You—"

"Fine! Then *you* go out and make the contact! *You* search out the information! I'll get out of the whole thing, and not get involved until I have been to more places."

"You know I can't be the one to—"

"No, Aram. I am too stupid. I haven't been enough places to do this. You go ahead. Just go walk up to Sarah and tell her you need to contact someone with interests against Robert."

"Calm down. I didn't mean—"

"I promise I'll try to visit you and Nestor in the dungeon."

"All right. I get it. It's just frustrating for me. I'm used to handling my own problems."

Jeannette continued to rub Daniel's back. The child cooed contentedly. "It's not just your problem."

"No, it isn't, is it."

Jeannette took in a deep breath.

Aram scowled. "It's hard for me—to need people."

"Well, you do!"

"I hate it." Aram turned toward Jeannette with his arms folded.

Jeannette glared at him knowingly. "It's easier to leave people if you don't need them."

Aram grunted.

"And you're thinking about it again," she said.

Aram's expression turned quizzical. "No." A sliver of satisfaction cut through his frustration as he considered her statement. "No. I'm not." He smiled. "I'm really not." His smile broadened. "It never even crossed my mind."

Jeannette eyed him.

"I'm telling you, it didn't." He held eye contact with her. "There wasn't even a hint of a thought." He nodded as he unfolded and dropped his arms. "There may be hope for me."

Jeannette set down their now-snoozing child and went to lay next to him. She settled into his arms for a hug. "Hope for *us*."

Aram chuckled as he nodded. "Yes."

"I know how important this is. And I have a good idea of some angles to get you in contact with the anti-Robert faction. It will be as soon as I can get it done—the right way."

Aram nodded. "Okay. But expect me to be annoying."

Jeannette nodded with a knowing smirk. "Don't worry, I do."

They kissed.

Late January, 1260
Aleppo, Northern Syria
Afternoon

"Still no response to the demand for surrender," Ketbugha said.

He and Hulegu looked out at the citadel defending the ancient city of Aleppo. Much of the stone structures surrounding the fortress were in various states of disrepair, but the citadel sat defiantly on a hill, dominating the surrounding area. Thick unyielding brown walls, though battered and chipped, still served their protective purpose.

"The old man gave us his response days ago," Hulegu said. "The response was defiance."

Ketbugha shook his head. "Pointless."

Hulegu's lips tensed. "Taking the citadel will not be easy. They can hold on there for days, maybe weeks."

"They cannot resupply," Ketbugha said. "Starvation will defeat them eventually."

Hulegu nodded. "Keep up the attacks."

"Of course."

Hulegu could see his breath, but the thick, crisp January air barely affected him—the winter steppes were much colder than this. He clenched his teeth. Anything flammable had been burned. Any structure easily destroyed had been disintegrated. Bodies lay in clumps that dotted the landscape. Smoke from fires lifted up in strands and columns, joining to create a haze over the general vicinity. "The rest of the city has been dealt with. Word will spread."

Ketbugha smiled. "We will encourage the word to spread."

An officer ran up to them. He bowed and, trying to catch his breath, said, "General. Il-Khan. Riders. From the East."

Hulegu nodded.

"Thank you," Ketbugha said.

"Another message," Hulegu said. "Let's greet them."

Ketbugha nodded. He was aware of Hulegu's concern, and had been working as hard as possible to learn all he could about the lands south of Aleppo in case they became his responsibility.

"This must be confirmation of the *kuriltai*, and that Kublai is the new great khan," Hulegu said.

"Yes," Ketbugha acknowledged.

Hulegu and Ketbugha led their trotting horses toward the entry route to Aleppo. Two riders approached.

The messengers dismounted and one handed the message up to Hulegu.

Hulegu studied the document. "He must have had to do it that way," Hulegu commented. "But it is not the right way."

Ketbugha waited for an explanation.

"They held the *kuriltai* out near the land of the Sung," Hulegu said. "They confirmed Kublai as the next great khan."

"That is irregular," Ketbugha commented. "But the result is correct. So if it is not contested…."

The second messenger handed another document to Hulegu and bowed. "From your representative. My instructions were to hand this to you after the first message is delivered."

Ketbugha raised his eyebrows.

Hulegu opened this paper and studied it. "Arigh-boke is contesting the *kuriltai* process. He maintains that the *kuriltai* naming Kublai the great khan is invalid. He has asked for a *kuriltai* in the homeland, preferably at Qaraqorum." Hulegu crumpled the paper slightly. "Arigh-boke." He looked down. "He has more connections close to the homeland than Kublai."

Ketbugha knew what was coming. But any sentiments had to be expressed by Hulegu. Ketbugha would not get near this issue.

"He is my brother."

Ketbugha kept his body language frozen and concentrated on maintaining a blank stare.

"But Kublai…." Hulegu stopped himself. Ketbugha sensed he was searching for the right words. "He is Kublai's junior. He is not the best choice." Hulegu's expression became stern. "He was prone to interfere with the Chagatai territories. I think he would be prone to interfere in mine." His eyes turned toward Ketbugha.

Ketbugha remained frozen, but suspected his expression could be broadcasting unease, maybe even some trepidation.

Hulegu nodded. "General, I understand and respect your silence. I have put you in a difficult position."

Ketbugha had to stifle a laugh. Difficult position? This was an impossible position. He either had to agree with Hulegu, agree with negative statements regarding a man who could become the great khan, or to disagree, which was never a good idea.

"General. Friend. I understand your silence if you do not agree with my sentiments. But if you do agree with me, you might as well say so. If Arigh-boke does become great khan, he will assume your loyalty is with me."

Ketbugha had to give the man credit. He made an astute point. "Arigh-boke would not be as good a great khan for you as Kublai would be."

Hulegu smiled. "Exactly. Which is why I need to pull the main elements of my army back up to our base near Tabriz. I need to be ready to move to the homeland if…." Hulegu again stopped, as if choosing his words. "If the succession issues become warped by faulty thinking."

"I am prepared to carry on here," Ketbugha said.

"I know you are. I will leave you a force of … ten thousand to twenty thousand men. You and I will meet with officers and establish the details. Secure Syria. Take what is available. Guard the conquests. Garrison the country. Secure these territories for my return. I will be back to complete this task when the succession is secure."

"It will be my honor to carry out this order."

Hulegu's lips tightened into what appeared to be a smile of satisfaction.

"What of Aleppo?" Ketbugha asked.

"Risk no more losses. Let starvation complete our victory here."

"And no mercy, to the garrison or the governor here?"

Hulegu looked off, apparently consumed in thought. "Hmm." His face tensed into a serious expression. "We have destroyed the entire city. We have reduced the population. The effects of this destruction are achieved. I think we will decide to honor a noble enemy, tough fighters to the end, admirable warriors. And this old governor here, the son of their Saladin, the great legendary leader of their dynasty … we will honor his position. Disarm them, and free them, and announce our respect for fellow warriors."

Ketbugha's eyes widened. He was unable to disguise his reaction to this idea.

Hulegu laughed. "Don't trouble yourself. This will not be a new policy."

Ketbugha still was not sure what to say. It certainly seemed like a new policy to him.

"My grandfather used violence against the soft city people, not out of anger, or an innate viciousness. He used it to facilitate his conquests. He used utter destruction as a tactic, to spread fear like a storm over his potential enemies. Fear is the greatest motivator because death is the ultimate consequence. But here, we have accomplished all fear will do for us. Aleppo is destroyed—the population slaughtered and enslaved. But we are about to pull the bulk of our forces out of the area. We will not distribute this news, but word will circulate. If we slaughter the garrison, and this old son of Saladin, we will only add a little fear; but we may add a great deal of determination for our enemy to strike back at us. Even now, we are receiving contacts from Syrian princes, falling over themselves to submit to us right away, with all haste. With a reduced force, I would much prefer to take territories through surrender than by risking that reduced force. By sparing this old son of Saladin, a senior member of the Ayyubid line who holds so much sway in this area still, we will collect those surrenders."

Ketbugha flashed a broad smile. "I understand. I will honor those noble warriors. Should we contact them for terms?"

"No," Hulegu barked, his face suddenly tensed with annoyance. "They must still be defeated. They must sense their slaughter is imminent, and that we spared them on the verge of death. Otherwise, our enemies may get the idea we negotiated instead of triumphed, and the fear we have established will wane."

"Yes, il-Khan. Of course."

Hulegu nodded. "Let's call the officers together. We have much to do."

Late January
Barza, Outskirts of Damascus
Afternoon

Baybars glared at al-Nasir Yusuf. "The citadel fights on against all odds. Saladin's own son, an *old man*, still defies the Mongols. Another prince still holds the pass into Syria for over a year! And we sit."

Al-Nasir Yusuf swallowed. His eyes darted as if he was a deer surrounded by hunters.

The men were part of a hastily convened conference in al-Nasir Yusuf's tent. His tent was smaller than the sultan of Syria's usual camp tent. Only a few of the decorations, the banners and frills, were on display. There were fewer cushions, fewer pieces of furniture, fewer objects of comfort than normally found in al-Nasir Yusuf's tent.

Baybars stood with a group of his inner circle. They were dressed in light armor, close to battle-readiness. "Give the order, Sultan," he said with a tone of authority. "Give the order and we will strike these evil creatures *now*. We will serve notice that our—"

"Your bravery is admirable; your willingness to engage our enemies is such a treasure." Baybars spun to face the source of these words. It was Zayn al-Din al-Hafizi, meticulously dressed in a light colored orange robe with a white turban. Baybars noted again what had always seemed to him to be a clean, nearly unmasculine look. Today, that look by itself irritated him. In addition, Zayn al-Din al-Hafizi's face exuded a patronizing grin. His expression was that of a father praising a small child. Baybars wondered if a fatherly pat on the head would be next.

Baybars sneered. "Sultan, I'm talking to you," he said as he turned back to al-Nasir Yusuf. "We can finally get into this fight. We can help that old man up in Aleppo. Four thousand. I know which units will be best for the job. We attack the fords of the Euphrates, up at al-Balis. This blow would—"

"Four thousand of our men against the whole Mongol army?" Zayn al-Din al-Hafizi shook his head as he smiled. "Your ambition is—"

"I am not talking to *you*," Baybars told Zayn al-Din al-Hafizi. "I am talking to the sultan."

"The fords of the Euphrates?" al-Nasir Yusuf finally asked. "Such a gesture could serve to provoke them without achieving any real gain."

"Gesture?" Baybars clenched his teeth and tried to contain his irritation, growing to anger. "I am not talking about a *gesture*. I am talking about getting into this fight! Of providing our support to those *already* in the fight!"

Zayn al-Din al-Hafizi told the sultan, "You need to concern yourself with feasible measures, with practicalities, not gestures."

Baybars' eyes narrowed.

"This sort of rancor from subordinates." Zayn al-Din al-Hafizi shrugged. "Wild proposals of battles behind the lines, up in areas already lost." He shook his head. "We have other matters to—"

"I'm not talking about a *battle*," Baybars insisted. "Four thousand horsemen would not engage in a battle. This would be a *raid*."

"Raid or battle, whatever you call it; it is a ridiculous idea," Zayn al-Din al-Hafizi said. "You waste the sultan's time with such silliness."

"It is a confirmation of your ignorance that you use the terms 'battle' and 'raid' interchangeably," Baybars said. He turned back to al-Nasir Yusuf. "This fool of yours is not a fighting man. His skills, if he has any, involve talking. Words against swords. Words against arrows. Words against siege engines. In this fight, the only words that will end the battle would be 'I surrender.' That is where his counsel is taking you. He deals in 'gestures.' He deals in speeches and points in a debate. He does not deal in eyeball-to-eyeball, sword-to-sword confrontation. He does not deal in *victory*."

"But even a raid, so far north…." The sultan sounded weak, as if he was whining.

"We strike at the fords, destroy their positions there, and return. The Mongol army runs on tiny ponies. They graze those ponies on the grasses of cooler, wetter areas. As they move deeper into Syria, into our home battlefield, they will find grazing difficult if not impossible. They will need supplies for this massive army, this rolling mass of humanity they are bringing against us. By striking the fords, we interrupt those supplies. It will not be a decisive blow, but it will weaken them, and assist our brave allies already engaged."

"Not a decisive blow?" Al-Nasir Yusuf sounded like a child deprived of a treat.

"That is an understatement!" Zayn al-Din al-Hafizi scoffed. "It is like poking a lion, a lion we do not need to anger at this time. Sultan, this long meeting is a waste of—"

"You will be the ruin of Islam," Baybars said to Zayn al-Din al-Hafizi.

"I take offense to—"

"You scheme to feed our sultan's fear with your counsel of indecision until his only option is accommodation. Accommodation is surrender. And surrender of these last positions of power held by the Faithful will be the ruin of Islam."

"I demand this man be punished!" Zayn al-Din al-Hafizi said to the sultan. "I will not tolerate these insults from a slave!"

Baybars sprung at the man, slamming his right fist into the man's ribs before any defense could be offered. Zayn al-Din al-Hafizi toppled to the ground. Baybars pounced on top of him, sitting on the man's abdomen. Baybars slapped Zayn al-Din al-Hafizi, once, then again, before the other man could get his hands up to defend his face.

"Get him off me!" Zayn al-Din al-Hafizi demanded.

Baybars punched him in the mouth.

The man's eyes rolled up. He uttered a short scream of pain.

Baybars slapped him again. "What 'gesture' should you use now? You sniveling little coward, you destroyer of the True Faith!"

Al-Nasir Yusuf's guards moved toward the altercation, but Baybars' own men pulled him off. Baybars did not resist their intervention.

Al-Nasir Yusuf looked at the scene in horror. His eyes followed Baybars as his men pulled him up.

Zayn al-Din al-Hafizi lay dazed on the ground. "Flog him," he said weakly. Servants brought water to the man and placed a pillow under his head. "I want him flogged. Flog the *slave*."

Baybars opened his arms. "Make a 'gesture.' Fire off some words. See if it gets you what you want."

Zayn al-Din al-Hafizi coughed and grimaced as he took some water.

"I await your orders," Baybars said to the sultan through steely eyes. "My men can move before the end of the day."

Al-Nasir Yusuf shook his head. "I will not commit forces to a meaningless attack miles away. I will not reduce our strength, our forces that we will need to protect us here, for such an adventure."

Baybars sneered and replied with a disgusted wave of his hand.

"Sultan, you must punish this man." Zayn al-Din al-Hafizi appeared to be in a great deal of pain, but with some effort he was able to get his words out.

Al-Nasir Yusuf looked at Baybars. His eyes widened, not from anger, but from fear. The sultan froze with indecisiveness.

Baybars motioned toward the tent's exit with a bob of his head. He figured he and his men should leave before al-Nasir Yusuf started to take the idea of punishment seriously.

"Correct me if I'm wrong," Baybars said to his men as they walked toward the Bahriyya camp, "but you could have pulled me off Zayn al-Din al-Hafizi more quickly." He smiled.

Sheepish grins were the reply.

"It would not have been God's will to interrupt the lesson you were so magnanimously providing for the venerable but misguided adviser to our sultan," said Sunqur al-Ashqar.

Baybars laughed. "Well said."

"Commander, what now?" Qalawun asked.

Baybars' smile disappeared. "We need to play this both ways."

The men waited for Baybars to continue.

"We must be ready to move whatever the outcome. We will prepare the camp for quick evacuation, though we must keep these preparations disguised from the sultan. We are now committed to treachery—no other interpretation exists."

"But if the outcome is unfavorable—"

"This is why we must be ready to move quickly," Baybars answered to Sunqur al-Ashqar. "In the event that our desired outcome does not occur before our treachery is discovered. Unfortunately, we are forced to rely on others. We do not control how this will turn out."

The men nodded.

Baybars shook his head. "We are drawn toward an unimaginable circumstance. This can only be the will of God. For months, this path seems more and more defined, determined, destined."

His men responded with knowing looks, with looks of understanding.

"My dear friends, companions in the defense of the True Faith, brothers in the last great hope of the True Faith—a question burns at me as I'm sure it also burns at you. Could it be God's will that we align with one devil in order to defeat a worse one?"

The men again silently offered expressions of understanding and approval, with nods and looks of recognition.

22

Late January, 1260
Acre
Late Morning

"No one ever came!" Aram said angrily just after he entered the quarters he shared with his wife and son.

Jeannette looked up from giving their son a bath.

"I waited the whole damn morning out there!" Aram slammed down a dented tin cup. A handful of coins rattled and two jumped out, landing on the floor. "I get up before dawn to make sure Robert's people aren't watching me. I dress in these *rags*." Robert motioned disgustedly at the torn, filthy, partially disintegrated clothes he had been wearing. "I wait, looking pathetic for hours. And no one showed!"

Jeannette released a quick sigh. "I told you, Sarah said they might not come."

"Then what is the point?"

"I'm not sure."

Aram grunted. "Neither am I. Just how reliable is this Sarah?"

"I don't think she got it wrong."

"Then what? They are toying with me?"

Jeannette shook her head and shrugged.

"I had hoped maybe they were checking my credentials out first," Robert said.

"That could be," Jeannette agreed. "Sarah said they're very suspicious."

"So why didn't they make contact?" Aram shook his head. "It still doesn't make sense." He began to take off the dirty clothes. "Doesn't Randolph ever … take responsibility for *some* hygiene?"

Jeannette chuckled. "Europeans don't bathe much. I think they set a day, once a season."

Aram kicked at the pile of clothing. "*Pff.* Maybe once a year."

"That's why I borrowed his clothes for you. They had the advantage of seeming dirty even after being cleaned."

"I am way too familiar with the odor of Randolph now, as it is permanently embedded in these rags." Aram dressed in his own attire.

"I'll get them washed."

"Believe me, anything I added this morning would have been an improvement."

Jeannette stooped to pick up the garments with one hand as she held their child upright in the washbasin.

"I'm not sure Sarah is the right connection," Aram said.

"Maybe not. It was worth a try." She made a neat pile from the dirty clothing.

Aram smiled. "I know you did what you could."

Jeannette smiled back. She lifted their son from the washbasin and toweled him off.

"I'll have to try to develop some contacts of my own. Maybe some people who I think—"

Aram's words were cut short by loud pounding on the door. "Aram! You are summoned for extra kitchen chores! Come immediately!"

Aram grimaced irritably. "What?"

Jeannette shrugged, but her eyes widened with apprehension.

"Extra chores?" Aram's mouth scrunched as he pondered this unusual request.

Another sequence of pounding struck the door. "Extra chores! Now!"

Aram shrugged. "Extra chores," he said to Jeannette. He opened the door and three guards greeted him. They did not appear to be armed, though Aram suspected they could have daggers nearby.

"Gentlemen." He greeted them with a smirk. "Um, I never try to shirk chores. No need for the, the escort."

One of the guards looked at another for guidance. "We're helping the kitchen," said the second one.

"Ah," Aram said, "so you'll be doing some chores with me?"

The man scowled. "No, we're only to bring you there."

Aram looked at Jeannette and shrugged. She looked back, clearly uncomfortable with these developments.

"Well, I'll be back ... after my chores...." Aram followed the guards.

"In case anyone cares, I think this platter is already clean!" Aram called. A white smock over his clothes, he stood alone next to a stack of plates, platters and trays. They all looked clean to him. A vat of water with some scented oil and a touch of lye soap sat on a table. "Like the rest of it!"

A man entered the kitchen and came over to Aram. He too wore a white kitchen smock, but was wearing it over what looked like a guard's uniform. "We need lifting, flour bags, pantry," the man barked in a German accent.

"Mm-hmm." Aram puffed air in his cheeks and tightened his lips. "In the pantry."

"Pantry."

Aram threw the rag he had been using into the water. "Bags to lift."

"With me," the German continued in his stilted speaking pattern. "In the pantry."

Aram followed. Something was not right about the whole situation, but he saw no basis for refusing to participate.

The pantry was a hall-like storage area filled with boxes and sacks of supplies.

"That stack. Move over to there." The man pointed at eight bags of flour then moved his finger ten feet to the left.

"We're moving that stack," Aram said.

"Yes."

"For no apparent reason."

"To make organized."

Aram looked at the stack's current location, then at the new location, and could divine no logic of organization that would warrant the move. But he shrugged and grabbed the first sack of flour. He took it over and plopped it down where the new stack would begin.

As Aram straightened up, something pinned his arms at the elbows. He turned his head and recognized it was one of the guards who had escorted him to the kitchen.

The man with the white smock demanded, in his thick German accent, "Where you early morning?"

"What?" Aram squirmed. "Let go of me."

"I asked where you go in this early morning," the man in the smock said.

"Answer!" said another guard Aram recognized. The man entered the pantry and moved around to face Aram. He slapped Aram. "Answer."

"What the hell!" Aram sneered at the man. "Don't you hit me! Someone wants to know something—ask nice!"

The two men in front of Aram glared at him and waited.

Aram's mind raced. Robert, or one of Robert's people, must have seen him go out that morning. What should he tell these men? What should he admit?

"You will explain your strange doing this morning," said the man in the smock. The man next to him pulled a knife and dangled it close to Aram's face.

Something was wrong about this. Only the man in the smock spoke, except for a single word out of the second man. Their German accents were extreme, almost caricaturish. Aram had been careful to avoid being seen all morning, and he had not seen any of Robert's men. He believed he was familiar with all of Robert's men, and he did not recognize these three men at all. Something about this whole scenario was not right.

"You are listening to me?" The questioner's face contorted with rage. "What were you doing this morning?"

"I don't want to say," Aram said. "I—" He paused "It's private."

The man brought his knife up to Aram's eye. "No private. You say now."

"I won't do Robert much good as a blind adviser."

The two men before Aram looked at each other. The interrogator bobbed his head toward Aram's hand.

The man with the knife grabbed Aram's left hand and put the blade against his pinky finger. Aram struggled against the man pinning his arms.

"You will serve Robert no trouble with four fingers."

Aram felt the blade of the knife pressing against his finger.

"All right. Leave my fingers alone."

The man with the knife pulled it back.

"It's hard to say, to admit." Aram cleared his throat as if to gather himself. "But Robert, with all due respect—Robert gave all my money to an irresponsible business partner. My family needs money. I was out begging for a few coins." Aram paused. He feigned shame. "I didn't want anyone to know." He looked at the man, summoning his most pitiful pathetic look. "Can you keep this between us?"

The interrogator's eyes bored in on Aram. His teeth appeared to clench. "You lie."

"You think I would lie about this? This disgrace of—"

The knife wielder brought the blade under Aram's chin.

"All right, all right," said a jovial sounding voice from behind a stack of boxes. A man emerged, wearing the black frock of a priest. "That's enough."

Aram recognized him. The man had sat at the far left of the table when Aram first interviewed for his position with Robert.

"You can go," the priest said to the guards.

The one holding Aram released him and the three guards left the kitchen.

"Did you actually collect some coins? They tell me you don't make a very convincing beggar."

"About as convincing as your fellow's German accent."

The priest smiled. "Fair enough." He looked around, as if inspecting the kitchen stores. Airily he said, "I understand you are dissatisfied with Robert."

"Dissatisfied?" Aram frowned in thought. "Wrong word. I am … uneasy about what I am signed on to do in his service."

"All right. Better way to say it."

Aram nodded.

"A number of us are also concerned about Robert. But he has credentials from the pope."

"Legitimate credentials?"

The priest shrugged. "From what we can tell. We have reviewed them closely. They look exactly, and I mean *exactly*, like every credential we have seen from the pope. And previous popes as well."

"What disturbs you about him?"

"His actions do not appear consistent with the mission stated."

Aram stood silently.

"He seems to be waiting for something. And he isn't explaining to us what it is. We thought he was possibly an agent of one of the Italian factions. But he seems utterly unengaged with any of them, even bored with their conflict."

"I have had the same feeling; that he's waiting for something. And I am not interested in an endless commitment here."

"Why not leave?"

Aram frowned. "He is holding me here. Holding my money, holding my friend hostage."

The priest's expression was dubious.

Aram added, "I would like to know more of what this man is about so I can complete my service to him and move on."

The priest nodded. "I see." He paused. "Those of us who feel as I do would like to see this man complete his business, whatever it is, and leave."

"But you seem to know little more than I do."

The priest raised his eyebrows. "I know he's a German."

"I figured that as well."

The priest seemed to think that fact somehow explained things.

"Are you suspicious of him just because he *is* German?" Aram asked.

"Of course."

Aram's eyes narrowed, inviting an explanation.

"This is not just a rote prejudice against a different nationality," the priest said. "A German is an unlikely special representative of the pope."

"Sir, I know almost nothing of European politics."

"Well, this pope has been trying to end the Hohenstaufen dynasty in Germany. They have been a terrible blight on Christianity for most of this century. Most are under excommunication.   But the Germans continue their encroachments into Italy, and their attempts to seize control of territory, and of Christianity itself. So it seems strange the pope would grant power to this man."

"I see." Aram thought a moment. "But what power does he actually have?"

"He has a seat at the table here, simply by virtue of his credentials from the pope. This gives him influence. This is a divided place; many factions compete for control. Old family rivalries, Venetians against Genoans … it goes on. We don't need this German here."

Aram rubbed his cheek. This was still not helpful.

"We have sent agents back to Europe to investigate this man. To check at Montpelier, to check with the pope's inner circle. Not a one has returned."

"How long have they been gone?"

"Five agents have been gone six months or more. Two more men left three months ago."

"So it seems some information is being concealed."

"Yes."

Aram nodded. "We have a common cause. The *end* of Robert's mission."

The priest grinned. "Yes."

Aram eyed the man. "And just who are *you?*"

The priest's head snapped back, apparently in response to the bluntness of the question. "Fair question. *Sixth* generation Outremer. A minor position, really, but one that has given me years of experience working with the various factions and power centers. I know everyone. They come and go, my family stays on, just trying to hold on to the shrinking Western Christian position here. A pragmatist, my dear young man. A problem solver."

Aram grinned. "Someone I can work with?"

The priest nodded.

"Those other priests I keep seeing at every meeting … who are they?"

The priest shrugged. "Two are Robert's men. The fifth one? The one with one arm? Charles the Slayer, from Tripoli. He was with Louis of France at Damietta in Egypt. Terrible defeat. That is where he lost his arm. Nearly died from the infection and fever. He prayed for God to spare him, and when he came through the fever, he joined the priesthood. But he has never let go of a fanatic, sometimes impractical hatred of all Muslims. His extreme attitude…." The priest paused in apparent thought. "It makes him difficult to deal with at times."

Aram nodded. "We will share information. I'll pass the word through Sarah if we need to talk. You can summon me through—"

"Sarah is not my preferred line of communication," the priest said. "Come to the kitchen. Ask them for Brother Adolfo."

Aram nodded, then smiled. "No more begging."

"I am sorry about that. You could have been part of a trap."

Aram nodded again.

Late January, 1260
Barza, Just Outside Damascus
Night

"It should be finished." Baybars' eyes darted off toward the road to Damascus. He stood around a smoldering fire with Qalawun, Sunqur al-Ashqar, and other close advisers and confidants. Baybars blew into his hands to keep them warm.

The men were fully dressed for battle in light armor, and swords at their sides. Helmets remained off, but were close by. "We should have received word hours ago," he added.

"Why do you think it is taking so long?" Qalawun asked.

Baybars shrugged. "Impossible to say. But none of the possible answers are good for our purposes."

Another of the men commented, "I wish we'd been the ones to handle it."

Baybars' lips tightened. He did not disagree with the man's sentiment, but sought to avoid any discussion about a decision already made, a discussion that would have no relevance to their current situation. "It couldn't be us," Baybars said tersely. "We've talked about that."

"It's just that, to rely on these Ayyubid princes to—"

"That is what we have to work with," Baybars said.

Momentarily, a squad of riders approached.

Baybars grunted irritably.

"They could be coming to inform us," Sunqur al-Ashqar said.

"Look who's riding with them!" Baybars pointed. A man with a rough resemblance to al-Nasir Yusuf rode in the midst of the squad, flanked by armed men on either side.

"That's him, isn't it?" Qalawun asked. "The sultan's brother."

Baybars nodded. "If they'd been successful, they wouldn't be riding back here."

"Commander," Sunqur al-Ashqar asked. "Treachery?"

Baybars squinted and examined the approaching squad more closely. "No…. They wouldn't come straight at us. They wouldn't come in numbers that would make it a fair fight." Baybars paused as the squad approached. "Stay ready, anyway."

The squad arrived, al-Zahir Ghazi surrounded by his protectors. He was younger and thinner than his older brother, al-Nasir Yusuf, although his nose was slightly larger. His helmet fit awkwardly on his head, as if he did not wear it frequently.

Al-Zahir Ghazi shook his head and addressed Baybars. "He got away. He did go out to the garden house, the way he always does."

Baybars sneered. A camp on combat footing was much too austere for the comfort-loving sultan, and nearby Damascus was too close for the sultan to resist. This routine had made him vulnerable.

"We thought we had him cornered," al-Zahir Ghazi continued. "But he climbed over a wall and escaped us into the city."

Baybars grinded his teeth. "You didn't surround the garden house?"

Al-Zahir Ghazi looked confused, uncertain how to answer.

"No matter," Baybars said. "The move failed."

"We are on our way to Gaza," al-Zahir Ghazi said.

Baybars gave a curt nod, acknowledging the information. He turned to his own men. "As we've discussed, al-Nasir Yusuf will assume we were involved. Service with al-Nasir Yusuf will no longer be an option for us."

"Meet us in Gaza," al-Zahir Ghazi said. He appeared to be asking a question as much as giving an order.

Baybars almost grinned at the man's lack of commanding presence. He nodded.

Al-Zahir Ghazi's squad withdrew and continued its journey away from Damascus.

"The Nasiriyya Mamluks will come with us," Baybars said. "I think they will also be ready to move. We need to pass the word to them."

"I'll take care of it," said Sunqur al-Ashqar.

Baybars nodded and Sunqur al-Ashqar headed for his horse.

Baybars turned back toward Damascus. No one was coming yet. He doubted al-Nasir Yusuf would have the resolve or the resources to act quickly. But Baybars and his men would need to leave that evening in case someone in al-Nasir Yusuf's service took charge. He faced Qalawun. "We all know where this is going," Baybars said soberly. "There really is only one answer. God wills it; this is more obvious with each passing moment. But we still need a few steps in order to get there."

Qalawun and the rest of the men responded with nods and looks of grim recognition.

23

January 31, 1260
Damascus
Late Afternoon

"Teacher! The rumors are true! It's happening!"

The shouting woke Dawud from a late afternoon nap. He turned toward the sound of his student's voice. A small stack of parchments rolled off his chest. Now he recalled what had bored him into dozing off. Calligraphy and commentary assignments, most of them dismally performed. The stack hit the ground and scattered. He grunted.

"At the walls! At the city walls!" The student's tone was insistent, urgent.

Dawud shook his head with a twitch. He looked at this young man who had completed an exemplary calligraphy and commentary assignment. Dawud smiled. "What's so compelling that it could prompt you to disturb an old man's afternoon nap?"

"The sultan's leaving Damascus!"

Dawud closed his eyes, rubbed them, then opened them again. "Al-Nasir Yusuf...."

"Yes. The sultan of Syria. Leaving us behind. Leaving the greatest city of Syria behind."

Dawud stood. "At the city walls?"

"You can watch his whole household, loaded up with everything they can carry."

Dawud nodded. He looked around his modest living quarters as he headed toward the entrance. He wondered if he should also grab whatever he could carry and follow the sultan's example. But for now, he would join his student. The walk would give him time to gather his thoughts.

Teacher and student moved briskly through the city. They were not the only ones heading in that direction. Dawud saw others, some with satchels and carts full of belongings, some without, also walking toward the southern walls of the city.

"Aleppo has fallen. The citadel is finally taken," the student said.

"I heard most of the city had already been plundered."

"But the citadel had still resisted. Resistance is over. The Mongols will come here next."

Dawud nodded. "Hmmm." He looked around some more. "Looks like a lot of people have had the same idea: to get out of here."

The student looked around. "Even some Christians."

"Hmmm." Dawud noticed a few beardless men leading their families, carrying belongings, even little children carrying at least a small quantity of light possessions.

"I thought Mongols favored Christians?" the student inquired.

Dawud squinted. "I suppose."

"Why would they flee?"

"How would I know?"

The student did not respond to the rhetorical question.

"I will hazard this guess," Dawud said. "When those Mongols start moving through a conquered city, they may not be very good at telling a Christian from a Muslim, or a church from a mosque, especially when Christian plunder is not distinguishable from the plunder of all the other peoples they have slaughtered. It is not far across to Tyre, along the coast, where the Mongols are not likely to go. This could be a very smart move for them."

The student nodded. "Yes. I can see that."

They continued toward the south walls of the city. Dawud raised his eyebrows. "Where is your family?" he asked.

"In our quarters. Preparing the evening meal. Getting ready for prayers."

"Why are you with me?"

The student's face showed a puzzled expression. "To tell you of this. To gain your insights and advice."

Dawud nodded. They had arrived at the south walls. Some stairs led the way to observation points up top.

Dawud grimaced.

His student noticed and said, "I should have thought of how the climb might be—"

"These old legs will carry me up there," Dawud stated firmly. He grinned. "As long as I don't have to carry you."

The student laughed. "I'll be fine."

"Good. Let's go."

They joined others who were also making the climb to the observation areas along the edges of the walls, overlooking the road leading away from Damascus. Some were heading the opposite way back down the stairs. Dawud's knees creaked a little with the protest of old age, but he was pleased at how little the climb taxed him. All this travel over the last year had improved his physical conditioning.

They arrived at a ledge lined with fellow citizens of Damascus. All watched the exit from the city to the road leading south.

"It's the sultan's baggage train," the student observed.

"Yes. Unmistakable. Escorted by his personal guards, no doubt as glad to leave this place as he is."

"He's a coward!" yelled a middle-aged man with a puckered expression, somewhat in response to Dawud's comments, but loud enough to be heard by everyone in the immediate vicinity.

Dawud looked around to see the reactions of his fellow observers.

"Coward!" another man yelled.

Yet another man took a worn sandal and waved it at the procession. "Run! Run away, you great leader of the Faithful!"

Dawud smiled. "Not a happy group of loyal subjects," he said quietly to his student.

"No."

Dawud looked out at the procession leaving the city. A few more guards came out, forming a squad.

"Is that him?" Dawud heard a woman ask.

"That's him!" a man's voice called out.

A din of taunts swelled from the crowd of observers. Dawud could hear angrier offerings with the rising tide of sound: "Coward!" "Loves only himself!" "Abandoner of the Faithful." "Unworthy of Islam." Some simply shrilled derisive syllables. The man with the old sandal threw it down at al-Nasir Yusuf. The shoe hit the back of a horse, not even causing it to flinch. More sandals and shoes flew from the walls.

Al-Nasir Yusuf, in a turban and a bright shirt, rode his trotting horse with his head fixed rigidly forward. If he heard the crowd, and the derision directed his way, he offered no reaction, not a twitch, not even a turn to look at his people expressing their sentiments.

Dawud wasn't sure what the man should have done. Maybe it was prudent to flee. But this seemed like a panicked departure. Dawud was certain—this was not the way a sultan should withdraw from one of the great cities of Islam, leaving so many of the Faithful behind.

"Let's go," Dawud said to his student. "I have had enough of this spectacle."

The student nodded.

The two headed back down the stairs, to return to Dawud's quarters. After they had covered a good bit of the distance in silence, Dawud finally asked, "What will you do?"

"I'm not sure," the student said. He looked at Dawud. "What will *you* do?"

"I hate the idea of moving again, forever in the path of these evil creatures," Dawud said. "But I think there is little choice." He shook his head. "I will pack to go." He took in a deep breath and sighed with exasperation. "Though I am not sure where I will go." He clenched his teeth. "Chased away by the Mongols. Again."

They rounded one last corner before Dawud's quarters.

"Teacher, I will speak to my family. I'm sure they will agree. Join us."

Dawud looked at him. He smiled. "I appreciate the offer." He hadn't considered the idea of joining someone. A brief feeling of relief surged through him. Maybe he didn't have to face this next dilemma by himself. His nose twitched. "And where will you and your family go?"

"I don't know," the student said. "Why don't you come over the first thing tomorrow morning and we will discuss it."

Dawud grinned. "I will be over after morning prayers."

As they approached Dawud's quarters, Dawud saw two armed guards at his door, milling around as if looking for someone.

Dawud froze and looked at his student. The student looked back with a puzzled expression on his face. Dawud shrugged.

The guards spotted him and one of them approached. "Are you Dawud the scholar?" the guard asked.

"Yes."

"The honorable servant of the Faithful, al-Zayn al-Hafizi, requests your presence at the palace."

Dawud looked at his student. "I will see you tomorrow morning."

The student nodded, but appeared nervous.

❧ ◆ ☙

"We understand you have had recent contacts with Mongols," al-Zayn al-Hafizi said with the tone of assured self-confidence bordering on pompousness. His seat was a throne-like chair set on a raised dais in the front reception room of the sultan's Damascan palace. Dawud noticed some bruises on the man's face, including some purple discoloration under al-Zayn al-Hafizi's right eye. A few guards were also in the room, along with other official-looking men seated on either side of al-Zayn al-Hafizi.

"Recent contacts," Dawud repeated. "I was taken into custody in Baghdad. I escaped."

Al-Zayn al-Hafizi looked perplexed by this response. "My information is that you are a learned man with knowledge of the Mongols. Is this incorrect?"

"I am a learned man. And I do have knowledge of Mongols."

"Ah. Good. We seek your counsel."

Dawud raised his eyebrows. "I will ... help to the best of my abilities."

"Yes, well, we have an embassy out to the Mongols to effect a peaceful surrender of the city. What can you tell me, from your experiences, to aid in this process?"

"So we will submit Damascus to Mongol rule...."

"Yes. Of course. That is the obvious choice facing us."

"You do not favor our sultan's 'choice.'"

"Because it was *unnecessary*," al-Zayn al-Hafizi said with a confident grin, with the tone of a professor lecturing a room. "We will not resist, so they will not destroy us. We will simply submit to their rule. They allow all people religious freedom. If this is managed correctly, we will come out just fine."

Dawud felt a surge of anger, but kept his outward expression neutral. "You are aware of what they did to Baghdad; to the place, and the people."

"Yes, because they did not manage it *properly*." The confident grin and professorial tone continued. "You survived. You can explain how you did that, and help us all behave properly, so we will survive."

"Survival?" Dawud's lips tightened. He had no desire to discuss how he had survived in Baghdad. "Do whatever they say. Give them whatever they want. And hope they have some reason for not killing you."

Al-Zayn al-Hafizi frowned and looked off, as if considering the advice. "Well, yes, that seems indicated."

Dawud said nothing.

Al-Zayn al-Hafizi smiled. "We have word that a portion of the Mongol army has moved north. I do not believe they want a big fight here. If we do not give them one, I believe we will be fine. The Faithful will live on. Islam will survive, even thrive."

Dawud was not sure what to say. He knew he couldn't express all of the conflicting thoughts this development raised. He had previously thought coexisting with Mongols was impossible. But maybe in a peacefully surrendered Damascus, a much reduced Mongol army would allow him to continue here as a Muslim scholar. He had no enthusiasm for running again, possibly only to the next place he would have to flee. This man al-Zayn al-Hafizi seemed hopelessly naïve about Mongols, but with Dawud's guidance, maybe this could be managed.

"Is there something you wanted to say?" Al-Zayn al-Hafizi sounded impatient.

Dawud realized he had drifted into his own thoughts. "Um, no, um, I would like to be involved with you on this, to help us make the transition."

"I would be pleased to have you, your experience, in our service."

"Yes. The main thing we need to understand about Mongols is their utter ruthlessness and brutality. If there is one aspect of the Mongols that can be easily—"

"Brutal and ruthless," al-Zayn al-Hafizi said. "Of course. We know. We will engage on this in more detail as their direct contact approaches."

Dawud forced a grin and nodded, even bowed slightly.

Al-Zayn al-Hafizi flashed a condescending grin and nodded in dismissal.

Dawud headed back toward his quarters. Twilight fell upon the city. As he moved through the streets he saw everywhere signs of people fleeing. He wondered if he was making the same mistake again, of staying in a city about to be taken by the Mongols. But this was a peaceful taking, by a smaller force. He would chance it.

As he approached his quarters, another thought sobered him. He would stay; he would risk his survival to retain his position as a Muslim scholar in a Damascus ruled by Mongols. But his student; he still had to convince the young man and his family to leave. He would not have the life of another admiring student on his hands, one who insisted on staying because Dawud was staying.

❧ ◆ ☙

February 1260
Acre
Afternoon

"It's a very specific request."

Aram overheard these firm words from a voice he thought he recognized. He approached the open doorway to a large meeting room. He had been brought to the Court of the Chain right on the coast at the inner harbor.

A messenger nodded to Aram.

"Here?"

"Yes."

Aram walked through the doorway.

"It's a specific request for specific actions." The man's words sputtered from his mouth with an adamant tone. He was dressed in a silk shirt with a broad brown hat. He stood up from a table at which a group of about twenty men sat. Aram recognized some of them as key leaders he had met during his early service to Robert. He suspected, from the distinctive upscale clothing, that these were nobles or other key leaders from the area.

The speaker continued, "We need to address these specific requests, understand them, discuss them, and react accordingly. There is too much indulgence in generalities. Too much wallowing in the superfluous."

"Perhaps you think I am superfluous!" challenged a dark-haired, shorter man who got to his own feet.

"Gentlemen." A third man stood with his hands out, motioning as if for quiet. "Let's not personalize this."

Robert looked at Aram, a puzzled expression on his face, and tilted his head as if in question.

Aram shrugged and looked back for the messenger who had brought him to the meeting. The man had gone.

"I asked him to join us."

Aram looked toward the voice, his eyebrows raised. So Adolfo was here, too.

Robert turned to Adolfo.

"I thought you would want him here," Adolfo said. "Your adviser, your expert on the Mongols."

Robert's eyes shifted up. He glanced away, then glanced back. "Of course. Good thinking."

"Well, that's nice," said the nobleman Aram had heard speaking as he first approached. "Another opinion to deal with. Just what we need."

"An informed opinion," Adolfo said. "From a man who lived in Baghdad, who has traveled east and dealt with Mongols and their authorities. Robert retained him, and I, too, think he could be helpful."

"I don't care what he says," the first nobleman said. "These Mongols are very dangerous people. To defy them because we are not currently threatened with proximity; to dismiss them"—the nobleman swept his hand as if shooing a fly—"because we face no immediate consequences. It is the shortsighted foolhardiness of a potentially fatal mistake."

Aram scrunched his lips to one side as he processed what he was hearing. "The Mongols contacted you?"

Robert spoke out. "Yes."

"Envoys?" Aram asked.

"No," Robert said. "A letter."

Aram raised his eyebrows.

"Yes, and it seems to be the consensus of this illustrious group that we should decline their requests," the nobleman said. "Perhaps it *would* be wise to hear from you. Enlighten this august group about what happened at Baghdad."

"I wasn't there when the Mongols took the city," Aram said.

The nobleman squinted at Aram, apparently not happy with his response.

The room settled into an uneasy silence. Men squirmed in their seats and looked away from each other.

Aram looked at Robert, hoping for a cue as to what he should do.

Robert cleared his throat. "Um, I can speak to Aram later about this…." Robert paused. "This development."

"I would like to hear this man's input," Adolfo said.

Robert nodded to Aram, and all eyes turned toward him.

"What did they request?" Aram asked.

Robert looked around. "Submission. They pronounced their superiority and demanded that we tear down our castles and defenses to the city."

Aram nodded.

"I advised against it," Robert said. "Most in the room agreed."

"Not all," the first nobleman said emphatically.

"Not all," Robert repeated.

"And you are deciding … how to respond?" Aram asked.

"And what to do," added Adolfo.

Aram shrugged. "I think it's an opening request. I think there will be more definitive requests in the future."

"Yes," the first nobleman said. "So we need *negotiations*.

These Mongols are the potential end of the Muslims, and their accursed religion. They may just be the best friends we could have. Defiance is a bad way to greet a possible friend."

"We don't want to spurn friends," said a new voice. It was Charles the Slayer, the former soldier who had lost his arm in battle with Muslims forces in Egypt.

Aram looked at Robert.   Robert nodded. "One thing I've learned from Aram, here, is that Mongols do not have real friends. They have enemies and subordinates. We should not consent to these requests."

"But an outright refusal—"

The first nobleman was interrupted by the shorter, darker nobleman. He directed his statement to Aram. "Shouldn't it be of some importance that there is information indicating a good portion of the Mongol army has withdrawn north? And that the rest appears to be moving south, past us, towards Egypt?" The man looked around the room at the entire gathering. "Gentlemen, we do not have to respond with a defiant refusal. We should offer pleasantries that say nothing, then strengthen our defenses, not lower them. They may decide we are not worth the trouble as they make their way down to Egypt to dispose of the Muslims."

Aram looked at Robert.

"Strengthen the castles." Robert wore a confident expression. "Do not defy but do not submit." He nodded. "I'm sure the pope would agree."

The first nobleman sat down. "As long as negotiations are not ruled out for the future."

Aram rolled his eyes at Robert.

Robert admonished him to silence with a small, subtle shake of his head.

Aram scowled thoughtfully, breaking into a small grin which he quickly decided to change into a neutral expression.

"The future can be spoken about in the future," the second nobleman said.

"Then it is decided," said another member of the gathering. He looked at Robert. "Perhaps your man here, your Mongol expert, can help us with the precise response."

Aram's eyes widened with apprehension. This was not a job he wanted.

Robert shrugged. "Of course." He nodded to Aram.

"However I can be of service," Aram acknowledged with a bow and a forced grin.

❧ ◆ ☙

"I was a little surprised," Aram said to Robert as they walked toward Aram's quarters. "Given your mission, I didn't expect you to opt for the more defiant response."

Robert shook his head. "It's not really defiance. Not direct anyway. There is still room for negotiations. You be ready. We may be on our way to meet the Mongols soon."

"Sure. And what will we tell them about the castles?"

"Whatever we need to tell them," Robert said. His eyes darted away from Aram's.

Aram looked ahead as they walked. "So it wasn't your idea to have me at that meeting?"

"No."

Aram frowned. Robert was measuring his words, with clipped responses and long pauses.

"I didn't think you were needed," Robert finally said. "I think Adolfo brought you in to irritate me. He seems suspicious and antagonistic lately."

"Why would my presence at the meeting be irritating to you?"

"I didn't say it would be."

"Well, why did Adolfo think it would be?"

"You would have to ask him."

"Maybe I should."

Robert turned and glared at Aram, then looked ahead.

Aram decided not to pursue this subject further. Robert was not going to offer any real answers, and pushing him would not help Aram's purposes.

"Did they formulate a good response?" Robert finally asked.

Aram shrugged. "I believe so. It serves the purpose: respectful while completely lacking substance."

Robert smiled. "Good." He stopped and looked ahead. "You know your way back to your quarters. I will contact you when we are ready to move out." He turned and left.

Aram stopped. He wondered if they would ever really follow through on a genuine mission to talk to the Mongols as representatives of the pope.

24

Mid February
Road Between Syria and Egypt
Night

"My mind is made up." Baybars, his arms folded over his chest, was speaking to Qalawun and Sunqur al-Ashqar as the three stood by a flickering camp fire. The Bahriyya tents occupied their own space, but not far from the Nasiriyya Mamluks. Baybars looked around, almost instinctively, to make sure they were alone. "The young man I am sending is well-trained, well-briefed—one of our best. I am not risking either one of you on this."

Qalawun shook his head. "Commander, we both know I am the one who needs to lead this squad."

Baybars took in a deep breath. He did not like to be contradicted. He rarely tolerated it. But Qalawun was different. He seldom expressed disagreement, and when he did, he couched that disagreement with respect. And he was usually right.

"I am prepared to join them," Qalawun continued. "I can leave with them tonight."

Sunqur al-Ashqar shook his head. "With respect to both of you, I am the one to go. This mission presents an extreme of negotiation and diplomacy. We all know I have demonstrated my skills in this area repeatedly."

Baybars stared past the campfire and out across the desert at the route his squad would take. "This will be dangerous. For either of you. You are both known to everyone."

Qalawun shrugged. "The squad will be clear of this camp before anyone notices," he said. "There is no real danger from anyone here."

Baybars said nothing.

"As for Qutuz, it is good he knows me."

"He may have you killed on sight," Baybars said.

"Commander, you have laid the foundations for this contact," Sunqur al-Ashqar said.

"We both know what our *optimum* circumstances would be," Baybars said. "We would ride against Qutuz at the head of an army gathered by a courageous Ayyubid prince, a leader understanding the need to resist the Mongols. A prince with the courage and determination to take power in Egypt and use those resources to save the True Faith."

Baybars studied Qalawun and Sunqur al-Ashqar. They seemed to be listening carefully, waiting for him to talk his way to the right decision.

"But," he said, lowering his voice as he looked around, "no such Ayyubid prince exists. We have bounced from one to another, chasing a wish, not a real person."

"Qutuz will be open to our approach," said Sunqur al-Ashqar.

"Just remember, the danger is not only from Qutuz."

"Yes, of course. We will be on an errand treacherous to the activities of this camp," Qalawun said.

Baybars shook his head. "Yes. If al-Zahir Ghazi discovers your mission, you are all dead men, and the rest of us may be fighting for our lives."

"I have helped set this up," Sunqur al-Ashqar said. "I am the one who needs to see this through."

Qalawun shook his head. "In any event, Commander, you can't send that … boy out to do this."

"Absolutely not," Sunqur al-Ashqar agreed. "It signals to Qutuz we are not serious."

"Qutuz knows of my importance to the Bahriyya mamluks," Qalawun said. "That is why it is essential for *me* to be the one."

Baybars gritted his teeth. "Stupid of us, to get tangled up in this coup. I should have known."

"Commander, you could not have foreseen just how selfish, short-sighted and treacherous these Ayyubid princes are," Qalawun assured him.

Baybars drew back as he took a deep breath. "Mongols are coming. Destroyers of Islam. We align with al-Zahir Ghazi to depose his weak, vascillating brother. Al-Zahir Ghazi asks for troops from Qutuz to help improve his position to resist the Mongols. And what does he do? Schemes to attack Qutuz on behalf of his brother, the very man we were supposed to depose! He played all of us, just to improve his position with al-Nasir Yusuf, the coward of Syria!" Baybars looked around to make sure his increased intenisty had not been detected by anyone nearby.

Qalawun's lips tightened.

Sunqur al-Ashqar nodded grimly.

Baybars' face tensed. "Yes. He has resigned himself to Mongol domination. He suspects his brother has, too. I should have seen it."

"Commander, what difference would it have made if you had?" Qalawun asked. "Even if you had anticipated this behavior—behavior so unworthy of a Muslim sultan that it would have been difficult to anticipate—even if you have anticipated this, our moves would all have been the same."

Baybars reflected a moment, then nodded. "You are right."

"I understand the mission well," Qalawun said. "I will make it a success. I will approach Qutuz with our great gift of information: the treachery of al-Zahir Ghazi. We will save Qutuz precious fighting men, men who will be needed when we battle the Mongols."

Sunqur al-Ashqar looked at Baybars. "If the mission takes a bad turn, you will need Qalawun here to assist you. Commander, I am important and experienced enough to complete the mission, and more expendable should it fail."

"Expendable?" Qalawun stated with disbelief.

"It has to be me," Sunqur al-Ashqar said to Baybars.

"That's just not—"

"Enough," Baybars said. "You've convinced me the young man I chose is not the one to lead. He will go, but not at the head of the mission."

Baybars paused.

Qalawun and Sunqur al-Ashqar waited, knowing a decision was coming.

Baybars looked at Sunqur al-Ashqar. "My friend, I am sorry." He paused, then grinned ruefully. "You are the one to go."

Sunqur al-Ashqar let a slight smile creep onto his face. "Yes sir. Thank you."

"Don't thank me. Just remember that Qutuz was responsible for the spectacle of watching our leader's head tossed down to us just before we fled into exile."

"Years ago," Sunqur al-Ashqar said.

"He is the same man."

"I will remember."

Baybars nodded grimly. "God is Great. Our fate, and the fate of Islam, will depend on your efforts."

Sunqur al-Ashqar nodded and walked away.

Baybars looked at Qalawun.

"I'll help them prepare," Qalawun said, "and explain the new situation to the man you originally assigned to this."

"Good."

"Sunqur al-Ashqar will do a good job."

Baybars smiled. "These Ayyubid princes were never serious about fighting the Mongols. Only Qutuz is. So we need him. And he needs us." Baybars let out a long breath. "I hope he understands that."

"So do I."

First Week March 1260
Damascus
Afternoon

"I was disappointed not to see some of your sultan's representatives upon our entry into the city," Ketbugha said to al-Zayn al-Hafizi. They stood just inside the entryway of what had been the sultan's main palace in Damascus. The high walls were white smooth stone except for some engraved patterns of alternating dark and light browns.

The smile on al-Zayn al-Hafizi's face seemed forced. As if he was a high-ranking dignitary greeting other high-ranking dignitaries, he was dressed in jewels and silks, and his turban was decorated with an intricate pattern. But behind the exterior trappings, the man looked uncomfortable. His eyes blinked excessively. His shoulders were hunched. His left hand fidgeted.

Ketbugha was glad he had worn full Mongol battle-dress, including his helmet. He was certain this would contribute to al-Zayn al-Hafizi's discomfort. With Ketbugha were a few other Mongol officers, including Shingkhor, the promoted security guard whose brother had been murdered by an old astrologer. A few Georgian and Armenian commanders also accompanied the visitors. "Um, no one, um, said we should be...." Al-Zayn al-Hafizi's voice trailed off. The interpreter offered the words as well as he could.

"You are the representative of al-Nasir Yusuf," Ketbugha stated sternly. "You did not see that it was your duty to offer us a respectful greeting?"

"Um, of course. That, that is what we are doing here."

"Hiding in the palace. In my palace."

Al-Zayn al-Hafizi swallowed. "Not hiding." He paused. "Here to offer the palace to you and your people."

Ketbugha squinted.

"I am very glad you and your forces are here," al-Zayn al-Hafizi quickly added. "There has been...," al-Zayn al-Hafizi stammered again. "Um, many of the Christians here...," al-Zayn al-Hafizi stopped, as if gathering his thoughts. "Some Christians have been taking liberties. They presume that your rule here will—"

"We recognize no distinctions among the faiths. All operate under the vast spiritual umbrella of the Eternal Blue Heaven."

Al-Zayn al-Hafizi's face seemed to drain of color. "I understand this, this idea. So one, um, religion, um, shouldn't be allowed to taunt and dominate another—"

"And a religion once privileged should not expect to maintain its present position over the other faiths, a position of domination and persecution they will no longer hold."

Al-Zayn al-Hafizi opened his mouth as if to speak, but then decided against it. He made a quick deferential nod, almost a slight bow.

"So tell me, then, what are these 'liberties' you are referring to?" Ketbugha asked.

Al-Zayn al-Hafizi took a long, deep breath. "Taunts. Desecration of Muslim holy places. Trimming the beards of the Faithful and ridiculing them. Public drunkenness and rowdiness, often at the expense of the Faithful."

Ketbugha raised his eyebrows. He wondered if al-Zayn al-Hafizi knew Mongols carried fermented milk with them and drank for hours on long rides, and that alcoholic drinks were a treasured pleasure for Ketbugha and his fellow soldiers. "I would like you to compile a list of specific complaints, with specifics as to who is complaining, and who the complaints are against."

Al-Zayn al-Hafizi nodded. "Thank you, General. It is reassuring to know that justice and fairness will be priorities for your administration of this great city. I can offer you—"

"Yes. Fairness and justice. Those making trivial complaints about the new circumstances are guilty of nothing less than rebellion. We will identify those unwilling to adapt to these new circumstances, particularly those who give voice to their objections, and we will make examples of them to keep others from forming bad attitudes." Ketbugha turned to Shingkhor. "See to it."

Shingkhor turned to al-Zayn al-Hafizi, and said in Persian, "We will work together on this. Order will be maintained."

Al-Zayn al-Hafizi's eyes flashed wider. He swallowed.

Ketbugha grinned. Al-Zayn al-Hafizi had been appropriately put in his place. He looked at Shingkhor. "You have mastered their language?"

"I know the words I need to know in Persian," he said.

Ketbugha turned to al-Zayn al-Hafizi and smiled. "He is an excellent security man; he has risen through the ranks by demonstrating great ability." He paused for effect. "Unlike what we have seen in so much of this part of the world, where privilege is doled out based on family connections and friendships."

Al-Zayn al-Hafizi did not respond.

"This is one of your many failings."

Al-Zayn al-Hafizi looked away.

"Like that miserable excuse for a religious leader, that Caliph of Baghdad."

Al-Zayn al-Hafizi seemed to tense as he drew a deep breath.

Ketbugha looked at Shingkhor with a smirk. The security chief radiated deadly seriousness.

Ketbugha raised his eyebrows.

Al-Zayn al-Hafizi looked at Shingkhor, then at Ketbugha. "We will leave this palace for you and your people." He bowed.

Ketbugha smirked again as he eyed al-Zayn al-Hafizi. "After you have assisted us by identifying who is complaining about the new situation."

Al-Zayn al-Hafizi's lips tensed. He nodded.

"We would hate to sense an attitude lacking in cooperation. We do expect you to inform us on who questions this regime."

Al-Zayn al-Hafizi looked at members of his entourage. "Please consider legitimate complaints."

With a surge of anger Ketbugha clenched his teeth. He lifted his chin. "We are in command here," Ketbugha said. "You will bring the complaints and the complaint-makers to us. You will do so now. We will proceed as we decide."

Al-Zayn al-Hafizi looked down and nodded. "As you request."

"One other matter," Shingkhor said. "It is my special task for the khan to track down fugitive criminals, those who have committed offenses against the khan but fled before facing the consequences of their transgressions. We expect cooperation from you on this issue as well."

Without any direction to do so, armed members of Shingkhor's squad moved to bar any exit.

"I have a personal stake in this issue." Shingkhor's eyes bored in on al-Zayn al-Hafizi. "My brother was murdered by such a criminal. An old man. He fled, and though we have pursued him, we have been unable to find him, or evidence that he has died. I want to know if he could have fled here. He professes to be a studying man, and the teacher of the religion of the Prophet. Coming here would be a logical place."

Ketbugha looked at Shingkhor's intense eyes, then at al-Zayn al-Hafizi.

Al-Zayn al-Hafizi swallowed. Then a look of realization seemed to come onto his face and he tilted his head up. "There is a man—" He frowned in thought. "It can't be him."

Shingkhor stared wordlessly at al-Zayn al-Hafizi.

Al-Zayn al-Hafizi looked over to one of his men. "Fetch that old man, the one who has been advising us about Mongols, the one who says he is from Baghdad."

"Dawud? Dawud the Teacher?"

"Yes."

"I will recognize this criminal if I see him," Shingkhor said.

Ketbugha nodded. "If this is the man, I will be impressed. It will convince me of your acceptance of this new situation."

Al-Zayn al-Hafizi smiled, apparently grateful for just the slightest hint of approval from his new Mongol masters. Ketbugha considered that the occupation of the most important city in Syria was starting off well.

25

First Week March 1260
Damascus
Afternoon

"Dawud!"

Dawud lay face up on the bed in his quarters. Pounding on his door had awakened him from a nap. He sat up.

"You are summoned," said the voice on the other side of the door.

Dawud closed and opened his eyes, then rubbed them. He stepped to the door and opened it.

"You are summoned to meet with al-Zayn al-Hafizi and the Mongols," the man said. The tone of voice was overly businesslike, overly impersonal.

Dawud studied the man's face. He recognized the man as one who had attended some of his informal study sessions for interested students of all ages. "Summoned," Dawud repeated, looking into the man's eyes, soliciting a further explanation.

"Yes," the man said. He looked away.

"To help with … what? With advice?"

The man looked back at Dawud. His expression seemed to soften, as if he was doing an unpleasant task, a task that had him pitying Dawud.

Dawud remembered a post-study session with the man. "This is not Baghdad," Dawud said gently. "No resistance was offered. That horror does not appear likely to repeat here."

The man nodded. "Yes. I see that."

"Then my friend, why the long face?" Dawud asked.

The man swallowed. "I…." The man looked around the room, then back at Dawud. "I am not sure it is God's will that I carry out this order the way al-Zayn al-Hafizi has issued it. I am not even sure it is al-Zayn al-Hafizi's will. But...." The man's lips tensed. "He seems to sense an opportunity to be cooperative with the Mongols."

Dawud shrugged. "And he needs me for this? Then I will join him."

"He's with the Mongol general."

Dawud scowled. This man was still not explaining his uncomfortable demeanor.

"And with a security man. A man who says an old Muslim teacher murdered his brother."

Dawud felt a surge of energy pulse through his body. He felt his eyes widen a moment, but sought to maintain an even demeanor.

"It *is* you," al-Zayn al-Hafizi's messenger said. "You *are* the one they're looking for."

Dawud squinted, but with anger, not fear. "It is possible."

"Then it is *not* God's will that I carry out this order. You must leave at once. I'll tell them I could not find you, or that you left—" The man's words sputtered to an uneasy break as he seemed to rattle off thoughts.

Dawud stepped to him and took him by the shoulder. "Panic is a bad idea right now. I appreciate your concern for me. I face an unpleasant fate if that Mongol security man is who I think he is. But we need to think this through."

"They are waiting for me."

Dawud nodded slowly. "Yes. You came here. It looks as if I have moved away. So you went to the mosque, but no one knew where I was. Go to the mosque and ask someone, to make your story plausible."

The man responded with a quick nod. He seemed completely willing to follow Dawud's instructions. But Dawud needed to keep them simple and easy to perform.

"Go to the mosque, then back to al-Zayn al-Hafizi. Tell them it looks like I have already fled the city. Offer to lead them back here to search. I will leave my quarters in a state that will confirm what you will tell them."

"And you will leave the city?"

"Not right away. They are certain to look for—" Dawud stopped himself. "It is best you do not know too much."

The man nodded again.

"They will ask who my closest associates are."

The man shrugged.

"You do not know?" Dawud asked.

"No, I do not."

"That's fine. It will take them some time to discover them. By then, I will have made my move."

The man seemed frozen.

"Go to the mosque."

"Right." The man left quickly.

Dawud looked around his quarters. He had given good advice to the messenger. Panic was a bad idea. Speed—deliberate, focused speed—was essential. He needed to act quickly, but maintained every morsel of steady concentration he could summon. What would he have taken, and what would he have left behind if he had gone a week or so before? He grabbed a satchel and pushed some clothes into it. He straightened his work areas, putting all his ledgers and books into neat order. He grabbed his copies of the Koran—he had four—and two ledgers he had been working on, along with a writing implement. That was it. He checked his quarters again. This could not look like a hurried departure. It needed to look like a departure taken deliberately, with a possible return in mind. He realized he should also take his prayer rugs—three. After this, he was satisfied he had accomplished what he needed to do.

Dawud took a deep breath, then stepped to the doorway. He looked out. The street was quiet.

With a few blocks to walk to his next destination, he would take them through less traveled back streets. Dawud walked at a quick pace, but not too hurried in case some official came upon him.

Dawud rounded the corner onto the only busy street he needed to travel to get to his next destination. This street, unfortunately, was not so quiet.

Two veiled women were surrounded by a group of adolescent boys—dark-haired, clean-shaven, wearing light-colored baggy shirts and dark pants. "Veils?" one yelled. He grabbed at one woman's dark blue veil.

She let out a sharp scream.

"No veils here anymore!" yelled the boy as he ripped it from her.

Dawud had only a moment to think about whether he should intervene before the two women ran off, escaping further abuse.

The group turned toward Dawud. Now he had his own problems.

"Hey, old man!" yelled the same boy who had ripped the woman's veil. "Hey! Come here! Bow down to Christ!"

Dawud walked toward them. There was no sense trying to avoid them, they would certainly enjoy the chase and his consequences would likely be worse at the end of it.

Dawud recognized one of them. "Demetrius. You and your friends enjoying yourselves?" he asked in Greek.

The boy who had yelled at Dawud looked at an apparently younger, but slightly larger boy. The older boy appeared to have a few whiskers under his nose while Demetrius had not sprouted whiskers yet. "You know him?"

"He's a teacher."

The older boy shrugged. "Oh. Well, he can bow down to Christ."

Dawud looked at the older boy. He nodded with what could have been interpreted as a low bow. "Jesus is honored in our faith as well."

"Then you will kneel to him," the older boy said, "after we trim your beard."

Dawud grunted, suppressing anger and impatience. He did not have time for this nonsense. "I would love to pray with you boys. But now is not the time. Join me for evening prayers."

"Now *is* the time," the older boy insisted. He pulled out a large knife. "I will cut that ugly beard, and then you will bow down to Jesus. Christians rule here now. St. Paul's memory lives. The Christian tradition will be restored forever. Kneel, old man." The boy stepped toward Dawud.

Two of the boys moved to pin Dawud's arms.

"*Mongols* rule here," Dawud told the boy with stern confidence. "They will not take kindly to any religion claiming superiority. They claim superiority to all. I am on my way, *right now*, to meet with al-Zayn al-Hafizi." He looked at Demetrius. "You know I have been advising him. My abuse, and your abuse of women on the streets by you thugs, will be featured in my conversation with al-Zayn al-Hafizi. I'm certain the Mongols will use you to set an example, to demonstrate their superiority and dominance."

"So I should kill you now," the older boy snarled.

"A stupid idea," Dawud told him. "Killing someone in service to the Mongols who is helping them take control here? But … if there is no evidence of abuse, I have nothing to report."

The boy smiled. He clenched his knife and chuckled with a taunting glee.

"Let him go," Demetrius said quietly.

The older boy turned and looked at Demetrius as if irritated by a fly buzzing around. "He's bluffing. The Mongols won't care."

"Let him go," Demetrius said more firmly. "He is a good man. He teaches me, about Greek learning, about many worlds and places he has seen."

The older boy's lips scrunched toward his nose. He relaxed his grip on the knife. "Oh, all right, Dim-Dim-Dimmy. You can have your little teacher of Greek learning." The older boy looked at Dawud. "Go on, old man; get out of here!"

Dawud nodded a quick thanks to Demetrius, then stepped away, resuming his determined walk.

"Run, old man!" the boy taunted as he stepped after Dawud. "Run away."

Dawud liked that idea. His old legs broke into a trot.

"Scared fool! He's not even going toward the Mongols!" he heard the boy call out derisively.

Dawud smiled as he trotted the rest of the way down the busy street he had been unable to avoid. The boy was certainly right about that : Dawud was not going toward the Mongols!

He turned the corner and found another quiet street. A block and a half to go. He slowed to a determined gait. He huffed and puffed, catching his breath. He felt sweat form under his clothes. He wondered how much of it was from exertion, and how much was from the pure stress of developing events.

At his destination he knocked at the door. His student-friend answered. His expression of surprise revealed that Dawud was the last person the young man expected to see.

"Who is it?" asked a male voice further back in the home.

"Dawud the Teacher!" the student called out.

"Shhh!" Dawud said as he raised his hand.

The student looked at him, apparently soliciting an explanation.

"There is no choice now" Dawud said. "I am in deep danger, and I'm afraid your family is also in danger. We need to leave Damascus. Together or separately, but we all need to leave now."

"What are you talking about, old man?" The student's father joined them at the door. "What is this nonsense? You have been trying to talk my son into fleeing our home, over and over. What now?"

"Mongols are looking for me. They will find out I was close to your son, and they will abuse all of you until you give them enough information to find me."

The student nodded grimly. "For what you told me happened up at—"

"His brother is *still* looking for me," Dawud said.

"It's time, father," the student said. "There are places near Jerusalem. The preparations are—"

"But the Mongols are here, and we are *fine*," the student's father insisted. "We could even have a good position here, after the Christians finish blowing off steam."

"If they ever do," Dawud said.

"I have an easier answer," the student's father said. "If you are a wanted criminal, then we should turn you in."

"No!" the student told his father. "You will not!"

The father turned upon his son and snapped, "Boy! You will do whatever I say!"

"I am not a boy. I am a young man. And I will not be a party to betraying a venerated man of the True Faith. I will not! I will not allow you to offend God with such an action!"

"How dare you! How dare you defy me!"

Dawud raised his hand. "Please. I did not come here to create a family rift. There is a way—"

"I will *not* turn you in to the Mongols," the student insisted. "I will flee with you and die with you; if my parents betray you, they will betray me!"

"You will stop your defiance!" his father yelled.

"There is a way!" Dawud repeated, with a sharpness of tone that surprised even him. Dawud looked at the student's father. "Stay here. Keep your position. The Mongols will come, looking for your son. Tell them he fled with me. Days ago. A few weeks ago. You're not sure. You do not know where. He defied you, and left on bad terms."

The father directed a malevolent expression of unbridled hostility toward Dawud, but he did not offer an argument.

Dawud turned to the student. "Grab your things. Make it look like a reasoned, deliberate departure, not a rushed one."

"Right away."

As the youth went to his room, Dawud told the other man, "I am sorry. I do not wish to create a son's defiance of his father. But sir, I suggest to you, you'll come to see this as the result of Mongol despotism and brutality. Do not judge your son too harshly. He is a fine young man—a future with greatness is within him. If at all possible, this will not be a permanent separation."

The man's face remained tense, but tears rolled down both cheeks. He nodded.

The student emerged, holding his belongings.

"Some food," said the student's mother as she came to the front room. She handed them some bread, a few oranges, some dried meat and nuts.

"Thank you," Dawud said.

"Thank you, mother," the student said. He kissed his mother and hugged her. He looked at his father.

His father extended his arms and they hugged. "Where will you go?"

"It is best you do not know," Dawud said quickly. "It is best you maintain that anger against your son's defiance. You must convince the Mongols. They must believe you have broken with your son."

The student's father nodded.

"Let's go," Dawud said. They left quickly.

"We need to leave the city soon, but not right away," Dawud said. "They may be on the alert for my departure if they do not believe I have already left." Dawud looked at his student. "Do you know of a good place to hide? A place where we will not meet up with anyone?"

The student smiled slyly. "I know a good place. I grew up in this city. As a young boy, I roamed the streets."

"Good. Pick somewhere we can find using back streets. We need to avoid … encounters with the wrong people."

"I know the place." The student started walking with a determined pace.

Dawud followed.

"The old man is gone," al-Zayn al-Hafizi's messenger said as he entered the palace reception room. "Gone maybe a week or two. I checked at the local mosque. They haven't seen him. His quarters looked abandoned. Not hurriedly, but as if he has left."

Ketbugha eyed the man. The man looked nervous. Was he nervous because he brought bad news, or nervous because he was a liar?

The security leader moved toward the messenger. "Did you warn that old man off?" he asked.

"Warn him?"

"Did you warn that old man off?" the security leader again demanded, moving right up to the messenger's face.

"Of course not."

"You have a choice to make," the security leader said, maintaining steely eyes. "You get that old man here now, or you suffer his fate. If he really has gone a week or two ago, then this will simply be your bad luck."

The messenger's eyes widened.

"Wait a moment," Ketbugha said. He looked at his security chief, then carefully guided the man out of earshot. He did not want anyone, especially the messenger, to overhear him countermand his security chief. "I have honored your persistence in searching for the criminal who killed your brother. I still think it most likely that the old man is long dead, rotting up in the hills of Azerbaijan. But I honor your desire for confirmation. And this old teacher here does fit the description. Loosely. Make inquiries. Investigate. But we need to govern these people; that is our first priority. Please do not let your inquiries become too fanatic or extreme."

"I think this messenger warned the old man away," the security chief said again.

"It is a suspicion without evidence," Ketbugha replied. "If you develop the evidence, proceed. But you are not to get carried away with this. I need you focused on rebellion against our authority, not a quest for murdering ghosts. Anything we do must be for public benefit, not private interests."

The security chief nodded. "Yes." He paused. "You said I am free to make inquiries."

"Of course, I told you, yes. But with discretion. Within reason."

The security chief nodded again. He looked at the messenger. "You'd better hope there is no evidence of your duplicity."

"I have the first complainer about the Christians—he had the nerve to come straight here," one of Ketbugha's men said. "He says Christians drew crosses in pig's blood on the door of a mosque."

"Hang him. Make sure everyone knows why."

"Yes sir."

26

March 1260
Cairo
Morning

"If I didn't know better, I'd say age had made you even taller," Qutuz said as he stood to greet his visitor. Baybars had just entered the reception area of the other man's palace in Cairo. Qutuz sat back down, his throne set upon a raised dais. He was flanked by two visibly armed, visibly well-conditioned guards. Other armed guards were set about the room. Bright banners hung from the ceiling. Qutuz displayed little wealth; only a few statues decorated the reception area, with no artwork, even with the abstract patterns acceptable to Muslims. One simple green jewel sat in the middle of his bright white turban.

Baybars looked at the man who had been the object of so much of his hatred for half a decade. He stood just before his own squad. Baybars counted it as a favorable sign that Qutuz had never asked Baybars and his men to disarm. But Baybars saw Qutuz was well-prepared if Baybars and his men had any intention of using their weapons at this reunion.

Baybars had prayed often to make peace with his impulse to bring justice to someone who had inflicted so much injustice on Baybars and his men. The moment was at hand, and Baybars was gratified his prayers had been answered. Baybars also was gratified to set aside his fears that this encounter masked a trap set by Qutuz.

Baybars looked at Qutuz, who wore a slight grin. He considered Qutuz's remark. "God grants me size and strength to destroy His enemies," Baybars finally said.

Qutuz's eyebrows rose and he replied, "May He grant you the strength to dispatch scores of Mongols to their deaths."

"I have offered that prayer more than once."

"God wills that we set aside our differences and unite in this struggle against the worst evil of our time."

Baybars nodded. "The worst threat to the True Faith since the Prophet brought the message of God to the people of the world."

"And we are the ones appointed to face it, resist it and destroy it."

Baybars smiled. His eyes started to moisten with tears. He did not resist the emotions taking hold of him. Emotions that came from releasing his hate against this man for a greater good. Emotions that came from the validation that leading his men to join this former enemy had been a good choice, a choice capable of fulfilling a holy purpose. Emotions that came from believing that this alliance, with this man and his forces, would bring success that would glorify God for all time. "You"—Baybars tipped his head with a shallow bow—"are the only leader who understands this."

Qutuz stepped off the dais. "Come forward."

Baybars made a show of undoing his sword belt and dropping it to the floor, so that there would be no doubt of his intentions to make peace. He took swift resolute steps toward Qutuz.

Qutuz opened his arms and they embraced.

Baybars felt a few tears roll down his cheeks.

Qutuz patted Baybars on the back and they released their embrace. The men around them broke into cheers.

"I do understand," Qutuz told his new ally. "And with the resources we have here, we will be victorious. For Good against Evil. For God."

Baybars smiled again.

"We do not need the others," Qutuz continued. "We do not want their wavering, uncertain, unreliable help. That attack you warned us about was the epitome of what their help has been."

Baybars grunted. "My old friend al-Mughith Umar…."

"Has submitted. I know."

Baybars shook his head. "No great loss."

Qutuz smiled. "As you would know."

"As you and your men demonstrated to me over and over."

Qutuz laughed.

"Al-Nasir Yusuf has all but submitted," Baybars said.

"Fleeing Damascus like a little girl. Lacking the courage even to make the submission."

"His resources could have helped."

Qutuz waved off the thought with a disdainful sneer. "We have what we need. We will focus on what we have, not on what we do not have. And now, we have you."

Baybars smiled.

"You are granted the Qalyub District, at the northeast end of the Delta, as your domain."

Baybars nodded. "I know the area. Thank you."

"The people have been notified, and should be honored to support the leadership of such great warriors for the True Faith."

Baybars nodded again.

"But, my friend, I do not expect you to spend a lot of time there. I need your men to drill with the rest of our forces, to train recruits, to help get us ready for the great battle to come."

Baybars nodded. "I will settle my wife and son, and settle the rest of the Bahriyya. Then...." He raised his right hand and clenched it into a fist. "God wills it. Death to Mongols."

Qutuz raised both fists. His nostrils flared and he sneered with defiance. "Death to Mongols!" he shouted.

The palace broke into a chant, with the pounding of swords, shields, and drums joining as it progressed: "Death to Mongols! Death to Mongols!"

Baybars raised his fist again, and offered Qutuz his own grin of defiance and confidence. The chant continued.

Qutuz nodded his dismissal.

Baybars nodded back and turned to rejoin his men, serenaded by continuing chants of "Death to Mongols!"

March 1260
Qalyub District – North of Cairo
Afternoon

"We haven't earned this yet," Baybars said to Qalawun. Sunqur al-Ashqar rode behind them as the three led a procession through the market district of Qalyub. They were followed by the squad that had completed the mission to contact Qutuz. People stood on either side of the main street, waving palm leaves and cheering. "But this is a nice gesture."

"Yes."

Both men smiled. Baybars waved. It seemed as if the entire district had flocked to produce this welcome.

Baybars looked back at Sunqur al-Ashqar, who was also smiling and waving.

As Baybars returned his gaze forward, he caught sight of a tall, thin, veiled woman to his left. His eyes fixed on her staring brown eyes.

She looked at him, then sneezed or coughed—Baybars couldn't tell which. Her veil dropped away from her face.

Baybars had never seen a more beautiful female in his life. She had olive skin, deep brown eyes, and a delicate nose on a narrow head.

The young lady quickly covered up.

Baybars gestured for one of his personal guards to join him.

"I want to meet that woman." He pointed to her.

The guard nodded. "I will see to it."

"Have her brought to me this afternoon."

The guard nodded again and went quickly to his errand.

"But Master, sir, she is set for betrothal to my partner."

Baybars sat in a plush chair in a reception room of a small palace. The young woman he had seen on the street stood next to her father. She was still veiled, quietly attentive to the discussion about her fate.

"You are bakers," Baybars said.

"Yes. Very prosperous bakers. He's a young man who came into my service recently. He will step into my shoes and care for—"

"I am the ruler of this district," Baybars told him. "I will prove to be a significant match for your daughter. God wills it. Perhaps you have another daughter to wed to your partner?"

"Um ... no. I just have one daughter. She's all I have. Her mother died giving birth. Thin hips. Like hers. Not worthy of—"

"I'll decide my own standards of worthiness. We will compensate your family. But Zahirah will be my second wife."

"She would be a first wife, and only wife—"

"Baker, this is not a discussion."

The man's nostrils flared as he seemed to fight tears. But he bowed his understanding. He turned to his daughter. "Life changes."

"I will be well, father."

He nodded. "I know you will. You have always been a strong, tough girl." He lifted her veil and kissed her.

Baybars caught another glimpse of Zahirah's striking face. His breathing quickened slightly.

Zahirah and her father hugged. He took one last, regretful glance at Baybars before leaving the room.

Baybars turned to a guard. "Summon the appropriate officials. I wish to complete this marriage immediately."

"Adiba!" Baybars burst into the room that had been designated as Adiba's quarters. Zahirah entered at his side.

Adiba was smiling, on the floor playing with their one-year-old son. "It's beautiful," she said, focused on the boy. "Al-Malik al-Said loves it here already." She looked up. Her smile shifted to a puzzled expression as her eyes moved to Zahirah.

"I am glad your quarters are good," Baybars told her, beaming back a smile. "Our circumstances are going to improve dramatically."

Adiba nodded. "I can see." But her eyes remained fixed on Zahirah.

"I've taken a second wife," Baybars told her, as if bringing home an extra loaf of bread. "Think of her as your sister."

Adiba nodded. She did not speak.

"I will be in my quarters." Baybars quickly ushered Zahirah out of the room.

"You dropped that veil on purpose," Baybars said to Zahirah, now that they were alone in his quarters.

She took off the veil. "Yes. Yes, I did. I was not meant to be the wife of the baker."

Baybars smiled. "No. I don't think so. You are the wife of a warrior."

"Yes." She walked to him. "A strong, powerful warrior."

Baybars kissed her.

Zahirah kissed back roughly.

"This was your idea, as much as mine."

Zahirah opened and closed her eyes seductively. "This was my idea *first.*"

Baybars laughed.

Zahirah stripped off her dress and the rest of her clothes.

Baybars had never seen a more perfect female form.

Zahirah then stripped Baybars, needing only slight assistance on his part.

They stood and faced each other. Zahirah looked down and seemed to smile her satisfaction. "A tall, strong warrior," she told him. She looked up. "My baker-husband would have been three inches shorter than me." She embraced Baybars. "Take me."

Baybars moved their pelvic areas into proximity. "You are pure…?"

"Yes," she said breathless and distracted. "But I know from other women how this is supposed to go, and believe me, I am ready."

Baybars took her to their bed and finished what had consumed him since he'd first seen her.

"I will never be able to compare to her," Adiba said. "She knows it. She walks around half-clothed, showing *me* her body, letting me know what she has that I can never give you."

Baybars upper lip rose as he suppressed a sneer. He was tired and in no mood to salve Adiba's feelings. "This is the way of things," he said. "I am an important man. As such, I will take more than one wife. You are my first wife. You bore me al-Malik al-Said, my first-born son. That is status enough. Accept your position. Don't whine to me."

Adiba sniffled. "Yes, my husband."

"Now send Zahirah back to me and go attend to our son."

She sniffled again, nodded, then left.

Baybars had always figured he would take a second wife. He had thought this would occur after the Mongol battle. But Zahirah, and God, had other plans. Adiba would live with it. And she would adapt. That was her strength, an ability she had proven many times over the previous few years.

March 1260
Marj-Barghuth, South of Damascus
Mid Day

"This Mongol general is a Christian," the one-armed priest said, with an optimistic gleam in his face and a bounce in his words. "He may view us differently than the absent Mongol ruler."

Aram's eyes widened and his lips bunched up. He looked at Robert.

Robert, with a slight shake of his head, communicated the message that Aram should remain silent. They rode on horses, side by side, and approached the group of nobles from Acre who were leading the excursion to meet the Mongols.

"We need this meeting, with these gifts to show these people we are their friends," the nobleman continued.

Aram looked at Robert again, but did not offer a comment, though he suspected his facial expression gave away his opinion of this idea.

"Of course it is wise to communicate with the new power in the area," Robert said.

"Of course. And your mission, from the pope, is now easier to accomplish," Adolfo said. Aram recognized the voice and looked over, then quickly looked back toward Robert before any signs of recognition between the two men became evident.

"As I have clarified before," Robert replied with an irritated edge to his voice, "my mission involves contacts with the Mongol rulers themselves, not their subordinates. But I am pleased to accompany and consult on this particular mission."

Aram stole a glance at Adolfo, who smirked.

"We will take the lead," one of the Acre noblemen said. "But it is kind of you and your people to be available, if we need you."

Robert nodded, with a grin of his own.

Aram knew Robert understood the remark well. It was unlikely this delegation would ask for any input from Robert. Aram was sure Robert knew this, and wondered why Robert had even gone along on the mission. Aram raised his eyebrows and let a slight grin creep onto his face.

"Young man!" Robert scolded as he looked at Aram. "You must not behave that way!"

Aram's eyes widened and he shrugged.

Robert looked at the Acre nobles. "I need to have a conversation with my subordinate," he said. He flicked his head toward a spot away from the group, motioning to Aram to join him.

The two men guided their horses away from the group. Robert looked back at them.

Aram saw that a few were watching them, but most faced the Mongol tents ahead.

"My apologies for that," Robert said gently. "I needed a pretense to speak privately."

"Mmm-hmm."

"They are not going to let me into this at all," Robert said. "I thought maybe…." Robert breathed out. "But this suits my purpose."

"Sir, I could be of more help if you would explain to me what your purpose is."

"The same," Robert said, as if it should be obvious. "Negotiations with the Mongols. An alliance against the scourge of Islam. An alliance for the—"

"Which these nobles, this delegation, will have a hard time pursuing the minute the Mongols ask why they have not yet dismantled their fortified positions. I know you are aware of that. We discussed it."

Robert seemed to search for words.

"So I ask again," Aram said, "what is our purpose?"

"I need a direct communication route to the Mongols. Around these fools."

Aram eyed Robert.

Robert shook his head. "These Acre nobles, and their competing entanglements with the warring Italian factions—it is impossible to present or even formulate a clear Christian position. I need my own distinct approach, not identified with this rabble."

Aram squinted. "And how do you propose we accomplish this?"

"Look for an opening," Robert told him. "Use your skills and savvy. Find me a way."

"And what will you communicate to the Mongols that this Acre delegation won't?"

"A less scattered, less provincial, stronger position from a stronger, more powerful potential ally."

Aram kept a blank expression. He did not want Robert to sense just how unsatisfactory he found that response to be. "Allow me a free hand. I may have an uncle here. Maybe he can help. But this will be tricky."

Robert looked at Aram with suspicion. "A free hand." He moved his lips around, then puffed them out. "Hm. Within reason, you have it."

Aram nodded.

Robert nudged his horse forward to rejoin the group.

Aram followed.

"Your gifts … are appreciated." But Ketbugha barely looked at the cartloads of goods the Christian delegation had brought to his tent. He was studying the Acre nobleman who was acting as the spokesman for the Christians. "Is there some other purpose to this visit?"

"Good relations," said the nobleman's interpreter.

Aram noted that the interpreter seemed nervous. And the translation was inexact. The nobleman had actually said "friendship", not "good relations", but there was no way to translate the word without implying submission.

"'Good relations,'" Ketbugha repeated. He grinned. "Yes. We have 'good relations' with al-Nasir Yusuf, now that we have destroyed nearly all of his military forces. The prince does seem to move from place to place a lot. But I'm sure his 'good relations' with us will be a formal submission, very soon."

"That is a basis for our good relations"—Aram again noticed the interpreter was translating "friendship" to "good relations" as the exchange continued—the war of Christian against Muslim."

Ketbugha smiled. "Christian? Against Muslim?"

"Absolutely. Certainly."

Ketbugha nodded. "I am Christian. From the Kerait tribe. That is my family's tradition."

"Tradition. And faith."

Ketbugha looked the Acre nobleman in the eye. "And my family has also served the Genghis Khan dynasty, the dynasty chosen by the Eternal Blue Heaven to rule the world. That authority does not recognize the supremacy of one religion over another."

The Acre nobleman appeared uncertain at how to respond.

Aram's eyes roamed over the entire Mongol delegation. He noticed a familiar face, a Muslim he recognized from his previous visit to Damascus. This man looked uncomfortable with the talk about a conflict between Mongols and Muslims. But the man seemed to fight off a smile when Ketbugha mentioned recognizing no religion's supremacy.

Ketbugha continued. "We have Christian rulers, and Muslim rulers, who dismantle their fortresses, pay tribute, and supply troops to aid our efforts when asked to do so. These are the 'good relations' we seek. These people are our friends, united under the rulership of the great khan." He motioned toward the carts. "But the gifts are appreciated, as a move in the right direction."

The Acre nobleman swallowed, then bowed.

Ketbugha turned to re-enter his tent.

Aram moved quickly toward the Mongol delegation, trying to weave in and out of people without calling attention to himself as he sought the Muslim man he recognized. With Ketbugha withdrawing, and the Acre delegation also beginning to leave, Aram was able to make his approach without much notice.

"Tarif," he said quietly.

Tarif turned, locked eyes with him, and seemed to go pale.

"Is my uncle still in Damascus?" Aram asked.

The man shook his head and gestured with his palms down, as if emphatically turning away the inquiry.

"My Uncle Dawud," Aram said. "The old scholar from Baghdad."

The man shrugged and again held his palms up. "You have me mistaken for someone else. I don't know your uncle. I don't know any old scholar named Dawud."

Aram followed Tarif's eyes toward two Mongol guards watching their contact. "Sorry," he said. "You look a lot like someone I know. But I can see now that I was totally mistaken. You look nothing like the man." He bowed. "Sorry to take up your time." Aram quickly withdrew to rejoin Robert.

"You still have Nestor," Aram said. He and Robert stood at the opening of a tent under construction. The late afternoon sun started to set on the Christian camp, not far from the meeting earlier in the day. "My wife and son are still in Acre."

"You couldn't care less about Nestor," Robert said. "And I'm not sure how much you care about that family of yours."

Aram bristled, but did not protest the implication that he did not care about his wife and child. "If you want me to try to set up a line of communication outside of—"

"I'm not so sure I'm interested anymore."

Aram scowled. "Well, if you want me to work on this, you're going to have to trust me."

Robert looked off, away from Aram. Aram sensed that trust from Robert seemed to be in short supply.

One of Robert's guards approached. With him was Tarif.

"They may be watching me," he told Aram without preamble.

Aram looked at the guard.

The guard said something to Robert that Aram figured was in German. Robert looked at Aram. "This man has sought you out."

Aram nodded, then looked at the man.

"They're still looking for him," Tarif said. "They may be watching me," he repeated. "He's in hiding, still in Damascus."

Aram's eyes widened. "You know where?"

The man looked around as if checking to assure his safety. "Yes." He glanced back toward the Mongol camp. "They drink a lot. In a few hours we should be safe to go see him."

Aram nodded. "I appreciate that."

Robert gave Aram a long scrutinizing look, as if trying to read his mind. Tarif continued to look around warily.

Robert let out a long breath. "Is there a line of communication to be had here?"

Aram paused in thought. "I doubt it," he finally said. "But I can give it a try."

Robert's lips tensed. "Very well. Go on. See what you can do." He paused. "Tell me about it when you return."

Aram nodded.

27

March, 1260
Damascus
Just Before Sunrise

"Uncle," Aram said. He smiled as he approached Dawud at the cavernous end of a tunnel. "You look terrible; I've seen beggars with a more presentable appearance." He raised a candle to get a better view.

Dawud grunted. His face was smudged with grime that seemed to be prominently tattooed on his cheeks and forehead. His robe, which may have originally been white, was stained with the dusty colors of dirt. Aram also smelled urine, and saw a pot which he suspected served waste disposal purposes. "You would look this way, too, if you were stuck down here for weeks," Dawud growled.

"Who is it?" demanded a young man with a similarly filthy appearance. "Who dares to confront you this—"

"My nephew," Dawud sneered. "Picking a strange time for a visit."

The young man jerked his head up. "Where did you come from? How did you—" The young man's expression showed fear. "Were you followed?"

"I was not followed," Aram said. "A concerned friend of yours gave me your location, with a recommendation that I help remove you from here as soon as possible."

"Who?" the young man demanded. "Who is this friend?

"Obviously an ally," Aram answered, with an impatient edge to his voice. "He could have easily led Mongols here."

Dawud smiled. He looked back at the younger man. "He's

right." With an outraised hand, Dawud identified the student to Aram. "This is a student of mine, traveling companion, friend." Dawud paused. "What brings you here?"

"I'm an envoy."

"Envoy." The student scowled. "For whom?"

"The Christians at Acre. We have a camp near here for our mission to give gifts to the new Mongol rulers in Damascus."

"From one of our enemies to another one of our enemies," the student commented.

"Smart fellow, your student," Aram quipped.

"Smart enough to—"

Dawud cut off whatever hostile comment his fellow fugitive was about to offer. "It will be all right," Dawud said to the student. "He is my nephew. And he is nobody's fool."

"Or student," Aram added.

"Hey!" the student objected indignantly.

"You have something in mind," Dawud said.

"You'll be envoys too, with me. You're a back channel contact. Come out of there—come with me now, before they've slept off the feast from last night."

The student looked at Dawud, shaking his head. "Teacher, I—"

Dawud interrupted him again. "We can't stay down here forever. I think this is our way out." He looked at Aram, smiling. "This tunnel goes under a church."

Aram nodded. "I have extra horses nearby. Let's go. Now."

"To join Christians?" the student asked.

"To get out of here," Dawud told him. "I'm not sure who we're joining yet."

"For the moment, you're working with me as part of my diplomatic mission here. We'll work out other details later."

Dawud began to collect his meager possessions.

"My advice to you is to stay with the man, and work out this 'back channel contact' if you can. It's a safe position, a good vantage point for you to discover exactly what this Robert-fool is up to." Dawud looked Aram in the eye. "Then, you can figure out the best way to extricate yourself—and your family—from this entanglement you're in."

They rode side by side, horses at a trot, just past the outskirts of the city. Dawud's student rode on the other side of his teacher.

The sun had begun to rise. It was going to be a warm day, a good day for travel.

"I am concerned that the Mongols will view Robert and me as complicit in a move of treachery," Aram said. "They despise treachery."

Dawud considered this. He scratched his itchy body, covered with accumulated sweat. He scratched his chin under his beard.

Aram explained, "I have heard it told that back in the days of Genghis Khan, out in Central Asia, some treacherous Muslim nobles betrayed a city the khan was trying to capture. The khan took the city, looted it, and destroyed the people he considered not to be useful, because the city had resisted his forces. He saved the most grisly, creative executions for the Muslim nobles who had betrayed their own city. He considered them the worst of all."

"But you are not the one engaging in any possible treachery; it is Robert."

Aram shook his head. "I am afraid that by acting for him, I will be seen as joined with his purpose."

Dawud grimaced, then after a moment his expression transformed into a grin. "True. And you're a clever young man, Aram. Make sure you present yourself as a mere servant to Robert's purpose. They will respect your loyalty to your superior, and if you do come under their power, they will value your knowledge and skill with language. Come now, Nephew; you're smart enough to manage it."

Aram nodded. "Yes...." He smiled. "Yes, that could work. And this Robert owes me a cartload of money—or should at some point. Yes, this is the best idea."

"Good."

Aram let out a deep breath. "It will be good having you, and your own cleverness to—" Aram's head suddenly jerked to their right, back toward Damascus.

Dawud looked in the same direction. "We need to flee. Now."

Aram shook his head. "We'll never outrun them, and fleeing ensures our deaths."

A squad of Mongol guards, six men, was moving quickly toward them. They would arrive in seconds.

"They're Mongols, not auxiliaries. Good." Aram looked at Dawud. "How's your Greek?" he asked.

"Good," Dawud said. He looked at his student, who nodded.

"Greek," Aram said. "Greek."

The Mongol patrol arrived. "You are taken. You come. Us," the apparent leader of the squad said in tortured Arabic.

"I am with the Christian delegation," Aram told them in fluent Mongolian. "I'm an interpreter, heading back to our camp."

Dawud understood a great deal of the Mongol tongue, but decided he needed to seem ignorant of that right now. He had observed repeatedly how clever his nephew was. He would now have to trust his life to that cleverness.

"What do we do?" Dawud's student asked, in nervous, heavily accented Greek.

Dawud was pleased his student had picked up the cue. "Aram will handle this," Dawud replied in Greek.

"These are not Christians," the Mongol squad leader barked. "They are Muslims. Escaping the city. One meets the description of a wanted criminal."

Aram first looked puzzled, then broke into a chuckle. "Muslims? You think these two are Muslims?" Aram shook his head. "Surely you don't think a Christian delegation from Acre would have Muslims in camp."

The squad leader appeared to consider this, but with a confused and suspicious gleam in his eye.

"They are Greek Christians," Aram told the man. "They came with us to advise. They became disenchanted with the evening worship service and went off on their own to pray. When my superiors did not see them this morning, they sent me to find them. Poor fools, they became lost and slept all night in the dirt."

Dawud liked this idea. "Why are we being stopped?" he asked in Greek.

"They think you're Muslims," Aram replied in Greek. "They think one of you is a wanted criminal."

"Criminal!" Dawud's eyes widened.

"Yes. Just let me talk to them."

"We are not criminals!"

"Of course not."

Dawud scanned the Mongol squad. He caught sight of one man who seemed to understand at least part of the exchange.

The squad leader shook his head. "I do not know of Greeks. Your gibberish could be a ploy. I will take you to my superiors. If this is the criminal we seek, I will be a hero."

Aram's eyes widened as he rolled his head. "Hero? You'll be a *fool* because you can't tell a Muslim from a Greek!"

The squad leader clenched his teeth. "Watch who you call a fool...."

"I'm trying to help you," Aram told him. "Better I say it than your superiors, and all your fellow soldiers."

The squad member who had seemed to understand the earlier exchange called out, "They speak Greek—I heard them." Dawud noticed a peculiar accent in this Mongol's words, but he couldn't place it.

The squad leader turned back. "Are you sure? Are you absolutely sure?"

"Yes. Clear Greek. With an Eastern accent, but definitely Greek."

Dawud wondered if the squad leader would follow up on the observation of the Eastern accent.

Aram spoke quickly. "You need to reward that man. He has saved you from embarrassment."

The squad leader looked at the man. "Yes." He looked at Dawud and his student. "Move along, back to your camp. We will escort you to the crossroads."

"Thank you," Aram said. "Say, if you want to be a hero, or at least an important man, I work for a high-placed member of the Christian camp who would like to have a private audience with someone highly-placed in your camp. You seem just the type who can help us."

Dawud fought a smile. His nephew wasn't missing any opportunity to follow his advice.

The Mongol squad leader's eyebrows lowered as his nostrils flared.

Aram added, "There will be gifts for all, including the one who brings us together."

The Mongol squad leader raised his eyebrows. "We will speak of it along the way to the crossroads."

"I'm not going back to your camp," Dawud said.

Aram watched the Mongol squad ride away. Dawud's gaze seemed to look further into the distance, as if peering into a distant future. About a half-mile to their left was the Christian camp. In the other direction was a road heading southwest, toward the Mediterranean coast.

Aram nodded.

"There is no place for me at your camp."

Aram nodded again. "I was trying to figure out how I would explain you and your friend."

Dawud chuckled. "I have no doubt you would have come up with something. Greek Christians." Dawud shook his head.

"A little luck...."

"Or maybe God's will...."

Aram shrugged. "Sure. Why not? But whatever it was, it worked for us that the Turk knew some Greek."

"Turk." Dawud nodded. "That's what it was."

"Sure was. He not only kept us out of trouble, but I may have the back channel I need. Not at this meeting, but some point down the line. Robert will be happy." Aram grinned. "At least, he will be pleased enough not to be too upset about the horses you two are going to take."

Dawud's eyes glistened. "Thank you." He reached over and grasped Aram's shoulder. "Thank you for understanding."

"I'm not sure I do." Aram placed his hand over Dawud's. "But I respect you too much to object."

Dawud let go of Aram's shoulder. He looked off to the southwest. "I keep telling myself, I am an old man; I have nothing to contribute. My days fighting for Islam—bloodstained, evil at times, ugly—are past. But Nephew, there's a confrontation coming. God—like the force of nature that pulls water from the mountains—God draws me to the center of this fight. I pull away; I travel far and wide to avoid it; but it follows me, it draws me to it no matter where I go or what I do. It is time for me to recognize God's will and move to the center of the fight."

Aram let out a deep breath.

"There is a village about a mile and a half down that road." Dawud pointed to the southwest. "I have friends there. They will let me clean up and provision for the trip I will take ... to Egypt. That is the last hope to save Islam, and as old and feeble as I feel, I will not be a bystander any longer."

Aram nodded. He handed over a satchel. "Here is all the water and food I have. It should get you to your village. I suggest moving quickly, at a gallop, while still in sight of Damascus. I think we met up with the only patrol, but you never know. God keep you safe, Uncle."

"He will. He has not preserved me this long to see me lose my life now." He raised his chin. "It is not my time yet."

Aram smiled. "Hey," he said to the student. "Take care of my uncle. I've given you a hard time, but you're all right."

The student raised his eyebrows. "And you." He seemed to think a moment. "I think you may be crazy."

They both laughed.

Dawud locked eyes with Aram. "I only ask—for your own sake, not mine—that you consider, dear nephew, where you will be when this confrontation arrives."

Aram's mind absorbed the titanic question, a question that jolted him, a question that had not occurred to him.

Dawud nodded, and almost bowed. He and his student turned their horses to gallop away.

Second Week of April, 1260
Near Tabriz, Azerbaijan
Mid Day

"You enjoyed reporting that news," Hulegu Khan said with a knowing leer. A messenger swallowed. He bore the signs of an apparent long trip: smudged uniform, hat askew, ears and lips red from the crisp spring air. He bowed deeply, then straightened up and smiled. "Yes, Your Highness."

Hulegu nodded. He was accompanied by a small squad of guards and a few officers. "I will have you tell it again."

The messenger bowed once more.

Hulegu turned to one of his officers. "Gather the commanders of every division. I want them to hear this. Bring them to the main campfire." Hulegu started to stride resolutely toward the campfire, then stopped. "Have Dokuz Khatun join us."

The officer looked puzzled at first, but then his eyes widened with understanding. "Yes, I will gather them all, il-Khan." He bowed again.

Hulegu resumed his march.

"The crossroads position of Mayyafariqin has finally fallen," Hulegu Khan said to a gathering of about thirty at a large campfire. He sat on a slightly elevated platform, his wife Dokuz

Khatun next to him. "My son, Yoshmut, and the troops under his command, have finally taken that position from the treacherous prince, al-Kamil Muhammad." Hulegu squeezed Dokuz Khatun's hand. "This al-Kamil Muhammad—supposedly of the blood of a great ruler of an empire that included Syria and Egypt—this al-Kamil Muhammad came all the way to Qaraqorum and expressed his submission to us. But when we asked for troops, and most importantly, when we commanded his surrender of Mayyafariqin to facilitate our passage into Syria, he refused us. He defied us after agreeing to submission." Hulegu sneered. "Such defiance can never be tolerated." Hulegu turned to the messenger, seated just to his left. "This man was there. He will describe the result of al-Kamil Muhammad's treachery." Hulegu nodded to the messenger.

The messenger bowed toward Hulegu, then stood. "First, al-Kamil Muhammad was taken and bound, and paraded through Mayyafariqin while our forces killed every living thing in his treasonous, defiant city; all men, all women, all children, all animals. Every creature that occupied this bastion of defiance, every creature with a sliver of life, was destroyed."

Hulegu smiled and enjoyed the messenger's flair for the dramatic. And his smile remained in anticipation of what was to come. He squeezed his wife's hand and raised his eyebrows as he exchanged a quick glance with her. Al-Kamil Muhammad's defiance of their young son was an indignity they had shared. He was certain she would enjoy this news as much as he had.

"We then invited al-Kamil Muhammad to dinner."

Hulegu laughed out loud. The messenger was embellishing the story in a most satisfying way.

The officers at the campfire looked puzzled.

Dokuz Khatun frowned. "Invited him to dinner…?"

"Yes," Hulegu told her.

"We made sure the great prince was dressed for the occasion," the messenger continued. "We plucked off his robes and turbans, down to what modesty demands we cover. We plucked him like the brainless bird that he is. But then, there is the dish, the dish for the feast for our honored guest. We roped his ankles to his wrists behind his back and raised him up over the cooking fire. The great prince whimpered with discomfort. Must be he was hungry, and needed to eat. Well, the dish was nearly ready. We made sure the cooking fire was strong, at a good heat to prepare the main course to perfection. We then peeled skin from his back and skewered it, grilled it over the cooking fire. He screamed. We offered him the meat. He held his mouth closed, but we would not take no from this poor, hungry prince. We forced his mouth open and shoved the wonderful meat in. We even moved his jaws to help him chew. He cried and vomited, but finally did eat some of the feast. Because he seemed to have such a hard time taking in the food, we kept feeding him. Finally, the man died. No one could say that he died of starvation."

Hulegu looked out over the group. He saw snickers and grins. He also saw some uneasy, forced smiles. This was fine with him. Let everyone inside and outside the ranks know what sort of fate, what sort of creative savagery, awaited the defiant and the treacherous.

Hulegu nodded to the messenger, who bowed and retook his seat.

Hulegu looked out at the group. "Everyone is to tell this story to no less than five people. And you are to command every person you tell to tell five more. All our people who are scheduled to travel are to tell the story in every village they go to."

Attentive faces looked back at him.

"We have defiant princes still out there," he said. "That example of wavering and indecision, al-Nasir Yusuf, still wanders about southern Syria trying to settle on a home and a decision. I want him to hear this story." Hulegu paused. "And the slave-soldier sultan of Egypt. He needs to know the price of defiance. I want this story circulated far and wide."

Hulegu slowly surveyed the faces of his audience then said, "You are dismissed back to your duties."

The gathering began to break up.

Hulegu looked toward the messenger. "You have earned some excellent gifts. I will see you are granted some fine choices from our storehouses. Your story-telling served well the purposes of the empire of the Eternal Blue Heaven."

The messenger bowed. "Thank you, Your Highness." He walked away.

Hulegu looked at Dokuz Khatun. "The defiance against our son has been avenged."

She smiled. "In a most satisfying and dramatic fashion. Thank you for sharing this result with me."

Hulegu grinned.

28

Early May, 1260
North of Kerak
Late Morning

"At long last, you have come to pay us a visit," Ketbugha said with a phony smile. He stood at the entrance to a tent in the midst of his army's camp. The surrounding turf was light brown, with very little vegetation. "I know we have been difficult to find lately, as we have progressed so quickly and so far south through the lands of Syria. Perhaps this is why we have not met up with you." Ketbugha flashed a mischievous gleam. "Though I am not sure how we could have missed you in Damascus."

Al-Nasir Yusuf swallowed. He trembled in worn and dusty military dress. A squad of Mongol soldiers stood around him; this group also look to have just taken a long journey. Al-Nasir Yusuf's hands were bound behind his back. "I am … at your service."

Ketbugha smiled again. "At our service. Good. You will be kind enough to demonstrate this 'service' by ordering and arranging for the peaceful surrender of the fortress at Ajlun." Ketbugha frowned, holding a stern expression a moment, then shifting back into a smile.

"Yes," al-Nasir Yusuf said with a slight nod.

Ketbugha's eyes narrowed as he frowned and scrutinized al-Nasir Yusuf again. He looked at the squad leader. "The hands. It is not necessary. This is our loyal subordinate now."

The guards began untying al-Nasir Yusuf.

However, Ketbugha was unsatisfied with al-Nasir Yusuf's attitude. The man was trembling, but too tight-lipped. Was he still trying to think of a way to hedge his bets?

Ketbugha locked eyes with the man, deliberately creating a silent, awkward moment. Al-Nasir Yusuf shook his wrists, now free from the rope bindings.

Ketbugha's face showed a sinister grin. "We are preparing a wonderful feast for this evening—in honor of your submission, at last, to the dynasty destined to rule the world by the Eternal Blue Heaven."

Al-Nasir Yusuf's eyes bulged and a shiver seem to undulate through him. "A feast?"

Ketbugha raised his eyebrows. Good. Al-Nasir Yusuf had heard of the fate of al-Kamil Muhammad. "Yes, of course. A feast. To celebrate the end of uncertainty regarding your position."

"Uncertainty? There was no—"

"Of course there was. You sent your son to us, with gifts, but with no clear message of submission. You failed to send troops we requested, or to facilitate the surrenders of Aleppo and Damascus. You have been roaming around southern Syria instead of seeking us out. It took an informant to determine your location. Were you lost?"

"Lost." Al-Nasir Yusuf stammered. "No, of course not. But I had ... submitted. Was that ... unclear?"

Ketbugha scowled. "Of course it was unclear." He quickly forced a smile. "But it is clear now. That is why the occasion demands a feast."

Al-Nasir Yusuf swallowed. "But I—" His lower lip trembled and Ketbugha wondered if al-Nasir Yusuf was about to shed tears.

"We like to celebrate these ... these occasions where issues are clarified." Ketbugha paused with the explicit purpose of magnifying al-Nasir Yusuf's distress. "There was a situation like this, up north. An uncle of yours? We had a magnificent feast at that—"

"But it's not like that." Al-Nasir Yusuf raised his hands, palms outward, as if to keep Ketbugha away. He rattled off words, syllables running into each other. "I did submit, I sent my son, I sent gifts. I didn't defy the il-khan at Aleppo or Damascus. It's not like I didn't—" His lips folded in as a tear or two streaked both cheeks.

"Oh, please." Ketbugha broke into a broad smile, then forced a huge guffaw for effect. "Oh, no. I think you may have the wrong impression."

"I am at your service. Command me." Al-Nasir Yusuf sniffled.

"Of course. You will surrender Ajlun. You will give whatever information we request. Then, you will make the journey up to see Hulegu, in Azerbaijan.”

Al-Nasir Yusuf looked like he wanted to say something. His mouth opened, but he quickly shut it and nodded.

“You were thinking of al-Kamil Muhammad? When I said feast?”

“N-no, um, because I did not defy the il-khan the way he did.”

“Defiance can come in many ways.” Ketbugha stared into al-Nasir Yusuf’s fast blinking eyes. “And can be dealt with in many ways. You have probably noticed—we can be very creative dealing with defiance.”

“Yes, well, um, you won’t need any of that with me. I’m telling you, I am promising you, vowing, in the name of Allah, the God of my faith. You will get no defiance from me.”

“Oh, I know. We are confident of that. The magnificent Hulegu, il-khan, grandson of the greatest ruler ever, Genghis Khan, has huge plans for you. No doubt, you will rule huge sections of Syria in his name.”

“I-I will be his loyal servant.”

“You can tell him in person.”

“About that, um, I think I can be more effective working in this area to—”

“Nonsense. You must face Hulegu and express your loyalty.” Ketbugha’s nostrils flared. “Or there could be confusion. Hulegu might come to view you as wavering, uncertain, which for him is the same thing as defiance.” Ketbugha paused, for dramatic effect. “Like the defiance of al-Kamil Muhammad.”

Al-Nasir Yusuf said, “We would not want that.”

“No. You would not want that. You will start on your trip to Azerbaijan; with our escort, of course, to protect you, to insure you do not become lost in unfamiliar territory, lost and wandering the way you seemed to be in Syria. You will leave immediately after the surrender of Ajlun.”

Al-Nasir Yusuf bowed his head with a set of quick, obsequious nods. “Yes, um, Your Excellency, um, General, sir.”

Ketbugha responded with a sly smile.

❦ ◆ ❧

May, 1260
Acre
Afternoon

"If Robert seems so indifferent, why are you still serving him?" Jeannette asked Aram. They sat in their quarters as Aram was putting on his shoes. "From what you say, Nestor is no good reason to stay if you don't want to, and you've said you think you could negotiate something for him. Why is Robert—"

"I'm not sure," Aram said. He straightened his second shoe and stood. "It's something Uncle Dawud said."

"Uncle Dawud." Jeannette sneered and rolled her eyes. "That old Muslim? What could he—"

"I keep telling you not to dismiss him so easily because of his faith." Aram narrowed his eyes. "I think a wise man looks at what a person does, not at what he says he believes. Robert says he's Christian. Some of the *Mongols* say they're Christians. But I would trust my old Muslim uncle over them."

Jeannette raised her eyebrows contemplatively and nodded. "All right. I see it. So what is it that your Uncle Dawud said?"

"He said a huge confrontation is coming. He has decided he cannot avoid its pull any longer. He will take sides—against the Mongols. He asked me what stand I would take."

"What did you tell him?"

"I didn't tell him anything. I don't take sides. I hadn't planned on changing that now."

Jeannette shrugged. "So? What is the problem, then?"

"Maybe sometimes we need to take sides."

Jeannette shrugged again.

"Well, that's been on my mind. And I've felt a pull toward events too. And the source of that pull is Robert."

Jeannette raised her eyebrows. "He's the only thing keeping you here."

Aram eyed her slyly.

Jeannette grinned. "Well, me too."

Aram chuckled. "Of course, you too."

"So what is so important about seeing Robert this afternoon?"

"I thought about this. Endlessly, maybe too much. But I keep thinking: if Robert is the pull, what is my purpose? Am I drawn to him to help him achieve his purpose? Or is my pull to this man at this time occurring because I need to thwart his purpose?"

"And just what *is* his purpose?"

Aram smiled. "That, my dear, is the question. That's what I don't know. That's what I *need* to know. I've been fishing around, throwing out lines, hoping to hook him into some revelations. I still don't know. This afternoon, I will ask. Bluntly. Openly. I should have tried this sooner. One thing I know as a student of history is that the chroniclers write about the big names—the generals, the princes, the kings, the sultans, the khans—but I know enough about history to know that it can be people in positions like mine, people who act as a bridge between two very different worlds, that can, at a key moment, have a major effect on events."

Jeannette nodded. "And you think approaching Robert directly will work?"

Aram's lips tightened. "I've been serving this man over two years. I've been on long journeys with him." Aram looked at her. "I'd like to think we have formed some connection that I can prevail upon."

Jeannette nodded. "It would be a good thing to find out, one way or the other."

Aram hugged Jeannette and gave her a quick kiss, then left their quarters.

"I'm not interested in a heart-to-heart talk," Robert said through a dismissive sneer. "I want my direct communication route to the khan."

"We've talked about that. If you're talking about the great khan, we are still waiting for Mongols to confirm who it will be. If you're talking about the il-khan, he is up in Azerbaijan and communications are—"

"All I ever hear from you are excuses and blather about complexity and difficulty. I am weary of it. I wonder sometimes why I retain you in my service."

Aram's eyebrows flicked up and down. If a direct, heart-on-his-sleeve approach would not be effective, maybe there was another way. "That's a good question, sir. Why *do* you keep me in your service? Why was your need for my services so compelling that you coerced me by holding my friend?"

Robert squinted through a stern glare. "You seemed more competent than you have turned out to be."

"Perhaps that is because my purpose is unclear, because I am not clear on *your* purpose."

Robert sneered. "What?"

"I am not clear on what you are trying to accomplish."

"I have told you." Robert seemed to grind his teeth. "I have told you repeatedly."

"You have told me you come from the pope on a direct mission to the Mongols. But when circumstances come up that seem to contradict—"

"Are you saying that I have not been sincere with you about my mission?" His eyes bulged and his nostrils flared. "Are you calling me a liar?"

"Absolutely not. No. Not at all. I am not calling you a liar. I would never call my superior a liar. I'm demonstrating my confusion. That is why I need a heart-to-heart discussion. To ease my confusion. To resolve my perception of contradictions so I can—"

"I have explained what I can. Your task is to aid my contacts with the Mongols. You know what you need to know."

Aram fought the frustration he was feeling. Showing anger, or even annoyance, would end the conversation without Aram gaining the information he sought. Maybe he should shift back to the heart-to-heart approach. "Sir, I am mired in indecision. I know my services have not been effective for you. I have wondered why you have not dismissed me. I have pondered asking for my release from your services. But I sense a monumental confrontation, and I'm here in the midst of it. I'm trying to assess my—"

"Do you think you are some prominent historical personage who will decide the fate of the world?" Robert's nostrils flared. "You are *my servant*. Your role in any so-called 'monumental confrontation' is a minimal role, a minor role, the role of a baggage handler, or a table waiter."

Aram felt a surge of anger. He knew this insulting diatribe was calculated to show utter disrespect for him, and to diminish his unique skills. He also suspected it was Robert's way to try to end the conversation. He took in a deep breath. "Do you need me to continue in your service, sir?"

"Yes. Yes I do. You may yet prove useful."

"Well, a baggage handler or table waiter would be cheaper, sir. You should be able to find one, or even more than one, quite easily to replace me."

Robert grinned. "All right. You have more value than they do." He shrugged. "Don't be so prone to offense."

"Mmm."

"Stand by. I believe I will need your unique skills because I believe contact with Mongol authorities is still likely. My objectives—the pope's objectives—if they are well served, I will commend you with a bonus, beyond the money Nestor has taken."

"Mmm hmm."

"Any other questions this afternoon?"

None that would be answered, Aram considered. "No. I think not."

"Stand by. I will summon you when your services are needed."

Aram nodded, almost a bow, then left.

"He seemed grouchy, grumpy. And hostile." Aram took off his cloak and sat down.

"Hostile...." Jeannette seemed to ponder the word.

"Yes."

"Why doesn't he dismiss you?"

"There's only one possible reason. The man truly needs me. Or believes he needs me."

"What for?"

"For whatever he is trying to do."

"And we still don't know what that is."

"No." Aram scratched his chin. "Not exactly. It has to do with contacting Mongols. That's what he thinks I can help with."

"Makes sense."

"But two things are certain. He is hiding something from me. And when I try to uncover his complete and true intentions, he gets angry and guarded with me. More than that, I am not permitted to know."

Jeannette nodded. "What do we do?"

Aram pushed some air out of his nose.

"I am ready to move on," she said. "Say the word. I am ready to leave Acre and settle wherever we need to go."

Aram smiled. He reached out to his wife and took her hand. "I appreciate that. But I have no idea where we would go. Uncle Dawud was right. A huge confrontation is coming, one that will change this area significantly. Until the results of that conflict are settled, it is difficult to know where we should go."

Jeannette nodded again.

Aram continued, "I see no choice. I need to stay in Robert's service. I'll keep trying to ferret out the meaning of his mission, as best I can. That will help me determine my place in this confrontation, and how we will come through it."

Jeannette smiled.

29

"'The Power of God, the Emperor of all men.'" Qutuz's upper lip curled into a sneer.

Baybars raised his head, keeping a neutral expression on his face. He understood Qutuz's emotions, and some of those same feelings stirred within him. But this called for a deliberate, calculated analysis.

They stood in the main room of Qutuz's Cairo palace. A number of the emirs had been summoned for an emergency meeting. Toward the back of the room was a group of five restless-looking men, dressed in the style Baybars recognized as Mongol warriors. A squad of guards surrounded them.

Qutuz held a piece of paper. "'The Power of God,'" he repeated. "It starts there, and the disrespect magnifies. He refers to me in most demeaning terms as a 'slave-soldier,' as if that makes me inferior right at the start. Then, he accuses *me* of fleeing, apparently confusing me with other rulers in this area. He brags as if"—Qutuz read from the paper—"'our horses are swift, our arrows sharp, our swords like thunderbolts, our hearts as hard as mountains and our soldiers as numerous as the sand.' Then he insults us: 'Only those who beg our protection are safe.' Beg! He is asking—no, requiring—that the sultan of Egypt 'beg' him for protection!"

Baybars looked around the gathering, and over at the Mongols. The general mood among the emirs seemed to be fear. The Mongol delegates wore arrogant grins.

Baybars saw Qutuz glance over at the Mongols for a quick moment. Qutuz apparently recognized the same arrogance: his reaction registered as a squint and tensing of his lips.

"What else does he say?" Baybars asked.

"Threats, threats, threats. And it ends with something else that is supposed to scare us. 'At present you are the only enemy we have to march against.'"

Baybars raised his eyebrows and allowed himself a slight grin.

Qutuz's eyes met his, then he looked back at the grinning Mongol envoys. "We will adjourn to my anteroom to discuss this."

Baybars nodded.

"I want to kill those insulting, supercilious, arrogant envoys," Qutuz said just as the last of about thirty men filed into the small room adjoining the main room of the palace. "Any objections?"

Murmurs of trepidation rippled throughout the room. Baybars caught some snippets: "Mongols avenge their envoys." "They've never been defeated." "We could be assuring our own deaths."

Baybars looked at Qutuz. "We know that last statement of theirs is false."

Qutuz tilted his head as he turned to Baybars. "Which?"

"The only enemy they have to march against. Christians have raided Mongol positions." Baybars shrugged. "I think they are reckless to do so. But the word is: Mongols are looking to retaliate."

Qutuz nodded. "Yes, yes, we know about this. But those raids are trifles. What does this mean to us?"

"I think the arrogance and bombast of this letter actually shows weakness."

Qutuz paused in thought a moment, then smiled. "Indeed it does."

"They're overstating their position, hoping to intimidate us into indecision and fear. We know the bulk of the Mongol army has withdrawn to Azerbaijan. Their overheated letter shows their fear. And those 'trifling' Christian raids show their control of the area is not so firm."

Qutuz nodded. "I think you are right. And that argues further in favor of killing the envoys and preparing to take on these godless creatures."

Mostly worried expressions radiated from the group of emirs.

"I'm not so sure of that," Baybars said. "What advantage do we gain by killing the envoys?"

Qutuz looked at Baybars. "You, Baybars? You want to negotiate with the Mongols? Treat these arrogant mites like honored guests?"

Baybars' smile snuck out through a steely glare. Qutuz deliberately evaded the question about what advantage would be gained. Baybars sensed the man did not want to explain the answer to the entire group. "I want us to move out right now and crush their bones into the desert sand. But we may gain an advantage by making them think we are in negotiations."

Qutuz looked around the room. "And what do the rest of you think? Shall we send love notes back and forth while we move out to crush them? Shall we ignore their arrogance completely?"

No one spoke immediately. Finally, one man offered an opinion. "I think we need to keep our options open. Not capitulate. No 'love letters', as you say. But I agree with commander Baybars. There is little advantage to be gained by killing those envoys, and if we do it will be hard to say we intend to negotiate."

Qutuz nodded, looking away from the group, holding a neutral expression. "And this seems to be the consensus?" He looked back at the emirs.

Baybars saw mostly nods, but a few frowns.

"We'll take a show of hands on this important matter," Qutuz said. "How many wish to keep our options open and send a reply back with the envoys?"

Most raised their hands. Baybars looked around. He did not raise his hand.

"How many vote to kill the envoys?"

Six hands went up.

Baybars added his to make it seven. He still did not see any advantage to be gained by the extreme action of killing the Mongol envoys. But he could tell Qutuz wanted to do this, and decided to offer his public agreement.

Qutuz seemed to notice and directed a knowing smile at him, communicating his gratitude for the support.

Qutuz shrugged. "So, we have a split." He chuckled. "A split." He smiled. "Some wish to negotiate, and some wish to kill the envoys for their rank arrogance and disrespect."

Baybars smiled, but his eyes narrowed as he wondered where Qutuz was headed with this. He did not believe Qutuz was actually interested in soliciting votes for his decisions.

"I have an answer that I think will satisfy all of us," Qutuz told them, sounding like a statesman.

Baybars did not believe the statesmanlike tone for one moment.

"You who want to negotiate with the envoys can negotiate with one half, and I will execute the other half."

Nervous murmurs rippled through the room.

Qutuz grinned.

"Sultan," one of the men called out, clearly distressed with the decision. "Killing *any* of the Mongols will incur their wrath!"

Qutuz nodded. "You are correct. And how would I choose which ones to negotiate with?" He paused, but Baybars sensed he wasn't really trying to reach a decision, just pausing for effect. "I will execute the top halves of the envoys, and you who wish to negotiate can do so with the bottom halves." He looked at his chief guard, at the door to the room. "Sever the envoys at their waists."

Baybars had to make an effort to stifle a laugh.

"I need to keep the top halves," Qutuz said. "Because I want the Mongol heads displayed for all to see so everyone here knows this government is powerful, strong, and not tolerant of insults or threats." Qutuz paused as he looked at the gathering.

Baybars saw shocked faces, except those who had voted in favor of the executions.

"The rest of you—those for negotiating—you're free to negotiate with the bottom halves. That is all."

The gathering started to disperse.

Qutuz moved to Baybars. He looked around, then said quietly, close to Baybars' ear, "The advantage, my friend, is that those timid old ladies know we are committed to fight. They know what it means to execute Mongol envoys. Now we will hear no more about 'preserving our options.'"

Baybars nodded and smiled. "It's done. Now, we go crush them."

Qutuz smiled broadly and slapped Baybars on the back.

July 1260
Tabriz
Mid Day

"It is a pleasure to welcome a visit from you at last," Hulegu Khan said to al-Nasir Yusuf. The Ayyubid prince seemed anything but regal as he emerged bewildered from between two purifying columns of flames at the entrance to Hulegu's tent. Hulegu sat in an ornate chair on a raised pavilion. The flames were visible through the tent opening.

Hulegu was surrounded by guards and high-ranking officers. Hulegu and his entourage sported colorful silks, but al-Nasir Yusuf wore a dirty robe and turban. He was flanked by two guards. "I trust your journey was not too difficult," Hulegu told him.

"Difficult ... um, no." Al-Nasir Yusuf squinted and rubbed his eyes. "I think I—" He appeared to stop himself. "It's all ... unfamiliar."

The two guards forced him down to a kneeling position. The irritation on their faces communicated to Hulegu that they had expressly instructed al-Nasir Yusuf to kneel as soon as he emerged from between the two purifying flames. Hulegu grinned at al-Nasir Yusuf's discomfort.

Al-Nasir Yusuf's eyes widened. He looked up at Hulegu apprehensively, as if he had suddenly remembered what he was supposed to do after passing through the fires.

Hulegu raised his chin. "It would be more familiar to you if you had come sooner, the way the other princes ruling under my protection and authority have come, instead of sending your son."

From his knees, al-Nasir Yusuf bowed. He started to speak, but seemed to cut himself short again.

Hulegu raised his eyebrows. "Yes?"

"It's just that...." Al-Nasir Yusuf appeared to measure his words. "I am needed. I am...." He paused. "My presence is important in my lands. So, I maintained my presence while sending trusted family and subordinates to handle...." He stopped himself again. "To complete other tasks that...." Al-Nasir Yusuf did not seem to be able to finish the sentence.

"That are less important?" Hulegu asked.

"Yes, um, no...."

"Yes? No?"

Al-Nasir Yusuf swallowed.

"What could have been more important than your direct submission to me?"

Al-Nasir Yusuf's lips tightened. "Nothing."

"So this was an error of yours, not to come and see me sooner."

Al-Nasir Yusuf nodded. "Yes."

"An error of disrespect you will never repeat."

"Yes."

"Good." Hulegu's jaw jutted out as he clenched his teeth. "Now, I need some information from you."

Al-Nasir Yusuf bowed. "Whatever I can help with."

"Who are these creatures, these 'mamluks' who control the land of Egypt? Are they prone to rashness?"

"Rashness? No, not that I—"

"Do you know what they did?"

"What they did…?"

"What they did to my envoys?"

Al-Nasir Yusuf shook his head. "No, Your Majesty."

Hulegu squinted. "Two riders just came in with the news. They cut my envoys in half and stuck their heads on display around the city of Cairo."

Al-Nasir Yusuf's eyes widened. "That seems extraordinarily foolish."

"And courageous, yes?"

"No. No, not at all. Foolish."

"But they are good warriors. Wouldn't this defiance make them courageous, in your eyes and in the eyes of others of your people?"

"It is not courageous to kill defenseless envoys. It is disrespectful and foolish." Al-Nasir Yusuf seemed to be working up to a reaction. "I am … angry. Angry that people of my faith could behave so horribly. It makes me want to rush back to Syria and mobilize forces to punish them—to destroy them!"

Hulegu eyed al-Nasir Yusuf. "You want to rush back to Syria." He smiled. "I have a very able general down in the area. I believe you met him."

"Yes. A very able fellow."

"So what do I need with you back in Syria?"

Al-Nasir Yusuf seemed unable to offer a response.

"I will tell you how you will serve me—back in Syria."

"Yes. Yes, that would be—" Al-Nasir Yusuf nodded. "I await your instructions."

"You will rule there, under my authority, after we have defeated all resistance."

"Yes. Thank you. I will be very effective ruling there—for you."

"You will simply need to collect the required tribute. As long as those obligations are kept current, we can anticipate a long, fruitful relationship."

"Yes, my lord."

"For now, I will retain your presence here."

Al-Nasir Yusuf opened his mouth, then closed it.

"I'm sure you would like us to resolve all dissident factions against our rule before you go back and try to take your position."

"I could be of assistance in those operations."

Hulegu shrugged. "The problem is, you took a long time to make this journey. Your actions in the area were ambiguous, subject to alternative interpretations. I have princes from your family who accepted our rule much more quickly, with no apparent equivocation. Princes who have supplied troops and ride alongside my forces as we speak."

Al-Nasir Yusuf did not respond. He seemed to be through with trying to offer any meaningful discussion, or any further arguments that he should return to Syria.

Hulegu sneered. "You will be kept in comfort here, as befits a future ruler in the great khan's empire. We will contact you when a change in your status is indicated." Hulegu motioned al-Nasir Yusuf's dismissal with a backhanded flick of his wrist.

30

Summer 1260
Cairo
Afternoon

"I'm sensing resistance to that idea," Qutuz said. He and Baybars stood over a table and looked down at a map. The tent around them was filled with top-ranking advisers and emirs, along with a small squad of Qutuz's personal guard. A few of Baybars' key officers stood beside him.

"It is the *right* idea," Baybars told him. "The *courageous* idea. The move that will give us the initiative."

"Yes. But it is not the *safe* move."

Baybars raised eyebrows as he nodded.

"They know we killed the envoys. They know we are committed to a fight. But I think many of them would like to wait it out as long as possible over here."

"I can see that," Baybars said. "But after the Mongol succession problem is resolved, we can count on Hulegu to come down here with five to ten times the force they have now. This is the time—God wills it—the time and circumstance for us to *defeat* them, to show our fellow believers they can be defeated, that we can drive them back out of our lands."

Qutuz smiled. "You do not have to convince me."

"I know."

"Your men are in extraordinary shape, no doubt a reflection of your leadership."

Baybars nodded. "Thank you."

"I wish all our forces were as ready as yours."

"From my observations, many are."

Qutuz paused. "I want your squads to help me identify those who are ready and to help me prepare the ones who are not."

"That would be my honor. We live to defeat and destroy God's enemies. And there is no worse enemy than the Mongols."

Qutuz clenched and raised his fist. "To victory."

Baybars smiled.

"I will assign drills to identify—" Qutuz broke off his statement and looked up as a guard walked in. Baybars' eyes followed Qutuz's.

"Yes?" Qutuz asked.

The man bowed. "Sultan, a patrol reports finding an old man and a younger companion up on the trail from Syria. We would not disturb you except that the old man insists he has just come from the Mongols."

"From the Mongols?" Qutuz scrunched his face in disbelief.

"From their territory. He insists he can be of help."

Qutuz frowned. "Is he here?"

"Yes. He and his companion."

Qutuz looked at Baybars.

Baybars shrugged. "Why not see what he has to say?"

Qutuz told the guard, "Bring them in."

Dawud and his student-companion entered. Their robes were filthy and their faces smudged. But the old man especially seemed to Baybars to have an energetic gleam in his eye.

"I am Sultan Qutuz, here with some key commanders in an important meeting," he said with condescension. "What do you have to offer that is important enough to interrupt?"

Dawud bowed. "My apologies for the timing, something I had no control over. I am Dawud the Teacher, originally from Jaffa. I would like to offer any assistance I can toward your defeat of the Mongols."

Qutuz scratched one of his eyebrows and chuckled. He looked at the guard who had accompanied the two men. "What have you brought me?" he asked, nearly giggling. "A new recruit for the infantry?"

"I have recently been through Mongol-held territories," Dawud said. "Perhaps I can help with information, with insight."

"So you are a spy," Qutuz said.

Dawud frowned. "No. Merely someone with information. I believe God is drawing me into this fight, and I need to make myself available to the warriors for the True Faith."

Qutuz squinted. "There are no Mongols in Jaffa. Only

Christians."

"I have not lived in Jaffa for many years. My father was a Christian knight; he fought against Saladin. In what seems so long ago it was a previous existence, I was a warrior for the True Faith. A dedicated warrior. A fanatic warrior. I feel some of that past passion coming back."

"I don't think we are so desperate that we need to start enlisting old men," Qutuz said. "You're an entertaining fellow, but we have work to do."

"I would like to help you with it."

Baybars watched the exchange. The old man was determined not to be dismissed.

Qutuz seemed to look him over, with the humor draining from his face. "They found you on the Damascus Road, old man. How can you help me with Mongols?"

"I was in Baghdad," Dawud said sternly.

"And that is your first and last mistake," one of Qutuz's advisers said. "They killed everyone in Baghdad. You're lying."

Dawud's nostrils flared. "I was *there*. They killed *many*, that is as true as truth gets. But they kept me. Because they thought I was an astrologer."

Qutuz looked at him. "But you're not."

"No. And when they discovered it, I had to escape or die."

Qutuz's adviser raised his hand to his mouth and snorted a laugh. "You? Escaped from Mongols?"

"I did," Dawud told them. "And again in Damascus."

Qutuz waved his hand dismissively. "I'm sorry, but I have no use for you. I do repeat that you're entertaining. But—"

"Maybe he's an envoy," the adviser said in a sly tone.

Baybars rolled his eyes.

"An envoy from the Mongols?" Qutuz repeated. "We have reserved special treatment for envoys."

A chuckle rippled through the group.

"How can I be an envoy if I escaped from the Mongols?"

"If you're an envoy, you'll be treated specially," the adviser said again. He looked at the young man next to Dawud. "You're an envoy, right?"

The young man looked confused.

"Being an envoy will get you special treatment," the adviser said again. "Tell us you're an envoy from the Mongols."

"We are not envoys," Dawud insisted. "We can—"

"Enough," Qutuz said impatiently. "That's enough." He turned to the guards. "Give them some food and water and point them toward the school."

Baybars looked at Dawud.

Dawud's nose twitched as he frowned. His head turned and his eyes met Baybars'.

"Wait for me," Baybars said. "I'd like to talk to you."

Qutuz raised his eyebrows.

"I like the old fellow," Baybars said as he grinned at Qutuz. "Like you said, he's entertaining."

Qutuz shrugged.

"Let's just take the food and water and go for a post in Cairo," Dawud's student-companion said quietly. They stood outside the tent.

Dawud shook his head. "You saw what I saw. That large man with the deep voice was the one the sultan was speaking with when we came in. He's an important man. Maybe it is God's will that we serve him."

"Or he wants to have sport with us."

"I don't think so."

"They apparently think we're stupid, or fools, or just … just targets for cruel fun, and don't know that those heads on the pikes belonged to Mongol envoys, Mongol envoys they sliced in half."

Dawud inhaled, then exhaled. "I don't know what that was about. But I did not hear the large one playing that game. I saw him studying us. Smiling, not frowning. Let's see where this goes."

"I would prefer not to have my head on a—"

The student stopped as Baybars emerged from the tent.

"Bury your fear," Dawud told the student.

The student offered what looked to Dawud like a nod, albeit a nervous one.

Baybars walked to them. "So, here's an old teacher, son of a Christian knight, warrior for the True Faith, citizen of Baghdad, escaping slaughter, escaping the Mongols…."

"I have had a complicated life." Dawud maintained a steely expression. He was tired of being toyed with and sensed that showing fear and weakness to this man would be a mistake. It was time for Dawud to demonstrate he was a serious man, to be taken seriously.

"If it is all true."

Dawud unflinchingly met Baybars' gaze. "All of it."

Baybars shrugged. "I can see that if it is all true, you could have value as an adviser for what is to come."

"And what is to come?" Dawud asked.

"I'll keep the details to myself. Just in case you're collecting information for the Mongols."

"And I will ride away, through all your patrols, to pass this information on?"

Baybars shrugged. "I don't know. Perhaps using the same miracles you used to escape from them and come all the way down here."

"That has been part of a long journey."

"I see. A journey that has brought you much knowledge and perspective."

"Yes." Dawud paused as he locked eyes with Baybars again. "I keep sensing doubts that I escaped the Mongols. Sir, *do not* doubt it. In my escape there is a lesson. They can be beaten. I killed one to get away. Me, an old man past my warrior days."

Baybars' raised eyebrows told Dawud he had the large man's attention.

"They found out I was not an astrologer. A particularly obnoxious Mongol took me to a killing ground and taunted me as he was about to behead me. He was going to enjoy butchering an old man. My only weapon was his arrogance, his utter failure to realize that all old men were once young men." Dawud clenched his teeth. "I threw an elbow into his knees and when he doubled over, I gained control of his weapon. I put an end to his life and rode away. His arrogance compelled him to deal with me alone, so when I disposed of him, there was no one to prevent my escape."

Baybars scratched his nose, but his eyes signaled his rapt attention.

"They came after me. They were still after me in Damascus. I suspect the man I killed has well-placed friends or relations, and my act was a source of embarrassment."

Baybars grinned. "No doubt."

"I can attest to my teacher's wisdom," said Dawud's student-companion. "And I can attest to the fact that Mongols were after him in Damascus."

"I am on a collision course with these monsters," Dawud stated flatly. "I now choose to embrace the collision instead of trying to escape it."

Baybars smiled. "And you have knowledge of this entire area. Mongols. And Christians."

"I know it seems fanciful. But it is true. I have serious connections with Christians through a close relative."

"You realize we killed the Mongol envoys, and are going out into Syria to seek a confrontation with the Mongols."

Dawud's face broke into a broad smile. "Good."

"And Christian territory could be involved."

Dawud bowed slightly. "I am at your service, sir."

Baybars turned to one of his guards. "Arrange quarters for these men. Fresh clothes. Food. Rest." Baybars looked at Dawud. "We will speak in greater detail later today. And you will tell tales of your days as a warrior for the True Faith," Baybars said in what Dawud perceived as an admiring tone of voice.

Dawud smiled and bowed again.

Summer, 1260
Acre
Dawn

"I am coming!" Aram said as he sat up in bed. Pounding on the door was once again interrupting the silence of the dawn. Jeannette remained on her side. Daniel slept.

Aram threw on some clothes. "Just … hang on a moment. I'm almost ready."

"What's this again?" Jeannette asked through a yawn as she turned onto her back.

"Some chore I'm to help with," Aram said. He rubbed his eyes. "Someone's figured out I don't do much around here."

"Regular chores…."

"Yes. Not a lot." Aram yawned. "I sure don't do much for Robert."

The door pounded again.

"I had better get going."

Aram stepped to the door and opened it. His eyes widened with surprise.

Adolfo stood there. "Yes. Let's go."

Aram nodded, suddenly wide awake.

They walked quietly through the halls toward an exit. "The stable-keeper is ill, at my instructions. So I have volunteered us to help him this morning."

"So we can talk."

"Yes. The chores are simple. Some of them mucky, but simple."

Aram shrugged. "And we will not be interrupted."

Adolfo smiled.

"So you have news?" Aram asked.

Adolfo shook his head. His pace increased. His head swiveled as he glanced back and forth. "Not here."

They emerged onto the street. Adolfo pointed ahead toward a stone building. "There's the stable."

Aram nodded. He knew where it was.

Adolfo looked side to side, then behind them as they walked through the street. "One of our people, sent back to Italy to find out about Robert, has finally returned."

Aram looked at Adolfo.

"We know a great deal more, but still have gaps in our knowledge."

Aram nodded. The stable was about twenty paces ahead. As they entered the structure Adolfo said, "Robert is German."

"That isn't new."

"You may not be completely aware of the significance. At this time, the Hohenstaufen dynasty is severely weakened, and the pope—not a German—is doing all he can to stomp it out."

"Robert is from that dynasty?"

"That is not clear." Adolfo looked at the stable. "Let's start with the stalls. We need to pile up the manure for use on the plots."

Aram nodded. He had little experience with chores of this type, but would follow Adolfo's lead.

Adolfo took hold of a small, two-wheeled cart. "Push this." Adolfo grabbed a pitchfork.

They moved toward the first stall.

"So who is Robert?" Aram asked.

"This is what we're still not clear on. There are some answers about what he is not. He is not really from Montpelier. He apparently attended the medical school there, briefly, before he found politics more to his liking. He likes to say he's from Montpelier because it is a known location throughout Europe, one with a cosmopolitan profile. This way, he can hide his true origins."

Adolfo stepped into the first stall and scooped out straw and horse turds, dropping them into the cart. "Also, he is not here on a mission from the pope to the Mongols."

Aram froze. That information sent a chill through him.

"That seemed puzzling to us from the first. But his credentials, his bearing, his armed companions...."

Aram's lips pulled together. "What is he doing? What am *I* doing?"

"The pope *did* send him out here. Robert had risen to become a fairly important man in the church. Robert volunteered to come out here, and the pope agreed, but only to get rid of a German with questionable loyalties. Our man reports he was given only one mission directly from the pope, and that was to deliver the news of excommunication to Bohemond."

Aram chuckled. "He clearly did not like that mission."

Adolfo moved to the next stall. "It was a thankless mission, maybe even dangerous."

Aram nodded. "So trying to set an alliance with the Mongols...."

"Not from the pope. The pope knows about Mongols. He's gotten reports, most recently a detailed and revealing report from William of Rubruck."

Aram raised his eyebrows as he nodded.

Adolfo grinned and shook his head. "The pope is calling for a Crusade against Mongols in northern Europe!"

"*Northern* Europe?" Aram puzzled over this.

"Out where the Poles are, the Slavs."

Aram barely knew where that was, or who those people were.

"The Slavs are not affiliated with true Christianity. But the Poles are. And Mongols have taken some of their lands. The pope is *not* looking for an alliance."

Aram's lower jaw jutted out, then pulled back as he clenched his teeth. "So what is all this nonsense from Robert?"

"He's working with someone, someone with resources. Two of our previous agents, sent to gather information, were intercepted and corrupted with lucrative positions. A more recent agent located them, and then found himself in serious jeopardy when he declined the same offer. His journey back here—well, I would call him a hero. He tells us messages come out of Rome, and from other locations, for Robert. But they are not from the pope."

Aram took his hands from the cart. "I'm packing my bags. This is not what I signed on for."

"We would prefer you don't," Adolfo said with a harsh terseness that conflicted with the apparent courtesy of the words.

Aram looked at him.

"We would prefer you stay in place with Robert and find out what he is up to."

Aram frowned thoughtfully as he continued to look Adolfo in the eyes. He wondered how he could tactfully ask *and what if I don't?* But his expression apparently communicated the question for him.

"You do not want to be without friends right now—you and your young family."

Aram paused. He looked away, then down. "I see." He took hold of the cart and they moved to the next stall. "I'll talk to Robert today."

"Good." Adolfo scooped another set of horse droppings and straw into the cart.

"So they know all about me now," Robert said with a sneer and a shrug. "So what." He sat at a table in his quarters looking over some parchments.

"So, just what is your mission, *sir?* And who are you working for? It's not the pope."

"No." Robert took in a deep breath. "It isn't." He smiled. "They sent you here to find out."

Aram forced a laugh. "They know all about you, Robert. They know everything! I would just like not to be the last one to know."

Robert shrugged again. "What does it matter? This place is so torn up with factions that it doesn't really matter." Robert looked at Aram with stern consideration. "The fact is, I still may need you. I'm not sure. But I am willing to maintain you here, at my expense, in case I do." He nodded. "And so, I should level with you. Maybe should have done it some time ago."

"You are right about that."

Robert nodded. "I grant you that. *Mea culpa*—absolution, please." He smiled slightly.

Aram let a slight grin sneak out. "What is it you want to tell me now, Robert not from Montpelier? How are you going to 'level with me,' after all this time—all this time of, of not so much leveling."

"You've heard I'm German."

"Figured it out long ago."

"Everyone probably thinks I'm with the Hohenstaufens."

"It's been said."

Robert chuckled. "I'm a bit mixed, actually. From Eastern France. That's where I got the French name. Early in my life, my family was fortunate enough to befriend, and offer services to, a German family. The family is on the rise, my dear Aram. I welcome the pope's efforts to end the power of the dying Hohenstaufen ruling house. My loyalties are with the up-and-coming power in Central Europe. The pope is simply clearing the way for them. And my political knowledge has been tapped by this family to assist their position. It will be Central Europe that dominates the true Christianity, Europe, and in time very possibly the world. At the time of Richard the Lionheart, before all he could do was fight Saladin to a draw, the great Frederick Barbarossa brought a massive army to the gates of Syria! A fluke accident took that great Emperor from this mortal world or this entire area would be German now! Central Europe has the resources, the masses of people, and the breeding—the blood of people never tamed by the Romans of antiquity, of people who eventually destroyed the Roman Empire. This is the future, and I am on the cusp of it. My benefactor is Rudolph the Fourth of Hapsburg. He and his agents in the German lands, and in Rome, are my partners in communication. The pope has been driven out of Rome while contending powers tug at him from every corner. I intend to work to make Rudolph of Hapsburg the dominant power."

Aram snorted through a smile. This speech was too heartfelt, too prideful, too arrogant not to be sincere. "I believe I finally have the truth from you. But one thing is still missing. What would your Hapsburg people want with Mongols?"

Robert shook his head. "Aram, Aram, Aram. I know you're a smart fellow, and if you thought about this for any time at all you would see this clearly. Mongols are going to destroy Islam. It is the clearest fact available to us, plain as the sunrise and sunset. Mongols never lose. They're on their way to taking Egypt. From there, it is a simple turn north and west to take the Mediterranean. God has sent this host to destroy the Islam scourge. I do not pretend to know or understand God's will. I do not pretend that this scourge against Islam does not bring evil in its wake. Mongols have attacked Europe as well. But Mongol victory is plain, inevitable, and irresistible. I have gone over this at length with my superiors. They are far more consumed with events closer to home, but have given me authority to set up lines of communication and negotiate on their behalf. The day will come when we will need to decide if we are friends or enemies of these base but powerful creatures. I prefer friendship. Then, I will pray God grants us the strength to bring these creatures to the true Christianity. God has seen this before, with the brutal pagan Vikings of Scandinavia becoming the fierce Christian warriors, the Normans. Such a transition may be God's will for the Mongols; we will pray for it. But I believe God has despaired of the hope that Christians from the West will ever destroy Islam. So He has conjured up this force of His will from the East."

Aram's face was tense. "You've seen what they do. You were there in Baghdad. You've seen what this 'force from the East' is about."

"Yes. It did trouble me—to see it up close. But, the facts remain."

"Invincibility?"

"Exactly."

"Sir, what if the Mongols are the devil's temptation?"

Robert's face went white. Aram sensed this had not occurred to him. "I don't think so," he finally offered weakly after a long pause.

"You don't think so."

"No," Robert said more firmly. "I don't. I have prayed, and I believe God.... I believe I have been, that I have understood God's will, God's will to be rid of Islam and his frustration with earthly powers, earthly servants incapable, incapable of completing the task."

Aram grunted. "Really." He shook his head. "Well, I am not of your mind on this. I am dismissing myself from your service. My family and I will be leaving. Please do not try to prevent this. I'll maintain my silence on these details. I have no desire to align with either—"

"Oh, well, certainly then. Go ahead," Robert said in a dismissive tone of voice.

Aram expected an argument. This took him by surprise.

"Where will you go?"

Aram's eyes darted. He wished he had a quick answer.

"Back to Baghdad? Maybe to Damascus?" Robert offered.

Aram's shoulders tensed but he did not reply.

"Oh, that's right. Both these places are under Mongol control. By your reckoning, possibly the devil."

Aram lowered his head.

"Egypt, perhaps? Europe?" Robert smirked. "What will you have to offer in those places? How will you sustain your young family?"

"I haven't thought this through, but I will." Aram wished the words had been stronger as he spoke them.

"You'll stay here," Robert told him. "I will pay you well. I will pay you *directly.*"

Aram tilted his head. He had to admit this was a valid alternative to consider.

"You don't like it, you don't want to admit it, but you're in the same position I am. There is a confrontation coming. Factions are choosing sides. One stupid faction from here is actually raiding Mongol territories! The fools! The consequences to them, and innocent Christians in the area, will be devastating! You're going to take your family out into that?" Robert shook his head. "No. You'll stay here with me, under my protection, earning good wages in my service, in the service of Rudolph of Hapsburg, until this confrontation resolves." Robert's eyes bored in on Aram.

Aram realized he hadn't thought through his impulsive desire to leave after finding out the truth about Robert. He hated the idea, but Robert seemed to be right. And he could stay safely at Acre, serving Robert and feeding information to Adolfo—though he suspected that wasn't even an issue, as Robert barely seemed to care if Adolfo's people knew everything. "I'll be in my quarters," Aram said.

Robert offered a smug grin. "I will contact you when I need you."

Aram nodded.

He walked through the halls to rejoin Jeannette. So he could not just pick up and leave as quickly as he wanted to. This would take some thought. Adolfo had been right. Traveling in the area without friends would be a risky activity. Robert had been right. He needed a clear idea of where he would go and what he would do. He wished he had someone he could confide in and ask for advice. He smiled and tried to remember the last time he had needed anyone's counsel, as if anyone could be wiser about what he should do than he was. Then he found himself wondering, out of want, and out of a whimsical curiosity, where Dawud was, and if he could contact his uncle somehow.

31

"Then let me add my voice to the others," said one of the emirs who had gathered in a command tent with Qutuz and Baybars. Dawud was also present, but he stood back from the others, observing events. "We should firm our positions in Egypt. Make the fiends come down through Syria, across the deserts of the Sinai, across the Nile, and then see how they fare against our rested armies and our fortified strongholds."

Qutuz sneered.

Baybars looked up and away.

Dawud shook his head.

The emir continued. "We can send harassing patrols to—"

"Are you volunteering for that duty?" Qutuz asked.

The emir stopped speaking, apprehension showing on his face.

Dawud was unable to suppress a small grin.

"We are committed to battle them," Qutuz said. "We can sit and wait, or take the fight to them."

"Of course we will battle them," the emir said. "The question here is what strategy we should use, whether we should—"

"The question here is whether you are *afraid* of this enemy," Qutuz stated starkly.

The emir bristled, but seemed to know he was not in a position to take offense. "You should know, Sultan, that my ideas on strategy are shared by many of my peers."

"By most of them, it seems," Qutuz said with steely eyes. "Our ranks are filled with troops fleeing these Mongol creatures—the

Turks, the Bedouins, the Kurds, along with Syrians who have fought under many different banners. We have skilled officers here training them in the most lethal tactics of combat and maneuver." Qutuz nodded toward Baybars, who nodded back. "We are out in this staging area, poised to move, and you think the best idea for all these circumstances is a *defensive* posture?"

The emir did not seem to know what to say.

"If the order is given, you will advance," Qutuz told him.

The emir's jaw tightened. "If the order is given, it may well be given over the trepidations of most of your officers."

Qutuz squinted. "You are dismissed."

The emir brought his legs together, gave a quick bow, and left the tent.

Qutuz looked at his other advisers.

"This is a common sentiment among most of them," one of his men said.

Qutuz clenched his teeth. "I need to give them some backbone. I need to remind them that we are committed to a fight to the death; for our existence, for the existence of the True Faith."

Baybars shook his head. "And they will say they are committed, but object to the strategy." He sneered. "You rule. You have the authority. You know what we need to do. You are dealing with fear, Sultan. Their fear of the Mongols. You need to counter that fear—with fear of *you* if they fail to carry out their duties under your command."

The tent became silent.

Qutuz appeared to process Baybars' words.

Dawud looked at the faces of the men in the tent. He sensed the silence was the result of no one having a better answer. Dawud did. Should he speak up? Baybars had brought him to the meeting to observe, without any overt encouragement to participate. But Dawud would not let any sort of fear stifle him. He had fled Mongols for two years, even killed one to survive. All he risked here was a potential rebuke. "Mix fear with shame," he said quietly.

Qutuz frowned.

Baybars tilted his head as his eyes narrowed, as if in thought. "Shame...."

"Yes," Dawud said.

"What is this old man saying?" Qutuz demanded of Baybars. "They already should be ashamed. I'm to harang them into shame about being afraid?"

"No, no," Dawud said. "Not with a speech. Words would be spoken, yes, but not as a direct scolding."

Baybars lifted his eyebrows. "We should hear more," he said to Qutuz. "I have found this old warrior to be one of the wisest men I have ever met. Experience, and God's gift of insight from that experience; he is a resource I am still learning about, but that I take seriously."

"Very well," Qutuz said as he shrugged. "Let us hear how your old refugee sage will shame the emirs."

"I am not going to make a long speech." Qutuz stood on a dais erected just outside his tent. He was alone, facing a large group of emirs.

Baybars was in the front row, facing the sultan. He glanced back at the diverse group of officers behind him. Some of them had been with Qutuz for many years in Egypt, but many were newly arrived, driven into the area by the spreading wave of Mongol conquest. He sensed these men were susceptible to whatever sentiment captured the group.

Dawud stood next to them. Baybars grinned at this old man, fast becoming a friend, fast becoming a man Baybars could respect. He hoped the idea for this appeal to the gathering, largely inspired Dawud's advice, would be successful.

"This is a battle for our survival, the survival of the True Faith," Qutuz told them. "Nothing less than that, my brethren. Right now, we are strong. Look at the mass of forces gathered here, all here to battle for God! The Mongol forces are *weak*, off worrying about who will govern their empire from some far-flung place. And God wills that we strike now! God will know where I was, and what I was doing when this battle was joined! What will God say about where you are now? What will your family say?" He paused and gazed over the crowd.

Baybars glanced around. Faces were attentive, but Baybars sensed the same uneasy mood he had gauged in the smaller group earlier.

"Here is what God will know about *me*," Qutuz told them. "If I have to fight *alone*, I will!" Qutuz put on his helmet and picked up a sword and a shield. He brandished the sword as he continued, "God and the Faithful will know where I stood, and God's will be done as to my fate!" He raised up his sword. "Who advances with me?"

Baybars stepped up immediately. "I advance with you," he said with his deep voice, filled with an understated but strong tone of resolution. "My men—every one of them—commits to advancing with you. If it is only us, we will be by your side."

Baybars' men began crowding onto the dais. "Commander Baybars, you've shown your commitment to the battle. And during our training over these last weeks, you have shown your grasp of tactics and ability to command. You will command the vanguard in this fight!"

Baybars bowed. "It will be my honor to be the *first* to engage these devils who come to our lands to destroy the True Faith!"

Qutuz nodded to Baybars, then looked back toward the emirs.

A few raised their hands and shouted their commitment. Baybars recognized most of those as newly arrived emirs, ones who had been committed to the fight long before this gathering. The Egyptian emirs continued to hold back. Baybars' lips tightened.

Baybars looked at Dawud, still standing in the crowd. Was this idea going to work?

Dawud grinned, then his grin broadened into a smile. As he took bold steps to the dais he yanked off his turban and flung it out to the crowd. Taking a place in the front of the increasingly crowded dais, he turned to stand facing the gathering. Dawud's white hair and beard showed his age. Murmurs rippled through the crowd.

One of Baybars' men handed him a helmet, which Dawud placed upon his head. Dawud's face scrunched with angry determination. Another man handed him a shield. Yet another, a sword. "I escaped the Mongols!" he shouted. "I survived Baghdad! I have seen seventy years! But I will ride with you, Sultan! I will defend the True Faith with my last ounce of blood, with my last years on this earth!"

"Who will join these men?" Qutuz demanded. "Who will join these warriors for the True Faith, and ride with me today?"

Shouts erupted from the crowd. Baybars smiled. The Egyptian emirs now bellowed their commitment to marching against the Mongols. The din of their yelling swelled to a point where individual commitments were hard to discern. Shouts of "God is great!" added to the growing sounds of determination and devotion. The dais was not capable of holding all the men, but soon, no one was facing Qutuz—they had all gathered behind their sultan.

Qutuz looked at Baybars. He smiled and nodded.

Baybars' eyes glistened slightly as he looked at Dawud.

"Ride out today, Commander," Qutuz told him. "Find them."

Baybars' face broke into a malevolent smile. "With pleasure."

Qutuz looked at Dawud. "Will you take the old man?" he asked Baybars.

Baybars chuckled. "I cannot imagine him agreeing to stay behind."

Qutuz looked around at the energized emirs, now arrayed behind him. "God wills it: we will crush the Mongols."

Early August 1260
Qalyub District – North of Cairo
Mid Day

"You two will get along," Baybars said to Adiba and Zahirah. "It is that simple." They were in the private quarters shared by Adiba, Zahirah, and Baybars' son, al-Malik al-Said. The two women were sitting cross-legged on the floor while Baybars sat in a chair. Al-Malik al-Said played nearby.

Adiba's upper lip trembled. "How long will you be gone?"

"I don't know. We are going out to take on the Mongols directly. I don't know how far we will need to go to catch up to them."

Adiba let two tears escape down her cheeks.

"See what I have to put up with?" Zahirah said. "Always the dramatic one. Always the martyr. Always complaining she has to do everything."

"*Does* she have to do everything?" Baybars asked.

"Not everything. But that's *her* son. Why should I have to—"

"Because I said so," Baybars said. "You will help. She is First Wife."

Zahirah smirked. "First in age. First in sequence. Not first in anything else." She looked at Baybars. "Not first in pleasing you."

"Stop that," Baybars told her. But he could not argue against what Zahirah was implying, that she was a pleasure dynamo, one he was still exploring at least once a day whenever he was with them. He hadn't visited Adiba in months, and the two women were aware of it.

Zahirah motioned disgustedly at Adiba. "Look at her."

Adiba's tears flowed.

"Yes, look at her," Baybars said firmly. "My first wife. Mother of my first son. And with authority over you while I am gone."

Adiba's expression changed. She looked at Zahirah with stern eyes.

"Consequences will flow if her authority is not respected," Baybars said.

Zahirah's expression froze. She nodded.

"I will return after the Mongols are defeated. Until then, you two will get along. I expect no reports to the contrary."

Baybars stood.

Both women moved to hug him.

He held both of them, one in each arm.

Second Week of August
Homs
Mid Morning

"They told me, but I still didn't believe it," al-Ashraf Musa said to Dawud as the latter was escorted into a small sitting room. The remnants of a morning meal were visible on a table. Al-Ashraf Musa motioned Dawud to a chair. "I am honored, teacher."

Dawud nodded. "Thank you." He took a seat.

"Bring the teacher some fruit and bread," al-Ashraf Musa called out to his servants. "And water."

Dawud smiled and nodded another thank you.

Al-Ashraf Musa was in his forties. His face showed signs of aging, but he had not allowed his body to become flabby with indulgences. And Dawud saw those same eyes he had known before, the eyes of a man constantly assessing, formulating; a man always prepared for the unexpected, and poised to find an advantage in it.

"I thought we lost you in Baghdad," al-Ashraf Musa told him.

Dawud raised his eyebrows and let some air out through his nose. "No, I would say God has gone out of his way to preserve this old life."

Al-Ashraf Musa chuckled. "You have a story to tell. I'm sure of that."

Dawud smiled. "No doubt of that."

"If that fool impersonating a caliph had submitted Baghdad to the il-khan, many might have survived."

"Under Mongol rule. Mongol slavery."

Al-Ashraf Musa raised his chin. "As I am."

Dawud paused, looked him in the eyes and said, "As you are."

Al-Ashraf Musa narrowed his eyes and grinned. "You never did mince words."

Dawud maintained eye contact. No, he most definitely did not mince words.

"You were my favorite teacher," said al-Ashraf Musa. He shook his head. "Baghdad, for me, was about you. My experience as a young man, acquiring knowledge in Baghdad, was an experience enhanced by you." He smiled. "You are one of the few I can think of to whom I would listen no matter how I might object to their words."

Dawud shrugged. "You were a great student. So smart. So clever. So enthusiastic to learn."

"Yes, well, those were different times, and different circumstances."

"Absolutely."

"What brings you here, now?"

"There is a battle coming. A battle for good versus evil. I want you to consider what side of that battle you will join."

"You must know, I've submitted to the il-khan. He will require my assistance against the Egyptian sultan."

"They scheme to destroy Islam," Dawud said.

Al-Ashraf Musa shrugged. "That is not my experience with them. They have allowed us to worship freely. They—"

"You should have seen what happened in Damascus. Christians were allowed to abuse the Faithful, and those who complained were cruelly and summarily punished. They would relegate the True Faith to equality with all other faiths—the religion of the Christ, the religion of the Jews, the religions of sun and moon worshippers dancing around campfires—all subject to Mongol whims under their Eternal Blue Heaven."

"Teacher, I have no choice. Al-Nasir Yusuf deposed me from my rightful position here. The Mongols have restored me. The Mongols have treated me better than my own Muslim kin! It is easy to sit in a classroom making remote observations of what needs to be done. The flesh-and-blood world demands decisions."

Dawud paused a moment, allowing al-Ashraf Musa's emotions to calm. Quietly he said, "Men always have choices."

Al-Ashraf Musa held a stern expression.

"You still have choices. If the time comes, and the fate of the True Faith is in your hands, I am here to remind you that human beings always have choices."

"Mongols do not take kindly to defections. Ask old al-Kamil Muhammad—turned into a chicken dinner."

"God's wrath could be harsher, and eternal."

Al-Ashraf Musa's eyes widened and his face seemed to turn white.

Dawud pulled his head back slightly, wondering if he had gone too far.

Al-Ashraf Musa burst into laughter. "You haven't lost a bit of your sharp wits, and your provocative lessons." He shook his head. "There is a place for you in my service."

Dawud let out a burst of air. "I have a position. Under a key commander for Sultan Qutuz."

Al-Ashraf Musa leaned back as his eyes widened again. "So this is from Qutuz?"

Dawud nodded. "He's making contact with you and al-Said Hasan. He implores both of you to consider the True Faith when the coming battle arrives."

"And he sends you?"

"I volunteered. I know you. I thought I would be best for this mission."

Al-Ashraf Musa appeared to consider the information. "Well, I do not have a real fight with Qutuz," al-Ashraf Musa finally said. "I respect that he has taken the time to reach out. I will send back word with you to tell him so."

Dawud grinned. "Good."

Dawud suspected al-Ashraf Musa was again hedging his bets, not wanting to alienate a possible victor in the coming clash. But whatever al-Ashraf Musa had in his mind, or in his heart, Dawud was satisfied that the message had been delivered. The idea had been planted.

"You are free to stay here under my protection during this battle. Mongols respect envoys—that is what I will tell them you—"

"I appreciate the offer, but I'm still hunted by Mongols for some, some trouble up near—"

"Don't tell me any more," al-Ashraf Musa said quickly. He laughed. "Oh my goodness. You are one of the greatest men I have ever crossed paths with." He stood.

Dawud got to his feet as well and they hugged.

"As it stands, I am subservient to the Mongols. I have an obligation to supply soldiers to contest Qutuz. But I respect your efforts here today."

Dawud nodded.

"Good luck to you, dear teacher. Whatever happens in the coming battle, I hope you remain well."

"You too, my friend."

"I'll have my men help you get on your way. You should go quickly."

"I appreciate that."

Al-Ashraf Musa called out to his servants, "Wrap up the food and drink for the teacher."

Dawud waited to leave, satisfied he had delivered the message to the best of his ability.

August 11, 1260
Sidon
Mid Day

"Your Excellency, your generalship, sir," the Georgian commander said as he dismounted from his horse. He removed his leather helmet and bowed his head, looking at the ground, averting eye contact. The brown-haired man wore a mix of Mongol and European battle dress. "These are Christians—men, some fighting men, some old and feeble—and women and children."

Ketbugha, mounted on his battlehorse and flanked by a squad of key subordinates, studied the coastal city of Sidon. They were perched on some low hills to the north of the city. All serious resistance to the Mongol move against the Western Christian city had been quelled. The sea castle, out on the water and connected by a causeway to the city, sat prominently in his view.

Ketbugha sneered. His eyes were hard. "Christians from this jurisdiction are responsible for the death of my nephew."

The Georgian commander seemed hesitant to reply.

"All of them," Ketbugha told him. "Kill all of them. Strip that city bare. Wreck it. Destroy it. Remove every living thing."

The man nodded, without ever raising his head to meet Ketbugha's eyes. He remounted his horse and rode back toward the city.

"It is a problem," one of Ketbugha's subordinates said. "Some of the prisoners—"

"Prisoners!" Ketbugha's lips tensed. "We are not taking prisoners here!"

"The auxiliaries—"

"I want the orders clear. No prisoners."

"We'll issue them again," the subordinate said. He looked toward a younger officer and gestured by tilting his head. The officer rode away. "But the auxiliary officers are reporting that John of Ibelin and Julian of Sidon may have been unaware that the territories they raided were controlled by us. There is no sympathy for the irresponsible raiders, but they would like to consider leniency, at least for the Christian women and children."

Ketbugha sneered. "And did they know it was us when they killed my nephew as he came to enforce our control over this region?"

The subordinate shrugged.

Ketbugha continued, "If they did, then they are paying the price. If they did not, their stupidity strains credibility. And in that case, they are are too stupid to make effective allies. This example will discourage others from similar stupidity."

The subordinate nodded. "Of course. But the lack of enthusiasm of our Christian troops...."

"Yes, I know." Ketbugha's face broke into a tense frown.

"They are not doing their duty. We had the city surrounded and sealed off before we breached the walls. But some have been allowed to flee. And the tasks inside the walls...."

"I understand," Ketbugha said. "We are undermanned, and need to rely on these auxiliaries." Ketbugha looked back out at the city of Sidon.

Smoke rose from various points inside the walls. He could observe a few scattered incidents of riders chasing fleeing inhabitants, but none of the methodical herd-and-slaughter processes his own Mongol regulars executed with systematic efficiency. He wondered what was going on up in Azerbaijan. He had relished the opportunity to bring glory to himself and his own family, in the tradition of Genghis Khan's masterful generals Subedai and Jebai, generals who had been entrusted with the command of huge Mongol armies and had added victories and substantial territories as a result. But his resources seemed stretched thin.

Ketbugha's eyes rolled up and down as he let out a deep breath. "Pull back all of the Georgian and Armenian auxiliaries to support positions. Use our Mongol regulars to finish the disposition of this city and its people. Use Turks or other non-Christian troops if needed."

Ketbugha saw nods of understanding from his men.

"This will require some reorganization; it will take some time," the subordinate said.

Ketbugha nodded. "I am aware of that. So I ask for quick action to prevent more of the people here from escaping the effects of the wrath of the empire of the Eternal Blue Heaven."

There were more nods of acknowledgement, and about half left to carry out the orders.

"This Christian state is small and weak, clinging to insignificant positions along the coast," Ketbugha said. "They're of little consequence to our objectives here, save the annoyance they have created by challenging our authority."

"This should teach a good lesson on the consequences of any sort of challenges to us."

Ketbugha nodded again. "Yes. This should drive them back into their coastal pens. We will then deal with the Muslims. After that, with Syria and Egypt under our control, we will reach back and sweep all resistance into the sea. Either into the sea, or into the empire."

"The destiny ordained by the Eternal Blue Heaven."

Ketbugha smiled.

Mid August, 1260
Gaza
Dawn

"Report!" Baybars requested with urgency in his voice as a small squad of scouts rode up. Baybars stood with his key lieutenants at the highest of a series of hills to the east of the Mediterranean coast.

"Small foraging parties," the squad's commander said as he brought his horse to a stop. "They appeared to be replenishing their ponies, with their soldiers milling about."

"Did they see you?"

"We don't think so. We got a look from a vantage point about eight hundred paces southwest. Commander, I don't think they expect us here."

Baybars nodded.

Qalawun asked, "Should we attack?"

"Get the men ready," Baybars said. He looked off into the sky, but not at anything in particular. He wanted to be aggressive. His instincts were always toward seizing the initiative. But an impulsive move without the proper consideration could play into the enemy's hands. "We still have three squads out." He looked back down at his lieutenant. "Get them ready, but stand by."

"We could attack them—catch them by surprise," Qalawun said.

Baybars lips tightened as he flashed a steely glare. "I like the enthusiasm," he said. "But the Mongols have a tactic of turning aggression against their enemies. Feigning weakness, drawing us in, then pouncing from the wings." Baybars paused. "I want the other reports. We won't fall into any Mongol trap."

Qalawun nodded.

Another squad approached. The pace of this squad's return was frenzied, with some hooting and howling.

"They know we're here!" the squad's commander yelled the minute he was in range.

Baybars waited for an explanation.

The commander of the returning squad brought his horse to a quick stop, kicking up turf as he joined Baybars. "We came over the rise." He breathed in and out to catch his breath. "We came up on some ponies grazing and a few soldiers. They were just there—we had no chance to disguise ourselves." He took in another deep breath. "We killed four, but four or five got away."

Baybars focused on the man's update.

"We did not follow." The man seemed reticent to admit this.

"Good. Your orders were to find information, not to try to defeat the Mongols alone. Did they re-form to attack? Did you see any other units?"

"No, commander. They did not seem to expect us. They seemed scattered, as if gathering sustenance."

Baybars clenched his fist. "We attack now!" he called out to his officers. "We will run them out of the area before they do form up!" Baybars looked at his subordinates until he found the man he was looking for. "Take a squad with word to the sultan. They're in Gaza. We're going to push them back, but the Mongols are in Gaza. And they are about to find out that we are here, too."

"Yes," the man nodded and left to carry out his orders.

"Form up!" Baybars called. "I want reconnaissance squads on our flanks reporting on any enemy units waiting in reserve! I do not expect to see any, but we need to stay alert for them! We will advance towards the positions that are not yet aware of us. I suspect the position we just skirmished with will already have been abandoned."

Baybars watched as the vanguard he commanded formed up to advance.

"Flank reports!" Baybars called out. "I want reports on the flanks immediately!"

Two officers left his side and moved in opposite directions.

"Another camp—hastily abandoned," said one of Baybars' men.

"And ten more stragglers, off to hell," Baybars added. He finally allowed a slight grin to appear on his face. "We see indecision all through the area."

"We caught them off guard," said another of the men.

"Yes. It won't last. But I want to clear and take control of the coastal road."

One man raised his eyebrows. "The coastal road?"

"Yes. Then we will have decisions only the sultan can make."

One of the two officers Baybars had assigned to inspect the flanks returned. "Nothing on the left flank," he said. "There will be no counter attack."

The second officer returned. "Right flank is secure," he added. "There was some fighting—some of them seemed inclined to resist. But our men pushed them back before they could get started."

"Excellent." Baybars looked at his men. "Deploy to take and secure the routes up the coast, and up the west side of the Syrian lands."

Officers nodded and left with a sense of urgency. Baybars' orders had created a lot of work for the men under his command, but he grinned as he looked out ahead. This advance could not have been more successful. Destiny was calling him, and the forces of the Faithful.

"The routes you speak of?"

Baybars looked back. It was Dawud, sitting on a warhorse. "Yes?" Baybars replied.

"They lead to the Christian territories—the Western European Christian territories."

"What are you doing here?"

"I finished my mission in Homs. I wasn't going to miss witnessing our forces going on the offensive against Mongols, watching Mongols retreat."

"And I'm betting you could handle a sword if you had to."

"If I had to. Maybe against one of their old men."

Baybars chuckled. "My modest friend. Some day I may see you in action. And I'll bet there will be regrets for whoever comes against you."

"Battles can be very unpredictable."

"Yes. But I have ordered you to remain out of harm's way."

"I have been."

"As to the territory, yes, Qutuz will need to decide how to use this route. If the Christians allow it, we can come up along those Mongol devils at the western flank of their forces. Or we could fight our way there and deal with the Christians at the same time."

Dawud shook his head. "You do not want two enemies right now."

Baybars sneered. "Yes, I believe Qutuz will agree with you. And I think that is wise, though I have little need for the lingering enclaves of the cross-worshipers."

Dawud raised his eyebrows.

"With your many-faceted background, I believe you may be of significant assistance during the next phase of this offensive."

"It will be my honor to serve, to contribute to the defeat of Mongols."

Baybars broke into a broad smile. "It will be done."

32

Mid August
Acre
Morning

"Brooding?" Aram sneered. "I'm brooding?" He hopped out of the bed he shared with Jeannette.

"Brooding. Sulking. Pouting. Whatever you want to call it. And I'm sick of it."

"That's what I'm doing? Couldn't be that I'm—"

"Aram, you should know by now, I am no fool!"

Aram's eyes narrowed into a quizzical expression. "I don't think you're a fool," he said quietly.

"I know we met in a peculiar way. But I came from a good family, a smart family, a prosperous family. I had two sophisticated parents before the foolish Italian faction battles took them away. I'm no fool. I know things. I understand things."

Aram took in a deep breath. "I know you do." He scratched the area above his lip. He had become aware of his wife's abilities, not expected from someone of her humble circumstances. Why was she so intent on making this an issue when he had such weighty decisions about the future on his mind? "I know you're an intelligent woman, tossed around by circumstances. But what does that have to do with—"

"Just ... get out of here!"

Aram's eyes popped open with disbelief. "What?"

"I'm sick of it, Aram. I'm tired of waiting for, for the inevitable! Just get out now!" Tears flowed from Jeannette's angry face.

"I really ... I don't know what's going on here...."

"Well, I do. I'm ready now, ready to be independent of you. I'm tired of guessing, and dealing with these moods of yours where I am left out of everything. I can do better without you. Daniel and I can do better without you!"

"Okay, let's just calm down here. I guess I have been a little preoccupied lately. Maybe I fell back into the all-to-myself pattern of thought again. But—"

"When it keeps happening, it doesn't make a difference whether you 'fell into it' or not. I'm done with this."

"You mean with me."

"That's right."

Aram gritted his teeth. "All right, fine." He stood and started toward a table with some of his belongings on it. "I'll gather my things and—"

"That's right. You gather your things. Just gather them and go. This is the life God has ordained for me! Everybody leaves me—my parents, my husband—everyone leaves me! That is my life!"

"But this time it's on you," Aram told her. "*You* are ordering *me* to leave."

"And you are quick to take me up on it!"

Aram felt like throwing his hands up in the air. "Do you want me to leave or not?"

"Doesn't matter. You want to. And it will happen sooner or later. So I say now."

Aram paused, then could not stifle a grin. "That is one of the silliest things I've ever heard."

"That's good, Aram. Make fun of me. Laugh at me."

"I'm sorry. I wasn't going to laugh. I said 'silly,' not 'funny.'" Aram struggled to stifle a chuckle.

Jeannette sniffled.

Aram tilted his head as he looked up. "Wow. Something strange just happened."

Jeannette sniffled again. "I don't care. You're still here. Go."

"I am still here. But for a split second, in my mind, when you ordered me out and I started to get my things to leave, I was gone."

Jeannette looked confused and impatient at the same time.

"In my mind, for a quick moment, I was gone. And something happened."

"Do I have to ask? You're going to tell me anyway, right before you leave."

"My options opened up. I had been sitting there trying to think of what to do next, and the choices seemed so limited before. If it was just me, there would have been many more options to consider."

"Then you have your answer, you despicable—"

"No," he said. "He moved toward her. "You have your answer. And you don't even know it."

"What are you talking about?"

"Because I never considered the option of just me. Not until this, this little argument. And I didn't consider it on my own. You put it in my mind."

Jeannette shrugged.

Aram stood face to face with her. "Back just a few years ago, I had so many options. Going with traders along the silk route. Doing translations in Baghdad. Transport and interpreting services up at the Mediterranean coast. Now where do I go if I decide to get out from under Robert? Back to Baghdad? Out with traders into a war zone? I can't do that with a family. And Jeannette, *I don't want to.*"

"Just go," Jeannette told him. Tears welled up in her eyes. She sniffed and sobbed. "Take all your options and go."

Aram reached out to her and took her in his arms. "You don't want me to go." He looked into her eyes.

Jeannette did not resist his embrace, but looked away.

Daniel whimpered.

Aram released Jeannette so he could pick the boy up, and patted Daniel on the back.

Jeannette watched him.

Aram held Daniel with one arm. He reached to Jeannette with his other arm, pushed her hair out of her face and dried her tears. "I'm not leaving you. That's not an option. And so I—"

"Of course it's an option, Aram! I beg you, don't toy with me! That's always the first option for you!"

Daniel cried. Aram squeezed him. He shook his head. "I need to make you understand—it never occurred to me. Leaving you and Daniel—it never occurred to me!" He looked at their son's tearful face. "I'm not leaving you." He looked back at Jeannette. "You've got to believe me, Jeannette. It *never* occurred to me!"

Jeannette scrunched her shoulders as if to make herself small. She sobbed.

"The fact that leaving you behind never even crossed my mind means I really have changed. I wish you could see that."

Jeannette's tear-stained face looked up at Aram. "I want to."

"You can. You can believe it."

Apprehensively, she said, "You're not leaving me here?"

"We leave *together*, or not all."

She smiled and squeezed him.

Daniel giggled.

Aram took a deep breath. "Thank a certain uncle of mine. An old Muslim. When I think back on this, he's the one who put me onto this way of thinking. I think I always thirsted for connections, without knowing. You came along, under less than ideal circumstances surrounding us. But happening onto that old fellow—he put me onto this whole idea." Aram looked into her eyes. "Then I realized my thirst for connections has already been satisfied. By you. And nothing within my control will ever separate us."

She looked at him, longingly, with vulnerability, but also with the power of deep affection. "I love you, Aram. I am lucky to have found you."

They embraced and kissed.

"I have a terrible fear of people leaving me," Jeannette said.

Aram nodded. "I can see that. I won't leave you."

Jeannette squeezed him.

"So, here are *our* options." He let out a burst of air. "If we just take no action, I have my employment with Robert. He's promised to pay me directly now, and we could walk away with a decent stake—for moving, for a business here, for maybe something we haven't thought of yet."

"That seems the safe choice."

"Safe." Aram nodded slowly, then tilted his head. "Well, it could be. But there is a conflict coming that is going to spread to this area. If I had to guess, I would predict that Mongols will crush whatever Muslim forces they encounter and then turn on this Christian stronghold." He shook his head. "Stupid people— affiliated with Christians here—attacked and provoked the Mongols."

"And they paid for it," Jeannette said. "I know people here who lost family in Sidon."

"And Robert—he's here to negotiate an alliance with Mongols. For some distant Central European authority."

"So you're in service to a man who wants to align with the winning side."

Aram nodded his head. "We are associated with him, yes."

Jeannette smiled.

"But it unsettles me," Aram said. "Mongols are as close to pure evil as I have seen in this world. What they did in Baghdad. What they do everywhere they go. The stories my uncle, Dawud, tells." He shook his head. "I feel I might be in service to an evil mission, if it is a mission that promotes the interests of Mongols."

"But Aram, what can we do? If they are to be the power in this area, what are we to do except try to make the best of it?"

Aram covered his mouth and chin with his hand as he looked at the floor and pondered the situation. "That's the language of practicality." He let out a burst of air. "That's also the language of collaboration. And isn't there a price to be paid for collaborating with evil?"

Jeannette nodded. "This is a difficult choice."

"Uncle Dawud made his choice," Aram said. "He tried to coexist. He tried to avoid the confrontation. But when I last saw him, he was no longer able to do so. He had resolved to engage with it." Aram paused. "I wish I had access to his counsel now."

"Me, too. He seems to be a very wise man."

"He is." Aram beamed. "He's my uncle. He's *our* uncle."

"A Muslim uncle?" Jeannette smiled. "Well, we need to consider this carefully. There is no sense in rushing. You have a secure position right now."

"And we will not know the precise ramifications of this clash of powers until it has resolved. There are many possibilities. We could mix into this in a variety of ways."

Jeannette nodded.

Aram looked at their son. He and Jeannette could provide this young child a life superior to their own. He relished the idea. He would make sure this boy—conceived with the woman that fate, or the God of someone's religion, had placed in his life—would have a great life, even amidst the turbulence of outside events. He and Jeannette could not control the results of Mongols clashing with Muslims, and how Christians—Western or Eastern—would mix into those results. But they could control their partnership, and their love for their son. They would take the deficiencies from their own backgrounds and turn them into Daniel's advantages.

A knock sounded at the door.

"Yes?" Aram called out.

The door to their quarters opened. A messenger Aram did not recognize stood in the doorway. Before Aram could chastise the man for opening the door without permission, the man said, "Aram? Aram, the translator?"

"Yes."

"You are to attend a conference. Envoys of the Muslim sultanate of Egypt have requested discussions with authorities here in Acre. You are to be present."

"Muslim envoys?"

"Yes."

Aram pursed his lips. "I am to assist Robert at this meeting? I don't recognize you as being with our group." Aram did not add that the man's accent lacked any of the harsh German twinges he had become accustomed to with Robert's men.

"Robert will not be attending. He is not invited. Your presence is requested by someone else."

Aram raised his arms, palms up, as he flashed an impatient look. Was this man going to tell him who? He looked at Jeannette, her eyes also trained on the man, waiting for the rest of the information.

"One of their delegation," the man said. "One of their advisers. His name is Dawud, recently of Baghdad—described as an old scholar. He has asked for you. He believes you can assist with whatever business they are bringing to Acre."

Aram's face broke into a grin.

He looked at Jeannette, who chuckled.

Aram looked back at the man. "I will be prepared to attend the meeting."

"You know this Dawud?"

Aram's lips scrunched then moved back into a grin. "Yes. He's my—" Aram quickly realized he was no longer talking to Jeannette, with whom he could share everything. Dawud's significance in Aram's life would not necessarily be understood, or tolerated, by Western Christian authorities in Acre. "I knew him in Baghdad. He's a learned man. A teacher."

"We will send word when they have arrived." The man turned and left.

Jeannette shrugged. Her eyebrows raised and she grinned. "Well, you did ask for your Uncle Dawud."

"That I did." Aram chuckled. "Not quite like this, but why should things start to follow an orderly process now?"

Mid August, 1260
Biqa Valley, Ketbugha's Camp
Twilight

"Is Baydara in camp yet?" Ketbugha asked. He and some key officers circled a fire to keep warm.

"Still a few minutes out, according to the latest returning squad leader," said one of his officers.

Ketbugha's left upper lip twitched. "Has anyone been able to find the messengers I sent to him?"

"They have not returned either," a second officer told him.

"So it's entirely possible he never got the message."

"Yes," the second officers said. "Likely."

"And the Egyptian slave-soldiers hold the territory they call Gaza, along the southern coast."

The second officer let out a deep breath. "Yes."

Ketbugha's lips tightened.

"He is a good officer—an aggressive commander," another of Ketbugha's officers said. "I'm sure if he—"

"I sent orders. They were not obeyed. I will hear his explanation," Ketbugha stated bluntly.

Ketbugha sensed doubt and apprehension from his officers. But none of them spoke.

Ketbugha's attention was diverted by an approaching horse and rider. He squinted to focus. It was Baydara on the horse.

Ketbugha folded his arms and raised his chin as Baydara dismounted and lowered his head.

"The enemy has taken the Gaza area, along with the coast," he said. "We have withdrawn to—"

"I sent orders to stand your ground," Ketbugha said through clenched teeth. "Why have my orders been disobeyed?"

Baydara took in a deep breath and swallowed. "I only received the orders in the last few days. The units were in full retreat by then. I considered with my officers whether we could regroup and contest Gaza. We simply could not form the units to engage effectively. I ordered the men back to camp."

Ketbugha did not like hearing how his orders had been disregarded, but he knew Baydara was a good officer. Maybe he could accept this explanation.

"General, these enemy squads—small, like reconnaissance squads—were extremely aggressive. We were spread out to collect supplies; we did not expect this sort of movement. I am sorry we were unable to—"

Ketbugha held up his hand. "Thank you for your report." He did not want to hear apologies or excuses. He did not want to feel he was being asked for favors. "Re-form your squads. Have them ready for our next move."

Baydara offered a quick bow and left.

Ketbugha looked at his officers. "He did a good job," he said quietly. "A lesser officer would have wasted men rather than using good judgment. And he had the courage to face me and defend his judgment."

Ketbugha observed what he sensed was relief on the faces of many of his officers.

"That brings us to the question: what should our next move be?" Ketbugha asked.

"Regroup and attack," an officer said.

Ketbugha nodded. "That was my first instinct. But we are considerably reduced with the il-khan up in Azerbaijan. Should we at least be discussing a strategic withdrawal, with the idea that when our main force returns, we then crush the Egyptians?"

Another officer raised his eyebrows. "In a way, it is the same choice Baydara had."

Ketbugha frowned. "Except we have no orders to hold our position."

"No direct order," the officer said. "But what would you rather bring to the il-khan? A retreat and regroup, or a victory?"

Ketbugha smiled. "No doubts on the answer to that."

The men said nothing further. Ketbugha saw expressions of grim determination on most of their faces.

"I will admit, when the il-khan entrusted these forces to me, I thought back to the great generals of our ancestors: Subedai, Jebe. I thought, this is *my* time." He shrugged. "What would *they* do?"

"They would attack," one officer said.

"They had the initiative," added another.

"So will we," Ketbugha said. "We will regroup here, resupplied, and we will move on them. Send out scouts; I want positions and levels of strength as complete as possible."

"We have some indications they are headed west, toward Western Christian territory."

Ketbugha grinned and considered this information. "Into the lands of their traditional enemies." He scratched his nose. "Whatever they are planning to do, it will take time. We will be ready for them. We will deliver a great victory to Hulegu, a present for him when he returns."

The men nodded and smiled.

"Send a dispatch to the il-khan with our decision." He thought a moment. "And ask for any information al-Nasir Yusuf has on this Qutuz. This man seems very aggressive. We may be able to use this against him as we gain our victory."

One of the men left to carry out the order.

33

"We have envoys for this," Qutuz said. "We have one of your own men—the old man you like—with my people. He's leading the group." Qutuz and Baybars stood in the command tent. Dawud and other officers and advisers were nearby, completing preparations to leave the camp. "I don't want my valuable vanguard commander going out on this type of mission."

Baybars maintained a steely expression. "I don't see this as a dangerous mission. Do you?"

"We could be fighting these people some day. If they find an opportunity to take a key commander into custody, who knows?"

"Even Mongols respect envoys. Christians, these land-stealers from Western Europe, have been observing flags of truce for generations. I'll be safe."

"I don't see the need for taking the risk, even if it is a small one."

Baybars nodded. He understood the sultan's concerns and was flattered to be considered so indispensable. But he wanted to go on the mission. "Sultan, you said yourself, we may be fighting these people—and in the near future. I would like to take the measure of them. I would like to see them with my own eyes. Yes, I know we'll get reports, detailed reports. But reports are never as good as a firsthand look."

Qutuz scowled.

Baybars did not sense Qutuz had been convinced. "I'll have them dress me up as a servant," he suggested.

Qutuz laughed. "My dear Baybars, you simply don't look like anyone's servant. Your towering stature. Your piercing glare. No one will be convinced. I suspect you would be more conspicuous as a servant than as an envoy."

Baybars did not argue.

Dawud walked up to them. He looked at Qutuz. "So my commander still wants to go."

"Yes," Qutuz said. "And he thinks he'll pass himself off as a servant."

Baybars shrugged.

"Paint him up as a Nubian bodyguard," Dawud suggested. "They'll never suspect a thing."

Baybars grinned.

Qutuz rolled his eyes and scowled, but seemed resigned. "One of my best officers, getting into costume."

"I know just the person to do it," Dawud said.

"Bring him along." Baybars said, "You can disguise me just before Acre."

Qutuz chuckled as he shook his head.

Mid August
Acre
Morning

"To summarize," Dawud said in slightly accented French, "we are not here on a mission of peace. We come on a mission of war, war against a great evil, an evil that threatens Christians as well as Muslims. We seek your help, help from people we have called enemies in the past. We seek your help against this evil."

Dawud and the delegation from the Egyptian sultan stood inside a tent that had been erected in sight of the walls at the southeastern edge of Acre. The site was close to the Knights of the Hospitallers quarter. The Harbor, and the Inner Harbor further down the coast, were visible from the outside of the tent.

Aram let a small grin come onto his face and nodded slightly. He studied the Christians he was with at this meeting, and wondered if they had any idea how impressive a man was speaking to them. He was proud this man was his uncle.

"You will not find a pro-Mongol attitude here," Adolfo said. "Not after Sidon."

"I think a claim could be made that we provoked that

retaliation," said Charles the Slayer, the one-armed soldier who had fought bitter battles against Muslims in the past.

"And if that claim was made, then the appropriate response would have been a raid in retaliation," Adolfo said. "Their rough treatment of Sidon was well beyond any provocation. They demanded we dismantle our defenses, for God's sake, in most arrogant terms."

"They are arrogant," Charles the Slayer said. "But terribly powerful."

"Their power is reduced," Dawud told them. "The master khan of the area is off dealing with succession issues. Now is the time to *crush* these arrogant, Godless creatures."

"You think *we* are godless creatures," Charles the Slayer said. "But we will serve your purpose to clean up this mess you've made."

Dawud seemed to gather himself for a careful response. The statement was undiplomatic, uncouth—rude. But Aram knew Dawud had the sophistication to stay out of the trap of matching rudeness with rudeness. The Muslims had come looking for friends, not partners with which to trade insults. This particular man seemed to be angling for a breakdown in communications between the Christians and the Muslims. Dawud finally replied: "We would never consider you 'Godless.' You are People of the Book. And the 'mess'? It is not a mess of our choosing. These creatures have come across the world to destroy us, and they have already accomplished much of their task. It is God's will … I daresay your God and my God … that these creatures be stopped now. Join us to make it happen."

"You didn't make the mess?" Charles the Slayer asked with a sarcastic edge to his voice. "You didn't slice Mongol envoys in half?"

Dawud turned to all the Christians. "The Mongols were coming after all of us. Dead envoys or not, they plan to conquer and rule all of us. We would like the honor of fighting side by side as we take on this evil foe. Short of that, we would like to request passage through your territories, with access to supplies. This terrible foe could serve a purpose in God's will: to bring us together."

"Muslims and Christians together?" said Charles the Slayer, gesturing as if waving Dawud's comments away.

"Of course together," Aram said. "This man speaking to us is my uncle." That statement surprised every person in the tent, but he continued before anyone could ask a question. "He and I lived with Christians and Muslims, and also Jews—all together in

Baghdad. Baghdad, a place that was converted by the Mongols into a smoldering collection of ruins, surrounded by the decaying bodies of thousands of people, people who did not do any harm to anyone."

"We've all seen the savagery of war," Adolfo said. "They should not—"

"Savagery of war?" Aram repeated incredulously. "This is the *routine* of war for Mongols. This is what they have done from the land of the Chin to the land of the Rus, along the Silk Road—"

"I'll not be lectured by the kin of an infidel," Charles the Slayer said, "an add-on to this group of dubious position. Not even a real Christian."

Aram's eyes widened. But he remembered his own observations of how this particular individual might be angling to sabotage the talks. He did not take the bait either.

Dawud looked amused. Aram sensed Dawud was stifling a laugh.

Aram found himself calming. Here they were discussing a fight to vanquish a monumental evil and this silly man was quibbling over what a "real Christian" was. It was amusing. He was grateful for Uncle Dawud's silent communication.

"I asked him here," Adolfo said. "He is the closest we have to an expert on the Mongols, and I want to include his insights in our deliberations about this matter."

"Insights." Charles the Slayer shook his head dismissively.

"I want to hear," Adolfo said.

"I'll tell you this," Aram said. "These people are here looking for an alliance, for friendship. Religious differences drive us apart at times. Sometimes with sad, tragic results. But let me tell you, Mongols don't have allies. They have slaves, or they have enemies. And they attack their enemies until they have slaves, or until they have bones bleaching in the sun. That is my best insight."

Dawud nodded at Aram, almost like a private comment to his nephew, an acknowledgement of pride. Aram enjoyed the moment.

"Well, I thank you for your visit," Adolfo said to Dawud. "We have much to consider and discuss." He motioned to some servants. "We have refreshments and some comfortable quarters for you while we discuss your proposal. We'll offer our response shortly."

"Thank you," Dawud said. "There are moments when fate calls, when the nature of human existence reaches a decision point. This is one of those times. I implore you to seize this moment with us—and change the world."

Adolfo nodded.

Servants led Dawud and his associates out of the room.

Mid August
Acre
Late Morning

"I did not come all the way to Outremer to fight alongside the infidels holding Jerusalem," Charles the Slayer stated. "Gentlemen, the principle is as old as the ancients: the enemy of my enemy is my friend."

"That's the dilemma, isn't it?" Adolfo said. "Which one of them is our enemy?"

Charles the Slayer scoffed. "The swarthy infidels who hold Jerusalem, who have held Jerusalem for decades."

Adolfo nodded. "A long chronicle of combat, no doubt. But not lately. They did not try to wipe Sidon out of existence."

A murmur rippled through the gathering.

Adolfo shook his head. "Maybe some wish to court these Mongol creatures. I know some of our own still cling to some bizarre notion that God has visited these creatures on us to rid us of the Muslims. But those of us who have seen them up close know they're not of God. They may be of the devil. A temptation."

"Or a force to be harnessed," said Charles the Slayer.

Aram wondered if these people had any chance of arriving at a consensus on how to respond to this very specific request. He had some thoughts to share, but was not sure if he should offer them.

"What are we considering here?" Adolfo asked.

"Whether we are to become allies with the infidels," Charles the Slayer said.

Aram moved closer and shook his head.

Adolfo asked, "You have something to offer?"

"Just a reminder. I hear talk of the enemy of my enemy being my friend. I remind you all, Mongols do not have friends the way we understand the term."

"Yes, yes, they will think we are subordinates," Charles the Slayer said. "Let them think it. Small price to pay to wipe out the infidel scourge that has haunted this area for centuries."

"Recall the temptation of our Lord Jesus Christ," Adolfo said. "The devil offered Jesus power and wealth. We should consider that the Mongols could be a temptation, a devil's offering, a devil's attempt to buy our immortal souls. But gentlemen, we are not here trying to decide if we're going to fight alongside the Mongols. We need to decide how to answer this pending request."

"I agree," Charles the Slayer said. "Reject it. That is simple. Then we can contact the Mongols and help them push the infidels out of this area."

"I believe we would be siding with the wrong side of the conflict if we did that," Adolfo said.

Aram took in a deep breath. A consensus seemed all but impossible. His sympathies were with the Muslims. But no one was asking for his opinion.

"Gentlemen, I have been a much shorter time in this area," Hanno Van Sangershausen said with a thick German accent. Aram had been wondering when the Grand Master of the Teutonic Knights, recently arrived at Acre after fighting Mongols in Eastern Europe, would enter the discussion. "But I have some thoughts to offer. I agree, best way to address this issue is to look at what is in front of us and leave larger issues for another time. The simple facts: we are not powerful enough to offer troops. We cannot offer a meaningful alliance to either. So do we let the Muslims pass? Do we help them? It is a yes or no."

"And we should consider the consequences of a flat refusal," Adolfo said.

Aram decided he had to speak. Hanno Van Sangershausen was guiding the discussion in the right direction. But there was another point to consider: "We also need to guard against making a decision that brings us two enemies."

Van Sangershausen raised his eyebrows. "My young friend is correct. Mongols have already shown us who they are with their activities at Sidon. Refusing Muslims here would likely provoke the Muslim army into attacking us to seize the travel route we are unwilling to grant." He looked at Adolfo. "I do not see that we have the forces to resist it."

Charles the Slayer scowled, but did not argue.

"We need to allow passage," Adolfo said.

Van Sangerhausen nodded. "At least that."

"More than that," Adolfo said. He looked at Van Sangershausen.

Van Sangershausen nodded again. "Yes. More than that. Mongols are killing Christians in my homeland and territories east. We need to resist them here."

"They attack us because we provoked them!" Charles the Slayer said. "We fail to see their potential for—"

"We provoked them by not submitting," Adolfo said.

A rolling chuckle flowed through the group.

Aram smiled and nodded. They understood—most of them, anyway.

Charles the Slayer frowned.

"Here is what would be practical," Adolfo said. "If we choose sides, we should help the Muslims defeat these soldiers of the devil, these Mongols. But we do not have the forces to offer. If the Muslims do not win this confrontation, and we are clear allies of their effort, we will share their fate. The stories are legendary of Mongol retribution. The only logical course that addresses all these concerns is to allow passage, and provide supplies. Make it easy passage for the Muslims on their way to contest the devil. But otherwise, we are not to be involved."

"And we state for the record that we are neutral," Charles the Slayer said.

Adolfo nodded. "Neutral. Yes, stated neutrality."

Charles the Slayer grinned slyly. "But allowing passage and offering supplies is not the behavior of a neutral party."

"It is if we say it is," Adolfo said.

Aram laughed along with others in the room.

Mid August
Acre
Late Afternoon

"That big man—he was not a Nubian guard," Aram said to Dawud. They sat together in a courtyard, unaccompanied by anyone else.

"No," Dawud admitted. "He is my current ... assignment. A quite talented commander and fighter."

"He wanted to be there for the discussions."

"Yes, to observe. I think he trusted me with communicating the message, but maybe not completely. It was all right with me—I was glad he was there. He saw that the response was not because of the way the message was delivered."

Aram shrugged. "You didn't really expect troops."

Dawud let out a long, deep breath. "I know Mongols. Up close." He breathed out again. "I suppose I can't expect others to understand what I know so vividly. But if they did...." His eyes glistened. He looked off, as if gazing into eternity. "If your people knew Mongols the way I do, they would have fallen over themselves to offer all their resources, not just passage and a few provisions."

"They're not my people, Uncle."

"Just who are your people?"

Aram raised his eyebrows. "Jeannette. Daniel. You."

Dawud smiled. "That is progress. When I first met you, you didn't have any."

Aram returned the smile. "You have helped me."

Dawud nodded, still smiling.

"So what is next for you, Uncle?"

Dawud shrugged. "I will stay with the man I serve—Baybars. A mamluk. A tough man. A man with many qualities that are needed right now to fight the Mongols: courage, resoluteness, calm in the face of adversity, and a willingness to do what must be done—without hesitation, without mercy—to achieve victory."

"You like him."

"Yes, for these times, I like him a lot."

"And he is a man who will be drawn to the fiercest part of the fight."

"No doubt."

"Uncle, you are not a young man. This does not sound like a good place for—"

"I know there is a chance I will die in the course of this battle."

Aram swallowed.

"I am resigned to this. I submit to God's will. God has moved me to this position, shifted me through territories, guided me. I am here at this place in time because I belong here. I'll offer this man, this Baybars, every insight I have to help him bring our people to victory. If it is God's will that I end my days during the course of those duties, I accept that."

Aram paused. "I don't know if I want to say farewell to you after only so recently finding you."

Dawud shrugged. "Then don't. We don't need such things. We have shared what needs to be shared."

Aram nodded. "I would like your advice, one last time."

"Sure."

"I am still technically serving this Robert character, from a land in Eastern Europe."

"Yes?"

"He was very unhappy with our decision."

"But not for the same reasons I was."

"No. For quite the opposite."

Dawud nodded.

Aram shrugged. "He wants to approach the Mongols about an alliance."

Dawud glowered at Aram. "And he wants you involved."

"Yes. He has told me: set it up." Aram shook his head. "He is held in such low esteem now that he wasn't even involved to the meetings today. I was asked for my expertise, but the fact is, I'm still a paid servant—well-paid now—of Robert."

Dawud sat back. "And what is it you want to do?"

"I hate the Mongols. I don't wish to work toward an alliance."

"And how long have you felt this way?"

"A long time, Uncle. A long time."

"But you have continued to serve this man."

"Technically. Yes."

"Technically," Dawud repeated. "Do you or don't you?"

"I do."

"You should have resigned."

"Maybe. But I didn't."

"That's right. So fairness dictates that you pursue this mission, with all the invention and expertise that you are capable of."

"I could resign now."

Dawud shook his head. "That would be wrong. To leave this man at such a crucial time would be a breach of your obligations."

Aram dropped his eyes and his lips tightened.

"You still like my advice?"

Aram grinned. "It's the right advice. And I don't want the wrong advice. I know it's counter to what you are working for. So it can't have been easy for you to offer. But it speaks to your integrity."

"And maybe, just maybe in the course of completing this mission, you will determine who 'your people' are."

Aram smiled and shook his head. "You realize how dangerous this is."

"Oh, yes."

"I mean, I could easily be killed by the Mongols before you."

Dawud laughed out loud.

"It's a mission of treachery," Aram said. "Robert will be making a proposal that contradicts his superiors, that works against their stated position. We spoke about the old Genghis Khan tale, how he executed traitors even when their betrayal helped him." Aram paused. "The Mongols could kill every one of us with Robert."

"You will be able to set this meeting?"

"Unfortunately, yes. I have the connections to do it."

"So you should complete the mission you have been hired for. Make it clear you are loyal to your superior—Robert. He is the one making the decisions."

"Even if they might kill everyone associated with such a duplicitous mission."

"I can't guarantee they won't. But they also respect envoys. Conduct yourself as one. As a loyal servant completing an assigned task."

"Suppose I am successful? That would work against your purposes."

Dawud shrugged. "It seems unlikely."

"But suppose it is?"

Dawud shrugged. "I believe in God's will."

Aram shifted his lips to the right. He nodded.

Dawud stood and Aram also got to his feet. "If we do not see each other again, Uncle, I have found our time together, our finding each other, to be a treasure in my life." He hugged the older man.

Dawud returned the embrace. "I have as well, Aram. I have as well. May God's will bring blessings to us both and allow us to see each other again in this life."

❧ *34* ❧

Mid August
Outside Acre
Evening

"We can deal with both factions right now," Baybars said to Qutuz through steely eyes. He wiped at some black face-coloring that had not been completely removed. Though darkness had ended the long day, the camp was lit by torches and bustled with activity.

"I know you cannot really be serious, Commander," Qutuz said. "So what I want from your unit is to—"

"I'm *deadly* serious," Baybars said. "They were *weak*. We have the forces to knock them out *right now*. We could cripple these Christian weasels, deal with the Mongols, then come back here and finish the job. We will be celebrated by the Faithful until the end of time."

"You were there with our men just now, yes?" Qutuz asked patiently.

Baybars' nose twitched but he did not respond.

"You saw them, wavering again. And again I had to give a speech to build them up. Weakness does not only permeate the Christian camp."

Baybars nodded. "The difference is, you have me and my men. We are ready for this. We will lead by example, and our own wavering old women will find their testicles and join the fight."

"But not against these Christians. Not now. We have what we need from them. We will fight one enemy at a time."

Baybars' jaw jutted forward. He scrunched his lips. He knew Qutuz was likely correct. Dawud, his chief negotiator, had been responding to Baybars' ideas with nearly the same arguments.

"The truth is, that old man of yours got us passage and supplies," Qutuz said. "He's been a good find."

Baybars nodded. "God's will brought him to us. But in this situation, it wasn't the negotiator that brought us this result. The Christians took the only course open to weaklings. If they denied passage we would have fought them for it, and they clearly feared any fight. And we surely are in a position to take any supplies we want on the way. By offering them some form of alliance, they control what we will get. 'Neutrality.' That's what they called it. It isn't even true neutrality. It's simply the least the weaklings could offer in order to avoid a confrontation."

Qutuz nodded, grinning. "All right, I'll grant you they're weak. But one enemy at a time, my dedicated warrior. One enemy at a time."

"I hate these Christians," Baybars said. He was resigned to the decision, but not necessarily unhappy with it; he just needed to vent his emotions further. "That Richard, with the lion's heart, would have known how to deal with Mongols. That man was a *warrior.* He would have seen the evil in the Mongols, and my understanding is he came to see the good in Saladin. They would have combined to create a glorious army that would have crushed the Mongols. Richard would have galloped right up to the Mongol commander and hacked him into vulture meat!"

Qutuz smiled. "They are not Richard."

"No. Not at all. And we lack the resources Saladin had."

Qutuz shrugged. "But I'm sure it has occurred to you—it certainly has occurred to me— that a victory over the Mongols will bring us those resources. Syria will not just fall to us, it will flow to us, like a thousand streams unifying into a mighty ocean."

Baybars nodded. A slight grin came onto his face. He wondered if Qutuz realized such a statement should be followed by a promise of reward.

"You will have a prominent part in such a Syria," Qutuz told him, evidently detecting Baybars' expectations. Even without the promise, Baybars would have fought against the Mongol curse that had shaped his life. But there was nothing wrong with letting Qutuz sweeten the incentives for him and his men. The sultan continued, "I will need good leaders for northern Syria while I control Egypt and the southern coastal territories."

Baybars nodded. "I could be very effective there."

"I have no doubt," Qutuz said. "Mamluks will rule a mighty empire of the Faithful. Slave-soldiers who, through God's will, have risen to be the main defenders of the True Faith. We will recapture Baghdad and restore the glory of Islam."

"And the Christians?"

"Eventually we will annihilate them, something Saladin was never able to do."

Baybars smiled.

"What I want from you now is to advance. Go out ahead of the main group. Find out where the Mongols are and find the best ground possible for our successful destruction of their army."

Baybars nodded. "I was born for this task, Sultan. My men and I will leave at sunrise."

Qutuz nodded and the men embraced.

"We will next speak at the battle," Baybars said.

Qutuz smiled with teeth clenched in murderous expectation.

Third Week of August, 1260
Ketbugha's camp near Damascus
Mid Day

"I'm a little surprised," Ketbugha said to Robert and Aram. He sat on a cushioned elevated chair in a huge tent. Robert and Aram, flanked by armed Mongol guards, stood facing Ketbugha. Robert's escort to the meeting waited outside.

"I thought your people had declared *neutrality*," Ketbugha said, and Aram interpreted his words to Robert. "What do you bring us under your flag of truce?"

Robert bowed. "I bring you what gifts we have available: some wonderful wine, and citrus from nearby groves," Robert said. Aram in turn was interpreting Robert's words. "I have come to tell you that not all Acre Christians agree with the declared status of neutrality. We believe this neutrality favors the Muslims ... your enemies. They should be our enemies."

"Yes," Ketbugha said with a matter-of-fact tone. "Anything short of full attack against the Muslim forces is not a friendly act. We have taken note of this. What of it?"

Aram interpreted the words. "I represent a faction of Christians that understands this completely," Robert stated. "We wish to pursue a different course."

Ketbugha took a moment to consider the words. Aram read suspicion on Ketbugha's face. Ketbugha appeared to be scrutinizing Robert for signs of treachery. "Are you a representative of the authorities at Acre or not?"

Aram told Robert what Ketbugha had said. Robert seemed to become energized. "I represent authorities from an emerging empire far from here, in Central Europe. This empire is destined to rule wider and wider territories up in Europe, soon to include possibly the position of *pope*." Robert smiled proudly.

Ketbugha's expression became severe.

Aram wished he could take a break from the negotiations to discuss Robert's approach, an approach that was wrong in almost every way.

"So you are *not* representative of the Acre authorities," Ketbugha stated in a careful tone. Robert's gaze wavered between Aram and Ketbugha as the former translated the words.

"I am attached to them at this time. But I represent a family with more power than anyone at Acre. An alliance between this rising Central European power and the great Mongol power to the east is the future. I know it. I'm here to set the terms."

Aram tried not to cringe as he interpreted the last few sentences.

"Interpreter," Ketbugha said. "Do you have discomfort?"

"No sir," he answered quickly, directly to Ketbugha. "Maybe from the travels. I serve Robert, and render his words to you faithfully, with all my capabilities."

Robert frowned, wondering why Aram and the Mongol general were speaking directly to each other.

Ketbugha turned to Robert. "You have a good man here," Ketbugha said to Robert. "He's transmitting your words accurately." Aram translated Ketbugha's words.

"I'm sure," Robert said, although he wondered if Ketbugha would really have needed to point that out. He looked at Aram. "Tell the general I'm not always sure you agree with my mission."

Aram's eyes flashed for a moment. He looked at Ketbugha. "Robert of Montpelier states that he believes I don't always agree with his mission."

"But you do serve the mission...."

"I am loyal to my superior," Aram answered directly to Ketbugha.

Robert frowned again, apparently unhappy with any words shared directly between Aram and Ketbugha.

Ketbugha turned to Robert. "He is saying he can serve your interests, and maintain his loyalty to your mission without agreeing with every element of it. As I said, he is a good man. You are lucky to have him." Aram translated the words, and the rhythm of Aram translating back and forth between Ketbugha and Robert was reestablished.

"Thank you."

"And what of your loyalty?" Ketbugha asked Robert.

"I am keenly loyal to the Central European family destined to rule an expanding empire."

Ketbugha nodded. "It sounds more to me like you serve a rival of ours. An expanding empire.... I know we have clashed with forces in Eastern Europe. Is this family of yours in arms against us?"

"Surely not the family I represent. That would be a mistake. Your people are destroying Islam, a mission we could not accomplish. Once that is done, we will all be friends presiding over a peaceful world unified through Christ."

"I am Christian," Ketbugha said.

"So I understand."

"But I do not recognize the pope, and I won't until he submits to the great khan in Qaraqorum."

"These are details that can be worked out."

"But haven't been," Ketbugha said. "In fact, your pope has seemed to believe he is superior to us, and that we should submit to him."

"Only spiritually. Certainly not militarily."

"Only spiritually." Ketbugha shrugged. "This has little meaning to us. In our lands, all religions have equal standing."

"Details to be arranged."

Ketbugha squinted as he chuckled. "Yes, I'm sure. Well, the beginning of that arrangement of details would be for your Central European family to come to Qaraqorum and submit to the great khan. If they control a mighty empire, we would expect significant gifts."

"I'll contact them. I'll see what can be arranged."

"Very good." Ketbugha smiled, then asked casually, "What of the Christians at Acre? You came in under their banner."

Robert shook his head disgustedly.

Aram held his expression. He suspected Robert was about to make a huge mistake, but there was nothing he could do.

"The Acre Christians are nothing compared to the forces I represent," Robert stated smugly. Aram translated the words accurately. He confined himself to professional and emotionally detached interpretations, taking care to avoid offering any inflections that would insert his own opinions about the exchange.

"Though you currently serve them," Ketbguha confirmed.

"In name only."

"But 'in name,' you do serve them...."

"Technically. And that position has allowed this approach to you, an approach that will lead to a world-changing association."

Ketbugha offered a confident grin. "Very well. You will come with me." He looked at Aram. "Stay here. I will communicate privately with your master about his offer."

Ketbugha stood and nodded to a squad of guards. They followed Ketbugha and Robert. Ketbugha whispered something to one of his guards.

The guard nodded and came over to Aram. He led Aram to an area just outside the tent entrance. "Wait here. It won't be a long wait."

"I have a gift for your superiors in Acre," Ketbugha said. He had returned after no more than ten minutes had passed. "Perhaps they don't deserve any gifts from me, given their position of 'neutrality'. But that is an issue for another day." He handed Aram a satchel. "I admire your loyalty to your superior. Perhaps we will meet again."

"Thank you, General." Aram frowned curiously. "Where is Robert?"

"He's joining you," Ketbugha answered casually. "Our response to his approach has been made quite clear. You may return to Acre. Join your men."

Aram bowed. "Thank you."

Mongol guards ushered Aram to his horse. It waited along with the rest of their escort to the meeting, a mix of Germans and Frenchmen from Acre. He looked at the satchel. It was a pouch-like leather container with thin leather strips as a handle. Similar leather strips were tied together at the top, drawing it closed. Aram raised and lowered it a few times. It was lighter than a stone, heavier than a pillow, maybe about the weight of a water bag.

What gift had the Mongols given to Acre Christians? And had Robert really managed to fulfill his mission at long last, an alliance between his German comrades and the Mongols? He looked forward to hearing the explanation from Robert when he returned.

"I think they want us to proceed," said one of Aram's traveling companions.

Aram looked around. A squad of mounted Mongol guards glared at them, hands close to swords. Aram shrugged. "Perhaps they have more to discuss, and will bring Robert to us along the road. Let's go."

"You do not give orders, interpreter," said one of the German members of the group. "We wait for Robert."

"It would seem prudent to wait elsewhere," one of the French traveling guards said, looking at the mounted Mongol squad.

"They did not say when Robert would be done here?" the German demanded.

"No. General Ketbugha just said that he'll be joining us," Aram answered.

"Let's start to slowly move toward the road," the French guard said. "I don't believe they're expecting us to wait here."

Aram looked again at the Mongol squad. He saw squints and glares. "No. I don't think so."

"We go to the edge of camp," the German posited. "But we are not leaving without Robert."

The French guard nodded.

The men began to move.

"What's in the satchel?" the German asked.

"A gift," Aram said.

"For you?" the German asked, suspicion on his face.

"No," Aram replied. He frowned as he thought about what Ketbugha had said. "He said it was a gift for the leaders at Acre."

The German guard said, "Open it."

Aram shrugged. Ketbugha had not told him to keep it sealed. He pulled at the leather strips sealing the pouch. He caught a glimpse of hair and flesh, then grunted and dropped the satchel. Robert's head spilled out and rolled along the ground. "God," Aram muttered through a wave of nausea.

The German guard brought the point of a sword to Aram's chest. "What did you tell them? How did you get him killed?"

The French guard drew his sword and confronted the German. "There will be none of that," he said. "They'll want a report. He's the only one who knows what happened."

"He got himself killed," Aram snarled as he jerked away from the German. "Damn fool. He sold out the Acre leadership and puffed on about a big empire in the east of Europe." Aram looked back at the German. "He did everything he possibly could to look like a traitor! The stupid fool!"

"Let's go," one of the French guards said in a panicked tone.

Aram dismounted. "We can't just leave"—Aram looked down at Robert's head—"*him*, here. It's a gift. They called it a gift. Their removal of a treacherous man for the leaders of Acre. They may consider it an insult to leave it." Aram reached down and took a handful of hair, then put the head back into the satchel and resealed it. Even though the hair he had touched had not been sullied by any blood, he unconsciously wiped his hand on his trousers.

Aram looked over and saw Mongol guards laughing.

"I repeat," the German guard asked. "What did you tell the Mongols that got him killed?"

Aram confronted the man with the most piercing look he could summon. "I spoke *his* words to them. *Faithfully. Accurately.*"

"And how did you manage to keep your head attached to your neck?" the German demanded.

"Because I am perceived as merely the loyal servant of a *fool*," Aram said.

The German lunged at Aram. "How dare you—"

The French guards moved their horses to block the German.

"We are lucky they didn't kill us all," the first French guard said. He looked toward the Mongol squad.

The Mongol guards seemed to take interest in the delegation, pointing and glaring.

"We need to leave," the French guard continued, "before that luck runs out."

The group left quickly as Aram hung the satchel with the Mongol "gift" from the side of his horse. He asked: "Is there any question, anymore, of who these people are, and who we should at least be rooting for in the coming clash of arms?"

No one answered.

35

Last Week of August
Tabriz
Morning

"What can you tell me about Qutuz?" Hulegu asked al-Nasir Yusuf. Hulegu sat on cushions in his tent.

Al-Nasir Yusuf stood facing him, flanked by two of Hulegu's guards. "He is a slave-soldier, one of those who stole Egypt by killing my family." Al-Nasir Yusuf's answers seemed clipped, as if offering the bare minimum of information.

Hulegu understood that al-Nasir Yusuf was unhappy with his detention in Tabriz. But he was not going to tolerate even a hint of petulance. "Surely you have more information than that."

Al-Nasir Yusuf shifted his weight. "What else do you want to know?"

Hulegu still did not like al-Nasir Yusuf's attitude. But rather than an evident expression of his dissatisfaction, he decided on a different approach to get the information he wanted, and to keep this cowardly fool in his place. "If I were to send you to assist in our efforts against this Qutuz, what would you do?"

"Send me? To Egypt?" Al-Nasir Yusuf's attitude seemed to brighten.

"Not Egypt. This Qutuz has actually moved against us."

Al-Nasir Yusuf seemed surprised to hear this. "I think we should use his arrogance against him. The slave-soldiers think they are the best fighters in the world. We both know your armies are superior. I would anchor my troops at a location that favors your forces, and let Qutuz's aggressive nature do him in."

Hulegu nodded. "And you would command a division against him."

"Yes. He has gotten—" Al-Nasir Yusuf appeared to correct himself. "He thinks he has gotten the best of me in the past. He will be overconfident if he knows I am—"

"So he has defeated you before."

"In skirmishes, but with your—"

"So you are unable to defeat him. I am not sure how your advice or leadership helps us."

"The resources of Egypt make the mamluks powerful," al-Nasir Yusuf said. "If they have come out of Egypt, they will be more vulnerable. I am intimately familiar with Syria and the Mediterranean coast. I can be—"

"I have heard nothing to convince me you would be of any help at all."

"I have to be there, to see conditions on the ground, to be of assistance. If you send me—"

"You have not convinced me you possess any information we do not already have," Hulegu said, shaking his head. "He is aggressive. Obviously. He tried to humiliate me by executing my envoys in an unseemly manner, spilling blood and guts all over." Hulegu's face tightened and his voice became angry. "What unique information can you offer me?"

Al-Nasir Yusuf swallowed. "He has accumulated forces, wandering into Egypt after your triumphs in northern Syria. This was occurring even before you took—" He appeared to rephrase his thought. "Before I joined you. These forces will not be reliable. If you show signs of victory, you can fragment them. Some of those forces are actually disaffected, previously cast-out fellow mamluks, sworn enemies of Qutuz. It is hard to imagine them working together."

Hulegu scratched his chin. "And you have relations with some of these factions."

"Yes I do. I can re-establish—"

"So here is the important question. Would you advise we fight Qutuz now? Or should my generals wait until I can bring larger forces from here?"

"There is no doubt," al-Nasir Yusuf said. "Qutuz cannot match the strength of your forces. Your generals will sweep him away."

"You seem confident. This has been a close question for us."

"Then let me assure you, the mamluks cannot defeat your forces. I would put my life on it."

"Really." Hulegu nodded through a slight grin. "What else?"

Al-Nasir Yusuf's lips tightened. He had the desperate look of a man wanting to offer anything—anything at all—to keep the conversation going. "I mentioned, um, I mentioned their arrogance, their over-confidence...."

"Yes," Hulegu said with a stern expression.

"Pride. Pride is their—-"

"Yes," Hulegu said. "I understand." He gestured with a dismissive wave of his hand. "We'll contact you when we need you again."

"So do I...." Al-Nasir Yusuf seemed to rephrase his words again as guards took his arms. "When do I go back to Syria?"

"I will let you know."

"But I could be—"

"Do not beg. It annoys me. I have told you that you will be put in an important position once we have taken the rest of Syria and Egypt. Your begging implies you don't believe my promise." He squinted. "That annoys me greatly."

Al-Nasir Yusuf swallowed. His eyes glistened, and Hulegu sensed he was holding back tears. The man disgusted him.

"I'll await your, your desire," al-Nasir Yusuf said, voice cracking.

Hulegu gestured again and guards led al-Nasir Yusuf from the tent.

Hulegu turned to one of his advisers. "Not of much value."

The adviser shook his head. "No."

"Have this information, particularly about the possible cracks in the enemy's unity, dispatched to Ketbugha." Hulegu shrugged. "But I got the idea from the last message from Syria that Ketbugha was going to fight, and fight soon."

The adviser nodded.

"This al-Nasir Yusuf puts his life up against a victory for our forces." Hulegu nodded. "That much of his information I believe. I doubt the slave-soldiers can stop even a reduced force under Ketbugha's command."

The adviser nodded again.

End of August
Acre
Evening

"You need to explain this," Adolfo said as he scolded Aram. Aram stood before a table facing a number of men, including Adolfo, Charles the Slayer, and Hanno von Sangershausen. The late Robert from Montpelier was the subject of discussion, and Aram was acutely aware this was a serious inquiry with him on the spot. "I did not always like the pope's representative. And I did not agree with him often. But he went out with you, and came back without a body. You need to explain."

Aram gritted his teeth. "Yes, well, the *explanation* is that I was a loyal servant on a fool's errand. I'm lucky my head didn't end up in that satchel with his!"

Charles the Slayer's eyes widened. "You would do well to guard your attitude."

"My attitude." Aram gritted his teeth again. "This Robert, whom I've served for *two years*, seemed oblivious to my advice, right up to the end. If you want to talk about attitude, I will tell you, *his* attitude got him killed, and could have gotten every member of our entourage killed."

Charles the Slayer glared at Aram a moment. "I have never been particularly fond of you," he said. "But I believe you are a competent young man, with valuable insights. That has kept you safe from the consequences of your ... other faults. But you would do well not to cross the line of insolence too far."

"My apologies, gentlemen, if I seem insolent. I suffer from the trauma of helplessly watching Robert do *everything* wrong, and praying his folly would not get all of us killed."

Adolfo said, "Robert brought gifts to them. He spoke for his own point of view, presumably for the pope."

Aram shook his head. "Robert offered an alliance with some German family back in the east of Europe. He seemed to be betraying both the pope and the leadership here in Acre."

Adolfo seemed frozen a moment.

Aram held their eye contact. It was Adolfo's move, to process the information and ask the next question. "I had no idea he would be so brazen," Adolfo finally said.

"Nor did I," Aram said quietly. "I couldn't believe the words he offered as I interpreted them."

"Then why did you not clean up his words, and save his life?" Charles the Slayer asked.

"If I had tried to reinterpret Robert's words as he spoke them, the whole contact would have become muddled, and *all* of us would have been killed. I did my job—what I was hired to do."

"Not very well," Charles the Slayer said.

Aram bit back a reply. He suspected Charles the Slayer, having nothing else to say but always needing to have the last word, simply threw out a verbal snipe to save face.

"Did he accomplish anything with the Mongols?" Adolfo asked.

Aram shook his head. "No. I can tell you, they seemed dissatisfied with our position of neutrality, but resigned to it for now. I suspect they see our neutrality as an issue they will deal with at a later time. I think they are focused on the Muslim forces coming their way."

Adolfo nodded.

Aram drew a deep breath. "I am now a man with no position, and few resources, as the man committed to paying me is no longer capable of doing so. My family and I will make plans to leave."

Adolfo shook his head and gestured with a slight wave. "We will find a position for you. Your knowledge and insights are valuable, and I'm coming to see there is little reason to blame you for Robert's fate."

Charles the Slayer's nostrils flared. He clearly did not agree. "I want him held in custody until we find out for sure what happened."

Aram stiffened. What more did this man want? What more information did he think would be available to them?

"Custody?" Adolfo asked.

"Yes. And I do not think we should be promising this man a position."

Adolfo scrunched his nose and mouth in apparent thought.

"I don't care about a position," Aram told them. "But you've no cause to hold me in custody. I've told you what happened. Unless you want to send a squad out to interview Mongols to get their side of the story, you'll have to rely on what I told you."

"So you keep saying," Charles the Slayer snapped back. "So you keep boasting; taunting." He turned to Adolfo. "You see it. His arrogance and insolence. He tells of plans to leave … into a war zone. He seeks to make his escape before we find out what really happened. He doesn't care about a position with us, he no doubt has himself a position—with Mongols, or with Muslims—already set."

"What?" Aram could not believe such a ridiculous notion had grown out of their discussion.

And worse, Adolfo's face registered doubt, and a sterner attitude. "Perhaps we will … think on this." He turned to Aram. "Confine yourself to your quarters. There will be a guard posted there."

"There is no call for this," Aram told him.

Adolfo looked at Charles the Slayer. "We will see. You are dismissed."

Aram started to state further objections to being confined to his quarters. His mouth opened, but then closed. He decided not to pursue the matter. They were not confining him to a cell in a dungeon, as he figured Charles the Slayer would have preferred, but simply asking him to stay where he was. He decided he had better wait until the controversy over the Mongol "gift" had died down.

"You always said this was dangerous." Jeannette was lightly crying as she held Aram. "I didn't understand until now."

Aram held Jeannette even more tightly. "I wondered what the Mongols would do. I felt like a man caught in the flow of a stampede, moving to the edge of a cliff, aware of the terrible danger, powerless to stop the momentum."

Jeannette squeezed him.

"It really hit me when Robert's head rolled out."

"God."

"I'm so glad to be with you and Daniel again. When I think of the last time—"

Jeannette put her fingers to his lips. "But it wasn't the last time. You're back. Safe."

Aram moved to Jeannette so they were face to face. He smiled and kissed her.

"What becomes of us?" Jeannette asked.

Aram embraced her again. "I don't know. We will need to figure it out."

"*We* will?" Jeannette said, looking expectantly at him.

"Of course. I will be dependent on you for a strong influence on what we will do. I value your instincts of family, of togetherness— so superior to mine."

Jeannette squeezed him.

"Our choice will be among three powers to live under: ineffectual Western Christians, whose days may be numbered; militant Muslims who may see the religion of our birth as a barrier to an amicable coexistence; and despotic Mongols, who see slaves or enemies with no middle ground."

"Is there a way for us to function out of the eyesight of all of these powers, to live our lives quietly in some corner of the world, somewhere?"

Aram smiled. "That may be what we need to look for, the best place to do that."

Aram could feel Jeannette nodding.

End of August, 1260
Southern Syria, Along the Jordan River
Mid Day

"Where are they?" Ketbugha asked. He greeted an arriving scout squad at his command tent, which was perched on a small hill with a view of the Jordan River before him.

The leader of the squad dismounted from his pony. "They're moving southeast, for the river."

Ketbugha grinned through a cold glare. "They are actually looking for us."

"I believe so."

Ketbugha chuckled. "There is a position southwest of here. A mountain, some springs, good grass for ponies."

"Yes, General."

"That seems like an excellent place for them to find us."

"I think it would be."

Ketbugha nodded. He looked toward his command tent at his key subordinate officers, who had listened to the scout's briefing.

"With all speed, gather the troops. We will establish position here," Ketbugha ordered.

"General, an idea," one of his commanders said. "Should we go out after them? Our strength is always our mobility. We're not usually the ones who take a fixed position."

Ketbugha laughed. "You are the one who questioned if we should engage them at all. Now you want to go looking for them?"

The man bowed. "It is my duty to point out alternatives."

"Yes, yes. And you do it well." Ketbugha shook his head. "If this was the regular Mongol army at full strength, we would go out after these creatures right now and destroy them." Ketbugha flicked his left hand in a dismissive gesture. "But we're not at full strength, and we have forces under our banners—Christians from Georgia and Armenia, Muslim princes from the area—who are not yet fully schooled in our tactics."

The man nodded.

Ketbugha continued, "We will set up good positions. They are looking for us. They came for a fight. So we will set the battle's location to our advantage."

"Wise, General."

"And have no fear, my friend. When the time comes to take the initiative, we will do so."

The commander's face radiated into a smile and he bowed again. "And after they are dispatched, there is nothing to keep us from Egypt."

"The il-khan will be extraordinarily pleased with our efforts here," Ketbugha said.

"Did you hear from him, General?"

"No. But I am certain we would have his blessing."

The commander nodded again.

The area around the tent began to bustle with activity as orders went out to gather the troops. Ketbugha looked at the leader of the scout squad. "I want constant reports on the enemy positions. Pass that order on to all the scout squads. I want to know when they get here, where they are, and how many of them have come."

"We will do our best. There are many hills and gullies in this area. I assume we do not want to be detected."

"Of course not."

The leader of the scout squad nodded, then mounted his pony and rode off to join the growing activity in the camp.

Ketbugha breathed out a burst of air. He had no doubt that victory against this seemingly impulsive enemy excursion from Egypt, its audacity exceeded only by its foolhardiness, was inevitable. Still ... with reduced troops, unfamiliar allies within his forces, and hills and gullies to disguise positions, he sensed that victory would take all of his skill.

36

September 2, 1260
Jezreel Valley, Northeast of Ayn Jalut/The Springs of Goliath
Afternoon

"They're already here," Baybars said through gritted teeth. "And they've spotted us."

Baybars tightened his grip on his horse's reins. They stood at the crest of a hill with a number of men from his advance cavalry squad. In the distance was a concentration of Mongol tents at the foot of Mount Gilboa, and the ground in between was covered with brownish-green shrub-like grass, dried out from the late summer climate. "They've got the springs, and a number of the hills around Mount Gilboa," he noted.

"That squad is still approaching," one of his men said.

"They're going to try to find out where our main camp is." Baybars' gaze traveled over the rolling terrain punctuated by large rocks, then toward the slopes of hills to the west. "I want them wiped out, or at least put to retreat. None of them follow us back to camp!"

"We won't be able to hide much longer."

"I know. But I want the sultan to know about them and have as much chance as possible to set a battle plan." Baybars' lips tightened with grim determination. "It's coming. As soon as tomorrow." He looked around at his men. "Attack that squad!"

Baybars waited behind as his men spurred their horses forward. As they charged they unleashed arrows toward the oncoming Mongols.

The Mongol squad seemed to waver indecisively. Some halted. A few turned, as if to retreat. Others reached for bows. One motioned with a wave of his arm to attack.

A return arrow missed one of Baybars' men. Another struck a

man in the shoulder, knocking him off his horse. "Take them!" Baybars shouted, though the action was too far off for his men to hear.

The Mongols did not advance to meet the charging Mamluks. They would have carried no momentum when the two forces collided, and had no real armor other than leather chest-coverings.

Two Mamluks lowered lances. The rest brandished swords.

A few more arrows were launched from the Mongol squad. Only one found its target, bouncing harmlessly off a shield.

The Mongol who had motioned his men forward now frantically signaled a retreat, waving his hand and shouting as he turned his war pony.

Dawud brought his horse up to Baybars at a trot. He was wearing a padded white jacket and white pants, but his flowing gray beard and the absence of shield or weapon—only a dagger hooked to his saddle—made him look out of place. "Not the time to chase them," Dawud said.

"Not today."

The Mamluks caught up to the slowest of the retreating Mongols and cut him down. A few squad leaders looked back at Baybars. He motioned them to return.

"We have much to discuss with the sultan," Baybars said to Dawud.

Qalawun rode over to them. "What you think that squad saw?"

"Enough," Baybars said. He grinned. "But not *too* much."

Dawud nodded. "Did you see how they were ready to charge right into our men, even though it was a superior force?"

Qalawun scratched his beard. "Arrogance. Overconfidence."

"And I believe that is what we can use against them," Baybars commented. A slight grin crept onto his face. "Withdraw to camp!" he called.

September 2, 1260
Foot of Mount Gilboa at Ayn Jalut/The Springs of Goliath
Late Afternoon

"There were too many of them, and we weren't in a proper attack formation," the nervous squad commander said as he reported to Ketbugha and a small group of key commanders outside Ketbugha's command tent. "We could not—"

Ketbugha raised his hand. "Their little victory today will be answered tomorrow. Go prepare your men."

The squad leader nodded and withdrew quickly.

Ketbugha smirked. The man had known he needed to make a report, but completed it as quickly as possible to avoid any potential wrath. Ketbugha was glad to receive the report, but did not want to praise the man. That would run the risk of looking like he was commending a defeat, even a small one.

One of Ketbugha's subordinates said, "He's afraid you'll scold him, or worse."

"If he'd stayed around long enough, I would have praised his good sense."

His subordinate's eyes widened.

"All right. Maybe not. But there would have been no reason for the entire squad to get wiped out. We needed their information."

"Absolutely."

"Glory will come tomorrow. We will avenge this little skirmish then."

"Of course."

"From the direction of their approach and attack, they must be up the river to the northwest," Ketbugha considered. "Summon the troop commanders for a meeting after the evening meal. We will go over our plan for victory."

"Yes," the subordinate said with a nod. "Glory to the Eternal Blue Heaven."

"For those of you who were born Mongol and have come a long way from home to achieve the destiny of your people, you know what tomorrow means. You have lived with your role in the world for generations." Ketbugha addressed an assembly of just over one hundred key commanders. The gathering took place in the light of large campfires. "My words now are for those who have joined us since our long journey west." Ketbugha looked through the crowd. He saw interpreters communicating his words to Armenians, Georgians, and Arabic-speaking locals. "I point out the good fortune fate has dealt you: of joining us, joining the inevitable, joining the unstoppable, joining the next succession of victories ordained by the Eternal Blue Heaven."

Ketbugha looked at the Arabic-speaking princes. He saw al-Ashraf Musa. Three other men stood with him, and Ketbugha assumed they were his key unit commanders. Al-Ashraf Musa, arms folded, intently stared at Ketbugha. He did not offer any hint of a reaction to Ketbugha's words as delivered by the interpreter.

"Look at us," Ketbugha continued. "All manner of peoples— Christians, Muslims, of different factions, of different tongues—all gathered together for this glorious venture. All peoples, living together in prosperity under the rulership of the Genghis Khan dynasty, within the glory of the Eternal Blue Heaven, embracing all peoples, all religions!"

Ketbugha saw al-Ashraf Musa shift his weight and resettle his arms. His eyes never wavered from their stare.

"Tomorrow, you will face those foolish enough not to embrace this destiny! They deserve defeat. They deserve annihilation. They deserve to be swept away! Your glory is that you are appointed at this hour to be the agents of this transformation, this new era. We will toast to it, feast to it, celebrate it with the passion of a larger purpose tomorrow evening, after our work is done! It will not be easy. But we *never lose*. Think about that a moment. Forces under the command of this glorious dynasty *never lose*. You have chosen well! You have chosen … victory!"

Ketbugha raised his arms. Cheers rippled and swelled through the group.

"Victory!" Ketbugha repeated again.

He looked at al-Ashraf Musa. The Syrian prince unfolded his arms and scratched his left cheek. His mouth remained closed, as was the case with his men—they were not joining the cheers.

"Victory!" Ketbugha repeated one more time. "Take this message to your men! We will reconvene tomorrow to celebrate it. Inevitable destiny. *Victory.*"

A final cheer arose.

As the gathering began to disperse Ketbugha turned to one of his key subordinates. "I want to see the unit dispositions in detail," he said with a cold seriousness. "The Georgians and Armenians—even the Persians— should be reliable. But the so-called Ayyubid princes…." Ketbugha shook his head. "Their units must be placed well into the midst of the formations. I want them to have no option but to fight for their lives tomorrow."

"Yes, I'll see to it."

"See to it and report the details to me."

The man bowed and left quickly.

❧✦❦

September 3, 1260
Ayn Jalut
Evening

"It is a superb plan," Dawud told Baybars as they walked away from the briefing. "We use their arrogance, and one of their own favorite tactics, against them." The two of them were surrounded by Baybars' key subordinates, including Qalawun. Dawud wore a long, slightly tattered and soiled white robe. The soldiers wore their uniforms without armor. None of Baybars' men made any moves to come between Dawud and Baybars, or seemed to object in any way to this newcomer's growing influence and his input on this important occasion.

"I think this is a plan for *success* against scourges from hell," Baybars replied.

Dawud nodded. "Who have had their way long enough."

"Tomorrow will signal the end for them."

"God wills it."

Baybars smiled.

Dawud returned the smile.

"The best part of the plan," Baybars continued, "is the use of the Bahriyya. We have the most prominent role."

"You are essential," Dawud said.

"The most dangerous role."

"To the most courageous."

Baybars smiled again.

He stopped walking and locked eyes with Dawud.

The other men stopped as well. Dawud sensed he was the only one who did not know what Baybars was going to say next.

"I'm having you assigned to Qutuz for the battle."

"To … Qutuz…." Dawud lowered his eyes, then looked back up with a quiet distress. "That is not necessary, Commander."

"Yes it is. I have marveled at your stamina, and how you have willed yourself to ride with us even though you're at least twenty years older than any of us. But tomorrow? It's different. It will be hard for the youngest, for even the spryest of limbs and strongest muscles."

"Commander, I am not afraid to die. I want my chance at them too."

Baybars shook his head. "I want you with me after the battle. I will not preside over your death to spare your pride."

"Commander, please, I know I—"

"It is decided. It is an order."

Dawud swallowed. For just an instant, he felt tears forming. But he knew how to take an order. And if this man, with all his responsibilities, had decided to issue this order, Dawud—even though he hated it—would obey. He would not whine and cry about it. There were more important considerations than his feelings at being reassigned by his commander.

"Yes, sir. Take the battle to them tomorrow, sir." Dawud's face tensed. "Destroy them. Ride to victory that leaves no doubt, that lifts the curse of their domination from this entire area."

Baybars grinned. "We will, most honorable seer. We will."

Dawud turned and the two men began to walk again, side by side. Quietly, Dawud said, "Qutuz has never been fond of me."

"Not at first, but I think that has changed. He will find an assignment for you. I told him I was—"

"He isn't going to think he has to protect me, is he? I would despise that."

Baybars snorted and shook his head. "No."

Dawud looked at Baybars, trying to figure out what Baybars was trying to say.

"He will simply put you somewhere … out of the way. That is what I think he will do."

Dawud stiffened. His lips tightened. He was an old man too useless to help during an important battle—this is how they thought of him.

"But I know what you will do," Baybars added.

Dawud looked at him.

"You will find a way to be important."

Dawud grinned. "Is that an order, too?"

"Yes it is, old man," Baybars said. "And I'm certain it will be of dramatic consequence."

Dawud wondered if Baybars was patronizing him. Then Dawud decided: so what if he was? Dawud would look for something he could do to influence the battle. If no one would assign him a task, he would find one, a good one, and assign it to himself.

37

September 3, 1260
Ayn Jalut
Afternoon

"It's him," the scout said as Ketbugha and a contingent of Ketbugha's commanding officers crested a hill that looked west onto an empty stretch of land. A series of rises and valleys rolled off toward the northwest. Dry grass dotted with an occasional bush made up the terrain. "I recognize him from yesterday. The big one."

Ketbugha frowned. "He is their commander?"

"I think so."

"Well, we found the scoundrels. So let us go get them!" Ketbugha addressed the officers with him. "Signal banners we'll attack. I want arrows up immediately. Send as many units as can swirl and swarm. Have them shoot arrows upward until our heavy cavalry reach."

"Which heavy cavalry?" one man asked.

"Send out the Georgians and Armenians along with a few of our own divisions."

"Two Arab divisions are with the frontmost Georgians."

"Send them."

Orders were given to the banner squad, which in turn signaled the orders to the entire army.

Ketbugha watched the Mamluks. They did not seem to be moving as a cohesive unit. He saw individuals look out toward the Mongol positions, move their horses a few paces back, then look around again. He saw what seemed to be a sauntering retreat, wavering and hesitant. "They seem indecisive at our arrival; confused."

"They're forming up quickly, though."

"Yes. We need to move *faster.*" Ketbugha looked around. "Come on! With all speed! Let's take them down now!" Ketbugha rode forward to lead the assault.

Arrows launched into the Mamluk positions.

Mongol tactics usually involved a much longer phase of swirling formations firing blankets of arrows into the enemy from a distance. But Ketbugha did not have as many regular troops as would normally be available. The Mamluks seemed to have been taken by surprise, so the time to bring in heavy cavalry was not after hours of withering arrow attacks, but immediately, to exploit the enemy's disarray.

Mongol heavy cavalry moved quickly down to the attack.

"Let's end this now!" Ketbugha cried.

"Here they come!" Baybars said. He looked up at a wave of arrows that arced toward them. "Shields!"

The Mongol riders were immediately moving into the attack.

Baybars stood at the middle of his lines. "Move out slightly to contest!" he reminded his men. "Wait for my orders!"

The barrage of arrows finished, and the two charging armies met in a clash. The fury of the Mongol attack slammed into the Mamluk lines, with the middle taking the heaviest damage. Baybars glanced at the flanks. They held. He had his best men there.

Baybars could hear the common sounds of battle: metal on metal, metal on flesh, metal on bone. Screams. It made no difference how brave a man was; if his body took the trauma of a terrible wound, he would cry out. And Baybars knew that would go for him as well. The only way to face that risk was to completely blot the possibility out of the mind, to concentrate on the task assigned, to assist the struggles of fellow warriors, and to dive into the moment. Stay in the present, away from a past to regret, or a future to fear. That ability, to stay in the moment, granted a warrior courage and glory.

The middle gave slightly. Arrows took a few Mamluks who were further from the front lines.

Baybars nodded. It was time to move the battle to the next stage. "Withdraw!" he yelled. "Withdraw!"

The middle gave immediately.

The Mongols poured through.

Baybars watched as the flanks fought a measured, disciplined withdrawal, positioning themselves behind some of the Mongol forces.

Baybars gestured sharply to a Mamluk messenger. "Tell Qutuz. They're coming to him. Right now."

The messenger bowed sharply and rode quickly toward the hills to the rear.

Baybars took a deep breath. His forces would re-form for further involvement. But the next phase of the battle was up to Qutuz.

"Take them! Kill them all!" Ketbugha ordered as the Mongol forces chased Baybars' retreating vanguard. "Get the ones on the flanks too!" Ketbugha could not believe how easily the victory had come. Although he had heard that the forces in Syria were inferior to his own forces, he was amazed how outmatched this enemy really was.

Ketbugha's troops plunged forward, exploiting the apparent rout, rising up the hill.

Suddenly a barrage of arrows ripped into the Mongol lines. Men and horses from Ketbugha's ranks screamed as they faced a sudden, unanticipated assault. Muslim forces sprang into action on the heels of the barrage.

Ketbugha avoided any wounds from the initial assault, but realized he had misread the situation. The force they had been chasing was only the vanguard of the Mamluk army. He had been taken in by a tactic for which the Mongols themselves were famous—the feigned retreat and counterattack. Now they were in danger of being surrounded.

Ketbugha looked around. How bad was the situation? His forces had been depleted, but not broken. Though he saw dead men and ponies on the ground, and others still wriggling and twitching, he also noticed the ranks of the formation that had charged in had not broken. Men not taken down by the surprise turn of events moved to fill the gaps created by fallen comrades. Years of militarized hunts had drilled an automatic adherence into the integrity of the formation. He looked behind his lines. They were not fully enveloped by Mamluks, but there was pressure from the rear. He allowed himself a brief grin. Had it been a

Mongol attack, the results would have been hopeless. The Mamluk attempt had created a problem, but the issue was far from desperate.

"I want everything we have—everything we can send—send it against their left!" Ketbugha commanded. The banner squads began waving the orders. "Get the word out! Everything! Hit their left! Their left!"

"General, we can still withdraw—"

Ketbugha backhanded the man so hard he was knocked off his horse. Ketbugha hadn't even looked to see who it was. "Death is inevitable! If we are to die today, then that is our fate within the Eternal Blue Heaven! But we will fight for this victory!"

If Ketbugha's forces could break out from their right, and swing around the Mamluk left, they might turn the attempted envelopment and drive the Mamluks south, toward the springs and the foot of Mount Gilboa.

"Deploy our best to the attack on their left!" Ketbugha commanded.

"What of the Arab units?" a subordinate asked.

"Just hold the right. Just hold it. Leave them there—with a few Georgians and Armenians."

"Yes sir."

Ketbugha led his troops toward the desperate fighting on his right.

"It worked," Baybars said as he watched from the hills to the west. "Now the question is where we can be of help."

He watched intently as Mongol forces, buckled by the counterattack, seemed to be reforming and pushing on the Mamluk left. He nodded. That would have been his next move. A breakout at the northern end of the battlefield, then push to the south against the hills, the springs, and the mountains.

"Form up!" Baybars ordered. "Stand ready for a counterattack at my command!"

Dawud stood on the hill watching the Mamluk counterattack and the Mongol attempts to break out on the Mamluk left. He wore some armor and a helmet, and held a sword and shield, but he had not been given access to a warhorse. He took in a deep breath, then let it out slowly. Baybars said he was sure Dawud would find a role in this clash. Yet here he stood, a pathetic old man holding a sword and shield, like a child wearing a costume. Worthless.

He had seen the Mamluks seize the advantage, and so wasn't concerned about being perceived as ineffectual as long as the Mongols were defeated. But as he watched, the Mamluk left was giving way more and more, thinning to a possible breaking point. What could Dawud do? Run down to the battlefield in his soldier's costume?

"Oh, Muslims!" Dawud heard Qutuz yell. Dawud looked out at the Mamluks, fighting for their lives against the Mongols. Qutuz felt it—the colossal importance of this fight. These moments could affect the future of the Faithful for centuries to come. His cry—his appeal to the True Faith—was an impulsive, emotional appeal to remind them they weren't just fighting for their survival. They were fighting for God.

Dawud looked over to see the sultan rip off his helmet and throw it to the ground. The left continued to thin and give way. The battle looked like it was about to turn. Qutuz sounded like a desperate man, a man who could not accept the tide turning toward defeat. What had happened to their advantage? Were Mongols invincible after all? That could not possibly be the will of God!

Dawud's lips scrunched together. He looked at the battlefield again. It was not God's will that he join the fray. He took his helmet off and threw it down, inspired by the sultan's action. He tossed aside his shield and sword. He fell to his knees and brought his forehead to the ground. "God is great," he said quietly. "God is great." He swallowed. "I submit to the will of God."

"We need to help on the left!" Baybars yelled. "It's giving way!" He pointed toward the spot where the Mongols started breaking through. The soldiers were fighting under Mongol banners, but also included tough, brutish Georgian and Armenian warriors. Had they actually turned the left?

Baybars and his men smashed into the widening breach and closed it off. Their infusion of forces reasserted Mamluk control on their left flank, and started pushing the Mongols back down, preventing a breakthrough and envelopment for the time being. Baybars continued his efforts, launching his way into the enemy forces, blood spattering up from sword wounds and bashed heads. Mongol forces desperately resisted every inch of this new Mamluk push.

"I want more reserves from our left!" Ketbugha yelled. "We can still hold our right with a few less. And we can still break through here!" He gritted his teeth.

Ketbugha circled back, looking for reinforcements and encouraging them into the breach. "When we break through, we will take them from the rear and annihilate them!"

The Mongols rallied again, and pushed on.

Baybars scanned the scene. This was it; there were no more reserves. They would win or lose right here, with this group.

He wiped sweat and blood from his face. He would throw himself into the fray as deeply as he could. If the Mongols were going to claim the victory, he did not want to live through the day. He would join God in paradise.

But just before he steeled himself to reengage, he caught sight of an amazing, nearly surreal image. It was Dawud riding a saddleless horse, a carthorse, along the crest of a hill. His gray-white beard was flowing, visible to anyone who looked his way. He was removed from the battle by a few hundred paces, but seemed to transcend it. He wore his white robe, and instead of a helmet he wore a white turban. He bore no weapons, no shield, nothing in his hands but a book: Baybars knew it had to be a Koran. Dawud had it raised in the air and appeared to be shouting something. Baybars, of course, could not hear the words, but Baybars knew the man, and knew what the words must be: "God is great. There is no God but God, and Mohammed is the Messenger of God."

Where was Dawud going? What was he looking at?

Then Baybars smiled in realization. Dawud was moving straight toward al-Ashraf Musa on the Mongol left.

"Men!" Baybars called out. "Just a few! With me!"

Baybars knew he could not take too many with him or he would weaken the line and allow a breakthrough on the Mamluk left. But if he saw correctly what was happening, only a few would be needed to do the trick.

Dawud continued his mystical, surreal ride toward the Mongol left, and al-Ashraf Musa.

And then it happened. Al-Ashraf Musa seemed to issue some orders, and as he did, his men deserted the field. First, a few. But in a short time, the whole unit.

Baybars yelled "Come on!" to the men who had joined him.

He and his men circled around and pushed through the gap created by al-Ashraf Musa's defection.

"They have nothing more," Ketbugha yelled out triumphantly. "And we are gaining the upper hand here! Keep pushing!"

The Mamluk left withered again, maybe for the last time. The Muslim soldiers fought desperately, but Ketbugha allowed a slight grin. He could sense his soldiers gaining the advantage and the enemy losing it.

"General! Al-Ashraf Musa has deserted the field!"

Ketbugha wheeled around. Suddenly his left was crumbling.

"We have to break through now! Our lives depend—" Ketbugha flew off his horse as it squealed in agony, an arrow having caught the poor creature in the neck. Ketbugha landed hard. He forced himself to his feet, but stumbled as his senses blurred and buzzed in a hazy disorientation. He shook his head, trying to regain reality.

Al-Ashraf Musa stood at the rear of his withdrawing forces. He made eye contact with Dawud, his former teacher. Al-Ashraf Musa bowed deeply and turned to leave.

Dawud clutched the Koran to his chest. "There is no God but God, and Mohammed is the messenger of God." Tears rolled down his cheeks. "God is great." A slight smile crept onto his face. He'd reminded an old friend of his faith. This was worth whatever happened now.

Dawud turned to examine the main clash points of the battle. If Mongols broke through and killed him, he would accept that. If an arrow flew up the hill and took him down, unshielded and unarmed, he would accept that.

But as Dawud scrutinized the field, he realized neither of these events was going to occur. The Mongols were scrambling to flee. The Muslim Mamluks were on the verge of victory. "Praise God," Dawud said quietly. "Praise God's will."

"Some of them have broken through back up north, through the Jezreel Valley," Baybars said.

"I saw them," Qalawun said.

"Have a few of our men let the sultan know: we are pursuing

these wretched creatures until I kill as many of them as God wills!"

Qalawun looked and saw a young warrior with a cut on his forehead, and his left arm dangling awkwardly. "Did you hear?"

"Yes."

"Inform the sultan."

"I prefer to join the pursuit."

"Not this time."

The soldier grimaced. "Yes, commander."

Baybars looked out at the bloody site. The fighting was over. Squads were collecting Mongol prisoners. Bodies of dead and wounded littered the field in piles. Some of the wounded squirmed and groaned.

"We own the field," Baybars said with understated quietness. "I thought they were invincible." Baybars let a slight grin sneak onto his face.

Qalawun smiled. "Not anymore."

Baybars took in a long deep breath. "Not anymore." He looked out toward the northeast. "Let's go get some more of them!"

Qalawun nodded, and the men pressed their horses into pursuit.

"I am Ketbugha, the general of these men who have fought you so bravely today, under the authority of the dynasty destined to rule everything. They will rule you. Not today, but they will rule you."

"On your knees," said the man who guarded Ketbugha. He started forcing Ketbugha down from the shoulders. Ketbugha sneered as he resisted.

Qutuz held up his hand.

The guard stopped pushing down on Ketbugha.

"You are defeated, General."

Ketbugha met the sultan's eyes, but did not respond.

"That's all right," Qutuz said. "We both know it to be true."

Ketbugha shrugged. "I know you. You are Qutuz, the one who slices envoys in half."

Qutuz nodded slowly.

Ketbugha continued, "I will die at your hands today. But two things are assured."

Qutuz chuckled. "What is *assured*, for a defeated general?"

"The great Hulegu Khan, ruler under the Eternal Blue Heaven, will exact terrible retribution from you, from your soldiers, from your family, from your soldiers' families, and from every living creature in your accursed land."

Qutuz shrugged, as if bored by the threat. "And your second assurance?"

"I will never be a slave-soldier who kills his master."

Qutuz looked at Ketbugha through a steely-eyed squint. "Your head will decorate my victory celebration tonight." Qutuz motioned guards to take him away.

Ketbugha never lowered his gaze. He never trembled. They wanted to take his head? They would. A sharp pain to his neck, maybe longer lingering pain if the executioner was sadistic or incompetent. But his troubles would be over soon. And as he went to his death, he was absolutely certain that Hulegu, or his sons, or his grandsons, or his grandsons' sons, would come back with a vengeance and kill thousands, maybe hundreds of thousands, maybe millions, to exact revenge for this aggrieved behavior against the power destined to rule under the Eternal Blue Heaven.

38

Second Week of September, 1260
Acre
Morning

"Thank you," Aram said to the guard in front of his door as he returned to his room with Jeannette and Daniel.

"It's fine," the guard said casually. "This is the easiest assignment here. I'm not even sure why you need guarding."

Aram grinned and shrugged. "Out of respect for the now-headless Robert, I guess."

"Those Germans left a while ago," the guard said.

"They did?"

"I think everyone is waiting to find out what is going to happen southeast of here."

Aram nodded.

Adolfo appeared down the hall, heading toward them. As he approached he said to the guard, "You are dismissed."

The guard nodded. To Aram he said, "Good luck to you. Think of me for any of those ventures you mentioned."

Aram smiled. "I will."

The guard walked away, giving Aram a friendly, salute-like wave.

"You have made friends with your guards," Adolfo commented.

Aram smiled. "I'm a friendly sort of fellow."

"The battle, to the south … it's over. The Muslims won, and from all we can tell, appear to be chasing the Mongols completely out of Syria."

Aram beamed a huge smile. "That is good news."

Adolfo raised his eyebrows. "Why do you say that?"

"You have to know Mongols. Up close. Then you would have no doubts."

"But the Muslims have been trying to wipe us off the coast since we got here, nearly two hundred years ago. This could set the stage for them to complete the task."

Aram looked steadily at Adolfo. "That's the problem with neutrality. You risk the wrath of whoever wins."

"You would have sided with the Muslims?"

Aram raised his palms in an exaggerated shrug. "I'm just a simple translator. I don't make such decisions; those are for you higher-ranking folks."

"Yes. That would seem to make you the epitome of neutrality."

Aram bristled. The man had a point.

"I argued with others to offer you a position here. I think there is much value in your abilities, especially as we address these new circumstances." He paused a moment, turned his head away, then back again. "I'm also embarrassed. I think we have treated you improperly, with no proof."

Aram was not sure what to say. He did not want to agree too fast, for fear of seeming to gloat. "You kept my … my confinement pleasant. I have no complaints."

"That is generous of you. I'm grateful."

Aram smiled and nodded.

Adolfo said, "I could not get all of our people to agree to offer you a position. There is no one who thinks there is any solid basis for accusing you of anything, but suspicions remain. Trust … there is no consensus for trusting you."

"I'm fine with that," Aram told him.

"Take your time making your next move," Adolfo told him. "Consider our continued hospitality to be recognition of your past service, and of our bad manners over the last few weeks."

"I appreciate that. Not all in your position would be so fair." Aram paused. "I will want to find out about my uncle. For that, I will go alone, without my family."

"Aram!" Jeannette looked annoyed.

Aram turned toward their room, not realizing that she had been eavesdropping. To assuage her fears he added, "I'll take a small contingent of armed men." He smiled at Adolfo. "I have made acquaintances with a few over these last few weeks."

Adolfo nodded. "Please pass along anything you find out as a result of your travels. Unofficially, of course."

"I will," Aram told him.

Adolfo left.

"I don't want you going out there on your own!" Jeannette insisted.

"I said I wouldn't. But I have to find out what happened to Uncle Dawud. And to see what connections are available to me with this change. It's not a mission for the whole family."

"It could be dangerous, you mean!"

"Not as dangerous as visiting the Mongol camp with the still-headed Robert." He grinned.

Jeannette's lips tightened, but she appeared to understand—reluctantly.

"I have an idea of what's next," Aram told her. "But I need to get some information." He raised his eyebrows. "And then make contact with our old friend Nestor."

"After all this, I don't want to lose you."

Aram embraced her and held her tight.

Second Week of September, 1260
North of Aleppo
Dusk

"How many?" Baybars asked. The sun had almost completely set. Baybars and his men were mounted and ready for action. A flat, dry terrain stretched out before them.

"Larger than normal. Almost a hundred," the returning scout answered.

"Do they know we're here?"

The scout shook his head. "No. It's a hundred men, but it's a rabble. About half are Mongols, with most of the rest Georgians and Armenians. Maybe a few Persians and Arabs. No sentries, no real unit discipline."

"Just a group still fleeing the battle."

"Exactly."

Baybars put on his helmet. "Are they in any sort of defensive formation?"

"No."

Baybars looked around. "No prisoners! All dead!" Baybars turned to the scout. "Lead us to the closest hiding spot. We'll attack from there."

The scout pointed. "There's a little cluster of bushes."

"How far from there?"

The scout shrugged. "Three hundred paces, maybe more."

Baybars called back to his men, "I want archers. Two volleys as the cavalry approaches. Then follow us in."

The Mamluks advanced, stopping behind the bushes. The glow of campfires lit the way to the fleeing enemies' position.

Baybars held his arm up. "Now!"

Arrows went up into the air and arced toward the enemy camp.

Baybars led the attack.

The second volley arced over and beyond the advance Baybars was leading.

Baybars and his warriors slashed into the encampment. They found panicked men in disarray, some pierced by arrows, some scrambling for weapons, some attempting to flee.

Baybars looked for one of his squad leaders. "Take some men around to the other side. No one gets away."

"Yes." The man nodded and moved to his task.

Baybars spotted a light-complected soldier, either Georgian or Armenian, brandishing a sword and poised to hack at the approaching cavalry. Baybars took a battle axe from a hook on his saddle. He flung it at the man and the axe sliced into his target's chest. A quick groan and he fell back, dead.

Baybars pulled out his sword as he saw a Mongol running toward a handful of ponies. He rode the man down and cleaved his head from behind. Brains oozed out from beneath his hair. Two other Mongols, also running for the ponies, changed direction to flee. Baybars hacked both of their faces, slicing deep. They fell, screams of agony on their lips.

Baybars looked around for other targets. Enemies lay dead everywhere. His men had accomplished their task.

Baybars spotted a dark complected Arab who was crouching, grabbing at something. He rode for the man, sword ready. The man came up, waving a white cloth of some sort.

Baybars' nostrils flared. He rode at the man and hacked him just below his chin. Blood gushed and squirted, soaking the attempted flag of surrender. The man fell back, his head mostly separated from the rest of his torso.

Baybars looked down at him. "Too late." Baybars raised his chin. "Way too late, for traitors against the True Faith."

The carnage was over in a matter of minutes.

Qalawun rode up to Baybars. "We got them all."

Baybars nodded. "I think we are just about able to declare all of Syria free of Mongols."

"Not many left around here, if any."

"What a victory, clear up past Aleppo."

"God is great."

Baybars turned to his friend. "We have seen a lot of God's justice over recent days. It has taken time, and God's will arrives at its own pace. But look at the fate of the Mongols, at the hands of Mamluks."

Qalawun smiled broadly. "It is a wonderful pleasure to be the agent of God's justice in this matter."

"All of us can take satisfaction. All of us who have taken this route to today. Generations ago, Mongols invaded the lands of the Kipchaks, destroying our people, pushing us into slavery. But here we rise again, from slave-soldiers, to deliverers of God's justice for their transgressions!"

"God spans the generations. God is almighty, all powerful!"

Baybars raised his sword. "God is great!" he called out to his men.

"Next will be the 'neutral' Christians," Qalawun said.

Baybars shrugged. "No doubt. But we need to see Qutuz come up with our reward. Aleppo would be ideal. We're already here. Our forces are gaining control of the area."

"But with the Mongol threat gone, will Qutuz do what is honorable? Or will he return to his efforts to destroy us?"

"Aleppo is far enough away. He should have no problem granting us this territory. The distance will prevent any friction. He fought well—brilliantly—at Ayn Jalut. So did we. We should all take that into account as we see what comes next."

Qalawun nodded.

Second Week of September, 1260
Damascus
Afternoon

"I should have known," Dawud said as he greeted Aram at the door to his room in Damascus. There were piles of scrolls and books around Dawud's room—on tables, on chairs, and on the floor. "Is your skin tanned from the sun, or did you smudge up your face?"

Aram entered the room. He wore a white ghutra that flowed from the top of his head down to his shoulders. "It didn't take you long to accumulate a lot of things, Uncle."

Dawud shrugged. "I have a lot of friends here, friends who survived the brief Mongol hold on this place. They helped me reaccumulate a lot of my lost possessions."

Aram studied the contents of the room. "Mostly the tools of scholars."

"And of religion, of the True Faith, yes."

Aram took off a padded jacket he was wearing and stepped to a basin with some water where he washed his face. "I started out here with an escort. But I quickly discovered passage is safer for a trader, traveling alone."

"A Muslim-looking trader."

Aram shrugged through a grin. "Yes."

Dawud seemed tired, with heavy eyes, and lacked words to say. But Aram saw a satisfaction, a deep spiritual satisfaction, as if Dawud was at complete peace with the world.

"You were there," Aram said.

Dawud nodded. "I was there."

Aram sensed his uncle would speak further, but that the words would come at his pace. "And I contributed," Dawud finally said.

Aram raised his eyebrows.

Dawud slowly closed, then reopened his eyes. His mouth was turned up in a smile of total contentment, maybe even hinting at a silent ecstasy.

"You killed a few Mongols?"

Dawud frowned and shook his head. "I prayed. And my prayer was answered. I prayed out in the open, with the battle raging a short distance away. I submitted to the will of God. We talk about it, but in those moments, I truly did it. Not just words. Not just hoping I meant it. I completely submitted and accepted God's will, whatever it meant for me—whether it meant imminent pain, the end of my earthly existence—I submitted and accepted." He looked up, as if watching his soul leave the room for a moment. "And God's will occurred. The Mongols ... this is a complete defeat for them, a complete victory for us."

"They will come back," Aram said.

Dawud looked into his eyes with an intense, piercing gaze. "If God wills it."

Aram felt a chill run up his spine at his uncle's intense spirituality.

"But I do not believe God wills it. I believe the Mongol days of evil glory, the Mongol days of evil domination upon the earth, have reached their apex."

Aram nodded.

Dawud motioned to some mats on the floor of his room. Aram took a seat and Dawud sat across from him.

"So what is next for you?" Aram asked.

Dawud shrugged. "Right now, I am a scholar and teacher again. But Commander Baybars and I are in contact. I believe he will call me back to his service soon."

"Baybars?"

"A very talented military man, high up with the Mamluks. He and the sultan were the keys to victory."

"And you...."

"Advised him. He seemed to appreciate my advice. It appears to me he'll be granted governorship of Aleppo. He has been all but promised it, and he is out there now, clearing the area of any remnants of the Mongols."

"You are extraordinary, Uncle. A scribe should write your story."

"There are not enough pages to contain it," Dawud said with a chuckle. "I have lived two or three lifetimes in the last two years. And that leaves another seventy years still to account for!"

Aram laughed.

"What of you? What will you do? Neutrality will not be easy— for anyone."

"Commerce, Uncle. I believe my future is in commerce. Among all types of peoples, all over this region, and maybe beyond. When commerce is done right, everybody gains and no one is an enemy."

"When it is done right...."

"I have to base myself at Acre," Aram said. "I have no wish to return to Baghdad where the Mongols and their proxies still rule, and to what is now little more than a struggling village. And I just can't count on Damascus, or the stability of these newly liberated areas."

Dawud's face tightened into a grim expression. "Acre." He pushed some air through his nose. "I believe Baybars will want to end the Western Christian presence in Acre as brutally as he dealt with the Mongols. He wanted to the day of our visit. He did not take their position of neutrality well."

Aram took in the information. "I think the Mongols are the much bigger threat right now. The new power in this area, if under Qutuz, or back under some local princes again, will be looking north; not west to the coast, at a tiny enclave too small to be more than a minor annoyance. And if traders can build mutual prosperity, they may come to tolerate the existence of Acre—as a gateway to trade with Europe."

Dawud shook his head. "Don't count on that. Such concerns are not priorities for these men. The same brutality that facilitated their defeat of the Mongols inspires them to seek victory over the Western Christians."

"I appreciate that, Uncle," Aram said. "But I see Acre as the best option—not perfect at all, but the best."

"There is another option I suspect hasn't even occurred to you."

Aram narrowed his eyebrows. He tilted his head, inviting Dawud to explain.

"You could adopt the True Faith."

Aram breathed out. "I don't think that's a practical idea. I would lose my Christian connections, possibly my marriage."

Dawud looked at Aram with the same slight smile of spiritual satisfaction Aram had seen before. "All right. It was God's will that I plant the idea. If you decide to adopt the True Faith, you will do so in your own time."

Aram nodded. "What sort of trade connections can I expect to establish here?"

Dawud grinned. He spread his hands, as if he were about to embrace the world. "This is a great city for trade. I can have you dining with some of the city's most capable merchants by tomorrow night." He smiled. "Commerce, done correctly, is honored here too."

"I have no doubt, Uncle." Aram smiled.

Dawud rose. "It seems to me you will be my guest for a time. I will pour us some lemon flavored water."

Aram stood. "That sounds excellent."

39

Mid September
Tabriz
Morning

"Is this what an il-khan does? Wait for news?" Hulegu Khan frowned as he looked at his wife for response. Strewn about the floor of their tent were breakfast scraps of dried meat, bread, and half-filled drinking containers of fermented milk.

Dokuz Khatun gave her husband a reassuring pat. "I am sure that at times the great khans have waited for news up in Qaraqorum."

"My grandfather took *action*," Hulegu said. "He did not wait for events."

"And neither do you," his wife said to him. "You have come to Persia, Mesopotamia and Syria, and you have—"

"And now I hover up here, away from my conquests. Waiting for news from the northeast, news from the southwest."

"Which will determine your next *action*, my husband. You do need to wait for this news. Especially from the northeast."

Hulegu grunted. "Kublai is the most obvious successor. I do not understand how Arigh-boke does not see this! He disgraces our grandfather's memory, and this family's history. We have remained ascendant all over the world because we have successfully navigated the types of dynastic squabbles that ruin other conquering families' continued dominion over their territories. Arigh-boke threatens it all! He threatens our favor under the Eternal Blue Heaven!"

"You may need to step in to help Kublai."

"Yes, of course. Otherwise I would be in Syria right now finishing our business there." He looked at Dokuz Khatun and smiled. "I have to be patient. And wait for news."

Dokuz Khatun chuckled.

A guard poked his head through the doorway.

"Yes?" Hulegu asked.

"A messenger. Just arrived. Wishes permission to see you immediately."

Hulegu looked at Dokuz Khatun.

She smiled.

"Granted. Send him in."

A young Mongol warrior entered. He wore a bandage on his face and a filthy, blood-spattered uniform. He bowed. "Il-Khan. It is my sad duty…." He trembled. "It is my sad duty to report…." He swallowed. "To report a terrible … defeat."

Hulegu's stomach churned. "Get on with it," he snarled. "Stop trembling. Stop stammering about like a drunken clown."

"Yes, my master, most exalted Il-Khan. The Mamluk soldiers destroyed the army led by Ketbugha at a place called Ayn Jalut. The army was utterly destroyed—scattered and fled through Syria, north. Ketbugha…." The young man took a deep breath. "Ketbugha was taken prisoner and beheaded."

Hulegu bolted up from the floor. He flew at the other man. "How! How could this happen!" He slapped the messenger.

"I … I believe they had more men than we thought. And … one of the Muslim princes in our ranks, at least, maybe more, left the field."

Hulegu shoved the man to the ground and kicked him. "This is an outrage!"

The messenger froze, remaining absolutely still.

Hulegu regained his composure. "Get up," he ordered.

The messenger quickly complied.

"Get me the chief security officer on duty."

The messenger bolted quickly from the tent, barely acknowledging the order.

"I ought to have that man flogged," Hulegu grumbled. "Trembling, crying … 'the army was utterly destroyed,'" Hulegu mocked.

Dokuz Khatun stood. "You have some business."

"Yes. Some *action* I can take, right now."

Dokuz Khatun started toward the tent opening.

"Stay. This won't take long."

The security leader arrived. "You asked for me, il-Khan?"

"Yes. Al-Nasir Yusuf, a worthless vassal of ours, has failed to secure Syrian loyalties, resulting in a temporary setback in the southwest. Execute him."

"Yes sir. Do you wish to talk to him first?"

"No. Do it immediately."

"Yes sir. Are we concerned about, about royal blood?"

Hulegu's face tensed. "Yes." He paused, then spat out the word, "Barely." Hulegu gestured casually with the back of his hand. "Use a few of his own rugs—those ugly, disgusting things he tried to pass off to us as gifts."

The security leader grinned slightly. "Yes."

"Do you see anything funny here?" Hulegu snarled.

The security leader's face became suddenly serious. "No sir."

"Then keep your grin to yourself and get on with my orders!"

"Yes sir." The security leader bolted away.

"I'll have him flogged next to that messenger."

Dokuz Khatun looked at her husband warily.

"What?" he demanded.

"Nothing, my husband."

Hulegu looked down. He kicked the breakfast scraps. "Once succession is resolved, I will rain down ruin on them that will rival what my grandfather did to the Khwarazm-shah in Central Asia after he killed our envoys. Every city will match Baghdad—there will be no mercy. They will learn the price for resisting the dynasty the Eternal Blue Heaven has ordained to rule the world."

Dokuz Khatun gave her husband a slight nod.

Hulegu kicked over a table covered with linens.

Third Week of September, 1260
Northern Syria, Outskirts of Aleppo
Mid Morning

"What does it say?" Qalawan asked.

Baybars stood in front of his tent, reading from a scroll he had just unraveled. Baybars squinted as his lips scrunched upward. "Not what we wanted it to say. Not what we had a right to expect it to say." Baybars looked at the messenger. "You're dismissed."

After the messenger left, Qalawan asked, "You think that man was looking for a reaction?"

"Yes I do," said Baybars. "And anything else he could overhear." He looked at Qalawan. "We need to gather the men. Leave a good force here in the north to maintain control. We have business in the south."

"So Qutuz is not coming north to Aleppo," Qalawan said.

"No. He proclaimed himself Lord of Syria while he was in

Damascus. His privilege, no doubt. But he remains silent on the governorship of Aleppo. I take this as a refusal. And his move south, away from my strength, shows he does not trust me, shows he sees me as a rival."

Qalawan smiled. "You are."

Baybars grinded his teeth as a grin snuck onto his face. "I was waiting to see—" He stopped in mid-thought. "Of course I'm a rival! I still haven't forgotten Aqtay's head and our years of exile and humiliation! Of course he still has grievances to answer for!"

Qalawan nodded and continued to smile.

"The simple truth is I hate Mongols more than I hate Qutuz."

Qalawan raised his eyebrows.

"Qutuz could have continued to channel that hate of mine to the northeast. Aleppo could have been mine, a powerful buffer state at the north of Syria, bumping up against Mongols. A state from where we could raid Mongols, slaughter Mongols, ruin their lands and push them further toward the steppes of Central Asia— where if the accursed creatures deserve to exist anywhere, they deserve to exist there."

"But the Aleppo state could have rivaled his own state."

Baybars grinned mischievously. "Maybe. Maybe over the years that would have happened." He paused. "But we will never know now, will we...."

Qalawan shook his head.

Baybars said, "Now it's going to be a matter of who kills whom."

Qalawan's eyes widened.

"He has signaled it." Baybars shrugged. "We can't even coexist in a vast swath of land extending from the Nile to the Euphrates. We cannot coexist in this post-Mongol world."

Qalawan nodded. "Yes. Yes, that is what his withdrawal south, without granting you Aleppo—that is what it means. He will go back to his pre-Mongol invasion policy—of trying to wipe us out."

"With me at the top of the list."

"Yes. But he knows of the loyalty to you among many who fought with you, and followed you up here. He will not trust any of us, even with you gone."

"So we know what needs to be done."

"Absolutely." Qalawan paused, as if gathering his thoughts before offering his next words. "But Commander, we need a small squad, of highly skilled specialists. Bring the rest down, but only partially south."

Baybars considered Qalawan's point. "Yes. We don't want to call attention to anything."

"Correct."

"And we need a contact inside the sultan's circle."

"There are some men loyal to us who could handle that specialty."

Baybars nodded again. "We will act. Now."

End of September, 1260
Acre
Mid Day

"I hear you've been looking for me." Nestor flinched as he said the words. Two armed guards flanked him, their hands ready to grab his arms at the least hint that Nestor would decide to turn and leave.

Aram looked at Nestor, He stood in the doorway of a small meeting room, in an inn just off the Inner Harbor. "You could say that. More accurately, I need to speak to you. I understand you've been avoiding my invitation."

"Avoiding? Um, no, not *avoiding.* Um, I don't think I ever understood that, well, that it was ... um, that *you* were anxious, I mean *urgent....*"

"Nestor, you've been avoiding me. You owe me a lot of money."

"And I think we're on the verge—"

"Nestor, I need you to be honest here. You took a lot of money that I earned, and you haven't paid me. This is why you're avoiding me."

"But this is—"

"Nestor. You see these gentlemen? The ones who brought you here? They're friends of mine. I have made many friends here. They're not letting you go about your business until I say you can. And I'm not letting you go about your business until we have a conversation. A *real* conversation. Understand?"

Nestor looked at the two guards. "I think so."

"You've been avoiding me, because you owe me a lot of money."

Nestor's eyes roamed, then came back to Aram. "Yes. And...." Nestor paused as his lips tightened. "And the work turned out to be a lot more involved than I thought it would be. I heard something about a satchel with a head in it." He grinned sheepishly. "I thought you might be a little angry with me."

"Now we're getting somewhere," Aram said. "Thank you," he

said to the guards. "I don't think I need you now." Aram looked at Nestor. "Do I?"

"No, no," Nestor assured.

Aram slapped Nester hard on the back, propelling him forward, nearly taking him off his feet. "Just good friends, getting reacquainted. Catching up." He motioned Nestor toward a chair at a small table.

Nestor coughed once and sat. "Right."

"I was a little angry," Aram told him as he sat opposite. "But really mostly about the money."

"And that might just be something I can—"

"Spare me. I know it's gone. When I renegotiated with Robert, I did very well. He actually set aside payment designated for me before he...." Aram paused. "Before he had his unfortunate dealings with the Mongols. I am not in a position where I need to worry about money. I'd more or less written it off."

"I really didn't just waste it," Nestor finally admitted. "I had it tied up in some excellent propositions. But the war hit—the Mongols— what a mess."

"I've forgiven you. You can pay me back out of a future venture."

Nestor perked up. "Future venture?"

"Yes. Absolutely."

Jeannette appeared at the doorway.

"Ah." Aram stood and motioned her toward another chair at the table. "Here she is, the reason I can't stay too angry with you. If you had never found me that employment, I never would have met Jeannette."

Nestor stood. "Oh. Well, I am charmed to meet you."

"Thank you." Jeannette sat at the table.

Nestor and Aram retook their seats.

"Here's what I want to discuss," Aram said. "I find I still have some good contacts out toward the East. Mongols are pretty much hands-off as long as the tribute's on time, taxes are paid, and you acknowledge their absolute control. I think I can set good trading contacts in their territories. I've also actually established a few contacts with traders in Syria, thanks to my uncle. I need to work toward some European contacts. But you already have contacts—Greek contacts, Italian contacts."

Nestor swallowed. "Some of those people"—Nestor forced a smile that quickly faded— "are also mad at me."

"Nestor." Aram shook his head. "You didn't burn all your contacts...?"

"No, of course not."

Aram looked down his nose.
"Some of them," Nestor said.
Aram's eyes narrowed.
"Many of them," Nestor said.
"Even if it's most of them, just tell me it's not all of them."
Nestor's eyes brightened. "I still have a few."
"Well, sometimes it starts with just a few."
"There is a family in Venice. The Polo family. They're looking for Eastern contacts."
"There we go. And they don't hate you?"
"No."
"And you have had business with them in the past."
"I have business with them now. They are on their way from Constantinople to the East; they're looking for trade with Cathay."
"Cathay? And what's your business with them?"
"I set them up with translators and advice. They paid me a small fee."
"The Mongols control Cathay right now. And they're still in a fuss over who's going to be the great khan."
Nestor shrugged. "The Polos don't expect immediate success. They're just exploring the opportunity."
"This is a family I need to meet."
"I will arrange it."
"Good."
"And I'm in for part of the profits of any venture?"
"Of course," Aram told him. "Of course, my old friend."
"I'll get to work on it." He stood.
"And other European contacts. Don't forget. Greek. Other Italians. French, and even Germans, if you have them."
"They're not all like Robert."
Aram shrugged. "I'm not going to say anything against Robert. He paid me well, and he paid a big price for his ... his deficiencies."
"True enough."
"Don't forget, I have a lot of friends here. Jeannette ... has a lot of friends. Keep things on the level between us. Don't avoid me."
"Now that we have had this talk, I don't want to. After all, you offer good opportunities."
Aram smiled. "Good. Times are in flux, but we can prosper."
"I believe you are right."
Aram stood. "Let me hear from you soon."
Nestor also stood. "You will, my friend."

They hugged briefly, and Nestor left the room.

"Well?" Aram said to Jeannette.

"Please tell me we're not trusting him with *anything.*"

Aram laughed. "Of course not. I don't trust him with any deal where he runs the money. And he will pay me back for what he took from me—and he'll be happy to do it."

"Good."

"But look what he can do. The Venetian family ... the Polo family. That's the kind of connection he has access to."

"If they exist...."

"There's no reason for him to make up something like that. I know the Italian merchant states are looking for Eastern trade. That's our future, too. Setting the conduits for those exchanges, and helping to make them happen."

Jeannette nodded. "And this is what we do, in a quiet corner, during these times of armies clashing all around?"

Aram shrugged. "It's what I'm best at. Contacts. Linking distant peoples and places. And this is how we can prosper."

"I know," Jeannette said.

"Commerce also can help immunize us."

"Or make us ripe for plunder."

"If we do this right, we will be too valuable for anyone to plunder. And each side of the various deals will be our protection, as long as our involvement brings everyone prosperity."

"Well, I'm glad you let me see Nestor."

"I wanted you to see what we are getting into."

"Thank you. For including me. For making sure I'm part of it."

Aram smiled, then reached over and took Jeannette's hand.

She leaned forward.

Aram and Jeannette kissed—this time not just a kiss of lust, or passion, but of enduring love.

40

October 1260
Between Salihiyyua and al-Arish
Late Morning

"This could be our chance," a young soldier told Baybars as he approached. "The sultan spotted a hare, and wants to hunt it. He is halting to go after it."

Baybars smirked. "Qutuz has always been a fool for a hunt— true from way back in the days of the Ayyubid sultans of Egypt." Baybars looked at the small group with him, which included Qalawun. "He will hand us the perfect circumstances for our purpose." Baybars' lips tightened. He and his group had caught up with Qutuz's army as it returned to Egypt. Baybars was ostensibly headed for the Qalyub district, but he had kept his distance from the main body of Qutuz's army while he placed surreptitious contacts in order to make his move against Qutuz.

"Lord of Syria, Sultan of Egypt, champion of the hunt," Qalawan commented.

"We need to be in the vicinity of that hunt," Baybars said. "Where was the hare?"

"Over along that ridge, just this side of the camp."

Baybars nodded. "Let's go."

The men brought their horses trotting over towards the area where they anticipated the hunt might be.

"We have two men in position," Baybars said to Qalawan.

"That should be enough," Qalawan said.

"His personal guard?" Baybars asked the young soldier who had reported on the sultan's whereabouts.

"He left them when he started chasing the hare."

Baybars shook his head. A fatalistic grin crept onto his face. Arrogance. Overconfidence. Maybe Qutuz's last mistakes.

"He knows you're here," Qalawan said. "We weren't able to keep that a secret."

Baybars' grin remained. "I am not one who escapes notice."

Qalawan chuckled.

"Qutuz must know I am here to complain about his decision on Aleppo, that I'm not happy about his attitude since Ayn Jalut. He must think we are close enough to home that he has all the moves."

"We will make ours now."

Baybars nodded. "Before he makes his, back in Cairo."

Baybars and his group of seven rode along toward the hunt.

They spotted Qutuz's group, five men chasing the hare as it scooted across the scrubby turf toward some bushes. "There it is!" Baybars called out. "To the right."

Qutuz's group was closer. A few of his men shot some arrows, but they missed the darting animal.

"It's in those bushes," Baybars said, pointing. "Let's join the hunt. Right now, we're not chasing Qutuz—we're chasing that hare."

Baybars' squad raced toward the bushes. One or two of them shot arrows into the clump of underbrush as Qutuz's men approached from a different angle, closer to the hare's apparent location.

Qutuz raised his hand, halting any bow shots as his group moved in close.

The hare suddenly darted out, from the side of the brush opposite Baybars' group. His men had no clear shots at the hare, but Qutuz's group was closer, and not screened by the bushes. The hare got about forty feet out when Baybars saw an arrow strike it.

"Got it!" Baybars said.

"His swordsman got it," Qalawan observed.

"That's *our* man," Baybars said.

"Yes."

"Let's move in," Baybars said. "Be ready."

He led his men toward Qutuz's group. "What a marvelous shot!" Baybars called out. "Superb!"

Qutuz looked at Baybars and his squad. "I thought the little devil was going to get away again!" He looked at his swordsman.

"Very skilled. Very skilled bow work."

"Thank you, my lord," the swordsman said. He dismounted and walked to the slain hare.

Baybars and his men eased their way among Qutuz's group.

"You have always loved a good hunt," Baybars said to Qutuz. "I should have known, when we started chasing it, that you wouldn't be far away."

Qutuz smiled. "You are right about that, Commander."

Two of Baybars' men were now within arm's reach of the sultan.

Baybars made a miniscule shake of his head. *Not yet.*

Qutuz's swordsman brought the hare to Qutuz. "I present our triumph," he said, handing the creature to Qutuz.

"Thank you. It was a magnificent shot. Thrilling. What prize can I offer you?"

"Well...." The swordsman broke into a sly grin. "There is a little Mongol slave-girl among those on their way to Cairo...."

"You will have your pick," Qutuz told him.

"Thank you, Sultan."

Qutuz extended his left hand, palm down, for a kiss of gratitude.

The swordsman reached to take the hand, but grabbed and yanked with his right.

"Now!" Baybars ordered.

His men unsheathed their swords.

Qutuz's swordsman put his hand on the sultan's sword to trap it in its scabbard. One of Baybars' men hacked Qutuz's neck. The swordsman unsheathed the sultan's sword and slashed at him with it.

Qutuz fell from his horse.

A few of his remaining loyal men reached for weapons, but Baybars caught their eyes and shook his head. Facing Baybars' men, poised and with drawn swords, they would certainly be killed.

Another of Baybars' soldiers stepped to the prone sultan and shot an arrow through his skull.

Baybars looked down at Qutuz. "It was going to be you or me," he said quietly. "I acted first." Baybars called out, "Qutuz is removed. We will discuss a successor. Our best and brightest will choose from among us to install a leader most fit to establish a Mamluk sultanate strong enough to rule wide territories and to defend against what will no doubt be a furious counterattack from the Mongols. Qutuz won the battle, but was on his way to failure by not moving north to secure the territory. We will choose a successor who will not make that mistake."

Two of Qutuz's men put the sultan's body onto his horse. The men rode back toward the main travel formation.

"You will be sultan," Qalawan assured him quietly.

"I know. Everyone in this group knows." Baybars took in a deep breath. "But this is a large realm we seek to rule. There are political considerations, powerful influential men to satisfy, to bring us together. We will guide the process, but we will make certain that we are not seen as coercing the process. I will take this power with the blessing of legalities, not just as some brute with more ruthless men and a more daring will. I want to begin a reign that will last."

"Yes. Good."

They followed the group with the assassinated sultan back to the main camp.

Late October, 1260
Cairo
Evening

"You wanted to talk to me. With Adiba." Baybars sat on a plush chair. The palace's private quarters had an ornate look, with complex tile patterns adorning the walls.

He wore silk night clothes. Adiba and Zahirah were in light-colored, full-length casual dresses. "This isn't more trouble between you?" he asked. From her expression, Adiba also did not know what this was about.

"No." Zahirah appeared to be fighting tears. "I need to tell you, to tell you both, something important."

Baybars raised his eyebrows, encouraging her to continue.

"I'm two months past my time," she said. "Since I was a girl, and started my bleeding, I have never missed."

Adiba took a deep breath. Baybars suspected she might not be happy with this news.

Baybars himself grinned. "That's wonderful," he said. "Another son."

Zahirah swallowed. There seemed to be something she wasn't saying.

"My mother died giving birth to me," Zahirah explained. "Look at me. I have the same tiny hips."

Adiba frowned, as if in thought.

"Look at you," Zahirah said to Baybars. She shook her head. "My baby with you will be huge." She sighed. "I'll never survive it."

"That's not a certainty," Adiba said. "Just because your mother died doesn't mean you will."

"We will have the resources of the nation to draw on," Baybars told her.

"I appreciate that," Zahirah said. "I know you will try. But I must face that this could lead to the end of my life."

Baybars wasn't sure what to say.

Zahirah turned to Adiba. "Please take care of my child if I—if I don't survive."

Adiba looked at her, at first puzzled, but then with sympathetic, almost pitying eyes. "Of course."

"I've been mean to you," Zahirah said. "I've tried to hold my beauty over you like some sort of superiority. I'm not superior to you. You are a fine woman, a wonderful sister, better than I should expect or deserve. I will not forget that again."

Adiba swallowed. Tears rolled down her cheeks. "I always sensed there was a decent girl behind all the bluster."

"I do not how you found that girl," Zahirah replied, "because I didn't find her until I realized I was with child. It's not a proud moment for me to only realize my bad behavior when facing adversity. But I have, and I will make amends."

"We will have every expert available working on this," Baybars said. "Small hips or not, we will do all we can to make sure you bear me this child, and others."

She nodded.

The two women left.

Baybars shook his head and smiled. He was glad to see his wives getting along. He would choose another time to tell them a third wife would be joining them all soon.

Late Autumn, 1260
Cairo
Afternoon

"Sultan."

"Almost," Baybars said to Dawud.

Dawud entered the ornate throne room. It was covered wall to wall with intricate mosaics, and colorful banners were hung from the ceiling. A carpet led up through the center of the room toward the shiny gold, jewel-encrusted throne. At the foot of the carpet, Dawud knelt and bowed, then walked toward Baybars. The Mamluk ruler stood as Dawud approached.

The room was empty except for the two men. Dawud wore his typical white robe and white turban. Baybars wore a colorful silk shirt and pants. A ceremonial dagger hung from his waist. A blue turban with a few jewels embedded in it sat atop his head.

"Almost?" Dawud asked as he reached the other man.

"I've had to share power here and there, with the idea of securing long-term control."

"Sounds prudent."

"How was your trip?"

Dawud shrugged. "Traveling is more difficult as I age."

"Thank you for making this long journey."

"I would not think of disappointing you."

Baybars paused. "I saw you at Ayn Jalut."

Dawud smiled.

"What you did—it was one of the most courageous acts I have ever seen on a battlefield."

Dawud shook his head. "It took no courage at all. I followed your command and looked for a way to contribute. And I submitted to the will of God."

"Are you still looking for a way to contribute?"

"Always."

"Rejoin my service. I have missed you."

Dawud's eyes darted to one side, then back. "Here in Cairo?"

"Yes. It is a great city for scholars; and not far from Alexandria, another great city for scholars."

Dawud nodded. "What can I accomplish for you here?"

"Advise me. I exist in a dangerous world. Potential enemies surround me. I must devise safeguards and layers of security that will prevent me from suffering the same fate as Qutuz." Baybars paused to gather his next words. "I have men, with me a long time, who I can trust to advise me on blood and treachery. But to be a great ruler, I need counsel from the seer who presided over a battle with nothing but the Koran, and his faith in God."

Dawud shrugged. "I'm not sure my advice would be helpful."

"Try. Tell me, what might I be missing?"

Dawud took in a deep breath. "What have you done to bring spiritual authority to your regime?"

"I have considered this, and have some ideas. What do *you* recommend?"

Dawud tilted his head. "There is no more Caliph of Baghdad. There is really no more Baghdad. Find someone to move into that spot."

Baybars nodded. "Can you help with that?"

Dawud shook his head. "Sultan, I am old, and cannot promise you the energy needed to do justice to the task. I will comment on what is being done, if you like."

"But what we need to do is bring the caliph role into *this* state."

"This is the logical place to reconstitute the position, while Baghdad is still controlled by non-believers. This state holds Mecca, and the great cities of Cairo, Damascus and Jerusalem. Islamic authority should emanate from here."

Baybars nodded. "We will work on that."

"What are your priorities for outside your borders and within your borders?"

"Outside the borders? Crush the Mongol threat wherever it exists, and drive them back to where they came from if we have the power. Destroy the Christian state planted in our midst once and for all. Inside the borders? Establish an enforceable authority throughout the realm, with brutal consequences for defiance, and stress organization with clear duties and expectations for subordinates."

Dawud looked down.

Baybars knew that Dawud did not approve of all of those goals. "That is what our world demands of us. We may need to look in strange places for alliances. Hulegu's brother Berke has adopted the True Faith. He is Mongol, that is true. But with his new religious affiliations, I may be able to set an alliance with him that will dampen Hulegu's desire to come back our way again."

Dawud was not sure how to respond. After what the Mongols had put him through, he did not trust any purported conversions to the True Faith, and could not countenance any sort of accommodation with them.

"What, then, would you suggest for me, as I seek to govern effectively over the long term?" Baybars continued.

"Look to the lessons of the past. I can help with that. Look to the last great ruler to establish control over Egypt and Syria."

"Saladin."

"Yes. He governed with a moral authority, with a spiritual authority—"

"I know about Saladin."

"Good, my sultan. His approach can teach you a great deal about—"

"Saladin's approach is a luxury we cannot afford. I cannot be a Saladin."

Dawud considered these words.

Baybars continued, "Saladin faced Western Christians, men like Richard the Lionheart. They were like a gentle tap on the back, a fly buzzing in the wind, compared to what we have faced from the East. Islam took some blows from them, no doubt. And we are taught that those Christian warriors threatened Islam." Baybars snorted dismissively. "At the time, Muslims believed it. But Mongols actually *did* threaten our entire existence. Mongols exceed Christians by magnitudes with their evil."

Dawud nodded.

"And the idea of Christian chivalry has deteriorated from the great warrior Richard the Lionheart to the motley group of vacillators and equivocators in Acre. Mongols are still out there, just beyond the northern edges of Syria, waiting to pounce on complacency, to crash through any weakness. Chivalry is over. It is worthless in this world. It was said Saladin was more chivalrous than Christians ever were. But there is no more room for Saladin's brand of kind and benevolent Islam; otherwise we will be swept aside by the evil around us. We need to have leaders now who pray to God, then go on to slaughter enemies without mercy. My dear friend, I will be one of them."

Dawud hung his head. This dose of reality jolted him out of a floating spiritual euphoria that really hadn't faded since the battle.

"You are disappointed."

Dawud shook his head. "No. I am … facing reality."

Baybars' expression invited explanation.

"I think you are a wise man. I think you are part of God's will—

the way you put aside your rivalry with Qutuz to drive away the Mongols." Dawud raised his eyebrows. "But at this time, I'm not sure I can help you."

"You are a treasure," Baybars said. "Your honesty is uncommon, and uplifts even when it is dissonant."

Dawud bowed in thanks.

"I know exactly what you will do for me, for my realm," Baybars said.

"How can I be of service?"

"You will return to Damascus. With your remaining years—and I hope you have many years ahead—you will train legions of men to think like you, to absorb your view of the world, your spiritual vision and knowledge, and you will send them to Cairo. And I will keep them on hand for when the world becomes a safer place, a place again amenable to the compassion and generosity of a ruler like Saladin."

Dawud's face slowly shifted into a gentle smile, a smile emanating from a deep spiritual satisfaction. "It would be my honor." He bowed.

Baybars returned the bow.

Dawud headed for the exit, then turned back after a few steps. "For me, the world has arrived at that spiritual place, with Islam."

"I hope I can join you there someday."

Dawud smiled and nodded. He had a sense that Baybars did not believe that day would ever come. But this was the best result Dawud could hope for. He turned and left the room.

Epilogue One

March, 1265
Damascus
Afternoon

"You are not permitted here!" insisted the young student. He was dressed in a white robe, and had a sporadic scraggly beard. "You are not of the True Faith."

"He is my uncle." Aram's nostrils flared. With Aram were Jeannette and three children; they had added another son and an infant daughter to their family. They waited just outside Dawud's modest quarters.

"You're not of the True Faith," the man insisted again. "This is the great Dawud, possibly in his last days! You will not defile his final moments!"

Aram's lips tightened. "Would you just tell him I'm here? We got word that time was short. That came either from my uncle, or from someone close to him. We hurried here, and I believe we have arrived in time. Now you presume to block us?"

"You'll not defile this great sage's final days!"

"At least talk to him. Tell him I'm here. With my family—*his* family."

The man folded his arms and glared at Aram.

Aram wanted to bowl the man over. But that would add violence to the situation, potentially escalating it, and upsetting his uncle who seemed to be on his deathbed. "Suppose my uncle, this great man whom you say you serve, sent word for me and my family to come and comfort him before his final breath. And suppose he passes to God, and you find out that you have thwarted his final wishes! How will you feel about your service to him then?"

The man swallowed, seeming to consider Aram's words.

"Tell him Aram his nephew is here. If he tells you to send us away, we will go with no further objection."

The man put his palms out. "Wait here." He went inside the room.

Aram looked at Jeannette. She shook her head. "How have you managed to do business here?"

"It hasn't been easy. Everything pushes and pulls for one faction, one group, one division or another. Trying to benefit everyone is a difficult concept. Most seem to believe that what benefits one takes from another, so God forbid a perceived enemy, or even a different group, ever benefits."

Jeannette nodded her understanding.

The young student returned. He bowed slightly. "Forgive me. The master has been waiting for you."

"Thank you."

Aram and his family entered the room.

Dawud lay in bed, covered in blankets. He seemed pale, almost frozen. His eyes followed Aram as he approached. "Praise God's will." Dawud seemed to labor for each word, catching his breath and regathering strength for each utterance. "One last time. Together."

"Yes, Uncle. We are all here. We are so glad to see you."

"My heart." Dawud closed his eyes. "Pains—all around it." He paused again. "I believe—" He grimaced. "I believe my time is very soon."

Aram nodded. "I understand."

"One thing." Dawud summoned the meager strength he still had. "No one can understand." He took in another breath. "But you."

"Tell me, Uncle. Tell me."

Jeannette gathered the children around the bed. The family huddled closely around Dawud.

"At this time, at the end." Dawud paused again. "Memories flood back—so many. Too many. Must sort—most important."

Aram waited as Dawud seemed to struggle for every word.

"'More than one path,' I heard—" He grimaced again. "I heard my father say."

"Your father, who was murdered by a Christian fanatic."

Dawud labored to nod. "I was just short of seven." He gathered strength again. "My father's friend—Rashid—he spoke of this as well." Dawud closed his eyes and seemed to sink back.

"He needs rest!" the student insisted. "You are tiring him! Leave! Leave now!"

Dawud shook his head, trying to lift it.

"He's trying to tell us something," Aram told the student.

"No rest." Dawud took another breath. "More than one path—"

The student looked at Dawud.

"—to God."

The student's eyes widenened in disbelief.

Aram smiled. The student had obviously been jolted by the decidedly un-Islamic idea. "I remember," he said to Dawud.

"Baghdad," Dawud said.

"We all worshiped freely, explored the world's knowledge," Aram said, nodding.

"It was my work there," Dawud said, now seeming excited, nearly breathless. He grimaced again. "I think … my heart is nearly done."

"Baghdad is gone. Those days are gone."

Dawud lifted his right palm. "My work. Buried."

Aram shook his head. "Buried. Burned. Wrecked. Devastated."

Dawud uttered a quick sigh. He sounded frustrated. He was apparently trying to make a point of some sort with his last words. "No. Buried."

"Sadly. Buried there. Lost."

Dawud slowly shook his head back and forth, as if it caused him pain. "Not lost. Buried."

Whatever Dawud was trying to communicate, Aram was not understanding. "My own work, commerce, seeks to thrive across the divisions, Uncle. We just recently brokered an invitation from Cathay for a prominent merchant family, Italian, from Venice. They are on their way. If there is to be a harmony—"

Dawud raised his head. "More than commerce. More than material." He closed his eyes. "I was on to something. Secret work. Dangerous. Had to be buried."

Aram shook his head. He still did not understand what Dawud was trying to say. "Your work here has been incredible. You have trained men in the best ideals of your faith. You have made your mark in a way that would please anyone's God."

Dawud smiled. "That is … more than one path." He closed his eyes again. "Baghdad. Will wait. To be un-buried." Dawud nodded as if accepting he had communicated as well as he could.

Aram took Dawud's hand.

Dawud squeezed it.

Aram motioned his family to surround Dawud. They quickly moved in, gently taking his hands and arms. Jeannette stroked the side of his head.

"He should—" The student seemed to stop himself, as if rethinking his words. "If these are his last moments, he should go to God hearing the words of the Koran."

"Yes," Aram said. "Of course."

"I'll get an imam to read."

Aram looked at the student. "Hurry."

Dawud opened his eyes a moment. "Not needed. I know the words. I want...." He closed his eyes, then smiled. A moment later he grimaced as his teeth clenched. He groaned slightly. His entire body seemed to relax, and the grimace loosened, morphing into that same smile Aram had seen from Dawud during their most recent contacts—that smile of spiritual satisfaction, of a spiritually perfect state.

Aram felt for Dawud's pulse. "He's gone." A tear rolled down his left cheek, then his right cheek. But as he looked at Dawud, he felt a gentle smile take over his lips.

Epilogue Two

April 6, 1291
Acre
Just After Sunrise

"They won't leave a soul alive."

Aram looked into the eyes of his oldest son, Daniel, as they stood at the walls of Acre. Aram shifted his view out from the walls at the Hospitaller Quarter toward the forces arrayed against them. Lines of Muslim/Mamluk troops ringed the land approaches to the walled city. Siege engines and catapults stood among the attacking troops. Nothing was going to enter or leave Acre from the landward side unless it was serving the purpose of the Muslims' capture of the city. If the Muslims had ever developed a state-of-the-art navy, the Western Christian positions would have been taken long before now. "It'll be worse than Antioch," Aram agreed as he looked out. "That's why we're leaving."

Daniel's head snapped around to look at his father, then back out. "I think you're right. It is time to go. It may be past time to go."

Aram nodded grimly. "It's over for the Western Christians out here." He let out a short breath. "I made a choice, years ago, to set up here. So, we will be swept away with them."

Aram's son closed his eyes, then reopened them. "We don't know Europe. We've been there. We know where it is. But we don't *know* Europe."

"Well, we'd better learn," Aram said. "We're better off than most. A lot of these people are crowding onto ships for Cyprus where they face uncertain, minimal prospects. We have prospects, in Venice: the Polos, and others. And we have wealth in Templar banks, and in our outposts around the area."

"Hm. When is the last time anyone heard from Marco?"

"Not for some time. We know he is safe in Cathay, good friends with the Mongol ruler, Kublai Khan. I wonder if he will ever return."

"If he does, I will seek him out," Daniel said. "I'll bet he has a story to tell, and he's the type who will love to tell it."

"That's right—you met him when he came through here, over twenty years ago now, I think."

"I was twelve. I remember it well."

Aram smiled. "The world grows together while it simultaneously bursts apart."

Daniel let out a deep breath. "Looks like I'll never get back to Baghdad."

Aram frowned in puzzlement with this statement. "Baghdad?"

"Something Uncle Dawud said."

"This again? You were five years old."

"Six. And I'm not just going on that. I'm going on what you told me."

Aram shook his head. "He didn't mean for us to go to Baghdad. He meant Baghdad as a state of mind, as a condition for coexistence—and that Mongols buried it, destroyed it with their brutality."

"I really think he meant something is actually buried there. Something he was working on. Something referring to 'more than one path,' that he was working on."

Aram shrugged. "Son, even if true, where would you look? Where would you dig?"

"I don't know," Daniel said, seeming resigned to the hopelessness of his quest. "You lived there, and you said you wouldn't even know where to start."

"When we went through there with the Polos twenty years ago, I could barely recognize even hints of familiar landmarks." He stiffened. "And anywhere you start digging, you go through a layer of bones."

Aram's son swallowed.

"We're going to leave as soon as possible," Aram said. "Hopefully tomorrow afternoon. We need to help your mother get things ready to go."

Aram's son nodded.

❧ ◆ ❧

Just Off the Shores of Acre
April, 7, 1291
Mid Afternoon

"This is almost like going home for you," Aram said to Jeannette. He had an arm around her shoulder. They stood at the rear of a Venetian merchant ship.

"Europe hasn't been home for me for a long time." She pointed out toward the coast. "*That* was home." She sniffled.

"Wherever we are together is home."

She smiled and squeezed his waist.

"One of the Templars was commenting—Richard, the king they called the Lionheart, left this place, on a ship like this, almost exactly one hundred years ago."

"He really was going home."

"With the idea he would come back and take Jerusalem for his version of Christianity."

Jeannette shook her head. "They're all gone, aren't they?"

"Who?"

"The sultan. Baybars. His son. The khan."

"Yes, and even Baybars' old friend Sultan Qalawun. It is *his* son outside these walls, there to complete Baybars' vow of annihilation." Aram smirked. "And Hulegu. He didn't even outlive Uncle Dawud!"

"They're all gone," Jeannette said. "But the fighting. The divides. That all lives on."

"And gets worse. We tried to bridge the divides with commerce. And here we are. Uncle Dawud's father thought he could bridge the divides with the 'more-than-one-path' to God idea. He lasted a much shorter time than we did."

Jeannette shook her head. "So much that could be done, so much potential goodness—lost in the divides."

Aram nodded.

"They'll kill everyone, won't they?" Jeannette said as Acre shrank into the distance, only its rough outlines visible behind them.

"Everyone left behind there, absolutely. Just like Antioch. And they'll brag about it." Aram raised his eyebrows. "To defeat the Mongols they have become the Mongols. And it's become a part of who they are. I wonder if the lofty purposes and principles of their faith will survive this."

"Their faith will live on, longer than we will. We can only hope that good people will rediscover those lofty principles some time soon."

"Until then, here we are." Aram gestured out to the city, a dot at the edges of the disappearing shore. "Leaving Acre. Leaving what I have heard people call the 'Holy Land.'"

Jeannette nodded.

Aram looked back one more time. *They had to become the Mongols to defeat the Mongols.* He turned and gently guided Jeannette to face him. They shared a brief kiss and walked toward the front of the ship.

Afterword

Hulegu, the il-khan, died in 1265 at age 48. Though Kublai Khan would win the battle of succession with his brother Arighboke to become the great khan, the Genghis Khan dynasty—for all practical purposes—broke into different states. Of course, Kublai Khan became the famous ruler of China. Knowing how Genghis Khan considered cities pointless, and city people useless, we have to wonder what Genghis Khan would have thought of his grandson's China. We can certainly suspect Genghis Khan's instinct would have been to attack and conquer the place, carting off its wealth and thinning out its citizens, particularly if there was any resistance.

Hulegu's son, Abaqa, continued his policies; but in 1295, the Ilkhanate adopted Islam, changing the nature of the state Hulegu established. By then, the fragmentation of Genghis Khan's dynasty was in full swing.

Baybars died in 1277, in his fifties; his exact birth year is not known with certainty. There is also some uncertainty about his death. Some accounts indicate he died from an illness. Others offer a strange story of Baybars trying to poison someone whom he perceived as a threat, but then he drank from the same cup and died shortly after the man he had poisoned. Baybars was not extensively mourned at his death—he was singleminded, even ruthless, during his rule. But his seventeen years of rule established the Mamluk dynasty as a major power in the area, and it would last for over two hundred years.

I found little information about Baybars' wives. One of my sources refers to an incident with Baybars' wife while he was in the service of al-Mughith Umar. I added details based on the circumstances at the time. Another source mentions Baybars having a four-year-old son in 1263, the future sultan al-Malik al-Said. So I worked my way back to create details about him. There is also a reference in my sources to Baybars' sons creating difficulties for future Mamluk Sultan Qalawun. From this, I deduced Baybars had multiple wives, and invented details based on the times and circumstances, along with some educated speculation concerning Baybars' character.

There is not a lot of information about Qalawun before the formation of the Mamluk state, but we can conclude he was a key ally of Baybars while the Bahriyya Mamluks went through their exile and reemerged to establish the Mamluk Empire. Sultan Qalawun died in 1290 as he was preparing to take Acre from the Western Christians, with the idea of ending the last vestiges of the "Crusader" presence in the Eastern Mediterranean. His son, al-Ashraf, would finish this task with a brutal, bloody capture of the city the next year (as referred to in Epilogue Two).

The historical Sunqar al-Aqsar was taken into custody around Aleppo in early 1260 and released in 1267. In the interests of maintaining the flow of the story, I did not incorporate that detail into *The Sultan and The Khan*. So Sunqar al-Aqsar participates in Baybars' approach to Qutuz in 1260. The historical Sunqar al-Aqsar does go on to be a major figure in the Mamluk state, eventually conflicting with Sultan Qalawun after Baybars' death.

Nasir al-Din al-Tusi was a talented scientist, caught throughout his life in the path of Mongol advances. He was in the Isma'ili castle of Alamut in 1256 when Hulegu destroyed it and killed all the inhabitants. Nasir al-Din al-Tusi was spared because he was a respected man of science. He convinced Hulegu to build an observatory in Azerbaijan, and was with Hulegu at Baghdad. I have given him an invented adminstrative role in his interactions with Dawud and Aram. He died in 1274 at the age of 73, with influential achievements in mathematics and astronomy.

Hulegu's decision to let the Aleppo citadel defenders live is described by historians as "surprising." Normal Mongol policy would have been to slaugher any forces offering resistance. The motives attributed to Hulegu in *The Sultan and The Khan* are offered by me, but are logical deductions based on the circumstances.

Qutuz did in fact order the Mongol envoys sliced in half at their waists and had their heads mounted after their approach to the Mamluk state in Cairo in 1260. And he did so even though a consensus of his emirs favored negotiations. The idea that he split them so one half could negotiate is my addition to the story, a creative leap on my part to explain this quirky method of execution. Some chronicles indicate Baybars was part of the killing of the Mongol envoys. Others indicate he had no part in it, but this might have been to soften Baybars' public image for later diplomatic approaches to the Muslim Mongol state of the Golden Horde. In light of this lack of a definitive record, I kept my portrayal of Baybars consistent with his personality, and consistent with his clearly expressed belligerent attitude toward the Mongols at this time.

In early August of 1260, in Salihiyya, Egypt, Qutuz did proclaim he would fight the Mongols by himself if necessary. Dawud's part of this episode is invented.

There is no historical record I am aware of that indicates the Hapsburgs ever sent an envoy to try to establish an alliance with the Mongols. The Robert character is entirely my invention, a way of dramatizing the changing power situation in Central Europe.

The story of Dawud influencing al-Ashraf Musa to defect from the Mongol ranks at a key moment during the Battle of Ayn Jalut is my invention. It is historically correct that al-Ashraf Musa did defect, and that this defection was a major factor in the battle. We can conclude that al-Ashraf Musa may have been inspired to defect when he realized he could help deliver a Muslim victory, and with his bitter rival al-Nasir Yusuf out of the picture, he could expect significant rewards for his action. (He was right—al-Ashraf Musa was granted rulership of Homs by the Mamluk state.) He seems to have been a skilled opportunist.

Some historians have argued that the Battle of Ayn Jalut was not a particularly decisive conflict, as the Genghis Khan Mongol dynasty was going to break apart anyway. There is some truth to this, but the Battle of Ayn Jalut was the first major defeat for the Mongols, a defeat they were never able to reverse. They had designs on Egypt, and from there could have swept west across North Africa, with Western Europe in their sights. This battle ended three generations of victories across thousands of miles of Eurasia. The fact that the Mamluk state had the courage and insight to make a stand against the Mongol wave of conquest decisively shaped history. Many Muslim and Christian authorities had submitted rather than risk resistance, but the Mamluks decided otherwise. This certainly shaped the Genghis Khan dynasties in Eurasia, and arguably shaped the sequence of events in the area with influence up to the present day.

The assassination of Qutuz is described differently by chroniclers. Various biases have no doubt slanted these accounts, including the tradition that the killer of a sultan is the one who should take the sultan's place. I have presented this episode using the most logical, most probable sequence of events, cobbling together the varied accounts, using common sense, and taking source bias into consideration.

Sources

MONGOLS AND MAMLUKS

Rashid al-Din (translation by John Andrew Boyle), *The Successors of Genghis Khan*, Columbia University Press, 1317/1971.

Safi Ibn Ali (translated by D. Ayalon, adapted by Paulina B. Lewicka), *Biography of the Mamluk Sultan Qalawun*, Academic Publishing House, Warsaw, 1284/2000.

Rueven Amitai-Preiss, *Mongols and Mamluks*, Cambridge University Press, 1995.

Eric Hildinger, trans. Friar Giovanni di Plano Carpini, *The story of the Mongols whom we call the Tartars:Friar Giovanni di Plano Carpini's account of his embassy to the court of the Mongol Khan*, Branden Publishing, Boston, 1252/1996.

John Bagof Glubb (Glubb Pasha), *The Lost Centuries*, Prentice-Hall, Upple Saddle River, New Jersey, 1967.

Peter Jackson, *The Mongols and the West*, Pearson Education, Harlow, UK, 2005.

Paul Khan, *The Secret History of the Mongols: The Origin of Chinghis Khan (expanded edition): an Adaptation of the Yuan Ch'ao Pi Shih, Based Primarily on the English Translation by Friar Woodman Cleaves*, Chang & Tsui Company, Boston, 1200/1998.

Abdul-Aziz Khowaiter, *Baibars the First: His Endeavors and Achievements*, The Green Mountain Press, London, 1978.

J.J. Saunders, *Mongol Conquests*, Routledge & Kegan Paul, 1971

Peter Thorau, *The Lion of Egypt: Sultan Baybars I & the Near East in the Thirteenth Century*, Longman, London, 1987.

CHRISTIANS/GENERAL SOURCES

Jonathan Riley-Smith, *The Crusades*, Yale University Press, 1987.

Jonathan Riley-Smith (editor), *The Atlas of the Crusades*, Times Books, London, 1991.

Stephen Runciman, *The History of the Crusades*, Cambridge University Press, 1951.

Christopher Tyerman, *God's War*, Belknap Press/Harvard University Press, Cambridge Massachusetts, 2006.

About the Author

Sadly, Richard Warren Field passed away before this book could see print. Although he dedicated *The Sultan and The Khan* to his father, the publishers would like to provide an additional dedication—to Richard himself.

Richard was born on November 16, 1954. He was the oldest of four children, including brothers Chris and Bill (twins) and sister Kathy. He was born in Rochester, New York and raised in Los Gatos, California. He went to Los Gatos High School where he ran for student body president, then graduated with honors. Next his education took him to the University of the Pacific, where he held a double major in Music and Political Science, and graduated in 1976 with a 3.8 GPA.

Richard was a creative soul who expressed himself through music as well as writing. He performed a number of self-composed recitals in high school and college, and his college recital ("Voyage of the Traveler") was a big hit. He recently produced albums of a genre of music he referred to as "mystic jazz," including a collection of covers and originals called "Songbook 1" and the spiritually-themed "Issa Music." Most recently he was working on "Songbook 2." The night he passed away he was going to perform at a local venue for aspiring singers and songwriters.

Richard's previous novel, *The Swords of Faith*, won the Bronze Medal in the 2011 Independent Publisher Book Awards; was a finalist for the USA Book News Award for Best Books of 2010 in the category of Historical Fiction; and was a finalist in the International Book Awards for Best Books of 2010 in the category of Historical Fiction. Other writings include *The Election*, a novel about a newscaster who runs for President that Publisher's Weekly called "a fast-paced … fantasy of third-party politics."

Richard also co-wrote the novel *Dying to Heal* with Dr. Alan Fluger, a fictional look at the interplay between conventional health care and chiropractic care.

On June 16, 2014, Richard passed away suddenly at his home. He is survived by his loving wife since 1989, Carrie, and their two children, Michelle and Ryan. Richard requested to have his ashes scattered at Walden Pond. He will be missed greatly, having been taken way too soon.

CPSIA information can be obtained at www.ICGtesting.com
Printed in the USA
BVOW04s0854050215

386402BV00007B/84/P

9 781932 045727